FOURTH EDITION

Exploring Religious Meaning

Robert C. Monk

Walter C. Hofheinz

Kenneth T. Lawrence

Joseph D. Stamey

Bert Affleck

Tetsunao Yamamori

PRENTICE HALL, Englewood Cliffs, New Jersey 07632

Library of Congress Cataloging-in-Publication Data

Exploring religious meaning / Robert C. Monk . . . [et al.]. — 4th ed.
    p.   cm.
    Includes bibliographical references and index.
    1. Religion. 2. Religious literature. I. Monk, Robert C.
BL50.E98 1994
200—dc20   93-25757
ISBN 0-13-299660-X   CIP

Acquisitions editors: Ted Bolen/Jennie Katsaros
Editorial/production supervision and interior design: Barbara Reilly
Cover design: Tommy Boy Design
Manufacturing buyer: Kelly Behr
Copy editor: Barbara Conner
Cover art: Valerie Jaudon, *Sebastapol*, 1982. Courtesy Sidney Janis Gallery.

 © 1994, 1987, 1980, 1973 by Prentice-Hall, Inc.
A Paramount Communications Company
Englewood Cliffs, New Jersey 07632

Printed in the United States of America
10 9 8 7 6 5 4 3 2

ISBN 0-13-299660-X

Prentice-Hall International (UK) Limited, *London*
Prentice-Hall of Australia Pty. Limited, *Sydney*
Prentice-Hall Canada Inc., *Toronto*
Prentice-Hall Hispanoamericana, S.A., *Mexico*
Prentice-Hall of India Private Limited, *New Delhi*
Prentice-Hall of Japan, Inc., *Tokyo*
Simon & Schuster Asia Pte. Ltd., *Singapore*
Editora Prentice-Hall do Brasil, Ltda., *Rio de Janeiro*

To the memory of

Mary Ida and Walter C. Hofheinz

With gratitude to

Carolyn Monk
Carol Lawrence
Sarah Stamey
Patsy Affleck
Judy Yamamori

Contents

Preface   xi

PART I   RELIGION AND RELIGIOUS TRADITIONS

Chapter 1   Toward a Definition of Religion   1

Introduction   1
Unit 1   Reliance on a pivotal value   4
Unit 2   Person-in-community   7
Unit 3   An individual and person-in-community   8
Unit 4   Other values subordinate to central value   10
Unit 5   Authentic to the individual   12
Unit 6   Religious tradition   13
Unit 7   Life-governing value   15
Unit 8   Understanding based on dialogue   17
Unit 9   Communication   18

Chapter 2   Religious Traditions   20

Introduction   20
Unit 10   Hinduism   21

Unit 11   Buddhism   25
Unit 12   Taoism   30
Unit 13   Confucianism   33
Unit 14   Judaism   36
Unit 15   Christianity   39
Unit 16   Islam   43
Summary   47

PART II   EXPERIENCING RELIGION

Chapter 3   Cases of Religious Experience   52

Introduction   52
Unit 17   God's call, Moses's response   53
Unit 18   Luther's religious experience   55
Unit 19   Gautama's quest for Nirvana   56
Unit 20   Sufi encounters   59
Unit 21   Saint Teresa's ecstasy   61
Unit 22   Juan Diego and Our Lady of Guadalupe   63
Unit 23   Mahatma Gandhi's religious journey   64
Unit 24   Pentecostalism and the charismatic movement   66

Chapter 4   Elements of Religious Experience   69

Introduction   69
Unit 25   The role of ritual in religion   70
Unit 26   Religious nurture and conversion   75
Unit 27   The role of symbols in religion   78
Unit 28   Mysticism in religious experience   80
Unit 29   Myth and religious insight   86
Unit 30   Magic: Theory and practice   88

Chapter 5   Religion in Artistic Expression   93

Introduction   93
Unit 31   Art as a symbolic vehicle   94
Unit 32   Images of Jesus as Christ in the early church   97
Unit 33   Luminous wholeness in Western European medieval
   architecture   103

PART III   THE DIVINE

Chapter 6   History, Revelation, and the Knowledge of God   114

Introduction   114
Unit 34   Revelation: General and special   116
Unit 35   Faith and reason   118
Unit 36   The anatomy of faith   122

Chapter 7   Ways of Conceiving the Divine   126

Introduction   126
Unit 37   The holy   127
Unit 38   The divine expressed in religious texts   131
Unit 39   Conceptualization of the divine   139
Unit 40   Spirit   141

Chapter 8   The Problem of Evil   146

Introduction   146
Unit 41   Why suffering?   147
Unit 42   Concepts of evil   149

PART IV   THE SELF AND RELIGION

Chapter 9   Understanding the Self   156

Introduction   156
Unit 43   The nature of humanity   157
Unit 44   On the meaning of *person*   161
Unit 45   Dimensions of the self and religion   165
Unit 46   Views of being human, East and West   167

Chapter 10   Freedom and the Self   170

Introduction   170
Unit 47   Responsible freedom   171
Unit 48   Human freedom   173
Unit 49   Concepts of Christian freedom and the dilemmas of decision making   176

Chapter 11   **Sin and Guilt   179**

Introduction   179
Unit 50   Roles of shame and guilt   179
Unit 51   Guilt and religious experience   181
Unit 52   Judeo-Christian concepts of sin   183

Chapter 12   **Death and the Self   186**

Introduction   186
Unit 53   How it feels to die   187
Unit 54   Attitudes toward death   190
Unit 55   Death and the afterlife: Cultural perspectives   193
Unit 56   Resurrection and monotheistic faith   195

Chapter 13   **Salvation and Redemption   199**

Introduction   199
Unit 57   Salvation   200
Unit 58   Eschatology: The coming fulfillment   202

PART V   RELIGION AND THE SOCIOCULTURAL CONTEXT

Chapter 14   **The Religious Matrix of Interpersonal Relations   211**

Introduction   211
Unit 59   The individual and the community   212
Unit 60   Love and duty   215
Unit 61   Act and motive   219

Chapter 15   **The Corporate Expressions of Ethical Concerns   222**

Introduction   222
Unit 62   Love and justice   223
Unit 63   Peace or justice?   226
Unit 64   Religion and the social status of women   228
Unit 65   Sexuality and human liberation   232
Unit 66   Poverty and race   235
Unit 67   Ethnic pluralism in contemporary American churches   238

Chapter 16   **Religious Traditions and Social Stability   241**

Introduction   241
Unit 68   Community of faith   242
Unit 69   Wholeness of life in a simply structured society   244
Unit 70   Wholeness of life in classical Greece   246
Unit 71   Japanese fondness for simplicity   248

Chapter 17   **Religious Traditions and Social Change   252**

Introduction   252
Unit 72   The challenge of world hunger   252
Unit 73   Religion, humanity, and technology   259
Unit 74   Secularization   262
Unit 75   Religious fundamentalism   265
Unit 76   Characteristics of modernization   267

PART VI   UNDERSTANDING RELIGIOUS KNOWLEDGE

Chapter 18   **Interpretations and Verification of Religious Knowledge   270**

Introduction   270
Unit 77   Factual statement   272
Unit 78   Verification   277

Chapter 19   **Authority and Tradition   281**

Introduction   281
Unit 79   Authority in religion   282
Unit 80   Tradition: Its meaning and function   284
Unit 81   Doubt   287

PART VII   RELIGION AND THE NATURAL ORDER

Chapter 20   **Order and Origins   290**

Introduction   290
Unit 82   Religious views on the origin of the universe   291
Unit 83   Religious vision and scientific method   297

Chapter 21   **Human Response to the Natural Process**   301

    Introduction   301
    Unit 84   Humanity and the world   301
    Unit 85   Nature and the natural   308

Chapter 22   **Time and Eternity**   312

    Introduction   312
    Unit 86   The mystery of time   313
    Unit 87   The temporal and the eternal   317

Index of Religious Traditions   324

Index of Names/Subjects   328

Preface

This book is intended to serve as a set of tools and resources for exploring the many dimensions of religion as a central activity of human beings. It was designed with introductory courses in religion, religion and culture, and the humanities in mind. It is useful as a supplementary text for courses in comparative religion, philosophy of religion, and sociology of religion. It is indexed in ways that suggest a variety of uses in classroom settings or for independent research. Both instructors and individuals interested in independent study will find the indexes useful.

The design of *Exploring Religious Meaning* suggests an approach to inquiry that may be called inductive and integrative. Many of the readings are taken from the Scriptures and classic literature of the world's great religions. Others are drawn from classic and contemporary sources that seek to interpret religion in its various dimensions—theological, philosophical, psychological, sociological, cultural. Some materials are drawn from areas of contemporary culture where religious experience and stances of religious commitment are actualized, appreciated, or criticized: cartoons, poetry, drama, motion pictures, news stories, song lyrics. The materials are presented in a variety of ways—in juxtaposition with interpretative commentary and questions—that seek to evoke encounter and insight.

Just as the authors of *Exploring Religious Meaning* do not always agree among themselves on questions of interpretation, readers will no doubt find themselves disagreeing with points of view expressed in the sources and in the interpretative commentary included in this book. We hope that readers will confront these materials, and the issues they raise, with questions and responses that arise from their own experiences. We hope that each individual reader will be stimulated to address uniquely personal questions and formulate personal responses in studying the issues.

To understand religion, religious phenomena must be seen in their wholeness, as they are manifested in society and in the lives of individuals. Religion is first of all something alive. Doctrinal formulations, institutional structures, traditional patterns and practices handed down from generation to generation—these are important aspects of religion. These aspects of religious experience received more attention in the third edition than in previous ones and receive even more in the fourth edition. But important, too, are highly individual elements of feeling, movements of protest and reform, the emergence of new patterns that may modify, give new life to, or put into eclipse the old and the established. We hope that the materials included in *Exploring Religious Meaning* will guide the reader to explore sources and issues that will lead to deeper understanding of and greater appreciation for the enduring and perennially renewed impact of religion on human life.

The major theme of the book is the all-pervasive influence of, and the constant interaction between, religious institutions, ideas, beliefs and practices and the human societies in which they are present and the lives of the individuals and groups who make up those societies.

In the Introduction a functional definition of *religion* is proposed. This definition suggests that religion is important to everyone because each person's life is shaped by—and all persons respond to—critical events that confront them in individual life and in society in terms of basic commitments. An individual's most basic commitments express what the individual values most, how that person defines the meaning and value of existence. Basic commitments, those involving a person's deepest loyalties and ideas about what is valuable and worthwhile, are—according to our proposed definition of religion—*religious*. The reality and meaningfulness of such commitments can finally be determined, expressed, and actualized only by the individuals who make them. But the study of religion—of religious traditions and religious phenomena—even as an academic discipline, may help persons clarify their own basic commitments and come to appreciate them more fully. The study of religion can also help persons come to understand and appreciate the religious commitments, attitudes, and behavior of others. As in all life, from the turbulent arenas of social and political controversy to the sometimes lonely realms of scientific and artistic creation, one must decide for oneself what is best in the realm of the good and the true.

However, one cannot understand the modern world or any of its parts without an understanding of the many ways that religious traditions and religious innovation affect all societies, from ancient to modern, from fifth-century BCE Athens or the Mesopotamia of four thousand years ago to the present-day former Yugoslavia or Waco, Texas.

Exploring Religious Meaning began as an attempt in the late 1960s to communicate these concepts to students in ways that would effectively and affectively speak to a student generation that was showing great interest in understanding religion both crossculturally and as a vital part of a person's inner and outer worlds. The first edition bore the marks of the pedagogical ideas of its time. Format and structure were highly energized, nonlinear, affectively "hot"—designed for a generation that seemed to call for multi-media, non-traditional stimulation. We have found that student generations change significantly in short periods of time. Though successful, the first edition of the text soon seemed to beg for more structure and unity and a less distracting format.

In accordance with our experience as teachers and the many helpful suggestions we received from colleagues across the country and from our students and their students, we made changes in format and structure in the second edition, producing a much more readable, useable book. This process continued in the third edition and now we think in the fourth edition has been brought much further. The second edition also added, by request of many instructors who had used the first edition, a new chapter (Chapter 2) offering brief introductory discussions of the major world religions. This proved successful and the chapter has been retained in the present edition with some updating and enrichment.

We have retained the basic structure and content of the book, which colleagues and students have told us work well. Overlapping themes, beginning with religious experience and proceeding to concepts of the divine, concepts of the self, group life and the cosmos are presented, usually with two or more chapters devoted to each. Each chapter deals with a major topic or subtopic by means of a brief explanatory introduction and a series of partly overlapping units. Some of the units raise major questions related to the topic (see, for example, Unit 47); some deal comparatively with ways in which different religions or religious and secular traditions treat one major aspect of religion (see Units 82 and 58 on creation stories in several ancient religions and beliefs about eschatology or fulfilled history, respectively). Some treat one major topic or theme in depth (see Units 77 and 69, which deal, respectively, with interpretation and the all-pervasiveness—nondifferentiation—of religion in the life of a very simply organized society). Some units illustrate a concept or a practice (Unit 33). Most of the units are comparative: some compare two things (Unit 50), some several (Unit 55). Throughout the book it is emphasized that each major topic mirrors and enriches the others. The structure of the book gives a large degree of freedom to instructors. Some instructors may want to omit some units or combine units from one chapter with units from another. But we believe the chapter introductions should be assigned.

Several new features appear in the fourth edition of *Exploring Religious Meaning*:

1. Significant improvements have been made in format and design, making the book more attractive, readable and useful.

2. There is substantial updating within the text, reflecting changes in the world and recent trends in the study of religion. The world has changed dramatically during the past decade politically, culturally, and in other ways.

The third edition for the first time gave more attention to religion in modernized and modernizing societies, as well as additional material dealing with non-Western traditions. There were several completely new units dealing with contemporary issues where religion and society interact: intensified religious concern about the threat of nuclear war and world hunger, the quest for human liberation, the rise of new or renewed religious movements, the new religious conservativism, issues related to the status of ethnic culture, women, minorities, and pluralism in contemporary societies. Many of these units have been updated. Also, we seem to be entering another period in which many students are becoming excited about the academic study of religion. We believe that the fourth edition of our text will appeal to and be useful with both the already and the not yet excited.

3. New material, dealing with non-Western religious traditions and with religious practices in simply organized societies, has been strategically integrated into existing units. (For instance, there is a much more in-depth treatment of Shamanism in Unit 30.) Here we have responded to the largest body of suggestions by reviewers and by colleagues from

across the country who have used the book. Accordingly, there are more illustrations taken from non-Western sources.

4. We have completed our rather modest set of theoretical tools that we began introducing in the first three editions. We do not want the book to be heavily laden with theoretical material, but found that, in addition to the basic definition of religion, adapted from such theorists as the theologian Paul Tillich, the philosopher William Blackstone, and the behaviorial scientist Clifford Geertz; the creed/code/cult/community typology, adapted from Joseph Fichter and other sociologists of religion; and the functional analysis of religion that pervades the book; we needed to complete our typology of orientations toward religion and put it in one place. This occurs now in the Introduction to Chapter 4.

5. Finally, there is for the fourth edition an instructor's manual which we believe will be helpful in explaining the book chapter by chapter, making its goals and objectives clear, suggesting ways and methods of using the materials, and giving some directions to supplementary materials.

We believe that *Exploring Religious Meaning* has greatly improved with each subsequent edition. For what we think is the most effective revision yet, the updated fourth edition, we want to thank especially the three reviewers of the third edition who were asked by our publisher to provide overall evaluations of the book and suggestions for its improvement. They responded with substantial and extremely useful critiques. We have incorporated many of their suggestions. Particularly helpful were the suggestions about new or neglected sources of materials from the religious traditions. We would like to mention in this connection the valuable comments and references given by Professor Dennis Lishka of the University of Wisconsin, Oshkosh, who has given us permission to thank him publicly.

We continue to be indebted to Jacques Bakke for the illustrations that have helped make the book successful.

We are greatly indebted to Professors William Barrick and Johnnie Kahl, colleagues at McMurry University, who have given us the benefit of their use of this text. Acknowledgement must be given to Dr. Joyce Carroll, formerly of McMurry University, for advice on earlier editions relating to contemporary films dealing with moral and religious issues, and to Professor Nell Senter of Texas Christian University for providing valuable information relating to contemporary moral problems, particularly those concerned with the status of women in society.

Finally, to our many students in the different colleges and universities where we teach, and to former students, some of whom are themselves now graduate students or professors engaged in the academic study and teaching of religion, we express sincere and abiding gratitude for suggestions, criticism, and encouragement.

Throughout *Exploring Religious Meaning*, dates of historical events are, for the most part, designated by the abbreviations B.C.E. ("before the common era") and C.E. ("common era"), which in most older sources and in some more recent ones were commonly abbreviated as B.C. and A.D.

CHAPTER 1

∾

Toward a Definition
of Religion

Introduction

From earliest times religion has been a pervasive social phenomenon. In our own complex society there is evidence of religion everywhere: religious holidays of particular groups (Christmas, Hanuka, Mardi Gras, Ash Wednesday, Passover, Good Friday, Easter), national holidays that have a distinctively religious component (Thanksgiving, the Fourth of July, Memorial Day), church buildings and synagogues, and even controversial social and political issues such as those concerning abortion and the legal and civil rights of homosexuals. Officials of religious denominations take part in public ceremonies, such as presidential inaugurations, and officials of organizations and private citizens advocating separation of church and state protest such participation.

Although in opinion polls people often say they believe that the influence of religion has declined, there is evidence that participation in organized religion in the United States has held steady for the past six decades at a high level for the overall population. But there is also in our society a new awareness of religious pluralism and an increasing diversity of religious groups. There seems to be, moreover, both a return to traditional religious practices—an interest in finding one's roots—and a new individualism in religion— the individual wants to be his or her own kind of Baptist or Catholic or Jew. Later units in the text will explore many forms of this two-sided phenomenon—for example, native Americans, many of them committed Christians, returning to older, tribal ceremonies, sometimes incorporating them into patterns of Christian worship; and Christian feminist theologians turning to elements long considered heretical among Christians, for instance,

1

gnosticism or "witchcraft" as authentic expressions of the feminine aspects of God and the Christian message.

At the individual level, many who have turned away from traditional religious answers or who have turned away from "organized religion" entirely, give evidence of deep religious concern. Increased involvement in "New Age" groups and writings continues an interest in Asian religions going back to the 1950s, along with astrology, forms of magic, the belief in previous incarnations, "channeling," and related phenomena. On the one hand, the rise of the religious right (especially in fundamentalist Protestant groups), with strong political concerns about prayer in public schools and abortion, was an important development of the 1980s. On the other hand, commitments to social justice; to peace; to the rights of women, minority groups, the threatened environment, and animal life; and to helping the starving, famine-threatened human populations of the world give evidence of a religious fervor and sometimes bridge the gap among Roman Catholics, mainline Protestants, and fundamentalists. The mainline Protestant groups, which declined in membership and prestige during the 1970s and 1980s, show some signs of revitalization. But the most rapidly growing religious groups in the United States at present are Islamic, with increases both from immigrant communities and African-Americans.

There has also been increased attention to the study of religion at the academic level. In many instances, as the successive editions of this book reflect, this has included a demand for increasing attention to the non-Western religious traditions, especially Buddhism, Islam, and Hinduism, and to ancient and contemporary religious traditions of simpler, premodern or preliterate tribal groups. But there is also increasing academic interest in religious developments and trends in our own society, evidenced by such studies as the ambitious *A Theory of Religion*; the comprehensive study of American religion and American life, *Under God*; or the insightful, provocative *The American Religion* by the controversial literary critic Harold Bloom.[1] It seems to us, the authors of the Fourth Edition of *Exploring Religious Meaning*, that not only has religion never before been practiced in a greater variety of ways in America but also it has never been studied so widely and with such a variety of methods and goals. Some people study religion to understand an important aspect of human behavior, some to find antidotes for what they consider human superstition and folly, some to find greater tolerance and appreciation of the varied traditions, and some to find saving truth.

We continue to believe that the investigation of religion must be broad enough to incorporate the most individualistic and nontraditional expressions of religious concern. While examining the major forms of established and emerging institutional patterns, we must be able to comprehend traditional patterns of religious expression, including those of societies other than our own. Affirming the need for such a broad perspective in religious inquiry makes especially necessary a concrete identification of the ways in which the term *religion* will be used in this book.

Religion is defined in many ways. Radoslav Tsanoff, in his book *Religious Crossroads*, conveniently summarized the linguistic data concerning the terminology used in

---

[1] Rodney Stark and William Sims Bainbridge, *A Theory of Religion* (New York: Peter Lang, 1987); Gary Wills, *Under God* (New York: Simon & Schuster, 1990); Harold Bloom, *The American Religion* (Simon & Schuster, 1992).

various cultures to designate what we call "religion." Tsanoff surveyed the major language stocks of the modern world and noted that no language group has a word meaning "religion" as a universal, inclusive phenomenon. Some languages have terms that designate "law," "devotion," "knowledge," and other components of what in the West has been termed *religion*. In fact, the Latin *religio* itself originally designated the ancestral customs and rituals of the early Romans. It was not until the emergence of a Greco-Roman culture, encompassing the area from North Africa to the British Isles and from India to the Atlantic Ocean, that the term *religio* began to denote a phenomenon of universal import. Tsanoff considered various ways of defining religion, several of which are enumerated and discussed: (1) theistic and other beliefs, (2) practices, (3) mystical feeling, (4) worship of the holy, and (5) conviction of the conservation of values.[2]

Everyone has had some experience of religion. Most people use the term on the basis of past experience, acquired beliefs, and favorable or unfavorable impressions. To one person, the word *religion* may produce good feelings. It may connote a close relationship to God—to the benevolent Being or Beings believed to provide life, security, meaning, and purpose. To another, the term may evoke fear or self-doubt or guilt. It may connote a threatening relationship to a stern or hostile or judging Power or Powers. People often reflect their own positive or negative feelings toward religion and toward their own past experiences of it when stating what they conceive it to be. On the one hand, the behavioral scientist—the psychologist, sociologist, anthropologist—may emphasize religion's *functional* aspect; psychologists may be interested in the role of religion in providing integration or in causing conflict in the individual personality and in the individual's group relationships. Sociologists may attempt to study ways in which religion may be a source of stability or change, unity or conflict, in societies. On the other hand, philosophers may be primarily interested in the *cognitive* claims of religion, in trying to understand the belief statements of particular religious traditions and in trying to discover what the functions and significance of those statements may be and how one might discover whether they are true. Theologians may seek to explicate the "meaning" aspect of religion, or at least of their own religious tradition. They will perhaps try to show that the religious tradition *is* meaningful and will provide for the adherent a framework, an orientation that makes sense of life.

The anthropologist Clifford Geertz has pointed to two major functions of religion: providing a comprehensive system of symbols for understanding the nature of reality and providing a system of values that demand complete devotion.[3] He sees these as inseparable. We may express his view by saying that ultimately we value the things we do because we see them as rooted in ultimate reality, and we see them as rooted in ultimate reality because we have learned to value them as having ultimate significance.

Accordingly, in *Exploring Religious Meaning* we will define *religion* as any person's reliance on a pivotal value or a group of related values in which that person finds essential wholeness as an individual and as a person-in-community. For that person all other values are subordinate to this central value (or to this group of values). The pivotal value spoken of in the definition is *authentic* (meaningful, real to that person, of great and unique importance to the person),

[2] Radoslav A. Tsanoff, *Religious Crossroads* (New York: E. P. Dutton, 1942), pp. 13–25.
[3] See Clifford Geertz, *The Interpretation of Culture: Selected Essays* (New York: Basic Books, 1973), pp. 89, 126, 140.

though it may not be meaningful to others. Here, "reliance on a pivotal value" includes trust in an unrivaled power or being. The pivotal value may be shared by others. In such cases we speak of a "religious tradition," such as Christianity, Buddhism, or Hinduism.

Generally when people profess to hold some pivotal value or values and their conduct seems to contradict their profession, we believe they are either hypocrites or hopelessly superficial and immature. For a person's professed religious commitment to be authentic, his or her life must be governed by the religion's pivotal value. People from very different religious traditions, in which the pivotal values at least seem to differ greatly, may therefore have great difficulty in understanding one another. An Orthodox Jew who emphasizes (whose pivotal value is) the living of all life in accordance with God's revealed law (the Torah) may find it difficult to understand or to sympathize with a Hindu mystic or a Christian Pentecostalist for whom an overwhelming sense of the presence of God within is the ultimate goal. Even within the same religious tradition this difficulty may appear. A Christian fundamentalist and a theologically liberal Christian may have a difficult time understanding and accepting the authenticity of the other's differing religious commitments, conduct, and belief.

However, a religiously committed person with an open and searching attitude may understand and empathize with a person of another faith by turning inward, to his or her own experience of religious commitment. At that moment a dialogue—in its truest sense—between human beings with different backgrounds and different mind sets allows them to open themselves to each other. We believe that such openness to others is important, even if the intellectual differences are sharpened. We believe that even when people continue to differ in major ways religiously, the value of life for each will be enhanced with greater understanding of the other's values and that the possibility of living in a more peaceful, constructive world, where many problems can be solved cooperatively in spite of, even because of, differences in religious understanding and commitment, will be enhanced.

This definition must be seen as a preliminary one. It will receive much qualification in the following units and sections of *Exploring Religious Meaning*. The immediately following units will both attempt to illustrate the definition of religion as "reliance on a pivotal value" and begin to qualify it.

UNIT 1   Reliance Upon a Pivotal Value

> We define religion as any person's **reliance upon a pivotal value** in which that person finds essential wholeness as an individual . . .

In answer to the question "What does it mean to have a god?" Martin Luther wrote, "Trust and faith of the heart alone make both God and idol. . . . Whatever . . . your heart clings to . . . and relies on, that is what really is your God."[4] It is sometimes said by religious persons that there are in reality no atheists.

[4] Martin Luther as quoted by H. Richard Niebuhr, *Radical Monotheism and Western Culture* (New York: Harper & Row, 1960), p. 119.

In what way is this statement true? In what ways—bearing in mind our definition of religion—might it not be true? Do you think that the way Luther talks about what a person's "real" god is makes sense? Is this a useful way of talking about "religious" commitment?

H. Richard Niebuhr was a twentieth-century Protestant thinker who accepted Martin Luther's definition of the concept of God—what one relies on, puts his or her trust in. Commenting on the definition, Niebuhr wrote, "If this be true, that the word 'god' means the object of human faith in life's worthwhileness, it is evident that men have many gods, that our natural religion is polytheistic."[5] Mr. Quimby, the golfer in Figure 1.1 might illustrate this belief. The object of his supreme devotion—his pivotal value—seems to be doing well at golf. In other cartoons in the "Lolly" series, he was equally concerned about wealth—he experienced severe emotional crises when the stock market fell or when it was time to pay his income taxes or when an employee asked for a raise. Are people frequently polytheistic? Do the terms *theism, polytheism*, and *monotheism* acquire new meanings—or at least other possible meanings—when *religion* is defined as "pivotal value"?

Niebuhr pointed out that an individual's pivotal value—that which the individual seeks or adheres to as the source of ultimate meaning or fulfillment—may shift from

Figure 1.1 Lolly by Pete Hansen. (Copyright © The Chicago Tribune. New York News Syndicate; Inc. Used by permission.)

[5] Ibid.

one value to another or may be composed of a group of values (such as health, wealth, and wisdom). The religions of the world propose supreme or pivotal values to their adherents as that which will bring fulfillment and security. In later units we will focus on some major religious orientations toward pivotal value. For instance, there is a *moral* orientation, which holds obedience to the will of a Divine Being (for many adherents of Judaism) or to an eternal code of right behavior (as in Confucianism) as the supreme value to be sought. There are also *mystical* religious orientations, which hold that a very intense sense of union with the Divine (Hinduism) or experience of the ultimate, overwhelming, transforming presence of God to worshipers whose will and personality are united to God in love (Christian mysticism) is the pivotal goal of life. We will speak also of esthetic, magical, and ecstatic orientations to religion. These need not be exclusive of one another, and this way of classifying orientations to a pivotal value is only a conceptual tool; it is not the only way of approaching the role of religion as the center of value and meaning in the lives of groups and individuals.

The following materials illustrate how the concept of pivotal value is present in three of the world's great religious traditions. In a passage from the Hindu *Bhagavad-Gita* (c. 100), the Lord Krishna calls for the entire devotion and loyalty of his devotee Arjuna. In effect, the Divine Krishna asks his follower to make devotion to Krishna the supreme, the pivotal, value of Arjuna's life.

> Cling thou to me!
> Clasp Me with heart and mind! so shalt thou dwell
> Surely with Me on high. But if thy thought
> Droops from such height; if you be'st weak to set
> Body and soul upon Me constantly,
> Despair not! give Me lower service! seek
> To read Me, worshipping with steadfast will;
> And, if thou canst not worship steadfastly
> Work for Me, toil in works pleasing to Me!
> For he that laboreth right for love of Me
> Shall finally attain! But, if in this
> Thy faint heart fails, bring Me thy failure! find
> Refuge in Me! Let fruits of labor go,
> Renouncing all for Me, with lowliest heart,
> So shalt thou come; for, though to know is more
> than diligence, yet worship better is
> Than knowing, and renouncing better still.
> Give Me thy heart! adore Me! serve Me! cling
> In faith and love and reverence to Me!
> So shalt thou come to Me! I promise true.
> Make Me thy single refuge! I will free
> Thy soul from all its sins! Be of good Cheer.[6]

In the Christian Apostle's Creed (c. 500), powerful expression is given to the Christian belief that the God of Christian worship is Lord of all life. God is confessed as being Creator, Savior and Redeemer, Deliverer, and Lord of all life, God and Lord in the present and in every future, eternally.

---

[6] *The Song Celestial or Bhagavad-Gita* Sir Edwin Arnold, trans., (London: Routledge & Kegan Paul, 1955), pp. 12.8, 18.64–66. Used by permission.

I believe in God the Father Almighty, Maker of heaven and earth. And in Jesus Christ his only Son our Lord; Who was conceived by the Holy Ghost, born of the Virgin Mary; suffered under Pontius Pilate, was crucified, dead, and buried; he descended into hell; the third day he rose from the dead; he ascended into heaven; and sitteth at the right hand of God the Father Almighty; from thence he shall come to judge the quick and the dead. I believe in the Holy Ghost; the holy catholic Church; the communion of saints; the forgiveness of sins; the resurrection of the body; and the life everlasting. Amen.

The following Muslim prayer gives graphic expression to the adherent's reliance on Allah as the Supreme Source of wholeness for the individual.

Thanks be to my Lord; He the Adorable, and only to be adored. My Lord, the Eternal, The Ever-existing, the Cherisher, the True Sovereign whose mercy and might overshadow the universe; the Regulator of the world, and Light of the creation. His is our worship; to Him belongs all worship; He existed before all things, and will exist after all that is living has ceased. Thou art the adored, my Lord; Thou art the Master, the Loving and Forgiving. . . .
O my Lord, Thou art the Helper of the afflicted, the Reliever of all distress, the Consoler of the broken-hearted; Thou art present everywhere to help Thy servants. . . .

O my Lord, Thou art the Creator, I am only created;
   Thou art my Sovereign, I am only thy servant;
   Thou art the Helper, I am the beseecher;
   Thou art the Forgiver, I am the sinner;
Thou, my Lord, art the merciful. All-knowing, All-loving.

UNIT 2   Person in Community

> We define religion as any person's reliance upon a pivotal value in which that person finds essential wholeness . . . **as a person-in-community.** . . .

TAOS, N.M. (AP)—An aging spiritual leader of the Taos Pueblo Indians, the sight in his 90-year-old eyes dimming, plans to take his tribe's plea for a religious sanctuary to the white man's Capitol.

He will renew the plea of the Taos Indians for title to 48,000 acres of forest land surrounding Blue Lake, high in the Sangre de Cristo Mountains of northern New Mexico, and sacred to the tribe.

"Our Blue Lake wilderness," Romero said, "keeps our water holy and by this water we are baptized. Without this, we have no life."

"If our land is not returned to us," Romero said, "if it is turned over to the government for its use, then it is the end of Indian life."

"Our people will scatter as the people of other nations have scattered. It is our religion that holds us together."[7]

In religion humans find wholeness not only as individuals but also as persons-in-community—persons unavoidably related to others, with whom the individual shares an identity, purposes, and experience.

[7] Associated Press.

After experiencing the Risen Christ on the road to Damascus, Paul in time felt compelled to preach to the Gentiles, whom he had previously regarded as alien foreigners. Sent by the church at Antioch, of which Paul had become a part, he went out into the Greco-Roman world with the message of salvation for all nations. For Paul the community was essential: "For just as the body is one and has many members, and all the members of the body, though many, are one body, so it is with Christ. For by one Spirit we were all baptized into one body—Jews or Greeks, slaves or free—and all were made to drink of one Spirit. . . . Now you are the body of Christ and individually members of it" (I Corinthians 12:12, 13, 27, RSV).[8]

From early Buddhist tradition, we learn the following:

> After the ecstasy (Enlightenment) had passed, Gautama was immediately confronted with a problem, a temptation. . . . He had attained to a Doctrine that was "profound, recondite, hard to comprehend." Were he to preach this Doctrine or Dhamma, and were others not to understand it, that would be labor and annoyance to him. After some struggle with himself, whether he should remain a Buddha for his own sake or become a Buddha for all, a teaching Buddha, he rose and went back into the world to communicate to others his saving truth. He sought out the five ascetics who had deserted him at Uruvela. The five ascetics were converted, and thus the Sangha (the Buddhist monastic order) came into being. . . . "I take refuge in the Sangha."[9]

This aspect of religion—in which the individual finds personal wholeness in community—raises profound questions about the significance of the individual's relationships to other human beings and about the meaning of human existence, about human nature generally. In addition, it raises questions about the nature of our avenues to truth: How much of what we consider knowledge, the belief systems of society, is simply the result of shared assumptions and a shared way of life? The point has often been stressed that most newborn animals are far better equipped biologically to begin life than humans are. Human beings, with their long period of dependency, literally have to learn from their human group how to be human.

The reality of human interdependency is clearly expressed by a student in her journal:

> So many people think that they can be an island and not depend on anyone else. But we have to have help; God did not mean for us to exist separately. I think that we can only find self-happiness when we can find happiness together.

UNIT 3   An Individual and Person-in-Community

We define religion as any person's reliance upon a pivotal value in which that person finds essential wholeness **as an individual and as a person-in-community.**

---

[8] *RSV* indicates the Revised Standard Version of the Bible.
[9] John B. Noss, *Man's Religions*, 4th ed. (New York: Macmillan, 1969), pp. 130–32, © 1949, 1956, 1963 by Macmillan, Inc., © John B. Noss, 1969.

For the Apostle Paul, living in an idol-worshiping society, commitment to Christ—as the pivotal value—eliminated the efficacy of idols. Therefore, it made no difference for Christians if the meat sold in the marketplace had been offered to idols. Nevertheless, Paul saw that although this might be true for him as an individual, as a person-in-community he had to consider other factors. "There are some who have been so accustomed to idolatry that even now they eat this food with a sense of its heathen consecration, and their conscience, being weak, is polluted by the eating." Paul as an individual was at liberty to eat such meat, but as a member of the Christian community he was ready to restrain himself. "If food be the downfall of my brother, I will never eat meat any more, for I will not be the cause of my brother's downfall." (I Corinthians 8:7, 13, NEB)[10]

Martin Luther King's last public speech was delivered in support of a sanitation workers' strike in Memphis, Tennessee. Adapting Jesus's Good Samaritan story to the current scene, King pointed out not only the social need of the time but also that individual wholeness is never separate from corporate wholeness.

> And you know, it's possible that the priest and the Levite looked over that man on the ground and wondered if the robbers were still around. Or it's possible that they felt that the man on the ground was merely faking. And he was acting like he had been robbed and hurt, in order to seize them over there, lure them there for quick and easy seizure. And so the first question that the Levite asked was, "If I stop to help this man, what will happen to me?" But then the good Samaritan came by. And he reversed the question: "If I do not stop to help this man, what will happen to him?"
>
> That's the question before you tonight. Not, "If I stop to help the sanitation workers, what will happen to all of the hours that I usually spend in my office every day and every week as a pastor?" The question is not, "If I stop to help this man in need, what will happen to me?" "If I do not stop to help the sanitation workers, what will happen to them?" That's the question.

The speech ends with King's premonition of his own death. Nevertheless, the dominant note is a firm confidence that no matter what happens to the individual, there is an abiding triumph that the individual shares when, under God, individual and group faith and action issue in corporate and individual wholeness—"the Promised Land."

> Well, I don't know what will happen now. We've got some difficult days ahead. But it doesn't matter with me now. Because I've been to the mountaintop. And I don't mind. Like anybody, I would like to live a long life. Longevity has its place. But I'm not concerned about that now. I just want to do God's will. And He's allowed me to go up to the mountain. And I've looked over. And I've seen the promised land. I may not get there with you. But I want you to know tonight, that we, as a people will get to the promised land. And I'm happy, tonight. I'm not worried about anything. I'm not fearing any man. Mine eyes have seen the glory of the coming of the Lord.[11]

King's personal commitment led to direct social action. Essential wholeness, however, manifests itself in various ways. This is seen in the experience of Dietrich Bonhoeffer, who sought meaningful wholeness as he wrote from his German prison. A committed Chris-

---

[10] Scripture quotations in this publication identified by the letters NEB are from *The New English Bible*. © the Delegates of the Oxford University Press and the Syndics of the Cambridge University Press 1961, 1970.

[11] Martin Luther King, Jr., "A View from the Mountaintop." Reprinted by arrangement with The Heirs to The Estate of Martin Luther King, Jr., c/o Joan Daves Agency as agent for the proprietor. Copyright 1963 by Martin Luther King, Jr., Copyright renewed 1991 by Coretta Scott King. Copyright © 1968 by The Estate of Martin Luther King, Jr.

tian preacher who would not silence his public witness for Christ despite Nazi commands to do so, Bonhoeffer was jailed and finally martyred. Until his death, however, he maintained his faith and his loving concern for others. Affirming Christ as the Man for others, Bonhoeffer interpreted faith as "Something whole, involving the whole of one's life."[12] Faith meant "taking risks for others."[13] For such a faith in Christ, Bonhoeffer risked himself—gave himself for others—and in this way, as he believed, experienced wholeness as an individual.

UNIT 4   Other Values Subordinate to Central Value

> We define religion as any person's reliance upon a pivotal value. . . . **for that person all other values are subordinate to this central value.**

Leon Trotsky, who with Lenin led the revolutionary movement that produced a communist government in Russia in 1917, was one of the most brilliant Marxist thinkers of the twentieth century. He did not become a Marxist all at once, however. The son of a prosperous farmer, Trotsky was drawn to various revolutionary movements popular among students who were concerned with improving the lot of peasants and industrial workers. After a period during which he argued strongly against the Marxist position, Trotsky was "converted" to Marxism while in prison for revolutionary activities. In the following passage of his autobiography, he describes how during a period of exile he found in his new position the key to understanding all the major aspects of life.

> Since 1896, when I had tried to oppose all revolutionary ideas, and the following year, when I opposed Marxism even though I was by that time already carrying on revolutionary activity, I had come a long way. By the time I was sent into exile, Marxism had definitely become the basis of my whole philosophy. During my exile, I tried to consider, from the new point of view I had acquired, the so-called "eternal" problems of life: love, death, friendship, optimism, pessimism, and so forth. In different epochs, and in varying social surroundings, man loves and hates and hopes differently. Just as the tree feeds its leaves, flowers, and fruits with the extracts absorbed from the soil by its roots, so does the individual find food for his sentiments, and ideas, even the most "sublime" ones—as Marxism states—in the economic roots of society.[14]

In Marxism, Trotsky found the key to the understanding of all life. For him, the "truth" of Marxist teaching was so central to life that it changed his understanding of everything else. He believed that for a Marxist, the ordinary relations and activities of life—work, marriage, friendship, hobbies, recreation—would be very different than they would be for non-Marxists: they would have different meanings and would call for differ-

[12] Dietrich Bonhoeffer, *Letters and Papers from Prison* (New York: Macmillan, 1958), p. 199.
[13] Ibid., p. 209.
[14] Leon Trotsky, *My Life* (New York: Grosset & Dunlap, 1960), p. 127.

ent behavior. For example, he saw marriage in a feudal society as a "sacred" relationship; in a capitalist society it was a contractual agreement; for Marxists, it would be a free relationship for companionship based on common political activities and friendship. Even after his expulsion from Russia and from the Russian Communist party, he believed that the Marxist theory fully explained why backward economic and social conditions in Russia had inevitably produced a deterioration of Russian communism into the Stalinist dictatorship. Trotsky remained a committed Marxist revolutionary. He was assassinated in 1940 by a Stalinist agent in Mexico.

We have stressed that religions provide a unifying value or system of values by means of which all other values and all parts of life may be interpreted. Did Trotsky's Marxist theory—his Marxist beliefs—express this kind of value orientation? Could Marxism for Trotsky be called a religious orientation? Note how Trotsky's beliefs about the central questions of life are interpreted by and subordinated to the central, unifying beliefs provided by Marxist theory.

The sociologist J. Milton Yinger has written,

> Major religious differences can persist in a functionally unified society only at the cost of sharp conflict on the one hand or by the reduction of the significance of these religions to their adherents on the other, or by some mixture of these processes. Insofar as it is reduction in the significance of traditional beliefs that occurs, men do not thereby give up the search for a unifying system of values. They develop a quasireligion to do the job. Most often in our time it is nationalism, sometimes pursued with an almost desperate sense of urgency for the conviction of unity.[15]

Sociologists often use the term *quasi-religion* to describe something—like nationalism or Marxism—that is ordinarily thought of as "nonreligious" in content but that functions or acts like a religion. What analogies are there between the unifying role that Marxism played in the life of Trotsky and the role that Marxism or nationalism might play in the life of a society? (See Figure 1.2.)

Figure 1.2
"Listen, I *love* my country and I'm *proud* of the flag, but do we *have* to pledge allegiance every time we get into the car?" (Drawing by D. Fradon. © 1969, *The New Yorker* Magazine, Inc., October 25, 1969.)

[15] J. Milton Yinger, *Sociology Looks at Religion* (New York: Macmillan, 1963), p. 31.

For both traditional religions and secular quasi-religions there will usually be symbols that express the meaning and importance of the religion's pivotal value or system of values. What might happen to adherents of a religion or quasi-religion when they perceive conflicts among the values their religious tradition or political movement advocates?

Religious symbols usually express and appeal to the emotions of the adherents of the religion in a powerful way. The cross for Christians; the words of the sacred Scriptures, the Torah, for Jews; the city of Mecca for Muslims—these are powerful religious symbols.

∽

Is the American flag as used in the cartoon seen by the cartoon characters as a religious symbol expressing a pivotal value?

Unit 5   Authentic to the Individual

> This pivotal value . . . **is authentic to the individual though it may not be meaningful to others.** . . .

In 1961 Secretary General of the United Nations, Dag Hammarskjöld, was killed in an airplane crash while on a mission seeking peace in a war-torn region of Africa. After Hammarskjöld's death, his personal journals and diaries revealed him as a man who had been motivated in his political career by insights of a deeply personal religious mysticism. He wrote, "In our era, the road to holiness necessarily passes through the world of action."[16] Others may not share this particular primary value. Nevertheless, we believe it may be useful to consider that all human beings have this in common—for each person there are values that are pivotal. The way these values fit together to become *the* pivotal value—if they do fit together—is the basis of the unity, the wholeness, of that person's life. We hinted in Unit 4 that conflicts among the values in the system of pivotal values in an individual's or group's life may result in the sense that wholeness is lacking. This may result in distress and a feeling of meaninglessness.

Cartoonists graphically reflect this awareness and at times draw their humor from unexpected conflicts in values (Figure 1.3).

∽

Is there any doubt about what is important to Lukey on this occasion? Are most persons as honest as Lukey in revealing their pivotal value?

[16] Dag Hammarskjöld, *Markings*, trans. Leif Sjöberg and W. H. Auden (New York: Knopf, 1964), p. 12:6.

Figure 1.3   *Snuffy* by Fred Lasswell. (© 1970 King Features Syndicate.)

UNIT 6   Religious Tradition

> **The pivotal value may be shared by others. In such cases we speak of a "religious tradition."**

Religion may be an intensely personal dimension of an individual's life, but even the most personal and individualistic religious experiences will have been drawn from the social setting. New religious movements, movements of reform or renewal or new direction in religious life, draw to some extent on a common body of beliefs and practices in the larger society. Thus we can speak of at least two important phases of religious tradition. First, it refers to those things handed down from the past that are shared to some extent by the members of a social group. In this phase, religious tradition becomes the basis of present and future religious life, for whatever new or deeper or repetitive elements an individual or group may experience. In a second phase, religious tradition may refer to that which, on the basis of the old traditions—perhaps in opposition to them, perhaps in the desire to renew them—becomes in a new way a religious possibility for people.

In the New Testament accounts of the origins of the Christian movement there is an interesting blending of these two phases of religious tradition. On the basis of traditional and newly interpreted expectations of Judaism for deliverance from foreign oppressors, for God's Messiah who would bring justice and salvation to God's people, many contemporary Jews responded to a call by John the Baptist for repentance, for a renewal of life and intention in expectation of God's soon-to-be-accomplished act of judgment and deliverance. According to the earliest Christian accounts, some of those who first responded to John's interpretation and reinterpretation of the traditional messianic hope of Israel then responded to the message and activity of Jesus. In the Gospel according to John there is the following account of how some of Jesus's first disciples or followers began to spread or hand on the beliefs and hopes they had acquired about Jesus:

> One of the two who followed Jesus after hearing what John said was Andrew, Simon Peter's brother. The first thing he did was to find his brother Simon. He said to him, "We have found the Messiah" (which is the Hebrew for "Christ"). He brought Simon to Jesus, who looked at him and said, "You are Simon son of John. You shall be called Cephas" (that is, Peter, the Rock).
>
> The next day Jesus decided to leave for Galilee. He met Philip, who, like Andrew and Peter, came from Bethsaida, and said to him, "Follow me." Philip went to find Nathanael, and told him, "We have met the man spoken of by Moses in the Law, and by the prophets: it is Jesus son of Joseph, from Nazareth." "Nazareth!" Nathanael exclaimed; "Can anything good come from Nazareth?" Philip said, "Come and see." When Jesus saw Nathanael coming, he said, "Here is an Israelite worthy of the name; there is nothing false in him." Nathanael asked him, "How do you come to know me?" Jesus replied, "I saw you under the fig-tree before Philip spoke to you." "Rabbi," said Nathanael, "you are the Son of God; you are king of Israel." Jesus answered, "Is this the ground of your faith, that I told you I saw you under the fig-tree? You shall see greater things than that." Then he added, "In truth, in very truth I tell you all, you shall see heaven wide open, and God's angels ascending and descending upon the Son of Man." (John 1:40–51, NEB)

In a similar way, later units in the text (Units 12 and 19) describe how Prince Gautama, dissatisfied with life and tortured by unanswered questions about human suffering, began the kind of religious quest that the Hinduism of his day taught those seeking religious enlightenment to pursue. He sought answers from the holy men and the teachers of philosophy. He withdrew to the forest, fasted, and meditated. A number of other seekers after enlightenment were so impressed by his devotion and his efforts to find the answers he was seeking that they attached themselves to him, hoping that when the answers came, they too would be enlightened through their contact with Gautama. When Gautama modified his approach, rejecting the prescribed fasting, mortification, and asceticism, these disciples were shocked and withdrew from him. But when the experience of enlightenment did come, they returned, became his disciples, and began to be part of a community that eventually preserved and handed on the teachings of Gautama.

A new religious tradition very often arises as a result of the activity and teachings of a powerful personality who has reinterpreted an older body of tradition. In later units of the book, such figures as Confucius, Martin Luther, Mohammed, and Teresa of Avila will be examined. In each case the pattern just described is present: Through a powerful reinterpretation of existing religious tradition, something new emerged, followers were attracted, and a new or renewed religious tradition began to be an effective influence in the societies and lives of individuals reached. Other such renewers, reformers, or initiators of religious tradition include Bernard of Clairvaux, George Fox, John Wesley, Alexander Campbell, Radhakrishnan, Joseph Smith, Brigham Young, and Charles Taze Russell. In more recent times there have been Mohandas Gandhi, Leo Tolstoy, Mary Baker Eddy, Sun Myung Moon, and Dorothy Day. From the work of each of these individuals who responded with various degrees of affirmation or rejection to existing religious tradition, new religious movements arose, and new and living religious traditions resulted.

Unit 7   Life-Governing Value

> For a person's professed religious commitment to be authentic, the person's life must **be governed by the religion's pivotal value.**

The value systems we consciously espouse as authentic may fail to coincide with those from which we subconsciously act. This inauthenticity is often transparent. The Hebrew prophet Amos lived in a time when many of his coreligionists made a show of devotion to God. Amos believed that their acts of worship often failed to express an inner reality of commitment to the God they claimed to worship since they were not concerned about God's demands for justice and compassion in society. Speaking for God, Amos condemned outward practices of religion that did not express authentic inner commitment.

> I hate, I despise your feasts,
> and I take no delight in your solemn assemblies.
> Even though you offer me your burnt offerings
> and cereal offerings,
> I will not accept them,
> and the peace offerings of your fatted beasts
> I will not look upon.
> Take away from me the noise of your songs;
> to the melody of your harps I will not listen.
> But let justice roll down like waters, and
> righteousness like an everflowing stream.
> (Amos 5:21–24, RSV)

Current criticism of religion usually concentrates on the hypocrisy of inauthentic religion, or pseudoreligion. It often finds expression in popular art forms—cartoons, TV sit-coms, songs. A song popularized a generation ago by the singing group Peter, Paul, and Mary is a good example:

> Sunday morning very bright
> I read your books by colored light
> that came in through the pretty window picture.
>
> I visited some houses where they said that you were living
> and they talked a lot about you

Figure 1.4   *Peanuts* by Charles Schulz. (© 1959 United Features Syndicate, Inc.)

and they spoke about your giving.
They passed a basket with some envelopes.
I just had time to write a note and all it said was
"I believe in you."

Passing conversations where they mentioned your existence
and the fact that you had been replaced by your assistants.
The discussion was theology
and when they smiled and turned to me
all that I could say was
"I believe in you."

I visited your house again on Christmas or Thanksgiving
and a balded man said you were dead
—the house would go on living.
He recited poetry
and as he saw me stand to leave
he shook his head and said
I'd never find you.

My mother used to dress me up
and while my dad was sleeping
we would walk down to your house
without speaking.[17]

Buildings, money, position, theology, and all the outward signs of religion are here subordinated to complete trust. But the song also seems to indicate that much that occurs in the worship service is not authentic. What one might do on the basis of an authentic religious commitment within this (Christian) religious tradition is not indicated in the song but possibly is expressed in a New Testament passage:

> Tell them [who trust in this world's goods and goals] to hoard a wealth of noble actions by doing good, to be ready to give away and to share, and so acquire a treasure which will form a good foundation for the future. Thus they will grasp the life which is life indeed. (I Timothy 6:18–19, NEB)

As should be clear from earlier units, though frequently people are not genuinely or fully committed to the religious values they profess, there are many examples of persons who have been authentically and powerfully committed to the values espoused by religious traditions. Hammarskjöld, Martin Luther King, Jr., and Bonhoeffer have already been cited, as well as others. In succeeding units people from a great variety of traditions—among them St. Teresa and St. Francis, Martin Luther, Gandhi, Moses, Martin Buber, and Gautama—will be presented, people whose lives were transformed in and through wholehearted commitment to the central values of one or another of the world's great religious traditions.

---

[17] "Hymn" by Karen Gold, James Mason, and Paul Stookey. © 1968 Pepamar Music Corp. All rights reserved. Used by permission of Warner Bros. Music.

UNIT 8   Understanding Based on Dialogue

For its adherents a religion usually is held to be absolute, not relative. This means **it is often difficult for one to understand the faith commitment of someone with a different faith perspective,** either within or outside one's own religious group or tradition. In this situation a religiously committed person with an open and searching attitude may understand and empathize with a person of another faith by turning inward, to his or her own experience of religious commitment. **What is demanded is willingness of the participants in dialogue to open to each other.**

Martin Buber, a twentieth-century Jewish philosopher and religious writer who had great influence on Protestant and Catholic as well as Jewish thought, recounts in the introduction to his book *Eclipse of God* two talks that involved him in religious disagreement with others. After one of Buber's public lectures, a French workingman presented an argument favoring atheism. Buber refuted the man's position. Then

> When I was through . . . the man . . . raised his lids, which had been lowered the whole time, and said slowly and impressively, " 'You are right.' . . ." Buber was dismayed. "What had I done? I had led the man to the threshold beyond which there sat enthroned the majestic image which the great physicist, the great man of faith, Pascal, called the God of the Philosophers. Had I wished for that? Had I not rather wished to lead him to the other, Him whom Pascal called the God of Abraham, Isaac, and Jacob, Him to whom one can say Thou? . . ."
>
> On another occasion, Buber and an older man whom he greatly admired argued about religion and never came to verbal agreement with each other. The older man criticized Buber for clinging to the use of the word "God." "What you mean by the name of God is something above all human grasp and comprehension, but in speaking about it you have lowered it to human conceptualization. What word of human speech is so misused, so defiled, so desecrated as this! All the innocent blood that has been shed for it has robbed it of its radiance. All the injustice that it has been used to cover has effaced its features. When I hear the highest called 'God,' it sometimes seems almost blasphemous. . . ." "Yes," I said, "it is the most heavy laden of all human words. None has become so soiled, so mutilated. Just for this reason I may not abandon it. Generations of men have laid the burden of their anxious lives upon this word and weighed it to the ground: it lies in the dust and bears their whole burden. The races of man with their religious factions have torn the word to pieces; they have killed for it and died for it, and it bears their fingermarks and their blood. Where might I find a word like it to describe the highest? If I took the purest, most sparkling concept from the inner treasure-chamber of the philosophers, I could only capture thereby an unbinding product of thought. I could not capture the presence of Him whom the generations of men have honoured and degraded with their awesome living and dying. I do indeed mean Him whom the hell-tormented and heaven-storming generations of men mean. Certainly, they draw caricatures and write 'God' underneath; they murder one another and say 'in God's name.' But when all madness and delusion fall to dust, when they stand over against Him in the loneliest darkness and no longer say 'He, He' but rather sigh 'Thou,' shout 'Thou,' all of them the one word, and when they then add 'God,' is it not the real God whom they all implore, the One living God, the God of the children of man? Is it not He who *hears* them? . . ."
>
> We cannot cleanse the word "God" and we cannot make it whole; but defiled and mutilated as it is, we can raise it from the ground and set it over an hour of great care.

> It had become very light in the room. It was no longer dawning, it was light. The old man stood up, came over to me, laid his hand on my shoulder and spoke: "Let us be friends." The conversation was completed.[18]

Buber believed that the first of these two talks had been a failure. Although he had communicated with the man on the level of ideas, the two had failed to meet at the deeper level that gave force and meaning to the ideas. In the second talk there was apparently little or no agreement at the intellectual level, but Buber and the older man had come to understand each other. Each had come to understand the force of meaning and personal depth of the other's beliefs and ideas about religion and the term *God*.

UNIT 9   Communication

The cartoon in Figure 1.5 illustrates an attempt at communication that fails because of the attitude of one participant toward the other. Failure to achieve meaningful communication generally rests on the inability of the persons involved to respect and trust each other. True dialogue and honest encounter mean willingness to respect each other and to share ideas without an attempt to minimize honest disagreements.

Some may wonder whether it is valuable or necessary for persons holding to different religious traditions or beliefs to discuss religion with each other. Won't differences and disagreements be minimized if people simply agree to be different in religion and concentrate on areas in which they *do* agree? In some cases, if the differences are great and mutually disturbing, can't people simply keep entirely apart from each other?

> Can you think of other options besides these—agreeing to disagree while leaving religious differences undiscussed, or keeping entirely separate from those whose religious beliefs or practices disturb us?

Figure 1.5   *The Born Loser* by Art Sansom. (Reprinted by permission of Newspaper Enterprise Association [NEA].)

[18] Specified excerpts from pp. 5–9 in *Eclipse of God* (Harper Torchbook edition) by Martin Buber. Copyright 1952 by Harper & Row, Publishers, Inc. Reprinted by permission of the publisher.

In the unit on Islamic religion in Chapter 2, it is suggested that if there had been better understanding of the meaning of Islamic religious beliefs and the value placed on them by their adherents, some present conflicts between the United States and the nations and groups in the Middle East might have been avoided, or at least lessened in scope and intensity. Many believe that in a world that is increasingly interconnected, and in a society as increasingly diverse and pluralistic in ethnic and cultural makeup as the contemporary United States, we cannot afford the luxury of failing to understand diverse and contrasting religious positions.

In addition, some ethical or religious positions adhere to and advocate the need to try to understand, in both of Buber's senses—at the level of ideas and at the level of personal depth—those who differ from us religiously, as did the Christians who formulated the following statement concerning dialogue with those committed to other religious traditions or positions. (Participation in the process does not assume that agreement in belief will be achieved or that all differences will be found to be unimportant.)

> We believe that Christ is present whenever a Christian sincerely enters into dialogue with another man: the Christian is confident that Christ can speak to him through his neighbour, as well as to his neighbour through him. Dialogue means a positive effort to attain a deeper understanding of the truth through mutual awareness of one another's convictions and witness. It involves an expectation of something new happening—the opening of a new dimension of which one was not aware before. Dialogue implies a readiness to be changed as well as to influence others. Good dialogue develops when one partner speaks in such a way that the other feels drawn to listen, and likewise when one listens so that the other is drawn to speak. The outcome of the dialogue is the work of the spirit.[19]

The Search for God at Harvard is the recently published, best-selling account of the author's becoming more open both to his own and to others' religious traditions. The author, Ari Goldman, grew up in New York and Connecticut in a very sheltered environment of Orthodox Judaism. He attended Orthodox Jewish schools, rather than the public schools, and then a Jewish university. He knew little or nothing about religious traditions other than his own; in fact, he had been warned to avoid them (especially Christianity). When he wanted to become a newspaper reporter, he was advised by many, including rabbis, that such work would be impossible for an Orthodox Jew living in full conformity to the commandments of the Torah. Nevertheless, Goldman tried to do both. Eventually he was put in charge of religious news for the *New York Times*; and he requested and received from the *Times* a year away from work to study the world's religions, including Buddhism, Hinduism, Islam, Christianity, and Judaism, at a Christian theological seminary. *The Search for God at Harvard* is Goldman's account of his developing awareness of the variety and diversity both among and within these religious traditions and an increasing appreciation of them as well as of his own Orthodox Jewish tradition.[20]

---

[19] The Kandy Consultation on "Christians in Dialogue with Men of Other Faiths" was held from February 27–March 3, 1967, at Kandy, Ceylon, under the sponsorship of the Division of Studies, Department of World Mission and Evangelism, World Council of Churches.

[20] Ari Goldman, *The Search for God at Harvard* (New York: Random House, 1992).

CHAPTER 2

Religious Traditions

Introduction

In the preceding chapter the term *religion* was given a functional definition. That is, *religion* was defined in terms of what it does, of how it functions in the life of an individual or a group. It was defined as that which provides unifying power, a center of meaning, a supreme, or pivotal, value in the life of the individual or group. It was also stressed, however, that religious traditions, clustered around the unifying center of a pivotal value, tend to crystalize, to develop and attain objective status, so that a religious tradition can be defined in terms of a number of characteristic features:

1. A set of beliefs (creed), which may be specifically formulated or rather informal and indefinite but is still important in shaping the lives of the religion's adherents
2. A code of conduct (code), which, again may be rigidly formulated in terms of taboos or may be relatively undefined, more a matter of life-style
3. A number of devotional or ritual practices for corporate or individual worship, meditation, or self-discipline (cult)
4. Conceptions of inclusiveness or exclusiveness of the religious group and the significance of belonging to it (community)

In this chapter we briefly examine seven of the major religious traditions of the world. We have two major purposes. The first is to provide relevant background material about seven of the world religions that are frequently referred to, discussed, or utilized in the later sections of the book. (The summary to this chapter contains a table of the major aspects of these traditions, as well as a table contrasting major emphases of Western and Eastern religious traditions.) Our second purpose is to illustrate the way in which the various features or elements of a religious tradition may cluster around its central emphasis— its pivotal value.

The seven units of this chapter are intentionally very brief and limited descriptions of multifaceted religious traditions, which will be augmented by later chapters. We do not include comments on the vast complex of prehistorical and preliterate religions, which are basic to many modern-day African, Latin-American, and South Asian cultures. Many of these religions embody an association of the divine with the natural order, a worship of nature, and a stress on humanity's cooperation with the natural order. Although some contemporary ethnic groups are presently attempting to recapture many of these traditions, they are too diverse for description here. Specific insights from such religions are discussed in later units (see Unit 87). Also, many elements of these traditions were absorbed in the major religions addressed in this chapter.

UNIT 10   Hinduism

Many would insist that oversimplification is always involved in trying to define the "essence" of a living religious tradition, that every living religion is a cluster of beliefs, practices, and attitudes held together in a certain bond of resemblance but without definable or essential identity. The philosopher Wittgenstein used the term *family resemblance* to characterize the way in which similar things—for example, games (football, baseball, chess, capture the flag)—may be like one another without necessarily sharing a group of precisely identifiable common features. Wittgenstein's term can apply to religions, and to no religion more than to Hinduism, which in one sense is not a religion at all (see Tsanoff's discussion of the term *religion* in Chapter 1) and in another sense is a whole family of religions—sects, cults, and creeds—and of religious practices.

Unlike some of the historic religions—Buddhism, Christianity, Islam, Confucianism—Hinduism has no specific founders. The complex of rites, images of the gods, and beliefs that characterize it stretch very far back into human history. Of the hundreds of millions of Hindus in the world today, the vast majority live on the subcontinent of India, though there are Hindus in other parts of Asia. During the nineteenth and early twentieth centuries, Hinduism, responding to contact with Western Christian missionaries, experienced a resurgence of vitality. Some intellectuals in Europe and America, attached to Hindu philosophy and spirituality, were converted to Hinduism. The broader world contact that has occurred since World War II has allowed various forms of Hinduism to become more widely known and accepted. Hindu sects, such as Krishna Consciousness (also known as Hare Krishna), have been particularly successful among young Americans and Europeans and claim adherents around the world.

To say that Hinduism has made converts itself involves a difficulty. The doctrines and cults of Hinduism are not exclusive, as are those of some religions of the world, nor is Hinduism dogmatic or doctrinaire in creed or code. It is not organized in any institutional way, though many of its sects, cults, and movements are so organized. Perhaps the prime characteristic of Hinduism is its tolerance. Willing to recognize truth in any religious creed or way of life, Hinduism grants that anyone who is sincerely religious—a Jew, a Christian, or a member of some other faith—is by the very fact of this religious sincerity also a devout Hindu. (Both Gautama the Buddha and Jesus the Christ are recognized by Hindus as among the *avatara*—incarnations—of the great God Vishnu.) Along with Hinduism's religious tolerance goes a certain skepticism and permissiveness in doctrinal formulation and practice. Since the ultimate Divine One—Brahman—is beyond all finite characterizations, almost *anything* asserted about the Divine is both true and false (incomplete). Hinduism has shown a remarkable ability to absorb and transform—to incorporate into itself—elements of other religions. Thus, though Buddhism began as a reform, and in some ways secessionist, movement in the India of the sixth century B.C.E., Hinduism was able to transform and incorporate elements of Buddhism, as it was to do millennia later with elements of Christianity.

Gods

Westerners may find Hinduism bewildering. In one sense it is extremely polytheistic, to the extent that literally millions of gods are worshiped in Hindu cults; but in another sense Hinduism is so purely monotheistic as to be monistic or pantheistic (see Unit 40). There is One Divine Reality and nothing else exists at all, since every reality—individual human being, cow, rock, tree—in its deepest essence (*Atman*) is not a separate entity or soul but is identical with the universal Self or Soul (*Brahman*).

The many gods, whose stories are told in bewildering detail in the Hindu scriptures, are themselves held philosophically to be aspects of the One Underlying Reality (Brahman), who is beyond all distinctions and characteristics, even beyond personality or personal existence. Though Brahman is described as the One or Supreme Self, Brahman is not to be thought of as a literal being or person, certainly not as having sexual character or personality. This nonpersonal understanding of the Divine is often difficult for Westerners, since it is almost always understood in the West as having personal characteristics.

Although Brahman is understood to be the One Universal Supreme Self, in Hindu tradition the manifestations of Brahman are myriad. The many gods of Hinduism were originally related to the natural order, to natural functions and natural processes of the universe. There were gods and spirits from the realms of animal life, for example, elephant gods, monkey gods, and human hero gods, and there was spiritual reverence for certain animals such as the cow. The roots of Hinduism go back to an ancient Indian culture, the Dravidians, whose gods often represented and corresponded to natural phenomena. When the Dravidians were conquered by Aryan invaders in approximately 1500 B.C.E., gods of the two groups, while certainly not identical, tended to merge and intermingle with each other and to preserve names and functions as well as to exchange and share them. At the popular level, modern Hinduism preserves a vast complex of gods and religious functions from these ancient periods.

Most important among the gods is the so-called Trinity of Brahma (Creator), Vishnu (Preserver), and Śiva (Destroyer and Renewer); each represents Brahman, the

Supreme Self. Brahma, as the Creator, is rarely an object of cultic worship and is often depicted as dependent on, or derived from, Vishnu. Vishnu and Śiva, in their many forms and with their female consorts, are of all Hindu divinities the most frequent objects of devotion.

Śiva is a god closely identified with the forces of the natural world, with fertility, the river, and the monsoon rains. (A Śiva temple is shown in Figure 2.1.) Though a part of the great Hindu Trinity, Śiva has several aspects. Known as the "destroyer," his destruction is for the purpose of renewal or purification, so that he not only destroys but also creates; he is often considered life itself, that is, the force or energy that sustains life. He and his many female consorts, such as Kali, a goddess particularly worshiped in her destructive and violent character, are popular objects of cultic worship.

Vishnu, the other god of the Trinity, is known for his compassion and is most often represented as the "preserver" of life. In this role, he intervenes in human history by means of *avatara*—divine representatives in animal or human form—showering humanity with benevolent love and compassion and exerting his influence on their behalf. Krishna and Rama, two principal *avatara* (incarnations) of Vishnu, are celebrated in legend and ritual, and their stories, along with those of their female consorts, are told in Hindu scripture and art. They themselves are objects of cultic devotion, even though they are derivative figures representing Vishnu.

Figure 2.1
A Śiva temple near Tanjore in Madras. (Courtesy of the United Nations.)

The patterns found in the worship of these and the many other gods of Hinduism are varied. There are important daily rites in the home and at the numerous temples where gods are honored. Elaborate religious festivals commemorate important events in history, honor natural phenomena, and celebrate the activities of divine beings. Purification rites are important in all worship, and pilgrimages to temple shrines and other sacred places, such as the river Ganges, are central in Hindu worship.

The Hindu scriptures (the *Vedas*) are an enormous body of literature of different types—from epic poetry to cultic rites and prayers—composed over several centuries. Among the *Vedas* the *Upanishads* contain the most characteristic statement of the philosophical concepts underlying Hinduism.

Karma

Some scholars have suggested that the basis of all later Hinduism is to be found in early rites of sacrifice, from which the concept of *karma* developed. Whether the source is in sacrifice or in other traditions, the belief in *karma*, and its complementary doctrine of *samsara*, is essential to Hinduism. In the Hindu view of life, the separate existence of particular entities is the result of a kind of ignorance (nescience) on the part of the individual. An entity, or *jiva* (*atman*, "soul"), becomes separated from the great ground of Being, Brahman, through ignorance of the nature of Brahman itself. In truth the Divine and the Self (Brahman/Atman) are one spiritual reality. However, the physical separation of individual beings (*jiva*, *atman*) leads to an illusion (*maya*)—an illusion that true life is the endless cycle of birth, death, and rebirth (as insects, animals, humans) that one experiences in physical life. This cycle is known as *samsara* and in Hindu teaching is what one must be released from to experience true spiritual life—the recognition that one is identical with Brahman, that the *atman* and Brahman are one.

How does one cast off such ignorance? The paths to release are many, but each involves *karma*. For the Hindu *karma* is a law of cause and effect. Every action, both spiritual and physical, carries consequences (*karma*); therefore, as one lives, good or bad *karma* accumulates. Good actions lead toward *moksha* (release) from the illusion of the rebirth cycle. Bad actions simply keep one trapped in that cycle (*samsara*) and may lead to lesser life forms. *Karma* then determines what one will be in a future life—whether one will rise or fall in the scale of beings when one is reborn after death in a particular existence. Release, *moksha*, or salvation from this cycle of rebirths and its illusion, is sought through a variety of paths or disciplines (each called a *yoga*, or "yoke"). Principal paths or yogas are the way of religious devotion to a particular deity like Vishnu or Shiva (*Bhakti-yoga*), the way of action or good works (*karma yoga*), the way of knowledge or intellectual enlightenment (*jnana yoga*), and the way of spiritual self-discipline through meditation (*raja-yoga*). Each of these paths eliminates bad *karma* and leads toward *mokska* (release) from the traps of *samsara* (rebirth).

Caste

The theory sketched above underlies the traditional Hindu caste system. According to the theory of *karma*, many incarnations—many births, lives, and deaths—may be required before an individual *atman* (*jiva*) achieves enlightenment and its resultant reunion with Brahman. Among humans there are four major states or levels of caste, although there developed over centuries a multitude of subcastes within the major groupings. One was born into a caste and could not leave it, except by becoming a complete outcaste, during a given lifetime. One's caste status determined what one's vocation would be, whom one could marry, and one's religious and social duties. Highest among the castes, traditionally, was that of the *Brahmins*, the priestly and intellectual leaders of India. Next came the *Kshatriyas*, the caste of political rulers and military leaders. Third were the *Vaisyas*, the caste of persons engaged in commerce and agriculture. Fourth were the *Śudras*, the servant caste. Below these and their numerous subcastes were the outcastes, those who had sunk to a level that excluded them from most opportunities to participate in society, whose very presence was religiously contaminating to members of the higher castes, and to whom only the most degrading and menial forms of livelihood were allowed.

Since India gained independence from British rule shortly after the end of World War II, the Indian government has attempted to correct some features of the caste system—outlawing, for instance, the outcaste status. Social change has also greatly modified the caste system; nevertheless, it continues to have great impact on Indian life.

Basically one's caste status specified one's religious duties. A vast number of rituals—often involving rites of washing for purification, sacrifices of various kinds, and prayers to be said or chanted—were associated with the various castes, particularly with the Brahmins. Also, though Hindus of every caste might choose a life of perpetual religious quest or devotion, a typical pattern of life for Hindus of the three highest castes—again particularly for those of the highest, Brahmin caste—was (and to some extent still is) to close a life that had passed through several stages (student, married person, head of family, householder, and participant in economic and public life—according to one's caste status) by finally becoming a religious pilgrim or hermit, a life of complete religious devotion or meditation.

Interconnection of All Things

Among the characteristic emphases of Hinduism, along with the stress on doing one's duty—moral, social, and religious—as defined by one's caste status or social roles, is emphasis on the kinship and interconnection of all things. According to Hinduism, one whose eyes have been opened, one who is sufficiently enlightened, always sees only the one true reality, the one divine and wondrous Brahman. From the lowest to the highest, everything is God, and life is therefore full of beauty and sacredness.

Unit 11 Buddhism

Buddhism, emerging in the sixth century B.C.E., began as a reform movement within Hinduism that sought to renew the essential core of the older faith during a period when Hindu vitality had become static and ritualized. Accepted by powerful political leaders and understood to have relevance to all people, it became a missionary religion. Over several centuries it spread through Asia, where it became an important, if not dominant, religion in China, Japan, Korea, Indochina, Nepal, Tibet, and Sri Lanka. Hinduism ultimately absorbed Indian Buddhism, so that in the modern world Buddhism is hardly represented in India. Buddhist groups in other countries were to become the conveyors and molders of modern Buddhism. Buddhism, in the last century, has experienced a resurgence of missionary zeal, spreading in some forms throughout the world.

The Buddha

The founder of Buddhism, Siddhartha Gautama, lived from 563 to 480 B.C.E. His life is surrounded by legend, yet it would appear that he was a member of the Kshatriya caste. His father protected him in his youth from the realities of suffering and evil in life—from *dukkha*, life's disjointedness and dislocation. Once Gautama discovered the realities of the world, he set out on a quest to discover why life should include such things and what they meant. Lasting several years, the quest led him through the disciplines of philosophy and religious asceticism, but he found no lasting solace in these. Eventually, through meditation, he became "enlightened"—that is, he found answers to the riddles of life—and subsequently began a new way of life. (For a more detailed discussion of his experience, see Unit 19.) He later would be called the Buddha, or the enlightened or awakened one; he became Gautama the Buddha and is referred to throughout history as Buddha.

Having found for himself release from the anxieties of life, Buddha chose to share this knowledge with others who had shared his quest. Five ascetics who had been with him accepted his new insights and joined with him to form a *sangha*, a monastic order, the nascent Buddhist movement. Enlightened at approximately thirty-five years of age, he spent the rest of his life in a wandering existence, teaching others the insights he had gained. Although he had gathered a large following by the end of his life, even to the extent of establishing orders for women, the development of Buddhism as a distinct religion became the work of his disciples.

Some of Buddha's insights certainly contrasted with the philosophical and popular Hinduism of that time; nevertheless, he also began with certain assumptions inherent in Hinduism. Hinduism's basic understanding of the universe was accepted:

1. The concept of the material world as an illusion (*maya*) to be ultimately discarded by the true believer;
2. The belief in reincarnation in a continuous round of existence (*samsara*) from which one is to be freed;
3. The law of karma—that the universe is governed by cause and effect, that all actions have their reward, good or evil, and that one's actions determine what one will be.

Accepting this framework, Buddha made major transformations in the religious thought of his own day. He was convinced that all persons, whatever their stage or station in life, could achieve the enlightenment he enjoyed. Consequently, he rejected the caste system of Hinduism, which required that one advance through a large number of reincarnations to a status where release would be possible. Philosophy in Buddha's time was also highly complex and intricate. Since Buddha saw no practical applications through these avenues that would offer enlightenment to ordinary people, he summarily rejected metaphysical speculation. He went so far as to reject any comment or speculation on the Divine because in his understanding human words or thoughts were not adequate. For Buddha all human discussion of divinity was speculation, and therefore impractical, since it could not lead to enlightenment. This hesitancy caused some later forms of Buddhism to question belief in the Divine and has sometimes raised questions about whether Buddhism should be considered a religion or simply a philosophical and ethical system.

Principal Teachings

The principal teachings of Buddha revolved around several insights into the nature of humanity and its life. He was particularly interested in helping people become "aware" of themselves and the world—the *dukkha* of life—and how they might overcome this disorientation. He is reputed to have said, "I teach only two things, O disciples, the fact of suffering and the possibility of escape from suffering." According to Buddha, one must recognize not only the reality of suffering but also that it is caused by ego-centered patterns—selfish desires (*tanha*). To alleviate suffering one must learn to redirect these desires until ultimately they are extinguished—so that one is not bound by mental, emotional, or physical desires but is released simply to "be."

To achieve release was not, however, a simple matter, for one must redirect one's whole attitude toward reality. The method was formulated in two direct steps. The first of these was the recognition of the truth discovered by the Buddha as expressed in the Four Noble Truths:

1. Suffering is an all-pervasive fact of life.
2. Suffering is caused by self-centered desire.
3. Suffering can be overcome only if attitudes of self-centered desire are eliminated.
4. Attitudes of self-centered desire can be eliminated only through a comprehensive and systematic effort.

The second step of the method taught by the Buddha involved a commitment to the required, systematic effort to overcome self-centeredness, an embarking on an Eightfold Path leading to enlightenment and ultimately to *Nirvana* (see Unit 19). Such insights into life and its realities meant that Buddha was far more interested in the ethical patterns of life than in religious rites, rituals, and theologies. In Buddha's teachings one is challenged to work out one's own "salvation," or release; others may help by pointing the way, but each person is personally responsible for the attitudes and patterns that determine one's ultimate existence. Though high ethical action is the method for moving toward enlightenment, that enlightenment is far more than simply a matter of ethics; rather, it is insight into the very essence of life and freedom to live on the basis of that insight.

A person who has experienced this insight or enlightenment has entered into a state of being most often described as Nirvana (extinction of desire). According to Buddha, when one enters Nirvana there is no need for a continuing soul or self; one simply *is*. Enlightenment also ends the round of reincarnations since, for Buddha, what is passed from life to life is the accumulated *karma* attached to one's consciousness. Having entered Nirvana, one no longer has need of individual consciousness.

Buddha's forty years of teaching elaborated these insights and others into a wealth of sayings and instructions. In his own eyes and in those of his immediate successors, he was only "the enlightened one," giving insights into life. In his own life he treated all persons and living things with compassion and taught others to do the same. Later, others were to make much more of his role and teachings, in some cases elevating him to divine status.

Immediately after his death, some of the leading monks among his followers joined in council and began to recite and memorize his teachings. The result was the formulation of dogma and tradition, which Buddha had criticized in Hinduism. These developments led, first, to the standardization of the teachings into scriptural writings and, second, to the formulation of two great branches or patterns of Buddhism.

The scriptures are written forms of the oral tradition passed down through the centuries. First written after a fourth council in the first century, they were recorded in the Pali tongue (an ancient Indic language). Today this text is a basic orthodox version of the scriptures. Other forms also emerged in Sanskrit, another ancient Indian language and the official language of the northern branch of Buddhism. Codifications of these scriptural texts have been numerous and controversial.

Buddhist Schools

The history of Buddhism as a religious tradition (in contrast to the teachings and life of Guatama the Buddha) revolves around changing answers to two basic questions: "What is a Buddha?" and "What is enlightenment?" Answers to these questions led to the development of several Buddhist schools, or branches, within the tradition.

Theravada, or the School of the Elders, understands Buddha to be one who points the way to enlightenment; he was a teacher who helped others by giving instruction, but ultimately it is by the individual's efforts alone that enlightenment can be reached. Enlightenment for the Theravadist essentially means wisdom—consciousness of human desire, the anxiety it causes, and the suffering it inflicts, accompanied by a personal commitment to follow the paths to the elimination of all desire. Such consciousness and commitment ultimately result in the abandonment of selfhood. The Theravadist, therefore, adheres to a strict interpretation of Buddha's teachings, insisting on an austere following of traditional rules and disciplines. The ideal followers in this form of Buddhism are the monks (known as *arhats*), who give themselves fully to the pursuit of enlightenment, usually through elaborate forms of meditation. Laypersons in Theravada understand their religious role as being primarily supportive of the monk's quest, yet any person may become a monk. In return for material support, the monks perform ritual and festival functions on such occasions as holidays, weddings, and funerals—functions often carried by priests in other religions—although the monks still stress meditation rather than these duties. Theravada became the religion of Ceylon, Burma, Thailand, and Indochina—the southern branch. Because of its austerity, Theravada is also known (by its adversaries) as *Hinayana* ("small vehicle" or "raft") since relatively few people (the monks) would be expected to follow its path immediately to ultimate enlightenment.

Mahayana ("large vehicle") developed from a different impulse within Buddhism. It stresses the infinite compassion of Buddha: his willingness to share his insights and his helping others achieve Nirvana. The goal is still the same—release—but within Mahayana, Buddha assumes the role of a savior and becomes deified, for he and others assist persons toward enlightenment. Buddha shares with others his divine grace or compassion. This branch tends to be much more flexible and allows a permissive attitude toward a number of developments in ritual and theology.

A most significant development within Mahayana is the concept of the *bodhisattva*, which refers to persons or beings who are "awakening" and are far along the path to full enlightenment such as that enjoyed by the Buddha. They have not fully achieved Nirvana but are close. What is distinctive about them is that they have chosen not to enter Nirvana but to share their insights and help those who have just begun their quest for enlightenment. The *bodhisattvas*, both male and female, are many in number and as bearers of a divine grace offer immense help to the ordinary believer and strength to achieve enlightenment. Compassion is their chief characteristic and they are destined to be future Buddhas. The layperson carries a larger role in the religious life of Mahayana, cooperating with the monks in elaborate and exquisite ritual patterns, art, and personal worship.

This form of Buddhism more readily adapted itself to native patterns and forms, often incorporating national or cultural emphases. As a result it took significantly different patterns in differing cultures. This pattern of Buddhism spread north and east into China, Japan, and Korea. It is called the large vehicle, or raft, for the obvious reason that many more might expect salvation.

Although these two branches of Buddhism have dominated the development of the religion, other forms have arisen over the centuries, and all branches have adapted many native customs and practices as the religion has moved through the various countries of the East. In the seventh century B.C.E., Buddhism was introduced into Tibet, where it took on a significantly different form, becoming a distinct branch. Although this form of Buddhism has been known by several names through the centuries, the most common being *Vajrayana* ("Vehicle of the Thunderbolt"), it is best described as a Buddhist representative of *tantric* religious patterns. Concerned with the interrelationship of all life, it asserts that the energies of the body as well as the mind and spirit may be used in the spiritual quest for enlightenment. Elaborate esoteric rituals perfecting body energies, *mandalas* (the use of sacred designs to focus the mind), *mudras* (hand rituals signifying feelings), and *mantras* (chanting or reciting spiritual formulas or words) all contribute to seeking enlightenment. Using these resources, the negative karmic patterns of life are transformed into the positive perfections of the Buddhas and *bodhisattvas* wherein enlightenment occurs as a perfect combination of wisdom and compassion. Their religious leader, known as the Dalai Lama, is understood to be the earthly manifestation of infinite compassion and wisdom, a *bodhisattva* now in his fourteenth successive human incarnation. In more recent times, other forms of Buddhism have arisen, such as Zen, which combines insights of both older branches, as well as elements of Chinese Taoist tradition and practice.

The diversity of Buddhism is evident, yet Buddha's basic insistence on enlightenment, which leads one from selfish desire to a state of selfless bliss and compassion for others, binds the various branches and interpretations together.

UNIT 12   Taoism

For centuries, the religious principle of the *Tao* (usually pronounced "Dow") has been intertwined with dominant attitudes and themes of Chinese life and culture. The term *Tao* itself designates both a way of living that humans should follow to be in harmony with nature and the Power or Principle or Overall Governing Presence that is manifested in the universe. Thus, to follow the Tao is to live in harmony with the Governing Power or Principle that brings harmony, unity, and balance to all things. For human beings to be striving, ambitious, self-seeking, overly refined, or overly civilized (artificial) disrupts the natural harmony according to which they should, unaggressively, blend into the life that flows through all things. Understood in this manner, the Tao, or "the way," lies at the core of all Chinese culture and is claimed by the two major religious traditions that arose in China, Taoism and Confucianism.

Equally important for Chinese culture and religion is the concept of *yin and yang*, the two major components or principles that must be blended to give reality to everything Figure 2.2 is an artistic expression of this concept. When they are blended harmoniously in accordance with Tao, peace, harmony, and fruitfulness result. Yang (in representations it is given the color red) is the positive, assertive, masculine force. It is the source of

Figure 2.2
Yin and Yang by Jacques Bakke.

warmth, brightness, hardness, dryness, firmness, and strength. Fire and sunlight are particularly associated with yang. Yin is feminine and dark, passive, cold, moist, and mysterious. Water, shadow, shade, and night are associated with yin. Neither of these is seen as evil. Both are necessary ingredients of all that exists. Yin and yang, in fact, contain each other in a hidden or scarcely discernible way. Anything possesses its own natural goodness and health when there is a proper balance of yin and yang in its makeup.

From very early times, Chinese society has been characterized by a reverence and a positive appreciation for nature and the powers, or spirits, supposed to inhabit it. Good and evil spirits were worshiped with rites and sacrifices to secure good fortune and ward off evil. The spirits of departed ancestors were worshiped in the belief that this would ensure good fortune in the present life. A failure to worship the ancestors would turn them into avenging Furies. Many natural phenomena, both real and legendary, were worshiped as manifestations of powers and spirits—mountains, rivers, and various kinds of animals. For instance, building one's home above the nest of a dragon was supposed to bring good luck. Ritual—sacrifices, celebrations, colorful festivals—was very important, both in placating the spirits and as enactments of the harmony between the earthly (human) and the heavenly realms, both seen as parts of one whole.

Lao-Tzu

The religious tradition that took the name of Taoism is often traced to the legendary writings and doctrines of Lao-Tzu, a teacher who was supposed to have lived during the first half of the sixth century B.C.E.; it also incorporates elements of much earlier Chinese tradition and has greatly influenced, and been influenced by, later religious movements, especially Buddhism.

Little, if anything, is known with certainty of the life of Lao-Tzu. This name literally means "the Old Boy" and is used affectionately to designate one who is revered as a master, teacher, or sage, whose life-style was marked by spontaneity, lack of pretense or pretentiousness, and a mischievous, paradoxical manner. According to tradition, Lao-Tzu was a government official who resigned his post after becoming convinced of the futility of a life of ambition, striving, and conformity to artificial social conventions. For Lao-Tzu a life of harmony with nature in its unvarnished simplicity was best. Again according to tradition, he was prevailed upon, before leaving the borders of the civilized world for good, to commit his doctrine to writing. This he is supposed to have done in the thin volume called the *Tao Te Ching*, one of the classics of the world's religious and mystical literature.

The *Tao Te Ching* is characterized by a style of thought and writing that is crisp, playful, profound, and paradoxical. The central concepts of Taoism are expressed in ways that show their continuity with earlier and later Chinese attitudes, foremost of which is a feeling of harmony and kinship with nature.

A basic virtue or positive quality stressed by Lao-Tzu's Taoism is *wu wei*, a kind of creative passivity, an attitude of selfless nonaction according to which one flows with the life present in all things. Just as Lao-Tzu is supposed to have withdrawn from the corrupt and artificially overcivilized world of his day to return to the simplicity of nature, there are many such stories of Taoist "conversions." In one, a harried government official, impressed by the teachings of Lao-Tzu, is supposed to have resigned his office and titles, stripped off his clothes, and walked naked into the woods to spend the rest of his days beside a stream quietly fishing without using bait (in order not to disturb the fish, the stream, or the peaceful harmony of the natural setting). Passivity; nonaction; the absence of striving; and the utility of quiet receptiveness, spontaneity, and appreciation of the simple beauty of life—these are the qualities exalted in the *Tao Te Ching*. In a sense, *nothing*—nonaction, nonbeing—is more useful than being: It is the empty space that makes a cup useful. The hardness of a rock may impress us, but a steady stream of water—what could be more yielding than water?—can wear down the hardest rock.

Chuang-Tzu

The teachings of Lao-Tzu were popularized by Chuang-Tzu, a disciple who lived in the fourth century B.C.E., whose accomplishment in the preservation and interpretation of Lao-Tzu's work was similar to that of Mencius in preserving and elaborating Confucius's teachings. Chuang-Tzu extended the teachings of the *Tao Te Ching* in his own similar small volume of sayings. For Chuang-Tzu two concepts were central: (1) All opposites and values are relative in the flow of change (the Tao) in the universe, so even death can be seen as only one more great change. When he was asked why he did not mourn the death of his wife, he simply suggested that just as she had changed in being born, so in death she changed again; therefore mourning is inappropriate because death is simply part of the Tao. (2) All religious insights and knowledge are real only when they are recognized and played out in the secular and daily activities of individuals. Cooking, crafts, art, and any other activity has at its core the activity of the Tao. The Tao is discovered or uncovered in all life (for an example of this teaching, see Unit 25).

Doctrine

The Taoist doctrine taught by Lao-Tzu and Chuang-Tzu is sometimes referred to as *philosophical* Taoism to distinguish it from *popular* Taoism, which has for centuries involved the worship of ancestral and other spirits and belief in and practice of magical and other rituals oriented to good luck and prosperity. A third form of (or really a third element within) Taoist tradition is sometimes designated by the term *esoteric Taoism*, which refers to teachings and practices of physical and spiritual self-discipline, resembling the meditation of Buddhist monks and Hindu yogis. Techniques of concentration and meditation, and claims of methods to attain remarkable physical as well as occult spiritual powers, are characteristic of this element of Taoism. Popular Taoism developed a priesthood, shrines, temples, cultic worship, and a number of divine beings to be worshiped, all to some extent modeled on Buddhist counterparts.

Taoism also interacted with, sometimes complementing and at times criticizing, Confucianism, the other religious tradition that arose in the same century and emphasized the social hierarchy, law, and rational order. If Lao-Tzu emphasized yin in order to temper an overemphasis on yang, Confucius was the great champion of yang tempered with yin. For many centuries, Chinese culture was characterized by the two traditions of Taoism and Confucianism, which more or less balanced or complemented each other. In fact, for most

Chinese there was no inconsistency in being Confucian (with respect to one's social duties), Taoist (with respect to elements of personal life-style as well as to secure good fortune in the present life), and Buddhist (particularly since many of the sects of Chinese Buddhism dealt with one's fate in a life *after* the present one).

Elements of Taoist philosophy influenced Buddhist thought, too, particularly Chinese and Japanese Zen sects; and elements of popular Taoism can perhaps be recognized in the traditional Japanese popular religion called *Shinto*. With the rise of Mao Tse-tung's version of Marxism in China after World War II, there were strong efforts to eradicate Chinese popular religion, including Taoism, Buddhism, and Confucianism, as well as religious philosophies such as Philosophical Taoism and Confucianism, because they seemed to be obstacles to the Marxist transformation, or modernization, of Chinese society. With the emergence of more permissive attitudes in post-Maoist communism, the opposition to traditional and popular religion has lessened. Citizens are now allowed to practice religion openly, although the official position of the regime remains atheistic.

UNIT 13   Confucianism

Of the two major Chinese religious traditions, Taoism and Confucianism, Confucianism, with its emphasis on the virtues of propriety and reverence for tradition, has been the more influential in Chinese civilization. The teachings of Confucius and his disciples and later interpreters molded the social patterns and mores that were to dominate the culture for centuries.

Confucius

Confucius was born during the middle of the sixth century (c. 551) B.C.E., apparently in humble circumstances. He worked diligently to acquire an education, studying the classics of Chinese literature and music and meditating on the virtues of the great teachers and sages of an earlier period, which he took to have been more virtuous and noble than his own time. The period into which Confucius was born was one that he believed to be characterized by moral and social anarchy caused by crude and selfish behavior, especially on the part of rulers motivated by vain personal ambitions—greed, desire for prestige and power, and self-indulgence. Confucius conceived the idea of a reformation of society through a reformation of its rulers. He believed that if princes could be persuaded to live exemplary lives and to show justice and compassion to their subjects, the whole of society might be reshaped in accordance with the good, tested ways of the past. Here Confucius reflected, in a more sophisticated way, the ancient and later Chinese belief that there should be a harmony between the heavenly and the earthly kingdoms and that the ability of the ruler to conform to the eternal pattern of the heavenly sphere determined whether his subjects would be blessed with peace and prosperity. Confucius himself sought positions in government to try to influence princes by precept and example. According to tradition, his moral standards, his insistence on propriety, were felt to be overly rigorous, and he spent most of his life outside government service as a teacher whose doctrines and personality attracted and influenced an increasing number of disciples.

Doctrine

The primary emphasis of Confucianism is on sincere adherence to a moral and social code of propriety. The Chinese term *li* designates one of the primary concepts (and virtues) exalted by Confucius. *Li* means propriety—the way things should be done. It refers to good behavior, that is, conformity to a moral and social code of appropriate behavior by doing what is customary, traditional, and required by social usage. In a more limited usage, *li* means rite or ritual. Confucius taught that the rites of Chinese traditional religion should be observed, not so much because he believed in the ancestral and other spirits to whom sacrifices were offered, but because he believed in the value of ritual, rite, and ceremony—a stylized pattern of life—for a society's stability. Confucius hoped to correct the anarchy of his own time by establishing a highly stylized, ritualized code of conduct according to which each individual at each moment of life and in any conceivable relationship or situation would know exactly what to do and would do exactly what was expected. Thus, the two meanings of *li* tend to converge in Confucian teaching.

Crucial to the Confucian concept of propriety are the five great relationships: ruler to subject, father to son, husband to wife, older brother to younger brother, and older friend to younger friend. In each case, one member of the relationship is dominant and the other subordinate, yet ideally there is reciprocity of respect. The ruler, the father, the husband, the older brother, and the older friend should show concern, courtesy, and consideration for the subordinate partner. The subject, son, wife, younger brother, and younger friend should show respect, reverence, and obedience to the dominant partner. The Confucian code is not unlike codes of chivalry of medieval Europe, in which the highborn and strong were supposed to protect the lowborn and weak, to care for them and show courtesy in all things, whereas the lowborn and weak were supposed to obey uncomplainingly and with gratitude.

In addition to *li*, Confucius spoke of other virtues and characteristics that one should possess. *Jên*, which he valued so highly that he spoke of it less frequently than he did of some other virtues, designates an attitude of benevolence that produces courtesy, good will toward others, and loyalty to those to whom loyalty is due. *Jên*, for instance, produces service to one's parents and to one's ruler. It includes an attitude of respect and good will toward others and a proper respect for oneself, for one's own dignity and value as a human being.

Another important Confucian concept is *Chun-tzu*, which designates a kind of ideal humanity—the kind of fulfilled humanity that one should seek to achieve in one's own life. *Chun-tzu* is sometimes translated as "Superior Manhood," "Ideal Man," "Man-at-His-Best" or even as "the Gentleman." The person who is a *Chun-tzu* is someone who possesses the Confucian virtues, who conforms to the code of propriety, who is generous, unselfish, benevolent, loyal, and courteous—the opposite of someone who is petty, selfish, grasping, and untrustworthy.

Confucius was convinced that the major means of acquiring this virtue, of becoming a *Chun-tzu*, was through study of and meditation on the classics of Chinese literature and music and through study of the ancient rites. Thus, Confucius placed great emphasis on correct education to create good character in individuals and to restore good order to society. Confucius, reflecting positive Chinese attitudes toward nature and the natural realm, believed in the essential goodness of human nature, an innate potential that can be realized through correct education in a well-ordered society. Confucius left sayings of his own as well as edited versions of earlier Chinese writings to provide a basis for an educational curriculum that for more than two thousand years shaped Chinese civilization. Mencius, a later interpreter of Confucius, did much to systematize the Confucian teachings, classifying the virtues—*li, Jên, Chih* (wisdom), and *I* (justice). Mencius taught that the seeds or origins of the virtues were "in the nature of things," the way the world was, and that their effects would restore harmony to the present world.

The question is frequently raised about the appropriateness of regarding Confucianism as a *religious* tradition. Is it not primarily a code of ethics and a social philosophy? Bearing in mind the definition of religion as a "pivotal value," one can see that Confucianism can be regarded as having a profoundly religious dimension. Being in harmony with and in conformity to the eternal moral code, that is, being in conformity with "heaven," *was* a pivotal value for Confucius. It should be remembered that for him even the rites of traditional religion were of value because observing them was demanded by propriety, the eternal moral code. Confucius, like Buddha, had nothing to say about the nature of heaven, the origin of the universe, and such matters. These questions simply were not relevant to how one lives in conformity to propriety. But for Confucius the moral code was itself a part of the very nature of the universe—a pivotal value.

Influence

The influence of the Confucian writings (some going back to Confucius himself; others, though attributed to him, probably coming from other hands) as a foundation of Chinese culture cannot be overestimated. Perhaps the best known outside China is the *Lun yü* (translated into English as *The Sayings of Confucius*), though in recent years the *I Ching* (sometimes translated as *The Book of Changes*) has received much attention in the West. In fact, the sayings of Confucius, many of them memorable proverbs and epigrams, as well as the other "canonical" Confucian writings functioned in China much as sacred writings have functioned in other societies—certainly as the basis of a moral and social code, as folk wisdom, as history, and as literary models, even (as the *I Ching* did and does) providing methods of divination, foretelling and deciding about conduct to meet future situations.

Because Confucian teachings sustained the traditional and, in Mao's view, decadent government and social patterns, Mao Tse-Tung, leader of the 1950s Chinese Communist revolution, frequently attacked the influence of Confucius and Confucianism, declaring that it had to be rooted out before China could be transformed into a progressive, politically and technologically modernized society. (At times he insisted that some of the Confucian virtues, such as certain forms of courtesy, were nevertheless necessary.) More recently the Chinese government has stressed the importance of Confucius and his teachings as an important part of China's cultural heritage.

UNIT 14   Judaism

Judaism, for the purposes of this unit, refers to the faith, worship, and life of the Jewish people. Judaism arose among Semitic peoples who lived in the ancient Near East around the eastern edges of the Arabian Desert. Migrating to the west, they settled in the Palestinian area of the eastern Mediterranean now occupied by Israel, Jordan, and Syria. After occupying this land for a number of centuries, the Jews began to scatter throughout the ancient Mediterranean world after a period of exile in Babylon. Their Palestinian community was destroyed by the Romans in 70 C.E. and again in 135, and Judaism thus became a religious community spread throughout parts of Asia, Africa, and later Europe and America. Its Palestinian homeland was not restored until 1948, with the establishment of the modern state of Israel. Modern Jews, bound together by their religious and cultural heritage, live over much of the world, with Israel itself comprising a relatively small number of the total.

Historically, Judaism traces its heritage to one patriarch, Abraham, and his family. Abraham was a Semitic wanderer who migrated into Palestine around 2000–1800 B.C.E. Central to his family tradition was the belief that he had been led into this migration by a God who promised him a land and that his family would become a "mighty nation." Some centuries later (1290 B.C.E.), again at God's instigation, Moses led the descendants of Abraham out of a period of slavery in Egypt. It is as a result of this exodus from Egypt and subsequent developments that the distinctive patterns of Jewish faith and life began to emerge. Whereas Abraham and his sons were patriarchs of the community, Moses emerged as the architect of later Judaism. Beginning as a familial and tribal grouping, Judaism later incorporated others into the community if they were willing to accept the requirements of the "covenant" that bound them to God.

The basic beliefs of Judaism are rooted in the historical elements that created the community. In Jewish tradition, Yahweh, the God who led Moses and Abraham, chose Abraham and his descendants (the Israelites) to be his unique and particular people. By acting in their history to form the community and by sustaining it through the centuries, Yahweh revealed himself as a God intimately related to the world and involved in its activities. Judaism also came to affirm that this God was *the* God of the universe (creator and all powerful), thereby establishing a monotheistic faith. In the exodus from Egyptian slavery, Yahweh further revealed himself and the nature of complete life through the Ten Commandments and the laws of Moses—the Pentateuch—the first five books of what Christians refer to as the Old Testament. He bound himself to the Israelites by giving promises of being "their God," and expecting that they in return would be "his people" by following the commandments and laws given. Created in this manner, Judaism expresses its loyalty and solidarity by a corporate life in which every aspect of life, public and private, is permeated by God's presence and human response to that presence. Through this relationship, Yahweh, although transcendent in the fullest sense, is revealed as being personal and exhibiting characteristics of love and concern as well as justice (when disobedience occurs). For Judaism this choice by Yahweh has still another implication: Through Israel God reveals himself and his nature to all humanity so that the estrangement that exists between himself and humanity can be overcome.

In Jewish understanding, humanity is created to be responsible for its actions and as such is given freedom of will—freedom to be obedient or disobedient to the universal laws established by God. Given this freedom, humanity has a propensity to be disobedient or self-oriented, thereby becoming evil. In receiving God's commandments and responding in faithfulness, Israel overcomes this propensity, thus becoming truly a "light to the nations." According to Jewish understanding, the Israelites have not always been faithful to this ideal and have been disobedient; yet the uniqueness of the relationship to God remains. In its best sense this is to be a source not of pride but of responsibility for the Israelites. Historically the relationship has produced among Israelites two perspectives often held in tension—an extreme exclusiveness and a sense of world mission.

Torah

The relationship depends ultimately on God's initiative, his gracious choice of the Israelites, with whom he seals the connection by giving them a *Torah*—"teachings," or more commonly, "the law." Through the Torah, all of human life is given a normative pattern by God's gracious guidance. In the broadest sense, the Torah is that guidance expressed in every aspect of life. In its written form it refers to Jewish scripture—Pentateuch, Prophets, and Writings. It may also refer to an oral tradition of revelation as well as to oral and written interpretations of the tradition (*Talmud*). This understanding of the Torah as a source of guidance is representative of Rabbinic Judaism, that form of Judaism that survived the Roman destruction of Jerusalem in 70 and 135 and was dominated by the rabbis—the teachers, ultimately the religious, social, and political leaders of the community. Rabbinic Judaism concentrated on interpretation of the law to adapt it to ever-changing social conditions and yet to retain its uniqueness. In the community, civil and religious law were not distinguishable from each other. Rabbinic Judaism took a traditionalist approach protective of distinctive Jewish ethical and ritual patterns. This set the members of this particular community apart from their non-Jewish neighbors (creating in Europe Jewish "ghettos," where the Jews lived apart from others), while at the same time guaranteeing the survival of the tradition that was severely tested through intense persecution in the medieval and modern periods. Ancient ritual and ethical practices, as well as demanding and exacting food laws established in the Exodus period and later, have survived into the modern day through this insistence on obedience to the Torah.

Rites and Festivals

The assumption that all of life is guided by God, added to the familial origins of Judaism, meant that the family emerged as a central element in the religion. Primary religious services and teachings, as well as the enforcement of ethical codes, take place in the home. Here the community of the faithful has its roots; therefore, some major religious festivals, as well as regular worship, take place in the home. Arising in the family is another central concern—insistence on education: to know and interpret the Torah and to prepare oneself as completely as possible for life. Related to the familial emphasis are several rites of passage: circumcision for male children as a sign of the covenant relationship; bar mitzvah, when the son, at age thirteen, recites Torah benedictions in the synagogue to mark his acceptance of the responsibilities of the covenant (also practiced among some Jews is bas mitzvah for girls); marriage, with appropriate rites and scripture readings; and burial, a simple but significant service. Each of these events, though a milestone in the individual life cycle, is also a family, and often a community, event celebrated in the synagogue. (The synagogue, formed by any ten adult male Jews, first arose as a place for teaching the Torah but became also a place of worship.)

In addition to these ceremonies, the feasts and festivals of Judaism play an important part in the religious life of the community: Pesach (Passover), commemorating the exodus from Egypt; Shavuot (Pentecost), celebrating the grain harvest and commemorating the giving of the Torah; Sukkot (tabernacles), an autumn harvest festival; Simchat Torah, concluding and beginning a new annual round of Torah readings; Rosh Hashana, celebrating the new year; Yom Kippur, the Day of Atonement; Hanuka, a feast of dedication commemorating victory in 165 B.C.E. over the Syrians, commonly celebrated by use of the seven-candle menorah shown in Figure 2.3; and Purim, celebrating deliverance from the Persian Empire. Other lesser festivals and fasts are also observed by many Jews. Central to all such cycles and to the regular life of the Jew is the Sabbath, instituted in earliest times as a day of rest and worship.

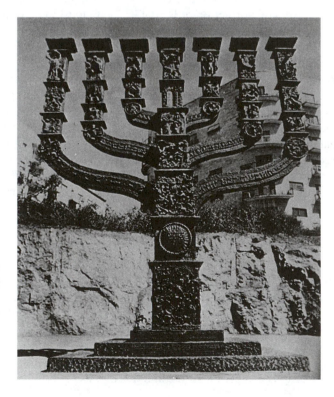

Figure 2.3
A menorah, used to celebrate the Jewish Feast of Hanuka. (Courtesy Consulate General of Israel in New York.)

Three Branches

The impact of cultural and intellectual developments in Western civilization during the eighteenth and nineteenth centuries drastically changed the economic and political situation of European and American Jews. For the first time they were able to move freely, and they gradually abandoned the ghettos to be amalgamated into the larger society. The results have been varied. Among the traditionalists, the heritage of Rabbinic Judaism has survived to become incorporated into modern Orthodox synagogues, where ancient ritual and ethical practices are still understood to be operative, though some modifications have been allowed to meet urban and nonghetto situations. Nevertheless, every decision and situation in life can be the topic of rabbinic interpretation. The intellectual ferment of the Enlightenment and its aftermath led some Jews, however, to question the ancient traditions and abandon certain of the laws (such as food laws and exclusive dependence on the Hebrew language in religious services) and to change some elements of their theological positions. These and other changes led to the establishment of Reform synagogues—those of the more liberal Jewish religious community. Reform Judaism basically abandoned dependence on a total religious-political-ethical code but retained emphasis on the moral law along with traditional religious practices when appropriate. Conservative Judaism forms a third major Jewish community, which, though willing to make concessions regarding certain aspects of the law, nevertheless insists on a more conservative formulation and practice than that found within the Reform community. Each of these major groups contains many smaller subgroups, which often reflect ethnic differences. With this diversification, there is still a strong cohesiveness among the Jewish community. The sense of a unique culture and relation to God is present. Although the unifying core of Jewish culture has traditionally been its religion, many modern Jews, through identification with patterns of Jewish culture, affirm their continuing identity as Jews without actively participating in, or necessarily accepting, the theological implications of the religious tradition.

UNIT 15   Christianity

Arising from Palestinian Judaism but separating from that foundation early, Christianity gradually spread throughout the Mediterranean cultures, becoming the religion of the Roman Empire by the fourth century. Dominating medieval Europe, Christianity became the major religious tradition of modern Europe and America, spreading from these bases throughout the world in the past three centuries. At present it claims the largest number of adherents (over 1 billion).

Jesus

Foundations for the religion were laid in the teachings and ministry of Jesus of Nazareth, a Palestinian Jew who lived in the reigns of the Roman Emperors Augustus and Tiberius Caesar. As a Jew, Jesus accepted without major modification many of the traditional Israelite beliefs: a monotheistic faith in one universal God, a confidence that this God acts significantly and graciously in human history, a belief in humanity's propensity to disobey the will of God, and a concept of salvation (restoration of loving relations between God and humanity) in which human disobedience can be overcome.

Jesus taught in the patterns and traditions of the Jewish rabbis (teachers), yet he reinterpreted the Jewish Torah on the basis of his own authority, claiming to teach what Yahweh originally intended in the insights and proscriptions of the Torah. He insisted on looking behind the multitudinous applications and interpretations of the Torah common among the contemporary rabbis to the *intent* of the law—the theological and ethical principles fundamental to that law and what they indicated about the relationship of God to humanity. Jesus also taught that the long-expected Jewish "kingdom of God" had begun in his own ministry. In this affirmation the popular Jewish expectation of an earthly but divine Messiah (anointed one of God) was substantially modified. Contemporary Jews expected a Messiah who would manifest God's graciousness within their own history by the restoration of a politically and religiously powerful Israel. For Jesus, God's kingdom was to come when God's will—the total commitment of one's life to God and the unrestricted love of one's neighbor—became manifest in the lives of the people. Therefore, the long-expected kingdom of God had already begun in those who, following Jesus's teachings, did God's loving will. It would come to full fruition in the future when all persons joined in living out God's will. Such teachings said little of the Jewish expectation of a politically restored Israel wherein one lived, according to Jesus, a restricted view of God's will. Added to these teachings was Jesus's ministry of caring—a ministry of healing and restoration to the wholeness of broken human lives.

Jesus's teachings and life-style, which accepted all persons as God's chosen people, were controversial among Jews. Many of the common people found in them great hope, but many, particularly the religious leaders, became his adversaries. After a brief ministry, he was charged with blasphemy by the Jewish leaders because of his claim to be speaking with God's authority. He was taken before Roman authorities and charged with treason for supposedly claiming to be "king of the Jews." Although crucified as a common criminal by the Romans, his followers testified that he arose from the dead and appeared to them on several occasions.

For Christians, this event of resurrection, along with Jesus's life and teachings, means that Jesus was the very incarnation of God in human form (a unique and unrepeatable event). In resurrection the power of death was broken not only for Jesus but also for all believers, so they were offered the promise of this gracious love in their own lives and the hope that their personal lives would continue in God's love beyond death. Christians also proclaimed that through this event God offers salvation to all humanity by overcoming disobedience and its consequences. They further affirmed that the God who had revealed himself in Jesus continued his ministry by actively participating in their daily lives and communities as a unique spiritual presence—the Holy Spirit. The later church would combine these insights into a doctrine of the Trinity: belief in God the Father (and Creator), God the Son (God manifest in Jesus the Christ), and God the Holy Spirit (God present in history)—a triune manifestation of one God. Subject to a great variety of interpretations by believers through the centuries since Jesus, these concepts form the core of Christian theology.

Christian Community

Immediately after the death of Jesus, his followers formed themselves into a community and in doing so provided an ongoing embodiment for his teachings and proclamations. Spreading the "Good News" (Gospel) of God's gracious love revealed in Jesus gave the new religious movement a missionary, or evangelical, pattern in a world where many religions sought adherents. Although at first made up of Jews, by the end of the first century after Jesus's death this community had gained converts throughout the Mediterranean cultures, and non-Jews were the majority in the movement.

As Jews, the first Christians retained profound respect for and dependence on the Hebrew scriptures—the Torah, the written forms of Jewish law, writings of the prophets, and historical writings. These became for the Christians the Old Testament (Covenant), embodying basic truths about humanity and God. Alongside these scriptures arose Christian writings recounting Jesus's life and teachings, expositions of faith, sermons, and apocalyptic materials. The most significant of these became the New Testament (Covenant) and were understood to be divinely inspired. Within the community these Scriptures constitute a principal source of information, inspiration, and interpretation of the Gospel. For some Christians, they are the sole authority in matters of faith. For others, along with faithful church tradition and the inspiration of the Holy Spirit, these Scriptures form one significant source of authority.

The diversity of the Christian community and its accommodation to hundreds of social settings have resulted in a great diversification of practices and patterns of worship. Most Christians accept at least two sacraments: baptism, a rite recognizing God's gift of his love and forgiveness, the acceptance by the believer of that grace, and the incorporation of the believer into the community of the faithful; and the Eucharist (the Lord's Supper, Holy Communion), a rite commemorating the life, death, and resurrection of Jesus, giving the believer an opportunity to participate symbolically in that event. Interpretations of the meaning and form of the sacraments have been numerous and often divisive, yet these sacraments remain characteristic of Christianity. Certain branches of the church (particularly the Roman Catholic and Orthodox) recognize other sacraments in addition to these two (usually seven in all). Though there is great diversity among Christian celebrations, the veneration of Jesus's life, death, and resurrection is embodied in Easter rites by most Christian churches, as is his birth at Christmas and the coming of the Holy Spirit to the first disciples at Pentecost.

The Church

Patterns of church organization, governance, and theology have also been diverse. From the earliest period, the church found itself ministering to variant groups with differing intellectual, cultural, and ethical impulses. The result has been the formation of many subgroupings, but most of them can be incorporated into three major branches: Orthodox, Roman Catholic, and Protestant.

During its first several hundred years, the church was a loosely organized community with local leaders (bishops) having responsibility and authority in local questions of doctrine and practice. When a universal or church-wide issue arose, representatives from the various local churches formed a council to make authoritative decisions. However, because the eastern and western sections of the Mediterranean represented differing cultural traditions, distinct theological and ritual practices emerged in each section. The differences between the eastern and western sections ultimately became acute, and two branches of Christianity emerged: Orthodoxy in the east and Roman Catholicism in the west. The process was slow, and an official final split did not occur until 1091.

Orthodoxy emphasized the spiritual aspects of worship by stressing the poetic and the mystical, accepted a loose regional autonomy of "equal" metropolitans (archbishops), and saw the Eucharist as the celebration of Christ's resurrection from the dead. Roman Catholicism insisted on a more precise rationalistic theology and on the authority of one bishop over the church (the bishop of Rome, known commonly as the pope) and understood the Eucharist as a remembrance and reenactment of Christ's redemptive death on the cross. Once separated, these branches had little contact with each other until modern times.

Called on to provide stabilization in the west as the Roman Empire disintegrated, the Roman Catholic church with its strong papacy and expansive monasticism became a primary component in the political as well as spiritual fabric of medieval western Europe. In the late medieval period (1400–1500), however, the hierarchy of the church had become rich, corrupt, and indifferent—out of touch with new intellectual, scientific, and spiritual trends in the society and removed from the needs of the common people.

In the sixteenth century, several Christian groups rose in protest against abuses of faith and governance in the church, a protest known in history as the Protestant Reformation. Basic to the protest was the rejection of the power of the pope, the insistence by Protestants that God's grace was available through faithful trust in him as well as through the sacraments, and the belief that the sole or primary authority resides in the Scriptures rather than in the church. Accompanying the protest was the resolute affirmation that a person is saved by God's gracious love recognized and accepted in personal faith, an affirmation that questioned the traditional capacity of Roman Catholic priests to define spiritual and moral works, which were understood to renew one's relation to God. Insistence on personal, direct access to God led to the development of numerous independent voluntary congregations and churches. Proliferation of separate denominations, each establishing its own interpretations, beliefs, and practices, became a hallmark of the Protestant branch of Christianity.

In modern times many of the differences among the three major Christian branches have been recognized by all involved as being historical, ecclesiastical, and cultural rather than substantial matters of faith. Recent changes in theology and practice within each group, the threat of secular culture, and competition with other religions have contributed in recent years to the rise of numerous ecumenical movements providing conversations, study, and joint projects among the variant Christian branches. Protestantism has during this period experienced a number of mergers and reunions of variant subgroups. It is to be expected, nevertheless, that a religion covering the many cultures of the world will continue to have major differences among its adherents.

Unit 16   Islam

In the sixth century the ancient civilizations of the Mesopotamian valley and adjacent areas had become decadent and were loosely governed by tribes living on the Arabian peninsula. The religion of these tribes was a polytheist amalgam of nature religions drawn from surrounding cultures. Prominent was the *Ka'ba*, a shrine containing many holy objects and images located in an important trade center, Mecca. One of the most conspicuous of these relics was a large black stone or meteorite.

Muhammad

Muhammad, the prophet through whose teachings the Islamic religion began, was born in 570 C.E., part of an aristocratic clan responsible for the care of the Ka'ba. Although closely identified with religious practices of the community through his family, Muhammad as a young man was repelled by the patterns of a religion in which caprice and change were prominent and sacrifices influenced or directed the divine spirits. Orphaned early and raised in the households of his grandfather and uncle, he traveled extensively throughout the region, working in merchant caravans. In these travels Muhammad was exposed to Judaism and Christianity and attracted to their monotheistic emphasis on the revealed will of *one* all-powerful God communicating through spokespersons (prophets). Concerned by issues of human existence and given to personal meditation, he was encouraged in his religious interests by Khadija, his wife. Once, while meditating in a desert cave, Muhammad had a vision in which the angel Gabriel appeared and commanded him to "recite." This was the first of a number of such occasions, which Muhammad came to see as direct expressions of God's will—the will of Allah, the Arabic high God. Khadija, with whom he shared these revelations, became his first convert to a new religion. Others soon joined her, forming a small community of believers in Mecca.

Central to Muhammad's teachings was the belief in *one* all-powerful, supreme God—Allah, on whom all creation depended. Humanity's proper relation to Allah was submission to Allah's will. The literal meaning of the word *Islam* is "submission." One who so submits becomes a *Muslim*. Allah's revelations to Muhammad were written down over a period of years and became the 114 *suras* (chapters) of the *Qu'ran*, the Islamic scriptures. These revelations, and therefore the Qu'ran, are looked on by Muslims as direct communications from Allah given through his greatest prophet, not as the original thoughts of Muhammad. The content of the Qu'ran is wide-ranging, from teachings about the nature of Allah and humanity to instructions for daily living.

When Muhammad began to preach his new message to the citizens of Mecca, it contrasted greatly with their traditional religious beliefs because it demanded that they abandon the worship of many gods to give devotion to Allah alone. Many responded with hostility, in part because they felt Muhammad's message was a threat to the economic benefits of the religious rites and shrines that attracted pilgrims to Mecca. For their own safety,

Muhammad and his followers abandoned Mecca, taking up residence in a nearby city, Yathrib. Here the citizenry was much more receptive to the Islamic message, and Muhammad was soon made governor. In Muslim tradition this escape to Yathrib in the year 622 became known as the *Hegira,* the "flight." From this Hegira Muslim calendars are dated. Yathrib's name was later changed to Medina, or "City of the Prophet."

Gaining support in Medina, Muhammad sought to reenter Mecca with his message. Conquering the city without a major battle, Muhammad's followers suppressed its polytheistic worship, cleansing the Ka'ba of all of its religious images and relics, with the exception of the black stone. The stone, in Muslim teaching, had been placed there by Abraham, forefather of Arabs as well as Jews, as a symbol of Allah; thus the Ka'ba became the holiest shrine of the new religion, and Mecca and Medina became holy cities. The Dome of the Rock Muslim shrine in Jerusalem shown in Figure 2.4 is the third most important Muslim shrine.

During the remainder of Muhammad's life and in the years after his death, the Islamic religion spread rapidly across the eastern Mediterranean and North Africa and into parts of Europe. Islam forbade wars of aggression, but recognized the right of defensive war and did not hesitate to suppress polytheism, while tolerating other monotheistic reli-

Figure 2.4   The Dome of the Rock. Located in modern Israel, this seventh-century building is still a sacred place to the world's Muslims. (Courtesy Israel Ministry of Tourism.)

gions, among conquered populations. During the seventh and eighth centuries Muslims occupied Portugal and Spain and a part of present-day France. Islam also spread across all of the Arabian peninsula, across large parts of Asia—covering present-day Turkey, Syria, Iraq, Iran, Afghanistan, and Pakistan and parts of India, Malaya, and Indonesia—and into China. Though Muslims were later driven from France, Spain, and Portugal, Muslim influence remained in the architecture, medicine, and philosophy of medieval Europe. At present, there are large numbers of Muslims in parts of southern and eastern Europe— Bosnia, Albania, and Bulgaria—as well as Africa and Asia.

Muhammad is regarded by Muslims as the last and greatest of the prophets in a line extending from Abraham and other figures whose lives and teachings are recorded in the Jewish scriptures down through Jesus. In no sense a divine being, Muhammad is regarded as the Seal of the Prophets. (Muslims recognize a kinship with Christians as well as with Jews since all worship the same God in a monotheistic way; nevertheless, Muslims are critical of elements that they consider polytheistic in Christianity—including the doc-trine of the Trinity and the recognition of Jesus as in some sense divine, the unique Son of God—and of what they see as the unfaithfulness of the Jews to the revelation that they received through their prophets.)

Duties

Combining the belief in one supreme, all-powerful, eternal God, creator of all things, with the concept of Allah revealing his will through Muhammad, the Muslim demand that one submit to Allah's will became the hallmark of Islamic doctrine. Based on this affirmation, Muslims are enjoined in the Qu'ran to observe five supreme duties, called the Five Pillars of Islam. The first of these incorporates the central belief—one is to con-fess (profess) and sincerely hold a belief in one God and in the revelation of his will through Muhammad. Anyone who can confess sincerely, "There is no God but Allah, and Muhammad is his Prophet" is regarded as a Muslim and has fulfilled the first duty of the Islamic religion.

A second duty is to offer prayer to Allah, at prescribed times, five times daily. Although ideally prayer is best offered in a *mosque* (a building dedicated to the worship of Allah), Muslims can pray anywhere. In Muslim countries followers are summoned to prayer by the chant of a *muezzin* (one who calls the populace to prayer, usually from the tower of a mosque). In prayer, Muslims, facing toward Mecca, prostrate themselves to sym-bolize their total submission to Allah, usually on a specially designed prayer rug (to sym-bolize or confer sacredness on the site where the prayer is made). Though women may attend services at mosques, it is especially important for men to do so; and if at all possi-ble, men and boys are present in the mosque for prayer at midday on Fridays, when an *imam*—a mosque official—leads the worship.

A third duty prescribed for Muslims is to give alms for the benefit of the poor and for the upkeep of the mosque.

A fourth duty is to observe a strict fast during daylight hours of the Muslim month of Ramadan, the month that marks the anniversary of the beginning of Allah's rev-elations to Muhammad. The month is intended to be marked also by special conscientiousness in fulfilling one's moral and religious duties. As much daylight time as possible is to be devoted to prayer and meditation, and food may be eaten only at night.

A fifth duty—the Fifth Pillar of Islam—is the duty of making, at least once during one's lifetime, a pilgrimage (called a *hadj*) to the holy city of Mecca. The hadj is supposed to be made with great reverence and with strict obedience to all moral and ritual requirements of the Islamic religion. A number of ritual duties must be performed during the trip to Mecca if the hadj is to fulfill its purpose. For instance, on arrival, the pilgrim must run around the Ka'ba seven times, each time kissing or touching the black stone. Only Muslims are allowed inside the sacred city. Muslim pilgrims often testify to the sense of brotherhood experienced by Muslims of many different national, racial, and cultural backgrounds during the hadj.

In addition to the Five Pillars, there are many moral and cultic requirements binding on Muslims. Demanded are justice, truthfulness, abstention from alcoholic beverages, abstention from eating pork, and above all abstention from anything that seems remotely connected with idolatry; no representations of divine, human, or animal beings may be made.

To those who are faithful to its moral and cultic demands, Islam promises endless rewards in a blissful Paradise after the present earthly life. The rewards are often presented as involving both material and spiritual benefits. Those who are unfaithful are threatened with endless punishment in Hell, represented in graphic physical detail in the Qu'ran (see Unit 58).

Branches of Islam

The rapid spread of Islam after Muhammad's death was accompanied by schism among Muslims. Some of these persist to the present day. For instance, *Sunnis* derive from those followers of Muhammad who accepted Abu Bakr, one of Muhammad's chief followers, as his legitimate successor. Abu Bakr was elected to succeed Muhammad after Muhammad's death and was given the title *caliph* ("leader"). Abu Bakr and his successor caliphs were largely responsible for the effective and energetic spread of Islam. Minority groups, however, have existed from the beginning of the religion. Members of Muhammad's family and their colleagues resisted the rule of the early caliphs, contending that leadership should have been retained among Muhammad's descendants. From this group arose the present-day *Shi'ite* branch of Islam, which places great emphasis on the charismatic qualities of their leaders, understood to be the proper spiritual heirs of Muhammad. This group is traditionally the more conservative of the two major branches in its refusal to accommodate Islam to the non-Muslim influences of the modern world.

In most Muslim countries there are rival Muslim groups and rival interpretations of the meanings of important aspects of the Islamic religion. There have recently been militant revivals of traditional, or "fundamentalistic," Islamic practices and beliefs in some Islamic countries, particularly Iran, in opposition to adoption of Western non-Islamic influence. The necessity of developing technological societies to meet the challenges of the modern world has created great tension, with the strongly felt need to resist Western encroachment and to retain distinctive Muslim patterns and traditions. The intensity of feeling among Muslims who have felt traditional patterns of belief and practice threatened by non-Muslim influence has often surprised outsiders, as has the bitterness between competing Muslim groups; Iran, for instance, is predominantly Shi'ite and has supported efforts, sometimes including violence, of Shi'ite minorities to secure greater influence in Muslim countries where the Sunni tradition is predominant.

Islam in recent decades has experienced significant revival both in areas where it has long been dominant and in many other areas of the world. Notable expansion of the tradition has taken place in Europe and America. The conservative renewal of Islamic cultural and social law has caused significant change, as well as conflict, in the present social and government patterns of many traditionally Muslim countries.

Another major strand of Islamic faith that has been influential in many forms of Islam is that of the *Sufis*, a pattern of religious mysticism that first arose in the ninth century and continues to the present. The influence and strength of the Sufi tradition has been varied throughout history and was strongly criticized and persecuted by more traditionally oriented Muslims in the nineteenth century. (See Unit 20.)

Muslim contact with the Christian West has often involved great tension, yet Muslim theologians and philosophers helped to preserve the teachings of the great Greek philosophers of antiquity, transmitting them, with monotheistic elaboration and interpretation, to the Christian philosophers and theologians of the Middle Ages. To the outside observer, the Islamic tradition may appear stern and demanding, yet rich and varied. It has supported and encouraged subtle and powerful expressions of religious devotion and creativity in the arts, in science, in poetry, and in speculative philosophical and religious thought.

Summary

Since this book does not seek to exhaust the content of all of the living religions, the charts that follow are intended to serve as aids in comparing and differentiating basic concepts and thrusts in today's major religions.

The material in these categories cannot be considered complete or fully representative of any of the religions in content and practice. One must constantly remember that there are problems in oversimplification. If one keeps in mind the complexity that is characteristic of any religious perspective, the chart may be helpful in reminding the reader of important emphases in the various religions.

In addition to the seven religious traditions found in Chapter 2, information is included here on the native Japanese religion Shinto, which is discussed in several units of *Exploring Religious Meaning*.

Basic Tenets of the Major World Religions

	HINDUISM	BUDDHISM	
		Hinayana	*Mahayana*
Creed			
What is the divine?	Brahman-Atman Eternal Spirit in world and individual	——	Cosmic compassion
What is man?	Eternal soul in bondage to a physical body through ignorance Reincarnation *Karma:* reap what you sow	Reincarnation *Karma:* reap what you sow	
What is nature?	Illusion arising from ignorance Unreal	Illusion arising from ignorance Unreal	Illusion yet reality, through which many may know compassion
What is salvation?	Being freed from bondage to illusion through Knowledge Works Devotion Asceticism	Achieving enlightenment through: Four Noble Truths Eightfold Path	
Code			
How should one live?	Meditation Doing one's duties Devotion to deity or deities	Eightfold Path Discipline Gentleness and kindness	Eightfold Path Gentleness Kindness and Discipline
Cult			
How should one worship?	Prayers Offerings Sacrifices Hymns Scriptures Meditation Ritual directed to deity or deities	Prayers Offerings Sacrifices Hymns Scriptures Meditation Ritual for the sake of discipline	Prayers Offerings Sacrifices Hymns Scriptures Meditation Ritual directed toward divine beings
What should one worship?	Powers of nature Brahman-Atman symbolized by images	——	Divine beings embodying cosmic compassion symbolized by images
Community			
How is the religious group understood?	Everyone	Those seeking enlightenment through self-discipline (monks) and, to a lesser extent, laypersons abiding by the rules	Those who express compassion
How is it related to others?	Tolerates others Holiest withdraw to live the life of religious hermits	Tolerates others Expresses wisdom to all	Tolerates others Expresses compassion to all

Basic Tenets of the Major World Religions (cont.)

	TAOISM	*CONFUCIANISM*	*SHINTO*
Creed			
What is the divine?	Tao: the Way	Cosmic order	*Kami:* Spiritual force in all things
What is man?	One among many natural beings Corrupted by aggressiveness and self-assertiveness	One among many natural beings Rational Able to do good or evil Moral Educable	One among many natural beings in whom kami is present
What is nature?	Ever-changing process in which the harmony and unity of the Tao is ever present	Real and dependable order in which harmony may be realized	Expression of the kami
What is salvation?	Becoming one with the Tao through mystical union and passivity	Restoring harmony within society and the universe by restoring the old ways	Recognition and veneration of the kami: the gods of the way
Code			
How should one live?	Social passivity; intuitive, mystical oneness with Tao	Harmonious relations with living, dead, and nature	Doing one's duty and honoring the kami
Cult			
How should one worship?	——	Prayers Offerings Sacrifices Hymns Scriptures Ritual Learning directed toward Heaven, ancestral spirits	Prayers Offerings Sacrifices Hymns Scriptures Ritual directed toward the kami
What should one worship?	——	Heaven Ancestors Spirits	Kami, which may or may not be symbolized by images
Community			
How is the religious group understood?	Any who seek union with Tao	Every thinking, sensitive person in society	Everyone
How is it related to others?	Withdraws from society	Is part of society seeking to establish harmony for all	Includes all society

Basic Tenets of the Major World Religions (cont.)

	JUDAISM	CHRISTIANITY	ISLAM
Creed			
What is the divine?	Yahweh (One God with personal attributes)	One God with personal attributes characterized by love and justice (often conceived of as triune unity—Father, Son, Holy Spirit)	Allah (one God with personal attributes)
What is man?	A being created in the image of God and directly dependent on him	A being created in the image of God, renewed in relationship to God and all men through Christ	A being created by Allah and dependent on him
What is nature?	Created physical order with a specific beginning, end, and purpose	Created physical order with specific beginning, end, and purpose	Created physical order with a specific beginning, end, and purpose
What is salvation?	Proper recognition of Yahweh and following his will	Freedom from alienation to participation in the Divine Love through relationship to Christ	Heavenly eternal reward for obeying Allah
Code			
How should one live?	Following the commandments of the Torah	In loving fellowship with man and God	Maintaining active obedience by following the *Five Pillars* and the instruction of the Qu'ran
Cult			
How should one worship?	Prayer Ritual Scriptures Offerings Festivals	Prayer Ritual Scriptures Offerings Festivals Preaching	Prayer Alms Scriptures Pilgrimage
What should one worship?	Yahweh	God	Allah
Community			
How is the religious group understood?	Those who recognize Yahweh and follow his laws Family	Those who affirm the Lordship of Christ and live by his precepts of love in community	Those who recognize Allah and Muhammad as his prophet
How is it related to others?	Lives peaceably with other faiths	Recognizes various approaches but seeks to convert others through basic message of faith	Recognizes Christianity and Judaism as legitimate religions; tolerates others

A Comparison Between Eastern and Western Religions

EASTERN RELIGIONS	WESTERN RELIGIONS
Hinduism	*Judaism*
Buddhism	*Christianity*
Taoism	*Islam*
Confucianism	
Shinto	

Oriented toward nature	Oriented toward history
Conceives of Divine Power(s) as impersonal	Conceives of Divine Power as personal
Places little emphasis on time	Places great emphasis on time
Believes world and humanity eternal and uncreated	Believes world and humanity created and not eternal
Believes truth is not bound to particular persons	Believes truth comes through particular persons
Tends to be inclusive	Tends to be exclusive
Has little interest in clearly defined doctrine	Has strong interest in clearly defined doctrine
Tends toward unity of reality	Tends toward duality of reality
Downgrades individual will	Exalts individual will

CHAPTER 3

❧

Cases of Religious Experience

Introduction

A flash of insight dawns as the Zen Buddhist is engaged in strenuous silent meditation; the Christian Pentecostal cries out in joyous ecstasy, in language unintelligible to the average listener, at the height of a highly active group experience. Through rational consideration and observation, the religious intellectual apprehends an orderly interrelationship of life forms and places this in the context of an awesome universe—such are the enormously wide-ranging personal experiences that may be termed religious. In the Introduction to Chapter 4, we have attached labels to these types of religious experience. The experience of the Zen Buddhist we have called mystical; that of the Pentecostal Christian, ecstatic; and that of the intellectual, aesthetic. We have also cautioned, and here caution again, that the labels should not be taken as absolutes and are at best indications of the various elements or dimensions of religious experience.

We can say the same concerning another way of distinguishing among types of religious experiences, namely, the distinction between something very private, belonging to individuals in solitude, and group experiences. Either type may be extremely intense or relatively calm. Either may be spontaneous or formally structured. And they may go together and reinforce each other. A person may experience a profound solitary sense of the Divine presence or absence, of being at peace or at war with oneself, as a result of positive or negative group experience, and vice versa.

This chapter presents representative examples of individual religious experiences. They have been selected from a number of traditions and periods not only to show the richness of diversity but also to allow the reader to observe the intensity and significance that the experiences held for the persons involved. Corporate expressions of religious experience are included in the study of structural elements in Chapter 4. Our purpose here is to begin with specific individuals who were historically influential but typical of the varieties of religious experience.

The following questions provide a framework for the examination of these cases of religious experience. They will also be relevant to the instances of religious experience described throughout the book.

1. How did the experience initiate, maintain, strengthen (intensify), or weaken the relationship of the individual or group to (a) pivotal value(s)?
2. What specific features did the experience have?
   Was it an experience of conversion, nurture, intensification?
   Was it sudden or gradual?
   Was it expected or unexpected?
   Was it sought (a quest) or unsought (a call)?
3. In what context did the experience occur?
   Did it occur in familiar or in unfamiliar surroundings?
   Did it occur in relation to familiar or unfamiliar persons?
4. Where was the religious experience centered—that is, what areas of the individual's or the group's life did it affect most? Least?
5. How did it affect the individual's or the group's relationships? How did it affect the roles the individual had in the group or the roles the group had in the larger society?

It should be remembered that many factors influence and are affected by individual or group experience. Most religions involve a belief, or credal component. Similarly, every religion contains some directives, moral or legal, relating to the way of life, or code of conduct, advocated for its adherents or the world at large. Most religions contain practices and prescriptions for public and private devotion, its worship or cultic aspect. Finally, every religious tradition contains some concept of the limits of the community—who is included and how one becomes included; who is excluded—united in (or divided by) their adherence to the particular tradition. Note how each of these factors, and others, may or may not be present in the cases that follow.

In accordance with our basic definition of religion, we define a religious experience as any experience that initiates or strengthens, maintains or weakens, or terminates one's reliance on or commitment to a pivotal value. In some religious traditions, such as some forms of Christianity, a religious experience is any experience that creates or strengthens, maintains or weakens, or extinguishes one's faith (in God or in Christ) or one's commitment. But we are concerned with language inclusive enough to cover any kind of ultimate or unconditional commitment or ultimate life or self-understanding.

UNIT 17   God's Call, Moses's Response

Moses was the leader of the Hebrews during their exodus from Egypt, perhaps sometime during the fourteenth to thirteenth centuries B.C.E. Born to a Hebrew woman but reared in the pharaoh's court, Moses enjoyed Egyptian favor until he impulsively killed an Egyptian taskmaster whom he saw mistreating one of his Hebrew kinsmen. Fearing Egyptian punishment for murder, he fled to "the land of Midian," where he became a shepherd and married the daughter of Jethro, "the priest of Midian" (Exodus 2:15–22). While in Midian, Moses received a "call" from God. As the following passage indicates, God initiates the relationship with Moses and defines its purposes.

While keeping his father-in-law's flock, Moses approaches the traditional holy mountain of God, Horeb. There he encounters a burning bush, which is not consumed by the fire, and having paused to investigate this phenomenon, finds God speaking to him.

> When the Lord saw that he turned to see, God called to him out of the bush, "Moses, Moses!" And he said, "Here am I." Then he said, "Do not come near; put off your shoes from your feet, for the place on which you are standing is holy ground." And he said, "I am the God of your father, the God of Abraham, the God of Isaac, and the God of Jacob." And Moses hid his face, for he was afraid to look at God. (Exodus 3:4–6, RSV)

Note that this is a personal direct encounter with God. Moses does not observe God himself but is clearly aware of his holy presence. In Hebrew tradition such encounters are normally for a particular purpose—a call to a mission or an instruction to the people. The Lord makes the purpose of this call clear.

> Then the Lord said, "I have seen the affliction of my people who are in Egypt, and have heard their cry because of their taskmasters; I know their sufferings, and I have come down to deliver them out of the hand of the Egyptians, and to bring them up out of that land to a good and broad land, a land flowing with milk and honey. . . . Come, I will send you to Pharoah that you may bring forth my people, the sons of Israel, out of Egypt." (Exodus 3:7–10, RSV)

Moses then responds in typical human fashion with a series of reasons why he should not be God's messenger. "Who am I that I should go to Pharoah?" The question is never answered directly. He is simply God's choice. Next Moses objects that he does not even know the name of the God who is giving the call. God then identifies himself as "I AM WHO I AM" and the "God of your fathers—Abraham, Isaac, and Jacob." The "I AM" designation indicates that Moses is here encountered by the transcendent, holy God whom the Hebrews had once followed but had forgotten. In giving Moses this "new" name, God is asserting that no explanatory name is adequate or necessary—he simply "is"—yet he is also identifying himself with the ancient God of the Hebrews and renewing his promises to Israel. Convinced that the Israelites will never believe what he has heard from God, Moses further objects.

God promises a sign to the people—a shepherd's rod or staff will become a serpent. Moses then points out that he is "not eloquent . . . slow of speech and tongue." God chides Moses, pointing out that he had made Moses's tongue, and he promises to be with Moses in his speech. Finally, Moses, driven to no more excuses, cries out, "Oh, My Lord, send, I pray, some other person." God, relentless in his call, only promises to use Moses's brother, Aaron, as his spokesperson. Moses reluctantly submits to the call.

God establishes the relationship, and yet Moses is free to struggle with his response to that call. Based on a personal encounter, the call is to a much broader community responsibility—the saving of all of Israel. The experience changes the direction of Moses's life and the immediate relationship of God to the people of Israel. In submitting to God's will, Moses becomes one of the central figures through whom the relationship of Israel and God is revealed and clarified.

UNIT 18   Luther's Religious Experience

Martin Luther's Europe of the late Middle Ages was marked by war, famine, plague, and death as well as by radical social change, indicated by the rise of capitalism in a feudal economy, population shifts from rural to urban areas, and the emergence of new technologies. The old values of medieval Christianity, which stressed that good works were rewarded by God's favor, although still embraced by many, no longer provided religious certainty in more sensitive people such as Luther.

As a young man, Luther began to prepare for a law career in accordance with the wishes of his strong-willed father. There was within him, however, a disturbing desire to find assurance that he was approved by God. The pervasiveness of death was a sobering and anxiety-producing reality in those times, a factor that no doubt haunted Luther and thus influenced him to leave the study of law and become a monk. He hoped to please God by such a move, even though it displeased his father greatly. Entering the Augustinian monastery at Erfurt in 1505, he assiduously pursued the monastic life. An overachieving monk who gave of himself unstintingly in seeking to experience God's grace, he quickly rose in his order and became a professor in the University of Wittenburg in 1512. Nevertheless, for all his close observance of the medieval way to salvation (serious good intentions, repentance, confession of sins, good works, and sacramental observance), he found no satisfying answer to his own growing question: How can one stand in holiness before the demanding righteousness of a just God?

During the period 1513–1519, Luther lectured at Wittenburg on the Psalms and Paul's letters to the Romans and Galatians. Through his constant dealing with these Scriptures, he discovered a new and vital meaning in the Gospel of Christ. He experienced what is classically known as justification by grace through faith—trusting in God's merciful love rather than one's own good works for salvation. His account of this religious experience follows:

> Though I lived as a monk without reproach, I felt that I was a sinner before God with an extremely disturbed conscience. I could not believe that he was placated by my satisfaction. I did not love, yes, I hated the righteous God who punishes sinners, and secretly, if not blasphemously, certainly murmuring greatly, I was angry with God, and said, "As if, indeed, it is not enough, that miserable sinners, eternally lost through original sin, are crushed by every kind of calamity by the law of the decalogue, without having God add pain to pain by the gospel and also by the gospel threatening us with his righteousness and wrath!" Thus I raged with a fierce and troubled conscience. Nevertheless, I beat importunately upon Paul at that place, most ardently desiring to know what St. Paul wanted.
>
> At last, by the mercy of God, meditating day and night, I gave heed to the context of the words, namely, "In it the righteousness of God is revealed, as it is written, 'He who through faith is righteous shall live.' " There I began to understand that the righteousness of God is that by which the righteous lives by a gift of God, namely by faith. And this is the meaning: the righteousness of God is revealed by the gospel, namely, the passive righ-

teousness with which merciful God justifies us by faith, as it is written, "He who through faith is righteous shall live." Here I felt that I was altogether born again and had entered paradise itself through open gates. There a totally other face of the entire Scripture showed itself to me. Thereupon I ran through the Scriptures from memory. I also found in other terms an analogy, as, the work of God, that is, what God does in us, the power of God, with which he makes us strong, the wisdom of God, with which he makes us wise, the strength of God, the salvation of God, the glory of God.[1]

Are there elements in Luther's experience that are also found in the experience of Gautama Buddha as described in Unit 19?

What is different about these two experiences?

What similarities and differences do you see in this experience and that of Augustine's conversion as described in Unit 26?

What was it in the experience that was most important for Luther, in your opinion?

UNIT 19 Gautama's Quest for Nirvana

Siddhartha Gautama is reputed to have been reared in a noble family in India, where he was protected from many harsh realities of the world. As a young man, he ventured forth into that world, only to discover and be staggered by extreme human suffering, disease, and death. Resolved to find answers to these realities of the human condition, he began a quest.

Like many before him in India, Gautama (born c. 560 B.C.E.), a contemporary of Confucius, began a life of spiritual searching, at first studying the philosophical and religious teachings of the highly educated Brahmins, then practicing the rigorous physical and spiritual exercises of the highly disciplined, self-denying ascetics. Even after six years of striving, his quest was not satisfied. Having exhausted the means suggested by the holy men of India, Gautama sat under the Bodhi Tree (the Tree of Wisdom) in meditation, determined not to leave until he had found a solution to the problem of suffering and the riddle of existence. Tradition says that during this "life and death" meditation, he received illumination. Thereafter, he was called Buddha, the Enlightened One (see Figure 3.1). A description of Gautama's religious experience and the Buddhist concept of Nirvana follow.

> Then I thought, it is not easy to gain that happy state while my body is so very lean. What if I now take solid food, rice and sour milk. . . . Now at that time five monks were attending me, thinking, "When the ascetic Gautama gains the Doctrine, he will tell it to us." But when I took solid food, rice and sour milk, then the five monks left me in disgust, saying, "The ascetic Gautama lives in abundance, he has given up striving, and has turned to a life of abundance."
>
> Now having taken solid food and gained strength, without sensual desires, without evil ideas I attained and abode in the first trance of joy and pleasure, arising from seclusion and combined with reasoning and investigation. Nevertheless such pleasant feeling as arose

---

[1] Excerpt from *Martin Luther, Selections from His Writings*, ed. John Dillenberger, p. 11. Copyright © 1961 by John Dillenberger. Reprinted by permission of Doubleday & Company, Inc.

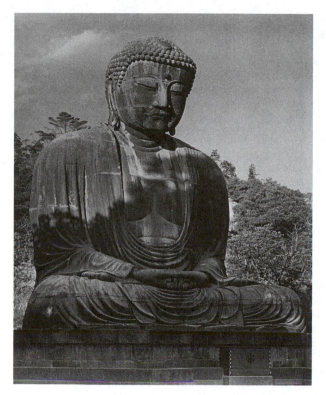

Figure 3.1
Amida Nyorai (Amitabha), known
as Great Buddha of Kamakura, thir-
teenth century. Kotokuin Temple,
Kamukura, Japan. (Photo by M.
Sakamoto; reproduced by permission
of Sakamoto Photo Research Lab.,
Tokyo, Japan.)

did not overpower my mind. With the ceasing of reasoning and investigation I attained
and abode in the second trance of joy and pleasure arising from concentration, with internal serenity and fixing of the mind on one point without reasoning and investigation.
With equanimity towards joy and aversion I abode mindful and conscious, and experienced bodily pleasure, what the noble ones describe as "dwelling with equanimity, mindful, and happily," and attained and abode in the third trance. Abandoning pleasure and
abandoning pain, even before the disappearance of elation and depression, I attained and
abode in the fourth trance, which is without pain and pleasure, and with purity of mindfulness and equanimity.[2]

Having progressed to a state of pure consciousness, Gautama came to several states of
knowledge. First, he reviewed his many former existences, in which he had gone through
thousands of rebirths. In these he came to understand each of his former lives and the
truth that there is rebirth in the normal order of life. Second, he came to realize that the
reason for this constant rebirth is the law of *karma*, wherein those who lead evil lives "in
deed, word, and thought . . . are reborn in a state of misery and suffering." Those who live
good lives are "reborn in a happy state." Having become aware of this truth, Gautama had
arrived at the basic Buddhist understanding of the nature of the world: Life contains suffering brought about by desire, and this suffering can be overcome through elimination of
desire—an insight that comes to be known among Buddhists as the Four Noble Truths (see

[2] Edward J. Thomas, *The Life of Buddha as Legend and History* (London: Routledge & Kegan Paul,
1927), pp. 66–68.

p. 27). This awareness of the nature of the universe, or "enlightenment," brought Gautama an immense sense of freedom and emancipation.

> As I thus knew and thus perceived, my mind was emancipated from the āsava of sensual desire, from the āsava of desire for existence, and from the āsava of ignorance. And in me emancipated arose the knowledge of my emancipation. I realized that destroyed is rebirth, the religious life has been led, done is what was to be done, there is nought (for me) beyond this world. This was the third knowledge that I gained in the last watch of the night. Ignorance was dispelled, knowledge arose. Darkness was dispelled, light arose. So is it with him who abides vigilant, strenuous, and resolute.[3]

Gautama then chose to share with others the freedom and knowledge obtained in this enlightenment. His experience and the teachings that arose from it became the basis of Buddhism. An ultimate state of freedom from the world and eternal bliss are taught by Gautama and known as Nirvana. Following are descriptions of this state and suggestions about how it might be achieved.

> A wanderer who ate rose-apples spoke thus to the venerable Sariputta:
> "Reverend Sariputta, it is said: 'Nirvana, Nirvana.' Now, what, your reverence, is Nirvana?"
> "Whatever, your reverence, is the extinction of passion, of aversion, of confusion, this is called Nirvana."
>
> (*Samyutta-nikāya* IV, 251–52)

> The stopping of becoming is Nirvana.
>
> (*Samyutta-nikāya* II, 117)

> It is called Nirvana because of the getting rid of craving.
>
> (*Samyutta-nikāya* I, 39)[4]

> We are told that Nirvana is permanent, stable, imperishable, immovable, ageless, deathless, unborn, and unbecome, that it is power, bliss, and happiness, the secure refuge, the shelter, and the place of unassailable safety; that it is the real Truth and the supreme Reality; that it is the *Good*, the supreme goal, and the one and only consummation of our life, the eternal, hidden and incomprehensible Peace.[5]

Gautama's Four Noble Truths:

1. That life inevitably involves *dukkha* (suffering)
2. That the cause of suffering is *tanha* (desire or selfish craving)
3. That the suffering can be cured by overcoming selfish craving
4. That the way to overcome selfish craving is through following the eightfold Way, or Path

The following steps constitute the Eightfold Path and lead to Nirvana:

1. Right View—Awareness of the need to overcome selfish desire.
2. Right Thought—Determination to solve this problem

---

[3] Ibid., p. 68.

[4] Edward Conze, ed., *Buddhist Texts Through the Ages* (New York: Harper & Row, 1964), pp. 92, 94.

[5] Edward Conze, *Buddhism: Its Essence and Development* (New York: Harper & Row, 1959), p. 40.

3. Right Speech—Abstention from lies and evil language
4. Right Action—Abstention from killing, stealing, and immoral conduct
5. Right Mode of Livelihood—Noninvolvement in the professions that harm living things
6. Right Endeavor—Suppression of wrong states of mind and creation of right states of mind
7. Right Mindfulness—Self-knowledge and self-mastery
8. Right Concentration—the experience of being freed from the false sense of selfhood and the isolation of selfish motivation

How does Gautama's religious experience compare with Luther's?

UNIT 20   Sufi Encounters

From its beginnings the general Islamic emphasis on the transcendence and omnipotence of Allah was supplemented by those within the tradition who also understood the necessity and centrality of a personal religious encounter with God—the intuitive, which cannot be captured by the rational, historical, or moral patterns of religion. Taking Muhammad's own personal encounters with Allah as an example, these Muslims stressed direct confrontation with God, an experience that often transported them beyond ordinary reality. Known as *Sufis* ("wearers of wool"; in their early asceticism they wore rough wool robes), through the centuries they have represented a distinct Islamic mysticism stressing the union of the individual with God. Concentrating on God's love as his primary category of being, their poetry and other writings reflect the personal character of devotion, often expressed through the symbols of love.

Their insights and teachings find voice in folklore, stories, and poetry. In the thirteenth century, Jalal al-Din Rumi, a Persian Sufi teacher and poet, speaks of the importance of feeling God in one's heart in the following tale in his *Mathnavi*:

> Moses saw a shepherd on the way, who was saying "O God who choosest whom Thou wilt, where art Thou, that I may become Thy servant and sew Thy shoes and comb Thy head? That I may wash Thy clothes and kill Thy lice and bring milk to Thee, O worshipful One; that I may kiss Thy Hand, and rub Thy foot. . . . O Thou to whom all my goats be a sacrifice, O Thou in remembrance of whom are my cries of ay and ah!"
>
> The shepherd was speaking foolish words in this wise. Moses said, "Man, to whom is this addressed."
>
> He answered, "To that One who created us; by whom the earth and sky were brought to sight."
>
> "Hark!" said Moses, "you have become very back-sliding; indeed you have not become a Muslim, you have become an infidel. What babble is this? What blasphemy and raving? Stuff some cotton into your mouth! The stench of your blasphemy has turned the silk robe of religion into rags. Shoes and socks are fitting for you, but how are such things right for One who is a Sun?"
>
> The shepherd said, "O, Moses, thou hast closed my mouth and thou hast burned my soul with repentance." He rent his garment and heaved a sigh, and hastily turned his head towards the desert and went his way.
>
> A revelation came to Moses from God—"Thou hast parted my servant from Me. Didst thou come as a prophet to unite, or didst thou come to sever? So far as thou canst, do not

set foot in separation: . . . I do not look at the tongue and the speech; I look at the inward spirit and the state of feeling. I gaze into the heart to see whether it be lowly, though the words uttered be not lowly, because the heart is the substance. . . . In substance is the real object. How much more of these phrases and conceptions and metaphors? I want burning, burning; become friendly with that burning! Light up a fire of love in thy soul, burn thought and expression entirely away! O Moses, they that know the conventions are of one sort, they whose souls and spirits burn are of another sort."[6]

Rumi carries the image further, expressing insight into the union possible between humanity and Allah.

> When God appears to His ardent lover the lover is absorbed
> in Him, and not so much as a hair of the lover remains.
> True lovers are as shadows, and when the sun shines in
> glory the shadows vanish away. He is a true lover of God to
> whom God says, "I am thine, and thou art mine."
>
> Let me then become nonexistent, for nonexistence
> Sings to me in organ tones, "To his shall we return."
> Behold water in a pitcher; pour it out;
> Will that water run away from the stream?
> When the water joins the water of the stream
> It is lost therein, and becomes itself the stream.
> Its individuality is lost, but its essence remains,
> And thereby it becomes not less nor inferior.[7]

Emphases on direct, dynamic, personal dedication and encounters with God are matched among Islamic Sufis by their awareness of the immanence of God in all of life's experiences. The traditional Muslim stress on outward prayer, pilgrimage, and alms is subordinated to the inward encounter with and dedication to God. In a story attributed to a tenth-century Sufi, Yahya Ibn Mo'adh, the teaching is clear:

> Yahye-e Mo'adh has a brother who went to Mecca and took up residence near the Kaaba. From there he wrote a letter to Yahya.
> "Three things I desired. Two have been realized. Now one remains. Pray to God that He may graciously grant that one desire as well. I desired that I might pass my last years in the noblest place on earth. Now I have come to the Sacred Territory, which is the noblest of all places. My second desire was to have a servant to wait on me and make ready my ablution water. God has given me a seemly servant-girl. My third desire is to see you before I die. Pray to God that he may vouchsafe this desire."
> Yahya replied to his brother as follows.
> "As for your saying that you desired the best place on earth, be yourself the best of men, then live in whatever place you wish. A place is noble by reason of its inhabitants, not vice versa.
> "Then as for your saying that you desired a servant and have now got one, if you were really a true and chivalrous man, you would never have made God's servant your own servant, detaining her from serving God and diverting her to serve yourself. You should yourself be a servant. You desire to be a master, but mastership is an attribute of God.

---

[6] John D. Yohannan, ed., *A Treasury of Asian Literature* (New York: Mentor Books, 1957), pp. 31–32.
[7] N. H. Dole and Belle M. Walker, *Flowers from Persian Poets*, (New York: Thomas Y. Crowell, 1901), pp. 216, 219.

Servanthood is an attribute of man. When God's servant desires a station proper to God, he makes himself a Pharaoh.

"Finally, as to your saying that you desire to see me, if you were truly aware of God, you would never remember me. So associate with God, that no memory of your brother ever comes into your mind. There one must be ready to sacrifice one's son; how much more a brother! If you have found Him, what am I to you? And if you have not found Him, what profit will you gain from me?[8]

Extravagant Sufi expressions of love for and identification with God along with significant asceticism through the early centuries of Islamic history often set Sufis apart from many of their fellow Muslims. Persecution of Sufi teachers and practitioners occasionally became intense. Abu Hamid al-Ghazali, in the eleventh century, sought to heal the rift between the legalistic religion of the Sunnis of his time and the insights of the Sufis. His work made it possible for Muslims to embrace the self-discipline, meditation, and intuition of the Sufis, practiced within the bounds of common sense, and at the same time participate in the demands of the Five Pillars, which were to flow from a heart identified with God's will. Modern Sufism most often embraces al-Ghazali's insight and follows his example.

UNIT 21   Saint Teresa's Ecstasy

Christian mysticism has never been more highly developed or widely appreciated than it was in sixteenth-century Spain. Central figures in the reforms brought to the life of the church by this mystical tradition were Saint Teresa of Avila and her younger colleague, Saint John of the Cross. Their writings on mysticism provide church standards for mystical discipline and have greatly influenced the tradition in all of its phases. For her preeminence in this field, Saint Teresa was declared a Doctor of the Church in 1970—a distinction granted to only two women by the Roman Catholic church.

Born in 1515, Teresa was a member of a prominent Spanish family. On her mother's death when she was fourteen, she began to turn to a more serious religious life, although its full fruition was a long time in coming. At the age of twenty, over her father's objections, she entered the Carmelite Monastery of the Incarnation at Avila. Except for periods of illness, she remained there until 1562. The Carmelite convent at that time allowed a rather lax religious life with a good deal of interaction with the secular community. From her early years Teresa had had visions, trances, and other spiritual experiences, which intensified through the years and made her uncomfortable with the convent's lack of a rigorous spiritual life. Beginning in 1555, as a result of an experience of intense compassion and sorrow at the sight of a statue of Christ's scourging, she turned to a life of spiritual perfection. Over considerable opposition, she was granted permission in 1562 to establish the Convent of Saint Joseph, to follow more strictly the original disciplines of poverty and spiritual life of the Carmelite order. The community became known as the Discalced (Barefooted) Carmelites, and over the next twenty years some thirty-two houses

---

[8] A. J. Arberry, *Muslim Saints and Mystics* (London: Routledge & Kegan Paul, 1966), pp. 181–82.

were established for both nuns and monks. The ultimate influence of the reforms instituted was to be felt throughout the whole Carmelite order. Teresa's mysticism became the example for dedicated spiritual life and, at the same time, was combined with an extremely active participation in religious reform. In later life her mysticism provided the motivation and power for her involvement in establishing and controlling an increasingly influential religious order. Mysticism did not lead her to inactivity or passivity.

To share her experiences, she wrote, at the urging of her superiors, several books. Her *Life* is both a recounting of her own early experiences and a manual for her sisters in the disciplined spiritual life. She describes several states of prayer, from the first beginnings in meditation to union with God. The metaphor of water is used to illustrate her experience. The first state of prayer is like drawing water from a well. It is difficult, requiring discipline when the result is small and slow. The second state is like the introduction of an irrigation pump. Divine aid is given and the reward is much greater. The third state is compared to a running stream. The stream runs at God's instigation and not that of the individual; one's faculties are reduced, in that one may participate in directing the flow but may have little other function. The final stage is likened to a gentle shower of rain, wherein the soul is freely watered by God without human effort. One's usual faculties are transcended so that the experience becomes indescribable. Ecstasy comes at God's instigation, is not granted to many, and results in influencing the person's subsequent life (this was the way Teresa distinguished between true and hallucinatory experience). Teresa insisted that although such experiences were of the greatest importance, they were not ends in themselves—the goal of life remained to do God's will.

The following passage from her *Life* recounts one of Teresa's best-known descriptions of an ecstatic mystical experience.

> It pleased the Lord that I should sometimes see the following vision. I would see beside me, on my left hand, an angel in bodily form—a type of vision which I am not in the habit of seeing, except very rarely. . . . It pleased the Lord that I should see this angel in the following way. He was not tall, but short, and very beautiful, his face so aflame that he appeared to be one of the highest types of angel who seem to be all afire. . . . In his hands I saw a long golden spear and at the end of the iron tip I seemed to see a point of fire. With this he seemed to pierce my heart several times so that it penetrated to my entrails. When he drew it out, I thought he was drawing them out with it and he left me completely afire with a great love for God. The pain was so sharp that it made me utter several moans; and so excessive was the sweetness caused me by this intense pain that one can never wish to lose it, nor will one's soul be content with anything less than God. It is not bodily pain, but spiritual, though the body has a share in it—indeed, a great share. So sweet are the colloquies of love which pass between the soul and God that if anyone thinks I am lying I beseech God, in His goodness, to give him the same experience.[9]

In the seventeenth century Saint Teresa's experience of the pierced heart was depicted in sculpture by Gianlorenzo Bernini (Figure 3.2). This piece was to become one of the best-known religious artworks of the day and the most famous representation of Saint Teresa.

---

[9] *The Life of Teresa of Jesus: The Autobiography of St. Teresa of Avila,* trans. and ed. E. Allison Peers (New York: Doubleday, 1960), pp. 274–75. Reprinted by permission.

Figure 3.2
The Ecstasy of St. Theresa by Gianlorenzo Bernini, in Sta. Maria della Vit-
toria, Rome. (Reproduced by permission
of Alinari—Art Reference Bureau.)

What distinctions do you see between Teresa's experience, described here, and those of Gautama (Unit 19)? How does it compare to Luther's or Moses's experience?

UNIT 22   Juan Diego and Our Lady of Guadalupe

In April 1519, Hernando Cortez and his Spanish army entered Mexico. The natives of Mexico were subjugated by the conquerors, who sought to force their culture and religion on the indigenous people in the name of the Cross of Catholicism and the Crown of Spain. The priests who accompanied Cortez represented the Roman Catholic mandate to missionize, evangelize, and win pagans to Christianity. During the decade following the conquest by Cortez, the Indians of Mexico resisted the Catholic faith. Then, in 1531, a mysterious event occurred—one that caused the Indians of Mexico by the thousands to embrace Catholicism. Virgilio Elizondo writes about this religious experience as follows:

> There is no scientific proof or disproof, or explanation, of the "apparition" of Our Lady of Guadalupe, but there can be no denying its impact on the Mexican people from that time to the present. Its inner meaning has been recorded in the collective memory of the people.

According to the legend, as Juan Diego, a Christian Indian of common status, was going from his home in the *barriada* ("district") near Tepeyac, a hill northwest of Mexico City, he suddenly heard beautiful music. As he approached the source of the music, a lady appeared to him. Speaking in Nahuatl, the language of the conquered, she ordered Juan Diego to go to the palace of the archbishop of Mexico, at Tlatelolco, and tell him that the Virgin Mary, "Mother of the true God through whom one lives," wanted a temple to be built on that site so that in it she could "communicate all her love, compassion, help, and defense to all the inhabitants of this land . . . to hear their lamentations and remedy their miseries, pain, and suffering."

After two unsuccessful attempts by Juan Diego to convince the bishop of the Lady's authenticity, the Virgin wrought a miracle. She sent Juan Diego to pick roses in a place where only desert plants grew. She then arranged the roses in his cloak and sent him to the bishop with the sign he had demanded. As Juan Diego unfolded his cloak in the presence of the bishop, the roses fell to the floor and the painted image of the Lady appeared on his cloak.

The subjugated Mexican people came to life again because of Guadalupe. The response of the Indians was a spontaneous explosion of pilgrimages, festivals, and conversions to the religion of the Virgin. Out of their meaningless and chaotic existence of the postconquest years, a new meaning had erupted.

The real miracle was not the apparition but what happened to the defeated Indian. In the person of Juan Diego was represented the Indian nations defeated and slaughtered, but now brought to life. They who had been robbed of their lands and of their way of life and even of their gods were now coming to live. They who had been silenced were now speaking again through the voice of the Lady. They who wanted only to die now wanted to live.

As at Bethlehem when the Son of God was born as Jesus and signaled the reversal of the power of the Roman empire, so at Tepeyac Christ set foot on the soil of the Americas and signaled the reversal of European domination. Tepeyac symbolized the birth of the Mexican people and the birth of Mexican Christianity. They were no longer an orphaned people and the new religion was no longer that of foreign gods.[10]

Every year, thousands of people make a pilgrimage to the Basilica de Guadalupe in Mexico City, where Juan Diego's apparition is believed to have occurred. There they recall the story and worship Our Lady of Guadalupe. The centrality of this story for the people of Mexico and Latin America cannot be overemphasized. One cannot understand Mexicans and the religious roots of Mexico without reference to Juan Diego, whose experience represents in an exemplary way how many Mexicans believe in God.

UNIT 23   Mahatma Gandhi's Religious Journey

Mahatma Gandhi led India to independence from England, not by the power and might of military strength, but by *Satyagraha* (nonviolent direct action). A world-renowned figure in his own lifetime, Gandhi, shown in Figure 3.3, was revered and admired by millions in both the East and West for his courage to renounce violence and his tremendous spiritual strength. Born in India in 1869 and reared a Hindu, he trained in England to be a lawyer and practiced law in South Africa for twenty years before returning to India. There,

---

[10] Virgilio Elizondo, *Galilean Journey: The Mexican-American Promise* (Maryknoll, NY: Orbis Books, 1983), pp. 11, 12.

Figure 3.3
Mahatma Gandhi. (Courtesy United Press
International.)

with creative power, he led his people to spiritual renewal and to political independence. In 1948, while on his way to prayer, Gandhi was assassinated. His last words, murmured as he was shot, were, "Hey Rama (oh God)."[11]

Gandhi's early glimpses of religion came from the Vaishnava faith, but that interpretation of Hinduism repelled him because of too much "pomp and glitter."[12] While a law student in England he studied the *Bhagavad Gita* and then the Bible, reading the Old Testament in boredom but the New Testament with deep interest, especially the "Sermon on the Mount," which he compared to the *Gita*. He was particularly impressed by Jesus's teachings:

> "But I say unto you, that ye resist not evil: but whosoever shall smite thee on thy cheek turn to him the other also. And if any man take away thy coat let him have thy cloak too," delighted me beyond measure and put me in mind of Shamal Bhatt's "for a bowl of water give a goodly meal," etc. . . . My young mind tried to unify the teaching of the *Gita,* the *Light of Asia* and the Sermon on the Mount. That renunciation was the highest form of religion appealed to me greatly.[13]

From that time forward, Gandhi increased his interest in religion, studying various religious writers.

While he was practicing law in South Africa, friends and colleagues sought to convert Gandhi to Christianity. He willingly submitted to hearing the Gospel, discussing doctrine, and being the subject of Christian prayers. He told a colleague, a Protestant lay

[11] Homer A. Jack, ed. *The Gandhi Reader* (Bloomington: Indiana University Press, 1956), p. 475.
[12] Ibid., p. 14.
[13] Ibid., p. 23.

preacher, that "nothing could prevent me from embracing Christianity should I feel the call. . . . I had long since taught myself to follow the inner voice."[14] He even attended a convention for Protestants, during which friends prayed fervently for him, but Gandhi saw no reason to convert, for he could not believe that Christianity was the only way to salvation. Although he did not feel that Christianity was the supreme religion, neither did he believe that Hinduism was perfect. He saw great value in both religions as well as in Islam, which he also studied.

The spirituality of Hinduism and Christianity intersected in Gandhi's religious quest. The teachings of Jesus were used by him in urging his fellow citizens to practice the ancient Hindu doctrine of *Satyagraha,* the postulate that nonviolence to all living beings is ultimately more powerful than violent action toward another living being. Convinced that all actions have consequences and either build up or tear down life, the Hindu doctrine of *karma,* he led a successful nonviolent revolution, ultimately gaining India's freedom from British rule. For *Satyagraha,* Gandhi suffered imprisonment, attacks on his life, long fasts that threatened his survival, and finally a martyr's death.

Gandhi's sense of obligation to the "inner voice" required him to live under intense obligations of faithfulness. He urged the use of nonviolent resistance to South African ordinances discriminating against Indians:

> We all believe in one and the same God, the differences of nomenclature in Hinduism and Islam notwithstanding. To pledge ourselves or to take an oath in the name of that God or with Him as witness is not something to be trifled with. If having taken such an oath we violate our pledge we are guilty before God and man. Personally I hold that a man, who deliberately and intelligently takes a pledge and then breaks it, forfeits his manhood.[15]

The tenor of his whole life expressed his faithfulness to the highest and deepest truth, the truth that he held to be not only divine but also essential for being human.

❧

How do you interpret Gandhi's religious pilgrimage?

How do you understand that he could be influenced by both Hinduism and Christianity to come to his religious convictions concerning nonviolent power as the force of love?

UNIT 24   Pentecostalism and the Charismatic Movement

Neo-Pentecostal experiences similar to the following have become more widespread in recent decades:

> I stand as one of the group of pastors who are desperately concerned and deeply disturbed and confused over the lack of power . . . there has been a growing concern in my heart, for

[14] Ibid., p. 35.

[15] Ibid., p. 62.

I knew that something ought to be there which was not there, and could not be found. . . . I read in the Bible about the early church and its supernatural power and I so longed for such as that. . . . This was about two years ago. Between seventy and eighty of our people have received this glorious experience. Men and women who wearily trudged to prayer meeting and drove themselves to be faithful have becoming flaming evangels for Jesus![16]

Another Pentecostal Experience. I continued to tarry for the Baptism. . . . On Sunday . . . I received the Baptism. The Holy Spirit came like a torrent, as though He would tear my body to pieces. One of my besetting sins has been my unwillingness to speak out boldly for Christ, but when the Holy Spirit came in He made me shout the praises of Jesus until He verily split my throat. However, as one brother said to me, the Lord is able to repair any damage He does to the old temple. After being tossed about violently for quite awhile until I was panting for breath and wet with perspiration, I then lay for quite awhile in blessed quietness and poured forth praise to God in tongues for over half an hour.[17]

These accounts indicate crucial elements of neo-Pentecostalism, now often called the Charismatic movement: dissatisfaction with perfunctory and powerless religious practice, the desire for an experience of supernatural power, baptism by the Holy Spirit, exuberant and emotional worship, contentment, and praising God in tongues.

Pentecostalism, the spiritual ancestor of the Charismatic movement, began mainly as a North American movement around the turn of the twentieth century and gave rise to new denominations, the Assemblies of God and the Churches of God in Christ, as well as other, smaller Pentecostal groups. These Pentecostal churches appealed initially to those of the lower economic stratum, were fundamentalist, emphasized a literal interpretation of the Bible, and called for the baptism of the spirit as recorded in Acts: "And they were filled with the Holy Spirit and began to speak in other tongues" (Acts 2:4, RSV).

The sure sign of receiving Pentecostal power has been and is "speaking in tongues" (glossolalia), as noted in I Corinthians 12:10, in which a person speaks ecstatically in words and syllables strange both to the speaker and to the listener.[18] An example of such utterances is recorded by John Kildahl: "Aish nay gum nay tays . . . aish nay gum . . . ash nay . . . anna gayna. . . . Ayna Ganna keena . . . kayna geena anna naymanna naymanna. . . ."[19] Kildahl's study includes some historical summaries, interviews with glossalialists, some psychological interpretations of the "tongues experience," and conclusions correlating speaking in tongues with hypnotism.[20]

The Charismatics of more recent decades claim that the baptism of the Holy Spirit fulfills Christ's promise to the apostles: "But you shall receive power when the Holy Spirit has come upon you . . ." (Acts 1:8, RSV). Convinced that the church will receive new power only by this baptism, Charismatics began to penetrate mainline Protestant denominations, including Lutheran, Presbyterian, Episcopalian, and Methodist, as well as Roman Catholic. According to a poll conducted by *Christianity Today* in 1980, approxi-

---

[16] Frederick D. Bruner, *A Theology of the Holy Spirit* (Grand Rapids, MI: William B. Eerdmans, 1970), p. 127.

[17] Ibid., p. 126.

[18] John P. Kildahl, *The Psychology of Speaking in Tongues* (New York: Harper & Row, 1972), p. 11.

[19] Ibid., p. 3.

[20] Ibid., p. 76.

mately 29 million Americans consider themselves to be Charismatic Christians.[21] Charismatic numbers have increased rapidly in Africa, Asia, and Latin America to become what some church leaders call "The Third Force in Christendom, ranging it alongside Roman Catholicism and Historical Protestantism."[22]

Current Charismatics differ from classical Pentecostalism at several key points. They include many people from the middle-class and upper-class economic strata. They may not identify themselves with any particular church and tend to be ecumenical. They recognize the diversity of spiritual gifts (Greek: *charismata*). Citing I Corinthians 12–14 as their guide, contemporary Charismatics believe that the Pentecostal power is available to all Christians and that it includes any one of the gifts—speaking in tongues and the ability to interpret tongues, prophesy, heal, and expel evil spirits.[23]

The locus of the gifts of the Spirit for Charismatics is in their worship together, where they share their gifts of tongues, prophesy, healing, and so forth. A highly participatory experience, their meetings include singing Gospel songs and choruses, perhaps music of an amateur church orchestra, joyous shouting, hearty handclapping, ecstatic prayer, communal witness, and testifying. A mood of joy prevails as they "sing not only with their voices but with their hands and their feet and their bodies." The rhythm of the distinctive "American folk beat" prompts the people to become one with the orchestra in praising God. In utter abandon the whole congregation may at some points in the service "descend to its knees" to "pray in vocal concert or cacophany." The sanctuary may fill up with sound during prayer as the people pray in tongues. In a time of mutual sharing, the believers witness to the Spirit of God, filling their lives with power. Their preaching of the Word becomes a community affair.[24] Although they "believe that the Spirit has baptized every believer into Christ" (conversion), they hope and pray that Christ will finally baptize "every believer into the Spirit" (Pentecost).[25]

Such modern "ecstatic" experiences of the spirit have many similarities throughout Christian history and in other religions. Comparable experiences have been integral to religious expression in tantric Buddhism and Taoism and in some forms of Hinduism.

Does Pentecostalism or Charismatic Christianity seem similar or different from mystical Christianity?

[21] Bruner, *Theology of the Holy Spirit*, p. 79.

[22] John Thomas Nichol, "The Charismatic Movement," *Christianity in a Secular Age: From the Depression to the Present*, ed. Mark A. Noll et al. (Grand Rapids, MI: William B. Eerdmans, 1983), p. 482.

[23] Nichols, "The Charismatic Movement," p. 483.

[24] Bruner, *Theology of the Holy Spirit*, pp. 133–36.

[25] Ibid., p. 60.

CHAPTER 4

❧

Elements of Religious Experience

Introduction

Religious experience may be characterized in various ways. It may be highly emotional or quietly mystical, ecstatic or born of suffering, gradually and rationally developed or sudden in origin. The materials included in this chapter focus on a number of aspects characteristic of a broad range of religious traditions. There are units that deal with the role of ritual, symbols, and myth in religion. There are also units that examine a number of contrasting religious orientations.

In the Introduction to Chapter II, we have attached labels to these types of religious experience. The experience of the Zen Buddhist we have called mystical, the Pentecostal Christian ecstatic and that of the intellectual aesthetic. We have also cautioned, and here caution again, that the labels should not be taken as absolutes and are at best pointers to the various elements or dimensions of religious experience. These orientations—the moral (or legal), the mystical, the aesthetic, the ecstatic, and the magical—may be present in various degrees in a given experience of religion. Some may be greatly prized and sought in some religious traditions and shunned in others. They may mingle and mix or appear in relatively pure forms in the lives of groups and individuals.

These five orientations will be illustrated in this chapter and throughout later sections of the book. To define them briefly,

The *moral (or legal) orientation* to religion seeks to subordinate behavior and attitudes to a pattern of conduct and intention held to have ultimate significance. This pattern may have been given through the commandments of a Divine Being or Beings. It may be held to be intrinsic to basic reality, the universe, or human nature. Or it may be the moral code of society.

The *mystical orientation to religion* attempts to negate or subordinate every reality, world, society, self, and all their relationships to Divine Reality—God or universe, absolute spirit or nature, truth, goodness, beauty—so that at its deepest level or core the self can realize oneness—union or unity—with the Divine Reality.

The *aesthetic orientation to religion* attempts to interpret all experiences in such a way that they are seen to manifest a divine or transcendental pattern as their underlying and guiding reality—God's mind or will, wisdom, truth, order, beauty.

The *ecstatic orientation to religion* seeks supernormal experiences that bring individuals or groups under control of or in close contact with transcendental power(s).

The *magical orientation to religion* seeks to discover and exercise methods that allow the control of transcendent power(s) for human purposes.

No doubt one may find other names for these orientations, and other or additional approaches to religion may possibly be identified. But it will be useful to keep these five in mind while reading this text. For instance, some experiences involve a moral or legal outlook, in which the individual or group seeks to subordinate self and world to a code of life and conduct expressive of the divine will. Conformity to this code becomes the pivotal value, or at least is closely connected with it. Confucianism is perhaps a good example of this type. Several units in other sections of the text (see especially Chapter 14) give examples of moral or legal approaches to religion. Further discussion of the five major orientations listed in the Introduction to Chapter 3 may help one to understand the nature of the experiences recounted in this chapter.

In studying religion, no aspect of religious concern should be neglected. Theologies, creeds, organizations, institutions, traditions—all are important. But it is probably at the level of personal experience—what happens to the individual or to the group, what is done or felt or believed—that the vitality of religion is most evident. Thus units in Chapter 3 are intended to present a variety of individual cases of religious experience. The units in this chapter are intended to provide a framework for understanding these and other instances of personal and group experience.

UNIT 25   The Role of Ritual in Religion

Ritual acts of piety and worship have from time immemorial been part of all recognized religions. Their variety is unlimited and their functions numerous. Because of their public nature and constant repetition, much of the content of a religion is handed down from generation to generation through ritualized religious rites; the acts and stories of ritual convey as much or more than formal religious teaching. Similarly, many apparently "secular" activities in society, for example, football and soccer matches and graduation ceremonies, are highly ritualized events and perform similar functions to "sacred" rituals in the life of a culture. Religious ritual normally falls into three discernable categories, which although distinct are not necessarily exclusive.

Ritual Directed Toward the Divine

Humanity, recognizing its own limitations and finitude, has through religious ritual sought to communicate with the divine power responsible for its creation and continuing existence. In early cultures it was only natural that ordinary events taking place in orderly patterns should become ritualized. Since religion permeated all aspects of life and was not separated from any event, the rites and rituals that emerged naturally had religious overtones and functions. Thus the cultivation of crops, creation of tools, tribal celebrations, warfare, and all other events in the life of a people carried ritual forms to recognize the gifts and guidance of the deities. Because such rites and rituals had religious implications, they often became elaborate, beautiful, and central to culture. As with symbols (see Unit 27), their importance and power were not limited to their particular form or ritual pattern. People often understood the rites to be humanity's participation in the divine drama of life itself. In sacrificial offerings human beings gave what was theirs, a part of themselves, in recognition of what had been given to them and to express community with the divine.

Although it arose in early cultures, such an understanding continued in sophisticated civilizations, as reflected in the words of Hzün Tzu, a Chinese philosopher of the third century:

> In general, rites begin with primitive practices, attain cultured forms, and finally achieve beauty and felicity. When rites are at their best, men's emotions and sense of beauty are both fully expressed. When they are at the next level, either the emotion or the sense of beauty oversteps the others. When they are at still the next level, emotion reverts to the state of primitivity.
>
> It is through rites that Heaven and earth are harmonious and sun and moon are bright, that the four seasons are ordered and the stars are on their courses, that rivers flow and that things prosper, that love and hatred are tempered and joy and anger are in keeping. They cause the lowly to be obedient and those on high to be illustrious. He who holds to the rites is never confused in the midst of multifarious change; he who deviates therefrom is lost. Rites—are they not the culmination of culture? . . .[1]

In many cultures the religious aspects of every event and act in life are often celebrated in ritual patterns; every religion has also developed specific patterns of worship and celebration to show devotion and commitment publicly. Often these rituals are obligatory for pious believers. The Qu'ran, the Muslim holy scripture, clearly illuminates this aspect of ritual. In the following passage Allah is speaking of the pilgrimage all Muslims should make at least once to the Ka'ba, or Holy Mosque, in Mecca (Figure 4.1).

> And when We settled for Abraham the place of the House [Ka'ba] We said: "Thou shall not associate with Me anything [idols or other Gods]. And do thou purify My House for those that shall go about it and those that stand, for those that bow and prostrate themselves; and proclaim among men the Pilgrimage, and they shall come unto thee on foot and upon every lean beast, they shall come from every deep ravine that they may witness things profitable to them and mention God's Name on days well-known. . . . Let them then finish with their

---

[1] Hzün Tzu, "Rationalism and Realism in Hzün Tzu," trans. Y. P. Mei, as quoted in William Theodore de Bary, ed., *Sources of Chinese Tradition* (New York: Columbia University Press, 1960), pp. 123–24.

Figure 4.1   Pilgrims at the Ka'ba in Mecca. (Courtesy of ARAMCD)

self-neglect and let them fulfil their vows, and go about the Ancient House." All that; and whosoever venerates the sacred things of God, it shall be better for him with his Lord.

We have appointed for every nation a holy rite, that they may mention God's Name over such beasts of the flocks as He has provided them. Your God is One God, so to Him surrender. . . .

O men, bow you down and prostrate yourselves, and serve your Lord, and do good; haply so you shall prosper; and struggle for God as is His due, for He has chosen you, and has laid on you no impediment in your religion, being the creed of your father Abraham; He named you Muslims aforetime and in this, that the Messenger might be a witness against you, and that you might be witnesses against mankind. So perform the prayer, and pay the alms, and hold you fast to God; He is your Protector—an excellent Protector, an excellent Helper.[2]

Personal Inward-directed Ritual as Transformation of the Self

Spiritual life expressed in public ritual is often complemented by personal ritual patterns, the purpose of which is not only communication with the divine but also discovery and transformation of the self. In religions such as Buddhism, personal discipline is

[2] Reprinted with permission of Macmillan Inc., from *The Koran Interpreted*, Arthur J. Arberry, translator, Sura XXII, verses 26–38, 75–77. © 1955 George Allen & Unwin, Ltd.

designed to "free" one from the delusions of *samsara,* the eternal round of individual existences (see Unit 11). Highly cultivated ritual patterns contribute to introspection, leading the devotee to release from *samsara* and thereby serving as a channel or means to personal transformation.

The fourteenth-century Zen Buddhist master Bassui Tokusho in the following passage recognizes the practical importance of personal ritual but also notes its transitory nature:

> To realize your own Mind you must first of all look into the source from which thoughts flow. Sleeping and working, standing and sitting, profoundly ask yourself, "What is my own Mind?" with an intense yearning to resolve this question. This is called "training" or "practice" or "desire for truth" or "thirst for realization." What is termed zazen [the actualization of the true Buddha nature] is no more than looking into one's own Mind. It is better to search your own Mind devotedly than to read and recite innumerable sutras and dharani every day for countless years. Such endeavors, which are but formalities, produce some merit, but this merit expires, and again you must experience the suffering of the Three Evil Paths. Because searching one's own mind leads ultimately to enlightenment, this practice is a prerequisite to becoming a Buddha. No matter whether you have committed either the ten evil deeds or the five deadly sins, if you turn back your mind and enlighten yourself, you are a Buddha instantly. But do not commit sins and expect to be saved by enlightenment [from the effects of your own actions], for neither enlightenment nor a Buddha or a patriarch can save a person who, deluding himself, goes down evil ways.[3]

Most religions include such pragmatic or practical personal rituals although they are not understood, as in certain forms of Buddhism, to be indispensable ritual patterns.

Ritual Spiritualizing of Ordinary Activities

For many religions the ideal devotee is one who recognizes and identifies the presence of the divine in the ordinary activities of daily existence. For these people the ritual patterns of daily life itself become an avenue for praise of and identification with the divine. Chuang Tzu, a third-century B.C.E. Taoist teacher, expresses the point quite well in his tale "Prince Wen Hui and His Cook":

> Prince Wen Hui's cook
> was cutting up an ox.
> Down went a shoulder,
> He planted a foot,
> He pressed with a knee,
> The ox fell apart
> With a whisper,
> The bright cleaver murmured
> Like a gentle wind.
> Rhythm! Timing!
> Like a sacred dance. . . .
>
> "Good work!" the Prince exclaimed,
> "Your method is faultless!"
> "Method?" said the cook

[3] Philip Kapleau, *The Three Pillars of Zen* (New York: Anchor Press/Doubleday, 1980), p. 169.

Laying aside his cleaver,
"What I follow is Tao
Beyond all methods!

"When I first began
To cut up oxen
I would see before me
The whole Ox
All in one mass.
After three years
I no long saw this mass.
I saw the distinctions.

"But now, I see nothing
With the eye. My whole being
Apprehends.
My senses are idle. The spirit
Free to work without plan
Follows its own instinct
Guided by natural line,
By the secret opening, the hidden space,
My cleaver finds its own way.
I cut through no joint, chop no bone. . . .

"There are spaces in the joints;
The blade is thin and keen:
When its thinness
Finds that space
There is all the room you need!
It goes like a breeze!
Hence I have this cleaver nineteen years
As if newly sharpened!

"True, there are sometimes
Tough joints. I feel them coming,
I slow down, I watch closely,
Hold back, barely move the blade,
And whump! the part falls away
Landing like a clod of earth.

"Then I withdraw the blade,
I stand still
And let the joy of the work
Sink in.
I clean the blade
And put it away."

Prince Wan Hui said,
"This is it! My cook has shown me
How I ought to live
My own life!"[4]

In Christianity this type of spiritualization of daily existence was practiced by Brother Lawrence, a monk who understood his dishwashing as an expression of praise and thanksgiving to God.

[4] Thomas Merton, *The Way of Chuang Tzu* (New York: New Directions, 1965). Copyright © 1965 by the Abbey of Gethsemani. Reprinted by permission of New Directions Publishing Corporation.

In some modern cultures religion has become only one element among many others, often losing its central place in ordinary life. Consequently, religious rituals have been modified and often limited to specifically religious functions or sometimes completely lost. Thus religious rituals have sometimes been reduced to particular rites or patterns, losing much of their dynamic quality.

∾

Are ritual forms and practices necessary for religious expression?

What rituals or rites are widely practiced in our own society?

Why have most religions stressed that participation in public rites of worship is a duty for the believer?

From your own religious tradition name the rituals that are most significant.

UNIT 26   Religious Nurture and Conversion

The term *conversion* is used in several different ways to characterize religious experience. It may be used to refer to leaving one religious group and becoming an adherent of another, as when someone is said to have converted from Protestantism to Catholicism or from Christianity to Islam. A second sense of *conversion* is used when someone who has not been an adherent or participant in *any* religious group or tradition joins one, as when someone speaks of the *conversion* of an atheist or skeptic or agnostic. In Europe or America, such usage usually carries the implication that the convert has become a member of some Christian group, though it may only mean that the person has become a believer in God or in some form of Christian faith. Finally, especially among some groups of Protestants, the term *conversion* may be used to describe an event of deepened or internalized participation in a religious tradition or adherence to its doctrines or way of life by someone who has previously participated in a more superficial or less committed way. For many Protestant groups, this experience is characterized as being "born again" and signifies that according to the group's understanding, the individual has for the first time made a full personal commitment to the truths that the group holds.

The development within Christianity, particularly in the last few centuries, of an emphasis on a distinctive religious conversion has been the focus of religious study. Historically, however, conversion is only one form of religious experience. A far more common experience is that of nurture, wherein one's religious faith is gradually matured through a variety of events, including religious education. A person is nurtured in religion by participation in numerous experiences within a faithful community. The older or more traditional Christian church bodies—Roman Catholic, Anglican, Lutheran—most often stress this form.

Horace Bushnell, a nineteenth-century American theologian, vigorously argued that religious experience and commitment are as legitimately the result of Christian nurture as they might be of a dynamic conversion experience.

Christian piety should begin in other and milder forms of exercise than those which commonly distinguish the conversion of adults; that Christ himself, by that renewing Spirit who can sanctify from the womb, should be practically infused into the childish mind; in other words, that the house, having a domestic Spirit of grace dwelling in it, should become the church of childhood, the table and hearth a holy rite, and life an element of saving power. Something is wanted that is better than teaching, something that transcends mere effort and will-work—the loveliness of a good life, the repose of faith, the confidence of righteous expectation, the sacred and cheerful liberty of the Spirit—all glowing about the young soul, as a warm and genial nurture, and forming in it, by methods that are silent and imperceptible, a spirit of duty and religious obedience to God. This only is Christian nurture, the nurture of the Lord. . . .

Children have been so trained as never to remember the time when they began to be religious. Baxter was, at one time, greatly troubled concerning himself, because he could recollect no time when there was a gracious change in his character. But he discovered, at length, that "education is as properly a means of grace as preaching," and thus found the sweeter comfort in his love to God, that he learned to love him so early.[5]

John Betjeman, a modern British poet, although raised a Christian, demonstrates that one can reject or lose the nurture Bushnell stresses but still return by a series of events to faith. For Betjeman, none of the events was identifiable as *conversion*, but each was part of a clear progression toward belief and commitment that may be described as a conversion process.

I was brought up Church of England, you know, and baptized and then, at Marlborough, I suddenly decided I was an atheist and refused to be confirmed. I used to think that religion was hymn singing and feeling good and not being immoral and always having a high moral tone and really rather priggish. Until . . . I remember one summer bicycling about in Cornwall and coming to a church, St. Irvin, in North Cornwall and meeting the vicar there who was a nice eccentric, and he said, I suppose you think religion is hymn singing in the chapel at Marlborough. And I said—Yes. And he said: Well—read this. And he gave me a book—Arthur Machens' *Secret Glory*, which suddenly showed me there were the Sacraments, and then I became very interested in ritual and I was first, I suppose, brought to belief by my eyes and ears and nose. The smell of incense, and the sight of candles, High Church services, they attracted me and I liked them. And at Oxford I got confirmed at Pusey House and went to Confession and lived the full life of a Catholic in the Church of England. And then found that one had gone so much off the rails one didn't dare to go to Confession any more, so I gave it up for a bit, and then went back again, holding on. Not finding it very easy to believe until only just lately. I do see that behind all the ritual and everything like that, the one fundamental thing is that Christ was God. And it's very hard to believe—it's a very hard thing to swallow. But if you can believe it, it gives some point to everything and really I don't think life would be worth living if it weren't true.[6]

These examples express a confidence in the developmental idea of Christian experience that has been most common. Yet the phenomenon of religious conversion characterized by a unique experience of enlightenment and change is a clear and significant tradition within Christianity. The experience of Augustine is a classic example.

So was I speaking and weeping in the most bitter contrition of my heart, when lo! I heard from a neighbouring house a voice, as of boy or girl, I know not, chanting, and oft repeat-

---

[5] Horace Bushnell, *Christian Nurture* (New Haven, CT: Yale University Press, 1916), pp. 12–13, 17.

[6] From John Betjeman's Diary as quoted in Derek Stanford, *John Betjeman* (London: Neville Spearman, 1961), pp. 25–26.

ing, "Take up and read; Take up and read." Instantly, my countenance altered, I began to think most intently whether children were wont in any kind of play to sing such words: nor could I remember ever to have heard the like. So checking the torrent of my tears, I arose; interpreting it to be no other than a command from God to open the book, and read the first chapter I should find. . . . I seized, opened, and in silence read that section on which my eyes first fell: Not in rioting and drunkenness, not in chambering and wantonness, not in strife and envying; but put ye on the Lord Jesus Christ, and make not provision for the flesh, in concupiscence. No further would I read; nor needed I: for instantly at the end of this sentence, by a light as it were of serenity infused into my heart, all the darkness of doubt vanished away.[7]

In this passage, a renowned Christian leader describes an event wherein an extraordinary religious experience served as a vehicle of confirmation of faith and trust in God. Augustine can call this his conversion. He had accepted some Christian beliefs and principles before this time, but now he could fully commit himself to God. In this description the crucial element is an awareness of acceptance by God, whatever one might be or have been. The concept that one's personal acts—one's own sins—are not a detriment to being accepted by God is that which allows total commitment and change of understanding and direction. Earl Ferguson has defined this type of religious experience as follows:

Religious conversion, from the psychological point of view, is an abrupt, involuntary change in personality in which the subject, under the pressure of resolving internal conflict or tension, surrenders the control of his life to beliefs and sentiments previously peripheral or repressed; the change occurs suddenly at a time of crisis and is not psychologically identical with the gradual process of growth or development.[8]

The categories of religious experience just discussed certainly are not exhaustive or exclusive but do illustrate common experiences among the Christian communities of Europe and America. Neither of these modes excludes the other, and they are often combined in a person's experience even if one may be emphasized more than another. Many other religions have similar experiences of religious nurture and conversion.

How well does Ferguson's definition of conversion apply to each of the three senses of the term discussed at the beginning of the unit? How well does it apply to the individual experiences cited in the unit?

Is an identifiable religious experience—whether by gradual nurture or conversion—necessary for religious consciousness and commitment?

Why in certain areas of America has conversion been the predominant form of experience?

Why among traditional and established churches would Christian nurture be predominant?

Does one type of experience provide a more personal sense of security than the other? Why?

---

[7] Saint Augustine, *The Confessions of Saint Augustine,* trans. Edward B. Pusey (New York: Random House, 1949), pp. 166–67.

[8] Earl Ferguson, "The Definition of Religious Conversion," *Pastoral Psychology,* 16, no. 156 (September 1965), 16.

UNIT 27　The Role of Symbols in Religion

Although many people have contributed to the growing literature on the analysis of symbols, this unit depends especially on the important contributions to contemporary understanding by Rollo May, a psychologist;[9] Paul Ricoeur, a philosopher;[10] and Paul Tillich, a theologian.[11] Each has had some influence on the conceptions presented here.

Symbols traditionally have been relied on by religions to express truths and insights that may not be simply rational. When we consider the origin of the English word *symbol*, we must turn to Greek. The Greek word *symballo* can be translated as "to place together" or "to bring together." Thus, we see that a central function of symbols in religion has been to unite or join truths with powerful, graphic representations.[12] Yet one problem in dealing with symbols is semantic. Some people may use the words *symbol*, *allegory*, *metaphor*, and other terms as if they are interchangeable. However, these words are different, and they carry differing connotations. A careful consideration of the functions of symbols requires that they be differentiated from other signifying phenomena.

It is a truism to say that most modes of expression serve primarily communicative functions. But in such communication, one frequently can separate the meaning from its vehicle. Consider a well-known metaphor, *the ship of state*. The intention of the phrase is readily apparent. Few would confuse a nation with a ship, that is, the vehicle with its meaning. Therefore, what distinguishes a symbol from a metaphor like ship of state is the peculiar representative function that a symbol serves. *That which is pointed to becomes one with the vehicle that serves as the pointer.* Thus, reality can become condensed in its symbol, enabling people to grasp part of a vast or transcendent reality so that at least they can participate in its symbolic form. However, metaphor especially is concerned with a linguistic procedure. It is developed to indicate what something is like.[13] But the symbol is multidimensional; it takes us beyond the semantic to roots deep in experience, which can be beyond words.

If symbols point to something beyond themselves, they also go further. A symbol fuses with that which it represents.[14] Because of this fusion, this joining, the symbol becomes a kind of autonomous reality because it points to and becomes a part of the larger dimension of which it is a representation. Thus, one may encounter an essential quality of the represented in the representor. The symbol elicits response that is both deep and strong from the person who perceives it. The symbol demands more than cognitive recognition; it functions at the affective (emotional) level as well. Therefore, people may experience symbols at the conscious as well as the subconscious level of their experience. Indeed, symbols may not be constructed by intention but may arise from individual and

---

[9] See Rollo May, ed., "The Significance of Symbols," *Symbolism in Religion and Literature*, (New York: George Braziller, 1960), pp. 11–49.

[10] See Paul Ricoeur, *Interpretation Theory: Discourse and the Surplus of Meaning* (Ft. Worth: Texas Christian University Press, 1976), pp. 45–69.

[11] See especially Paul Tillich, *Dynamics of Faith* (New York: Harper & Brothers, 1957), pp. 41–54.

[12] See also Erich Kahler, "The Nature of the Symbol," in May, *Symbolism in Religion and Literature*, p. 70.

[13] See also the more extensive discussion of metaphor in Ricoeur, *Interpretation Theory*, pp. 46–53.

[14] Cf. also Tillich, *Dynamics of Faith*, p. 42.

group unconscious experience. Further, symbols change as individual and group needs change.[15] Symbols grow or sometimes are replaced by new and more functional ones.

Specifically, religious symbols may represent the ultimate—God. They can serve to make the vast, awesome, transcendent deity perceptible to us. They are part of the language of faith. Religious symbols can have a power that distinguishes them from other symbols; they deal with issues that are the deepest of all concerns a human may have, with ultimate meaning.[16]

Religious symbols are supported by communities and therefore are socially rooted. Most societies support special institutions such as churches, synagogues, mosques, or temples, whose function is to maintain and develop their tradition of religious symbols.

A religious image or concept that has achieved the level of symbol may eventually become an idol for a person or group when it no longer represents the deity for a worshiper. That is, it can be perceived and treated as the deity itself. Such an image or concept can function as a symbol only when some difference is discerned between the representation and the represented, between the object and the actual ultimate. When this is known, a person becomes capable of employing a symbol to point to the ultimate, to serve as an "arrow" to the Divine. It is in and through the symbol that the divine is encountered and known. The symbol serves to "telescope" the transcendent Divine, to make it accesible, to serve as vessel or vehicle and yet not *be* the totality of the Divine. The symbol serves functionally as a revealer, though it cannot reveal the totality of the Divine. In many living religions, the symbol is of God in terms of its intermediary, representational function, but the image and the words remain less than that to which they point.

Many contemporary commentators on the role of religious symbols have observed that people sometimes become so immersed in the models and symbols they produce or inherit that they forget their function. A symbol represents that which it is not itself. It is a form that arises from the depths of human experience and stands for something vast, something not fully under rational control, something at the edge of one's ability to comprehend. Yet the symbol embodies some essential characteristic or quality of that which it represents (see Figure 4.2). As has been suggested, it "telescopes" the represented into a manageable form; hence, the represented is encountered within the symbol; it is *there*. However, the symbol always points beyond itself to the represented. Both models and symbols are functional. They facilitate connections. They are not absolute substitutes for what they represent, but the essential of the represented may be contained in them.

Certainly, a large part of human religious experience is mediated through symbols. The cross, the Bible, the Wailing Wall in Jerusalem, the Ka'ba in Mecca, a footprint of the Buddha, the sacred Ganges River in India—all are powerful religious symbols, expressive of the Divine that is apprehended through them, in them, or behind them by adherents of the religious traditions involved—Christian, Jewish, Muslim, Mahayana Buddhist, and Hindu, respectively. The same may be true of works of religious art and architecture. They often function powerfully in human religious experience.

One primary mode of religious orientation, the aesthetic, may be particularly closely dependent on symbols, on seeing the religious-symbolic significance of things—

---

[15] See also the characteristics of symbols, ibid., p. 43.

[16] Ibid., pp. 44–47.

Figure 4.2
The Ancient of Days by William Blake,
1794. (Reproduced with permission of
the Library of Congress, Lessing J.
Rosenwald Collection.)

parts of the natural and human world, persons and historical events as well as works of
art—as the intrinsic element in religious experience. According to this view, the aesthetic
type of religious orientation is that which seeks to discover the presence and disclosure of
God or the Divine Powers in the world, others, and the self.

Most modes of religion depend heavily on symbols as expressions of God or the
Divine, even though it may be held that no finite symbol—thing or work of art—can fully
or adequately express the Divine that transcends all symbols. The magical mode of religion and magic generally are heavily dependent on symbols. Perhaps only the mystical
mode of religion attempts finally to dispense with all symbols and to know God directly.
But even in the mystical mode, symbols may have an important role in the preliminary
stages of the religious life. Later they may be used to communicate some sense of the mystic's experience to others.

UNIT 28   Mysticism in Religious Experience

An account of the religious experience of Teresa of Avila is given in a previous chapter
(Unit 21). Teresa's experience is a classic instance of religious mysticism.

One day, being in orison . . . it was granted me to perceive in one instant how all things are seen and contained in God. I did not perceive them in their proper form, and nevertheless the view I had of them was of a sovereign clearness, and has remained vividly impressed upon my soul. It is one of the most signal of all the graces which the Lord has granted me. . . . The view was so subtle and delicate that the understanding cannot grasp it.[17]

Mysticism as a type of religious experience has been frequent in Christianity. It is also highly characteristic of the Eastern religions—Buddhism, Hinduism, and Taoism—and has been represented by the Sufis in Islamic religion. The Greek philosopher Plato believed that the highest knowledge of reality must be gained in a flash of mystical insight.

Even so, this organ of knowledge must be turned around from the world of becoming together with the entire soul, like the scene-shifting periact in the theater, until the soul is able to endure the contemplation of essence and the brightest region of being.[18]

As we suggested in the Introduction to this chapter, mysticism is one of the major forms of or orientations to religious experience. It involves the attempt to negate the relation to self, others, and the world in order to give God or the Divine Reality complete power in and over the self. The result is that the self is completely surrendered to, or in union with, the Divine.

As a hart longs
for flowing streams,
so longs my soul
   for thee, O God. . . .
When shall I come and behold
   the face of God?
My tears have been my food
   day and night,
while men say to me continually,
   "Where is your God?"

Why are you cast down, O my soul,
   and why are you disquieted within me?
Hope in God; for I shall again praise him,
   my help and my God.
                 (Psalm 42, RSV)

Evelyn Underhill, an important twentieth-century British writer on mysticism who was herself a Christian mystic, defined mysticism as follows:

Mysticism, according to its historical and psychological definitions, is the direct intuition or experience of God; and a mystic is a person who has, to greater or less degree, such a direct experience—one whose religion and life are centered, not merely on an accepted belief or practice, but on that which he regards as first-hand personal knowledge.[19]

[17] Saint Teresa of Avila, as quoted in William James, *The Varieties of Religious Experience* (New York: Longmans, Green and Co., 1912), p. 411.

[18] Plato, quoted in Walter Houston Clark, *The Psychology of Religion* (New York: Macimillan, 1958), p. 261.

[19] Evelyn Underhill, *The Mystics of the Church* (New York: Schocken Books, 1964), pp. 9–10.

In describing the phenomenon of mysticism in religious experience, the psychologist and philosopher William James found these four characteristics:

1. *Ineffability.*—The handiest of the marks by which I classify a state of mind as mystical is negative. The subject of it immediately says that it defies expression, that no adequate report of its contents can be given in words. It follows from this that its quality must be directly experienced; it cannot be imparted or transferred to others. In this peculiarity mystical states are more like states of feeling than like states of intellect. No one can make clear to another who has never had a certain feeling, in what the quality or worth of it consists. One must have musical ears to know the value of a symphony; one must have been in love one's self to understand a lover's state of mind. Lacking the heart or ear, we cannot interpret the musician or the lover justly, and are even likely to consider him weak-minded or absurd. The mystic finds that most of us accord to his experiences an equally incompetent treatment.

2. *Noetic quality.*—Although so similar to states of feeling, mystical states seem to those who experience them to be also states of knowledge. They are states of insight into depths of truth unplumbed by the discursive intellect. They are illuminations, revelations, full of significance and importance, all inarticulate though they remain: and as a rule they carry with them a curious sense of authority for after-time. . . .

3. *Transiency.*—Mystical states cannot be sustained for long. Except in rare instances, half an hour, or at most an hour or two, seems to be the limit beyond which they fade into the light of common day. Often, when faded, their quality can but imperfectly be reproduced in memory; but when they recur it is recognized; and from one recurrence to another it is susceptible of continuous development in what is felt as inner richness and importance.

4. *Passivity.*—Although the oncoming of mystical states may be facilitated by preliminary voluntary operations, as by fixing the attention, or going through certain bodily performances, or in other ways which manuals of mysticism prescribe; yet when the characteristic sort of consciousness once has set in, the mystic feels as if his own will were in abeyance, and indeed sometimes as if he were grasped and held by a superior power. . . .[20]

R. C. Zaehner, in a classification of three types of mysticism, feels that in all of them, the quality or kind of experience is perhaps similar—like that described by William James—but that the object or content is different. The first type of mystical experience described by Zaehner is *nature mysticism,* sometimes called pantheism—the feeling of union or identity of the self with objects in the natural world or "nature" as a whole.

A second type of mysticism is that typical of certain Eastern religious traditions, particularly Vedantic Hinduism, in which the self feels itself as identical with the Absolute Self, Brahman, the One Reality beyond the natural world of mere appearance and in which the individual self is totally merged with, absorbed in, the Absolute. The third type is described as follows and is illustrated by Figure 4.3:

Thirdly there is the normal type Christian mystical experience in which the soul feels itself to be united with God by love. The theological premise from which this experience starts is that the individual soul is created by God in His own image and likeness from nothing and that it has the capacity of being united to God, of being "oned" to Him as the medieval English mystics put it. Here again we have a third type, distinct, it would appear, from the other two. . . . No orthodox Christian mystic, unless he is speaking figuratively or in poetry as Angelus Silesius does, can well go farther than to say that his individual ego is melted away in God by love: something of the soul must clearly remain if only to experi-

---

[20] James, *Varieties of Religious Experience*, pp. 380–81.

Figure 4.3
A vision of the resurrected Christ is presented by an artist of the High Renaissance, Matthias Grünewald, in this section of his triptych, the *Isenheim Altarpiece* in Musée Unterlinden, Colmar. (Photo courtesy Musée d'Unterlinden.)

ence the mystical experience. The individual is not annihilated, though transformed and "deified" as St. John of the Cross says: it remains a distinct entity though permeated through and through with the divine substance.[21]

∾

What difference does Zaehner see between Christian and Vedantic mystical experience? Between both and nature mysticism?

∾

Although Zaehner's threefold division of the types of religious mysticism is useful, it probably represents a simplification that, taken too far, is misleading. This can easily be seen by considering Zen Buddhism, which is based on a form of mystical experience, prepared for by instruction in rigorous techniques of meditation by a Zen teacher (or master), and leads to an experience of enlightenment called *satori*. In many ways Zen enlightenment results in attitudes similar to those of nature mysticism, a sense of overcoming the division between the self and the whole, as well as between the self and the individual

---

[21] R. C. Zaehner, *Mysticism: Sacred and Profane* (London: Oxford University Press, 1961), p. 29.

concrete presence of things. Zen is rooted in Buddhist traditions that derive from Hindu pantheism (though Buddhism generally and Zen particularly do not have theological or metaphysical theories of pantheism or, for that matter, of the nature of things). Christian writers have found profound analogies between the Zen approach and that of the Hebrew-Christian Scriptures and parts of Christian mystical tradition and practice.[22]

Following is a Zen play presenting the experience leading to the Zen enlightenment of Bodhidharma, an Indian Buddhist monk who became the founder of Zen, a movement that spread to China and is now most frequently associated with Japan. The play, entitled *Bodhidharma*, is by Saneatsu Mushakōji. It is a good illustration of Zen mysticism, which is in some sense uncategorizable as one of Zaehner's types. Nevertheless, it resembles all of them, particularly if one realizes that even with the emphasis in Christian mysticism on devotion to an absolute object, most Christian mystics have stressed that God as experienced in mystical union cannot be "known" (as a subject-knower might know—perceive or understand—an object of finite experience). Note that entrance into enlightenment is the culmination of extreme personal discipline but does not depend on that discipline or reason; it comes in the intuitive moment, in this case symbolized by a blow on the head.

The characters are A, B, and Dharma. In front of a small temple where Dharma sits in meditation, A and B enter.

A: Do you know the fellow that lives here?

B: I don't.

A: Don't you? There's a peculiar fellow living in this temple.

B: What is he like?

A: A fellow who has sat staring at nothing but the wall for eight or nine years.

B: Staring at the wall for eight or nine years? What for?

A: If we knew what he was doing that for, he would no longer be considered peculiar. But there isn't anyone who knows what he is staring at the wall for. People say he must be an idiot.

B: If you talk in such a loud voice, the fellow inside will hear you.

A: No fear. He's an idiot, and besides, he's deaf.

B: Is he deaf?

A: He is deaf.

B: Is that why he only stares at the wall?

A: Yes, that's why he only stares at the wall.

B: How does he eat?

A: His neighbors make a point of bringing meals to him, it seems.

B: How thoughtful of them!

A: I suppose they sometimes forget to bring the meals. They told me that once they purposely didn't bring his meals for three or four days, but he stared at the wall as usual as if nothing had happened. . . .

B: But is he really an idiot? I can't believe that he is.

---

[22] See Thomas Merton, *Mystics and Zen Masters* (New York: Farrar, Straus & Giroux, 1967), and J. K. Kadowaki S.J., *Zen and the Bible: A Priest's Experience* (London: Routledge & Kegan Paul, 1980).

A: But an intelligent person could not go on doing such a thing for eight or nine years at a time like this, could he? For what is the good of staring at a wall? It can't do any good, can it?

B: I think you're right. However, are you sure he didn't change color when he was beaten? Don't you think he was just pretending?

A: No, I assure you he didn't change color. I watched him intently.

B: But you saw him at some distance didn't you? Then you couldn't possibly see him roll his eyes.

A: Then I'll strike him on the head now, so watch closely.

B: Is it all right to strike him? If the fellow should suddenly roar you look as though you'd be paralyzed with terror. For we seldom see such a fearful face, you know.

A: Don't worry. Now watch me, I'll strike him.

B: Are you sure it's all right?

A: Of course it is. Watch me closely.

B: The more I look at him the stranger his face looks. He looks as if he'd choke you to death and eat you if he once got angry.

A: No, he is a mild fellow really. He looks terrible only in the face. Now I'll strike him.

B: All right.
     [A strikes Dharma on the head.]

A: How was it?

B: Strange. It surely is strange. Please strike him again. [He draws nearer.]

A: All right. [He strikes him again.] . . .
     [He approaches Dharma . . . and raises his arm. Dharma turns his head]

A: [falling on his knees.] Please forgive me. Please forgive me.

DHARMA: What day is it today?
          [A and B are struck dumb. They try to say something but cannot.]

DHARMA: Are you two deaf?

A: No, no.

DHARMA: What day is it today?

A: Yes, sir. Today is the twelfth day of December.

DHARMA: Is it? Then I have been here exactly nine years!

A: Yes sir.

DHARMA: [Standing up.] Dullard as I am, I have at last attained enlightenment after nine years! What the Buddha said was true. Thanks! Thanks!
          [The two watched in amazement.]

A: Then you are not deaf?

DHARMA: No, I am not deaf.

A: Please forgive us our rudeness a while ago.

DHARMA: You haven't done anything rude to me.

A: But we struck you on the head . . .

DHARMA: Oh, then it was you? I must thank you for it. I was able to attain enlightenment because you struck me on the head. The Buddha kindly entered into you and beat me.[23]

Zen as a religion is purely a religion of human realization, or self-awakening. It teaches us, human beings, to attain *satori* and live a new life in this world as new men of *satori*. It insists that this inner conversion should be carried out by oneself, that one can attain his

[23] Umeyo Hirano, trans., *Buddhist Plays from Japanese Literature* (Tokyo: Cultural Interchange Institute for Buddhists, 1962), pp. 1–2, 4–5, 7–8. Used by permission.

Zen personality by oneself by searching inwardly, not relying on anything outside. It declares that man has the potentiality for attaining *satori*. This should be happy tidings for human beings.[24]

The following excerpt from a longer poem expresses in poetic form the classic Zen insight into the universe and life.

All beings are primarily Buddhas
Like water and ice,
There is no ice apart from water;
There are no Buddhas apart from beings.[25]

Unit 29   Myth and Religious Insight

The term *myth* is often used in ordinary conversation to mean "something that is widely accepted or believed but that is in fact false." A second common use of *myth* is to designate stories that arose in primitive or naive societies that involve personified forces of nature, gods and goddesses, and legendary heroes, for example, the familiar Greek myths. In a third sense, *myth* is sometimes used to mean "primitive" beliefs about nature and the universe, "prescientific science"; for instance, the Babylonian cosmology (still the basis for systems of astrology) is sometimes called a mythological scientific system. Finally, the term *myth* has been used by recent political or social thinkers—R. M. MacIver and Bronislaw Malinowski among them—to refer to any basic belief or system of beliefs involving value claims and commitments. Thus, MacIver defines *myth* as the "the value-impregnated beliefs and notions" that sustain and give unity to society. Malinowski called such myths the "charters of belief" that validate the customs and practices and code of society.[26]

In this unit, we will suggest that a simpler and better way of trying to understand *myth* is to begin by remembering that the word often refers to a kind of story. The story is not always about gods and goddesses or the forces of nature personified or even great legendary heroes and heroines. For example, an American myth is associated with the life of Abraham Lincoln. It tells a story of a man who grew up in poverty; who experienced hardship and failure; but who through determination, hard work, and personal integrity, rose to the highest office in the nation. This story embodies one of the great myths of American society, the belief that by hard work and personal integrity, a person may rise from poverty to economic and social success. The myth is rooted in historical experiences such as that of Lincoln, in which such a rise in status did indeed occur.

Myth has a very important role in the life of the individual and in society. Often, it is by means of myths that societies and individuals define or acquire their sense of identity, which is why myths have an important role in most of the world's religions. It is mis-

[24] Zenkei Shibayama, *A Flower Does Not Talk* (Rutland, VT: Charles E. Tuttle, 1970), pp. 30–31.
[25] Ibid., p. 65.
[26] See David Bidney, *Theoretical Anthropology* (New York: Columbia University Press, 1953), p. 297.

leading to think that myths necessarily involve falsity. They may be stories about profoundly deep, underlying truths.

Perhaps one of the more helpful scholars is the anthropologist Claude Lévi-Strauss, who has studied the functions of myth in both preliterate and literate societies. According to Lévi-Strauss, the essential characteristic of myth is that its structure is historical or narrative in character. A myth is the narration of a sequence of events. These events may be historical or legendary, but they are presented as being, and are felt to be, ahistorical and "eternally valid." A myth is a pattern of timeless relationships combined in a temporal sequence and related to one another by means of transformations. The result of the transformation of the elements of myth is that unlike or contradictory elements of human experience (including life and death, agriculture and warfare, and maleness and femaleness) are enacted and felt as being essentially identical. The myth allows the integration of differences that are potentially disruptive to society or to the individual because of their contradiction with other elements (such as beliefs, values, interests, expectations, and desires). The mythical resolution of the contradictions of life is not reached or apprehended reflectively or discursively; it is enacted and lived in feeling, imaginatively and affectively.

Contemporary biblical scholars have written extensively about the use of myth in the Jewish and Christian Scriptures. John Knox, a contemporary Christian New Testament scholar, has referred to such biblical images as "the pre-existence of Christ, his decision to come into this world as a man, his struggle with demonic powers and his triumph over them, his ascension to heaven, where he reigns at God's right hand" as part of a mythological framework used by early Christian writers to express the *meaning* of the *historical events* of the life, death, and resurrection of Jesus.[27]

Some Christians have objected to the use of the term *mythological* to characterize these or any parts of the message of the Bible. Other Christians, like Rudolf Bultmann, have asserted that mythological elements must be interpreted in such a way that the message of the New Testament can come alive in a meaningful form today. Thus, he argues that the Bible must be "demythologized." Still others, including Paul Tillich, have insisted that all religious expression must involve certain mythological elements, since myth is a necessary symbolic medium in expressing reality that is transcendent. Such Christian commentators agree with the anthropologists that myth functions to preserve and reinforce "unexpressible" truths. According to them, myth in its religious use does not denote that which is false or fabricated. Instead, it suggests that which is most significant.

Following is a description of a Vietnamese myth. This mythical story illustrates features that cause myth to be an extraordinary communication of profound truth in the experience of the people.

> The myth of the birth of the Vietnamese race goes back to the misty Bronze Age during which De Minh (a great grandson of Than Nong, the God of Agriculture) met, in the course of one of his inspection tours in the southern part of China, a Tien (fairy), and married her. From this union a son, Loc Tuc, was born. And when De Minh was too old to rule his vast empire, he divided it into two territories: the North, which he gave to his eldest son, De Nghi, child of his first marriage, and the South (Vietnam), which he gave to Loc Tuc. Loc

---

[27] John Knox, *Jesus Lord and Christ* (New York: Harper & Row, 1958), pp. 51–53, 255–59.

Tuc became Emperor Kinh Duong Vuong and married the daughter of Than Long (the Dragon God). From this marriage between the descendant of a fairy and a dragon there came a son who would be Emperor Lac Long Quan. Indeed, the Vietnamese often call themselves the children and grandchildren of a dragon and a fairy. Lac Long Quan's marriage to Au Co, another fairy, resulted in the birth of one hundred male children. He told his wife one day: "I came from the race of Rong (Dragon), you came from the race of Tien. We are as different as water is to fire, and it would be unwise for us to continue to live together. We have to part." Fifty children then followed their mother to the mountains and fifty marched with their father to the south seas. Lac Long Quan then handed over his throne to his son Rung Vuong, who founded the Rong Bang Dynasty and named his kingdom Van Lang.[28]

With regard to this myth, Tran Van Dinh further comments,

From this recital of legendary origins, one can see that Vietnam considers its fate determined by:

1. A contradiction—the marriage between the descendant of a fairy (sweet, gracious, beautiful) and a dragon (powerful, aggressive, and hard-featured). These two contradictory aspects still prevail both physically and mentally in the Vietnamese people, and especially among the women who are slender but tough, durable and aggressive but romantic and gracious. The fairy virtues seem to be most apparent and persistent, however. . . .

2. An internal division—the first Vietnamese family was a divided one (fifty children went with their mother to the mountains and fifty accompanied their father to the seas). Division and disunity became Vietnamese national problems in the past as well as at the present time. And the division is not only between the North and South but also between the minorities which live in the mountains (Montagnards) and the majority dwelling the pallins of the sea coasts. . . .[29]

Thus, this myth of Vietnamese origins incorporates a story. But it goes beyond being a simple story to express a deep truth found in the very fabric of Vietnamese culture. Societies frequently communicate their most important truths and beliefs through myth, which functions to preserve and reinforce "unexpressible" truths. *Myth* in its religious use does not denote that which is false or fabricated but that which is most significant.

∽

What insights do Lévi-Strauss's view of myth give into the purposes or functions of the myth of the birth of the Vietnamese race?

Examine the Babylonian and Japanese creation myths presented in Unit 82, and also examine some of the familiar Greek and American Indian myths in the light of Lévi-Strauss's discussion of the way myth functions.

UNIT 30   Magic: Theory and Practice

As myth plays a unique role in culture and is often related to religion, so too has magic frequently been associated with religion. Many recent authors have argued that there is a fundamental difference between magic and religion and between religious and magical orientations to our lives and transcendent reality—divine beings or powers.

[28] Tran Van Dinh, "The Foundation of Man," *"Story" in Politics,* ed. Michael Novak (New York: Council on Religion and International Affairs, 1970), pp. 55–59. Used by permission.
[29] Ibid.

In contrast to this view, we have suggested (see the Introduction to this chapter) that there is a magical orientation to religion and that it can appear in its pure form—as a way of cultivating spiritual power by individuals or groups, a way of self-development and self-discipline (self-transcendence)—or be mixed with other forms of religion, such as the moral or the aesthetic. However, the two views are not as incompatible as they may seem, and in much of this unit we will examine the view of the sociologist Bronislaw Malinowski, who held that there is a fundamentally sharp distinction between the goals and functions (orientation) of religion and magic. We believe that Malinowski's theory reveals more about the magical orientation to religious experience and why in many religious traditions the magical orientation has been shunned or condemned. Malinowski, in *Magic, Science and Religion*, argues that

> There are no peoples however primitive without religion and magic. Nor are there, it must be added at once, any savage races lacking either in the scientific attitude or in science, though this lack has been frequently attributed to them. In every primitive community, studied by trustworthy and competent observers, there have been found two clearly distinguishable domains, the Sacred and the Profane; in other words, the domain of Magic and Religion and that of science.
>
> On the one hand there are traditional acts and observances, regarded by the natives as sacred, carried out with reverence and awe, hedged around with prohibitions and special rules of behavior. Such acts and observances are always associated with beliefs in supernatural forces, especially those of magic, or with ideas about beings, spirits, ghosts, dead ancestors, or gods. On the other hand, a moment's reflection is sufficient to show that no art or craft however primitive could have been invented or maintained, no organized form of hunting, fishing, tilling, or search for food could be carried out without the careful observation of natural processes and a firm belief in its regularity, without confidence in the power of reason: that is, without the rudiments of science.[30]

In the societies that Malinowski studied, people used scientific—or technical—procedures in situations in which there was little natural danger or unpredictability. They used magic only in situations that involved uncertainty, great difficulty, or hazard:

> "It is most significant that in lagoon fishing, when man can rely completely upon his knowledge and skill, magic does not exist, while in the open-sea fishing, full of danger and uncertainty, there is extensive magical ritual to secure safety and good results." Further, even when magic is used, the individual "never relies on magic alone, while, on the contrary, he sometimes dispenses with it completely, as in fire-making and a number of crafts and pursuits. But he clings to it, whenever he has to recognize the importance of his knowledge and of his rational technique."[31]

Although Malinowski saw a significant role for magic in dealing with the unknown and dangerous elements of life, he believed that there is a clear difference between magic and religion:

> While in the magical act the underlying idea and aim is always clear, straightforward, and definite, in the religious ceremony there is no purpose directed toward a subsequent event. It is only possible for the sociologist to establish the function, the sociological *raison d'être*

---

[30] Bronislaw Malinowski, "Magic, Science and Religion," *Science, Religion and Reality*, ed. Joseph Needham (London: Society for Promoting Christian Knowledge, 1925), pp. 17–18.
[31] Ibid., pp. 48–52.

of the act. The native can always state the end of the magical rite, but he will say of a religious ceremony that it is done because such is the usage, or because it has been ordained, or he will narrate an explanatory myth.[32]

The sociologist, Malinowski thought, will see that whereas magic is directed to specific ends—for example, a good catch of fish—religion is less specific in terms of goals. But religion will tend to express and promote the cohesiveness of the community. This can be seen by considering the social function of the funeral ceremony, a religious rite found in most societies.

> The mortuary proceedings show a striking similarity throughout the world. As death approaches, the nearest relatives in any case, sometimes the whole community, forgather by the dying man, and dying, the most private act which a man can perform, is transformed into a public, tribal event. . . . There is always a more or less conventionalized and dramatized outburst of grief and wailing in sorrow, which often passes among savages into bodily lacerations and the tearing of hair. This is always done in a public display and is associated with visible signs of mourning, such as black or white daubs on the body, shaven or disheveled hair, strange or torn garments.
>
> The immediate mourning goes on round the corpse. This, far from being shunned or dreaded, is usually the center of pious attention. . . .
>
> . . . Man's conviction of continued life is one of the supreme gifts of religion, which judges and selects the better of the two alternatives suggested by self-preservation—the hope of continued life and the fear of annihilation. . . .
>
> Thus the rites of mourning, the ritual behavior immediately after death, can be taken as pattern of the religious act, while the belief in immortality, in the continuity of life and in the nether world, can be taken as the prototype of an act of faith.[33]

According to Malinowski, then, magic and religion can be sharply distinguished. Magic seeks to tap transcendent or mysterious powers for specific goals (safety, health, wealth, love, success) of groups or individuals in order to manipulate the environment when technological or commonsense knowledge is not available to achieve these goals. Religion is directed toward transcendent powers, or beings, or even a Being, by a community for relatively nonspecific goals—or perhaps for no goals at all but merely out of a sense of obligation or necessity, perhaps to obey the will of, or to express reverence toward, some transcendent Being. However, we spoke earlier of a magical orientation (in contrast to moral, mystical, and aesthetic orientations) toward religion, and many religious traditions contain magical elements or at least allow their adherents to participate in semimagical practices. We may define the magical orientation toward religion as one in which control of transcendent or divine power is sought so that it may be used for manipulation of the religious adherent's environment for personal or group purposes. Because of this manipulative element in magic, many modern and some ancient religious traditions, such as Judaism, have rejected, or have come to suspect and repress, magical elements.

We can also see why some religious traditions have highly valued the magical orientation as a vital element in their religious traditions. If we examine the role of the shaman (or "medicine man"—not always a man—or "witch doctor" or "oracle") in many

---

[32] Ibid., p. 38.
[33] Ibid.

societies, we can see that the "expert" in magic was often highly valued. Often the term *shaman* is associated with preliterate or at least rather simply organized societies, such as those whose economic life is built on hunting or fishing or undiversified agriculture. But the expert in magic is not confined to simpler societies and may be highly valued for two reasons. The shaman, or expert in magic, will be seen as someone who through demanding disciplines—often physical as well as intellectual or spiritual—has acquired transcendental powers and may be seen as a kind of saint. The shaman will also be valued for the ability to provide cures for the sick and success in war or love or agriculture. However, there can also be harmful magic, and some magical experts may be seen as extreme dangers to the individual or group; among the Navajo, for example, people who are believed to practice destructive witchcraft are feared and hated. Even so, the belief in malicious witches provides some relief to suffering individuals or the group: It "explains" illness, bad luck, and misfortune, thus making them more "rationally" acceptable and understandable. The belief in malicious witches also gives suffering individuals something positive to do, namely, to find a "good" shaman who can counteract the malicious witch's spells.

Still among the best sources for learning about beliefs and the practice and acquisition of the shaman's art are the fine essays in Lévi-Strauss's *Structural Anthropology*.[34] But two fictional accounts, one of them recent, do much to bring to life the shaman's powers. The first is the Nigerian novelist Chinua Achebe's *Arrow of God*, a vivid depiction of the conflict between traditional ways and modernity, in which an Igbo leader of great authority uses his reputation as a man of magical power to try to stem the erosion of tribal customs.[35] The second, *Coyote Waits* by Tony Hillerman, tells the story of a Navajo tribal police officer, Jim Chee, whose deepest desire is to become a singer, one who can exercise the healing power of one of the Navajo "ways."[36]

At one point in the story Chee remembers the ceremonial curing—an Enemy Way (a Navajo ritual conducted to cure people from contamination by contact with things "foreign" to Navajo life, such as strangers or enemies)—he attended as a child.

> The cure had been conducted by a *hataalii* who had been very tall and had seemed to him then to be incredibly ancient. The patient had been Chee's paternal grandmother, a woman he had loved with the intensity of a lonely child, and the event had formed one of his earliest really vivid memories. The cold wind, the starlight, the perfume of the pinon and juniper burning in the great fire that illuminated the dance ground. Even now, he could see it all and the remembered aroma overpowered the mustiness of this office. Most of all, he remembered the *hataalii* standing gray and thin and tall over his grandmother, holding a tortoiseshell rattle and a prayer plume of eagle feathers, chanting the poetry from the emergence story, making Old Lady Many Mules one with White Shell Girl, restoring her to beauty and harmony.
>
> And restore her it had. Chee remembered staying at the old woman's place, playing with his cousins and their sheepdogs, seeing his grandmother happy again, hearing her laughter. She had died, of course. The disease was lung cancer, or perhaps tuberculosis, and people with such diseases died—as all people do. But it had been that cure that had caused him to think that he would learn the great curing ways, the songs and the sand paintings, and become a *hataalii* for his people.[37]

[34] Claude Lévi-Strauss, *Structural Anthropology*, Vol. 1 (New York: Basic Books, 1963).

[35] Chinua Achebe, *Arrow of God* (Garden City, NY: Doubleday/Anchor Books, 1969).

[36] Tony Hillerman, *Coyote Waits* (New York: Harper Paperbacks, 1992), pp. 191–92. Copyright © 1990 by Tony Hillerman. Reprinted by permission of HarperCollins, Publishers, Inc.

[37] Ibid., pp. 191–92.

Chee had wanted so much to become a singer who could bring benefits to his people that he had taken lessons from a highly regarded shaman and learned the curing ceremonial called The Blessing Way. As he tells a non-Navajo character in *Coyote Waits*,

> I'm a would-be shaman. A singer. A medicine man. *Hataalii* is the Navajo word for it. I was going to be one of the people who conducts the curing ceremonies to restore people to harmony. Or I was trying to be. Nobody seemed to want my services.[38]

Chee's comment shows both the power of the belief in shamanistic magic and the effects of modernism in corroding that power. But if we look at even the most highly modernized societies, such as the United States today, we can find remnants and pockets of belief and reliance on magic, in southern Louisiana, for instance, where voodoo is practiced, or in southern California, where magic by many names and in many forms flourishes.

---

[38] Ibid., p. 178.

Chapter 5

❧

Religion in Artistic Expression

Introduction

The two preceding chapters have concentrated on the nature and character of religious experience, using examples that are mostly verbal descriptions of religious expression. In our time, many people have difficulty in grasping the full import or meaning of value statements or religious expression in art forms because they do not understand verbal and visual texts. Yet anyone who considers carefully the nature of communication in modern societies realizes that an enormous number of the messages transmitted today are primarily in a visual format; that is, they are visual texts. Part of our difficulty rests in our lack of formal education in analyzing and consciously "reading" these visual statements with which we are bombarded—from television, film, advertising, architecture, and various forms of mass art. Yet in reality, human religious experience probably has been as readily expressed, perhaps even more adequately expressed, in the various arts (in addition to the verbal and literary forms). People of all ages and in varied cultures have sought to express in painting, sculpture, architecture, and music, and in our time, film and television, their deepest values, including, in symbolic form, their sense of encounter with the Divine.

Some people have suggested that artistic expression is the most reliable of all the forms of communication. John Ruskin, in the nineteenth century, said that cultures present their own "autobiography" in three books. The first book is the "book of their deeds," that is, their histories; the second is their literature, or "the book of their words"; and the third is "the book of their art."[1] He argued that "not one of these books can be understood unless we read the two others" as well. Furthermore, "the only trustworthy one is the last: the arts." In the contemporary era, British art historian Kenneth Clark agrees: "Writers and politicians may come out with all sorts of edifying sentiments, but they are what is known as declarations of intent. If I had to say which was telling the truth about society, a speech by a Minister of Housing or the actual buildings put up in his time, I should believe the buildings."[2]

The purpose of this chapter is to look at some examples in which religious experience and meaning have been communicated in visual arts, including painting, mosaic, stained glass, sculpture, and architecture. In Unit 31, we explore some of the ways in which art serves as an avenue, a vehicle for the expression of religious meaning. To become more explicit on this subject, Unit 32 discusses briefly how visual images were used to interpret Jesus as savior (Christ) in the very early centuries of the Christian church. Next, a process central to the expression of virtually all religions, the *translation of ideas into visual form*, is considered in Unit 33. To attempt to clarify that process, the unit focuses on the emergence of medieval Gothic architecture in the history of Christianity, especially in France. Thus, this chapter considers the many and varied art forms one encounters daily that may communicate values or religious meanings.

UNIT 31   Art as a Symbolic Vehicle

The arts are among the most reliable means of knowing the true characteristics of a culture or a time. The twentieth-century Spanish painter Pablo Picasso, who evidently did not wish to theorize about his work, is reported to have said that "art is a lie that makes us realize the truth."[3] If, indeed, Picasso did utter this interpretive statement, his phrase urges us to consider how the *form* of art has everything to do with its *content*, that is, its meaning. An artist or composer designs or composes or constructs, fabricates, a form that in a literal sense is an illusion, albeit a carefully constructed one. Yet, it is in this art form that one may encounter imaginatively something that is vastly more than the form itself. The art form may serve the function of symbol; the art object may gather into itself qualities or significance that transcend (go beyond) the object. That is, the art object may contain some essential quality of that which it represents, and thus we "see" or "know" that characteristic through the art object. Then, one may argue that art is a form of "disclosure."[4]

When we look at paintings created by prehistoric, "primitive" peoples, often in caves, we are not viewing art objects that are intended to be mere reproductions of something. Instead, ancient artists have interpreted that which is represented. This can be argued to be true of virtually all art objects. Even photographs, including those that are not intended to serve an artistic function ("record shots" or "snaps"), still include some element, no matter how little considered or fleeting, of the photographer's interpretation and

[1] Quoted in Kenneth Clark, *Civilization* (New York: Harper & Row), p. 1.
[2] Ibid., p. 1.
[3] Roger Hazelton, *A Theological Approach to Art* (Nashville, TN: Abingdon Press, 1968), p. 16.
[4] Ibid., p. 17.

composition. Consequently, when we attempt to address art as a symbolic vehicle, we speak of the way humans create symbols (some form or concept) that point beyond themselves, represent that which they themselves are not. Thus, in the symbol is an image that we have created (albeit often unconsciously) of some larger, complex reality.[5]

Representation in art perhaps reaches its greatest depth in objects that can become spiritual icons. When a picture or other art representation of a religious tradition, person, or story becomes so identified with the spiritual truth it depicts that it comes to be venerated as sacred itself, it becomes an icon. In such cases, the art is not just an external display; rather it involves both internalization and participation on the part of the viewer.

The power of art as icon is illustrated by the experience of some university students who were studying religious art and architecture in Greece a few years ago. One day the group of North American students found themselves in a major square in downtown Thessaloniki, where there is a large Greek Orthodox church. The students entered the narthex (entrance area) and discovered that the many people coming and going were stopping in the church for quiet meditation or prayer rather than for a worship service. Of particular significance to the students was how virtually all the people would pause before a large painting of Jesus Christ and Mary, his mother. The people gazed up into the faces in the image and frequently would begin to mutter or whisper quietly. This action would be followed by gestures made with their right hands, touching their heads and chests; the movements formed the shape of a cross. Often, though not in every case, the individuals would kneel before the painting, kiss their own hand, and place that hand on the bottom of the image. Then they would rise and advance toward the sanctuary inside.

Some of the students wanted to know how these religious people felt about the painting or image or what their thoughts about it might be. They asked some individuals whose behavior they had observed. In most cases, the people responded in a friendly manner and explained in several ways that the painting was an icon for them and that it served as a focal point for their devotional acts. The object had a sacred quality because it represented something central to their religious perspective. They did not worship the object itself; rather the object "captured" an image of people in the history of their faith through whom God was made known. The picture was revered because of the power of its representative function. They encountered the respresented in the representor, and thus it had become an icon.

Much contemporary art has highlighted this participational characteristic. Some plays, films, paintings, and sculpture require involvement in order to be fully understood. For example, widely varied responses have been evoked by the works of the surrealist artist Salvador Dali. In 1955, he painted *The Sacrament of the Last Supper* (Figure 5.1). No doubt people viewing the painting have verbalized perceptions and responses to it that Dali did not have in mind when he painted it. For most viewers, the work evokes a response; some enter into it, participate in it. They may see a truth to which this symbolic representation points.

A student, Judy Covington, describes her reponse to *The Sacrament of the Last Supper*, a painting in which subject matter, form, and style all convey religious meaning.

---

[5] See also the discussion of symbol in Chapter 4, Unit 27.

Figure 5.1   Salvador Dali, *The Sacrament of the Last Supper*, 1955, The National Gallery of Art, Washington, DC. (© 1993 Demart Pro Arte, Geneva/ARS, New York.)

I saw this painting for the first time while I was still in junior high school, and the thing that grabbed me then is what still grabs me now—it's so realistic that it's unreal. I thought at first it was a retouched photograph, because of the preciseness and detail with which the scene is portrayed—the refraction of light within the cup and foldmarks on the tablecloth, as well as the sharp lines of light and shadow across the table and the disciples' robes. But I realized that the figure of Christ, although very human-looking, was transparent. And even though it seems logical to assume that the light would have its source in him—he casts no shadow on the table in front of him—the shadows of the disciples indicate that the light comes from somewhere behind him, from what would be the body of the enlarged arms and chest visible above and behind Christ. That caught my attention, too—it was the first time I had ever seen "a painting of God" as such. I was a little overawed—who was this Dali character to think he could imprison a likeness of the Almighty on canvas? But looking at it now, I can understand that Dali must have felt that men need a "see-able" God, and not some vague apparition floating around in the clouds. Most of the body is invisible, but the chest, shoulders, and arms seem firmly anchored—there's nothing vague about them. Dali does not go further than the shoulders—I imagine he did not quite feel up to painting a face—that would have been nearly profane. Just from that part of the body which is there comes a sense of peace. There is a feeling of anticipation, not necessarily sorrowful, either. It is as though Christ has raised his hand and stopped time for a moment, stopped to remember himself and so that the disciples may remember, too. The transparent beams which support without enclosing add to the contrast between real and unreal. Christ is definitely the center of the painting, with the lines of light on the table and the beams on either side and above Him outlining the nucleus of the painting. His is the only visible face, and his expression is one of calm. There is no sorrow in his eyes, only certainty. He looks as if he is remembering all the good things in his life, as if he will not die in vain. Dali has taken a traditional scene out of the structured, dark upper room, out of an anxious, melancholy mood, and set it on a plateau overlooking the world, almost, with God the Comforter watching over. The painting is so personal a statement of faith and painted with such clarity that it almost hurts to look at it, I wanted to sit still so as not to disturb anything or spoil the image.[6]

Dali's meticulous painting technique paradoxically records as if it were objective fact the most subjective elements. His dreamlike compositions include the mixing of seemingly unrelated objects, solid forms that appear soft or distances that seem immeasureable.

In addition to the response of Judy Covington, there are a number of possible interpretations. The background of dawn in the picture, the Sea of Galilee, and the fishing boats may point to the coming of the Easter event. The outstretched arms of the raised figure could represent the crucifixion of Jesus (yet to come). Thus, the painting encapsulates the Last Supper of Jesus with his followers, the Crucifixion, and the Resurrection sequence. It powerfully expresses both historical events and symbolic-interpretive dimensions.

UNIT 32   Images of Jesus as Christ in the Early Church

Conceptions of the incarnation of deity have played an important role in several of the major religions of the world. Yet one could argue that possibly Christianity has placed greater emphasis on the incarnation of God than any other religion. From this central affirmation that the essential quality of the Divine is fully present in the man Jesus comes the rest of the doctrine of Christianity.

Central to the Christian perspective is Jesus of Nazareth's affirmation that unqualified love has the power within itself eventually to elicit a response of the same kind. His capacity to express this "no strings attached" love (Greek: *agape*) is exemplified in his forgiveness of those who were crucifying him even while they were doing it. The early Christians saw in this process the presence of God fully manifest in the man. Hence, the cross representing crucifixion became the central symbol of the religion, though several hundred years would pass before it did so.

To the earliest Christians, Jesus had taught that the one God in whom they placed their trust was the deity who was sovereign over all the universe, perfectly just, and personal in quality, and God could be characterized most completely as unconditional love (*agape*). They further observed that Jesus *was* what he had taught, that personally he exemplified perfectly what he had said about the nature of deity. Thus, the faith claim emerged that God is incarnate in Jesus, to whom they gave the title Christ (Saviour).

Throughout the history of Christianity, followers have developed conceptions of Jesus the Christ as saviour and as mediator of God's love and will. Soon after Jesus's time, Christians began to express their understanding and experience of Christ in verbal (written) and visual statements.

Controversies arose early and have often recurred in the church regarding Christology (ideas on the nature, person, and work of Christ). Historic creeds were devised

[6] Judy Covington, journal notes. Used by permission.

affirming both the humanity and divinity of Christ. Just how these characteristics were mingled, without confusion, has remained a point of continued discussion, although Orthodox Christianity affirmed that Jesus was fully a man in whom God was fully present.

Quite early in the history of Christianity, artists expressed varied understandings of Christ and his ministry through painting, mosaic, and sculpture. Particular characteristics are emphasized in these works of art, which sometimes communicate with greater depth than words. The combination of the figure of Jesus Christ (especially the manner in which he is portrayed) along with various symbols and actions can be one of the most effective means of communicating conceptions of his significance.

As in Figure 5.2, one of the most frequent modes of depiction of Jesus Christ in the earliest Christian art is as the "good shepherd." Quite consistently he is presented as youthful, a common mode at that time to suggest vigor and power. Also, he is clean shaven, with a Caesarian haircut, and in the *contraposto* pose frequently employed in ancient Greek and Roman art to present an active hero or deity figure. Generally, the clothing is that of a Roman shepherd with the loose-fitting tunic and short skirt (to allow rapid movement) that was so familiar in the Greco-Roman world. This shepherd's clothing (in fresco paintings) frequently is white with vertical purple stripes down the front, a connotation of authority in early Roman society. Thus, though he is presented as a shepherd caring for his flock (the church), he is exalted with authority. Such depictions of Christ began to appear as early as the second century C.E.

In the figure, Jesus Christ is the shepherd, the deliverer from death, of his flock (the Christian community). He is carrying a sheep over his shoulders, an idea that may have as its source the parable of the lost sheep, which appears in the New Testament books of Matthew and Luke. (The style of this visual presentation was familiar at that time because it had been employed in pre-Christian art.) Further, Jesus is shown carrying a container of water (representing the water of new life or baptism?), and his arm is extended in a very natural manner because of the weight of the object. He is surrounded by other sheep, which represent the community of the faithful (the church). Frequently, such scenes are placed in a pastoral setting; in this fresco painting, the lines suggest the earth on which the figures are standing and the trees on either side (almost lost to view by damage from moisture over the centuries).

The whole scene is enclosed in a circle, which helps to complete part of the total design. Circles frequently were used symbolically to represent the eternal. Thus, the suggestion is made that Jesus, the good shepherd, is eternally Christ the Saviour.

Figures called *orants* often appear in enclosed sections of a fresco composition near an image of Jesus. (They are similar to the orant figure in Figure 5.3.) The orant, in early Christian art, was a symbolic representation of the "disembodied soul"[7] and consistently was presented in an attitude of prayer, with the hands uplifted, as shown here. Indeed, a scholar of early Christianity, Walter Lowrie, has suggested that the orant is exhibiting faith since prayer is a typical expression of it. It can be argued that the orant in such catacomb depictions prays for herself or himself, asking "God for deliverance or giving thanks . . . for it."[8] Thus, the souls of the faithful are related to the eternal Christ, their shepherd and deliverer from death to eternal life.

---

[7] Walter Lowrie, *Art in the Early Church* (New York: W. W. Norton, 1969), p. 45.
[8] Ibid., p. 46.

Figure 5.2   *The Good Shepherd*, fresco, third century. Detail from the ceiling of the Vault of Lucina, Catacomb of San Callisto, Rome. (Photo by K. Lawrence.)

In the fresco painting in a lunette above a crypt in the Catacomb of Saint Domitilla at Rome, we begin to notice significant shifts of emphasis in the depiction of Jesus Christ (see Figure 5.4). It may be dated perhaps a century later than the visual text in Figure 5.2. The artist has arranged the disciples of Jesus so that attention is focused on the Christ figure. Their gestures and their gaze suggest his importance in their company and have the effect of exaltation. Christ is presented with an air of authority; his right hand is extended in a gesture of communication or address and he has an intense gaze. He wears a white, togalike garment with the dark stripes that suggest authority (cf. the costume in Figure 5.2). His disciples, through association with him and through his authority, gain a similar importance, as is suggested by their clothing. In this image, Jesus Christ is no longer presented in the earlier, familiar shepherd format but like a teacher and lawgiver, as *pantocrator*, Greek for "universal ruler."

In Figure 5.4, two figures stand behind Christ, holding up and extending what appears to be a mantle (similar to the modern conception of a cape), with a field of blue with scattered stars. This design was subsequently used in Christian art to refer symboli-

Figure 5.3
Orant, fresco, Catacomb of
Priscilla, Rome, late third cen-
tury. (Photo by Max Hirmer.
Used by permission.)

cally to the cosmos; and by being placed behind the figure of Christ, it came to refer to his
universal significance. The position of these figures and the way they seem to lift the
object suggest the possibility that they will place it on the shoulders of Jesus Christ, a gesture associated with a kind of investiture. In the church, it became eventually one act in
the investment of Christ's authority in his vicars (representatives), the bishops of the
church, who were being set apart even in New Testament times for special functions.
Thus, a more exalted interpretation of Christology is suggested by the entire composition.

In C.E. 313, the Roman Emperor Constantine issued the Edict of Toleration at
Milan. Through this act, the Christian religion was officially recognized by the state. This
act allowed complete freedom of worship and the erection of churches, and persecution of
Christians was to end. Though the emperor seems to have adopted the new religion, and
members of his family, especially his mother, Helena, were active in it, for a long time
many were opposed to it, including some important senatorial families. Nevertheless, with
an imperial sanction made official, the church could grow openly and organize itself
throughout the empire. It would supplant officially the old Roman religions in the 380s.

At Ravenna, on the northern Adriatic coast of Italy, some of the finest examples
of Christian art of the fifth and sixth centuries are preserved. Among these is the little Mausoleum of Galla Placidia, erected probably in 424 or 425. Originally dedicated in honor of

Figure 5.4   Christ as *Pantocrator* with disciples, fresco, Catacomb of St. Domitilla, Rome. (Photo by Max Hirmer. Used by permission.)

San Lorenzo (Saint Lawrence), an early Christian martyr, the building, according to a long-standing tradition, was used as a mausoleum by Galla Placidia, sister of the Emperor Honorius (who temporarily moved the western capital to Ravenna), for Honorius after he died in 423. Tradition suggests that Galla Placidia may have been entombed there as well.[9]

In an interior tympanum (in this case, an arch above the doorway), there is a mosaic of Christ as good shepherd (see Figure 5.5). This mosaic contains some of the finer workmanship of the period; and although strong Byzantine influences are present in this transitional work of the latter part of the early Christian era, the good shepherd figure recalls some Roman catacomb art.

This mosaic was created in time of enormous controversy in the Christian church throughout the empire over the interpretation of Jesus as Christ (Christology). This discord made necessary several church council meetings, and finally the great Council of Chalcedon was convened in 451 in an attempt to clarify and settle the matter. An essential ingredient in the creed produced at Chalcedon included the insistence on Jesus Christ as

> . . . the same perfect in Godhead and also perfect in manhood; truly God and truly man . . . the property of each nature being preserved, and concurring in one person (*prosopon*), and one subsistence (*hypostasis*), not parted or divided into two persons, but one and the same Son. . . .[10]

[9] For more detailed discussion of this structure and its mosaics, see Kenneth Lawrence, "An Iconological Analysis of Mosaics in the Mausoleum of Galla Placidia, Ravenna," *ARTS, The Arts in Religious and Theological Studies*, III, 3 (Summer 1991), 19–24.

[10] Williston Walker, *A History of the Christian Church*, rev. ed. (New York: Scribner, 1959), p. 139.

Figure 5.5   Christ as good shepherd, mosaic, Mausoleum of Galla Placidia, Ravenna, Italy, ca. 425. (Scala/Art Resource, New York.)

Although the mosaic was produced before the Council of Chalcedon, it can be argued that the elements under discussion, regarding the manner in which Christ was understood to be simultaneously fully human and fully divine, are presented by the artist in this image.

Presented in a pastoral setting, tending and caring for the flock (the community of the church), as frequently was seen in early Christian images, Jesus Christ is reaching in Figure 5.5 across his body, warmly responding to one of the sheep (by chucking its chin), an intimate gesture. The flock of sheep look to the shepherd. Also, his face is rather Roman, instead of Eastern, in character—a facet of classical art.

At the same time, the setting is elevated, not only because the tympanum mosaic is above the entrance door, but also because the location suggested is like a dais, a raised platform. (Note the clifflike escarpment suggested at the bottom of the image, in the foreground of the picture plane.) Rather than the typical Roman shepherd costume, Christ wears a different, more priestly garb. His clothing is long, flowing, and golden, with royal purple stripes on either side of the front—suggesting an exalted figure of authority. One might expect the staff he holds to be a shepherd's crook; instead it becomes a crucifer, like the cross carried in Christian liturgical processions. In the time frame of this depiction, it should probably be interpreted as a symbol of authority, as a sceptor.[11]

[11] Lawrence, "An Iconological Analysis," p. 23.

Jesus is seated on three graduated rocks, a thronelike arrangement. The three sheep on each side are geometrically arranged. There is an aureole, or halo,[12] around his head. The complex symmetry of the composition, the concern for order, may reflect the need for clarity in the thoughts of the church, which was so urgent at the time.

In the vault above the tympanum image, we see a strictly ordered decoration with a deep blue background and starlike designs. Is this a symbol of the cosmos, and by association, does it suggest the universal saviour significance being assigned to Jesus the Christ? The colors, geometric balance, and concern for order blend with those of the tympanum image. "Thus, in this image, in *simultaneous mutual interaction*, we observe a presentation of both the human and divine."[13]

During the reign of Emperor Justinian II (from Byzantine Constantinople), a remarkable, if small, church was constructed in Ravenna about 547. In its mosaic-encrusted sanctuary apse, there is the scene shown in Figure 5.6.

Heavily influenced by imperial court ceremony, the mosaic puts Christ at the center, enthroned as *pantocrator* ("universal ruler," "sovereign"). He is presenting a martyr's crown to Saint Vitalis (at left), to whom the church is dedicated.[14] An angel (second from left) is presenting the saint to Christ. At right, another angel is presenting Bishop Ecclesius, the founder of the church,[15] who in turn is ceremonially presenting a model of the church to Christ. A broad study of the art of the early church demonstrates that by the time of this building, the saints and martyrs were being represented in the very formal, ceremonial clothing of the era.

Christ himself, now more exalted in the thought of the church, is seated on a sphere, whereas the other figures are standing with their feet on the ground. Below the Christ, the four rivers of Heaven flow. He holds the Book of Life and is endowed with a bejeweled halo that incorporates the shape of the cross. The light depicted by brilliant colors on the clouds behind Christ possibly suggests sunrise. The brilliant gold background (which becomes a convention in art of this type) and the strong colors have a dazzling effect on the viewer below and connote both the preciousness of the function of Christ's church and its authority.

UNIT 33   Luminous Wholeness in Western European Medieval Architecture

How are perspectives of religious meaning expressed in physical structures? How are concepts translated into physical form? The writings by an extraordinary leader of both church and state in medieval France and other available sources make it possible to trace

---

[12] In classical mythology, an aureole was a shining cloud sometimes surrounding a deity when on earth.

[13] Lawrence, "An Iconological Analysis," p. 23.

[14] Everett Ferguson, "S. Vitale," in *Encyclopedia of Early Christianity*, Everett Ferguson, ed. (New York: Garland Publishing, Inc. 1990), p. 828.

[15] Ibid., p. 828.

Figure 5.6   Christ as *Pantocrator* with Saint Vitalis, Bishop Ecclesius, and archangels. Mosaic in apse of Church of San Vitale, Ravenna, Italy, ca. 547. (Scala/Art Resource, New York.)

the development of form in one particular circumstance. What today is called western European Gothic architecture arose in the twelfth century. Central to its development was the decision to reconstruct the Royal Abbey Church of St. Denis in the Île-de-France, near Paris.[16] Numerous and complex factors, summarized below, contributed to this development. Our discussion is based on the publications of H. W. Janson and Erwin Panofsky, art historians, and Max Miller, lecturer at the Chartres Cathedral, France, as well as on our own direct study of numerous medieval buildings.

[16] For a most useful analysis as well as a translation of original documents by the person who more than any other brought about the creation of Gothic architecture, see Erwin Panofsky, ed., and trans., *Abbot Suger on the Abbey Church of St.-Denis and Its Art Treasures* (Princeton, NJ: Princeton University Press, 1946). Though many analyses and commentaries on medieval Gothic architecture are available, an especially clear introduction to the form, its origins, and the surrounding religious, social, and political circumstances is provided by H. W. Janson, *History of Art* (New York: Harry Abrams, 1962), pp. 229–39.

There must have been many people who contributed to the creation of a "new" architectural statement in the first half of the twelfth century, but we are able to distinguish the experience, thoughts, and religious and political circumstances of one man: Abbot Suger of the Royal Abbey Church of St. Denis. Suger attended the school at this abbey, where he became a close friend to the prince and future king of France. One may assume that their friendship from student days provided a basis for the later great trust accorded Suger when his friend was king. Suger's efforts and later role in both the church and the state would make him counselor to yet another king.

After schooling and ordination into the priesthood, eventually Suger found his way back to St. Denis, a place of learning, contemplation, and worship. Before considering further the role of the royal abbey church and the new architectural form, we should turn our attention to this place, the Abbey Church of St. Denis. According to ancient tradition, a man named Denis was the apostle to France; that is, he brought Christianity to Gaul (France), as well as several important theological ideas, which would later be used to make a physical structure a "text," a medium for expressing theology and faith. Tradition (in error) assigned the origin of these ideas to Dionysius the Areopagite, a follower of St. Paul, the great missionary, teacher, and theologian of the earliest church. (That the ideas should have been assigned to a later fifth-century theologian, now referred to as the "pseudo Dionysius," probably did not matter in terms of the tradition.)[17] The remains of Denis, the Christian apostle to France, were enshrined in the abbey church dedicated in his honor.

When Suger accepted the role of abbot at the Abbey of St. Denis, it had long been a place where pilgrims came to venerate the saint who had brought the Christian faith to their land. Suger also inherited a monastery in need of reform among the monks and physical restoration of the buildings. Suger poured all of his considerable energy and talents into sustaining the important role of this abbey, favored of monarchs. Erwin Panofsky speaks of the manner in which Suger submerged himself into the abbey and its honored saint:

> Thus Suger, conceiving of himself as the adopted child of St.-Denis, came to divert . . . the whole amount of energy, acumen and ambition nature had bestowed upon him. Completely fusing his personal aspirations with the interests of the "mother church," he may be said to have gratified his ego by renouncing his identity: he expanded himself until he had become identical with the Abbey.[18]

Suger not only identified himself with the abbey and St. Denis but also with the nation of France. It is argued that he developed an almost "mystical nationalism," and "the French word *chauvinisme*" has been applied to him.[19] Suger saw the king as having divine responsibility for concord in the land, for defending it, and especially for preserving the church and seeing to the needs of the poor. Suger's dear friend, King Louis *le gros*, vowed "at his coronation in 1108" to fulfill these roles.[20] Thus, for Suger, the abbey, St. Denis, and the central authority of the realm, invested in the king, were effectively merged.[21]

---

[17] See further discussion on this subject in Janson, *History of Art*, p. 231.

[18] Panofsky, *Abbot Suger*, p. 31.

[19] Ibid.

[20] Ibid., p. 2.

[21] Ibid.

The dukes of the regions forming the French nation often were rather independent in their behavior, and the central authority of a monarch with a cooperative court was not easy to maintain. By imbuing the investiture of the monarch's office with a holy task, Suger succeeded in forming an alliance, even a union, between the mother church and the royal office.[22] And the Abbey Church of St. Denis, with its holy relics of the apostle to France, was steadily forged into a symbol of that union. "Suger wanted to make the Abbey the spiritual center of France, a pilgrimage church to outshine the splendor of all the others, the focal point of religious as well as patriotic emotion."[23]

Suger set out to achieve this goal partly by restructuring the church building, and from this project emerged a striking architectural accomplishment: the new style that we have come to call *Gothic*. Suger assembled the great designers and builders of the land, and gradually there emerged a physical form that reflects the theological ideas Suger drew from St. Denis. Whoever served as chief architect must have been singularly responsive to Suger's stated desires to express theology in stone. Architect and theologian must have collaborated continuously to realize this form.

Two salient features of Gothic architecture that are especially revelatory of theological meaning are (1) *mathematical harmony*, the clear demonstration of perfect ratios and geometric planning that result in a structure in which all the parts are interdependent; and (2) *luminosity*, the use of natural light to flood the structure, especially through stained glass, with a brilliance that invades the interior space like a revelation.[24] The perfect harmony, the rationality, clearly perceptible in the building's balance and ratios, symbolizes the very mind of God. It suggests the order and balance in the God-created universe, as perceived by medieval humanity. The new form allowed the creation of huge spaces for windows, making possible the admission of great shafts of light. The deep coloration of the stained glass of the period served to transform the light, to diffuse and filter it—to change the very quality of daylight and endow it with special character. The luminosity could then symbolize the "light of God," especially seen in Christ, so that humanity might be enlightened.

How was this accomplished through the structure of a building? Before the emergence of Gothic architecture, Western buildings used for public gathering and/or worship tended to be characterized by great mass. They appeared often as powerful and sometimes majestic edifices, which seemed to rise out of the ground. Roman building principles, long used by the church in some form or other, produced a fortress quality. It was necessary to use the Roman arch or a post and lintel system and heavy walls and small windows to support the weight of the roof. If one wanted to make a building taller, it had to be widened as well, to retain stability. Otherwise, the roof weight might cause collapse since it tended to exert pressure downward and outward. Thus, one was conscious of an enclosed, fortresslike space.

Innovation was required for Suger's goals to become possible if they were to be translated into structural form. It appears that architects under his supervision were experienced in the fairly recent development of the groined arch system used in some

[22] Janson, *History of Art*, p. 230.
[23] Ibid.
[24] Cf. discussion on this subject by Janson, *History of Art*, p. 231.

Figure 5.7   Cathedral of Notre Dame, Paris, facing east. (Alinari/Art Resource, New York.)

Romanesque (Roman-like) churches of fairly recent construction. In planning the new building, they employed this system in the direct support of the roof (see Figure 5.7).[25]

The weight of the roof would fall onto a *boss* (a round, latchlike ornament) positioned at intervals along the center of the peak of the pointed arch. Radiating out from the boss were curved *ribs* to support the vault and disperse the weight in at least four directions to four or more *capitals*. Then, a fourth of the weight on the boss was received at the capital and projected down a *column* to the *column base*, which rested on a *plinth* (a square or rectangular base for the column). Thus, part of the weight was transferred to the foundation. However, because the architects wanted to open huge sections of the walls to windows, so that the symbol of light could be used, the resulting tall, pointed arch system (a kind of skeletal structure) required further support to avoid collapse. It appears that the architects calculated that the weight and pressure received at each capital, pressing down and out, needed to be met in precise ratio by an object pressing in and up. Thus, we have the invention of the *flying buttress* (see Figure 5.8).

Thus, a structure is possible in which the walls play a comparatively small role in its overall stability. Examination and contemplation of the exterior and interior of the

Figure 5.8   Cathedral of Notre Dame, Paris, exterior detail: flying buttresses at apse. (Photo by Kenneth Lawrence.)

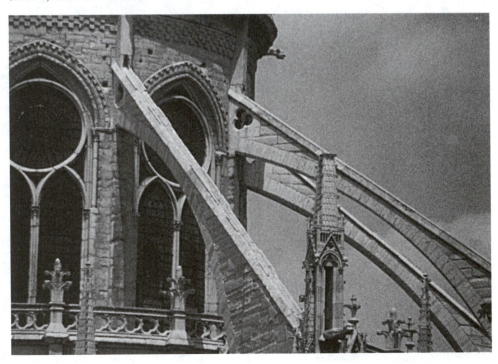

[25] Because the Abbey Church of St. Denis has been altered considerably since it was constructed, we are using pictures of Notre Dame, in Paris, which clearly exemplifies the Gothic form developed by Suger and his associates.

structure reveals to the viewer the interdependence of all the parts. The balance of ratios and the visually exhibited geometric planning—the rationality of it all—eventually may overwhelm the viewer with its seeming harmony. The building no longer suggests a fortress, a great pile of stone; instead it seems to reach up, to suggest a vast order, a unified wholeness rather like the universe in microcosm (see Figure 5.9).

Now the walls of this great, skeletal structure could be opened for windows. Frequently the glass was stained or painted to present pictures of persons, events, and symbols important to the history of Christianity. Stone tracery formed an intricate support system for sections of glass, which were further divided into small segments held together by lead. Much of this glass was so refined that it gathered light rather like a lens and transformed it into dazzling rays of widely varied colors that were projected into the interior. The luminosity, symbol of the Divine Light, invades this universe.

Though certainly not unique to Christianity, from the very beginnings of the faith, the symbol of light has been one of its central and most active symbols (see Figure 5.10). This very ancient symbolic reference is also so deeply rooted in culture that language is thoroughly permeated with it. W. Mark Gunderson, an American architect, articulates the deeper levels that give that architectural form spirituality.

Figure 5.9   Cathedral of Notre Dame, Paris, exterior from west. Note especially the system of buttresses and windows. (Photo by Kenneth Lawrence.)

Light is a building's breath.
Day and night are inhaling and exhaling.
Light invests form.

. . .

It becomes difficult . . . to speak of quality of
light in a room which reflects no regard for
daylight (to say nothing of moonlight).

Lucid thought, *clarity* of idea, *shedding light* on
a subject, *illuminating*, etc.; all of these metaphors
reiterate the importance of Light as requisite for
understanding—for the need to "*see clearly*,"
literally and figuratively. Without a discipline
it is impossible to *enlighten*.

Order allows light into situations which light would
avoid through no prejudice of its own.[26]

The sense of the splendid balance of ratios and of harmony and the invasion of
space by dazzling light are exhibited especially well by the Cathedral Church of St.
Andrew at Wells, England. Smaller than many Gothic cathedrals, Wells may be judged a
superlative statement of the Gothic perspective. Upon entering the nave of the church,
one immediately perceives the two major ideas of the Gothic conception (see Figure
5.11).

Striving for a coherent and balanced whole is also characteristic of the facade of
the Cathedral of Siena, Italy. The formal architectural discipline employed in the construction of the cathedral embraces both the mosaics and the sculpture. Each part has a
definite role within the unity of the total framework (see Figure 5.12).

While Christian thinkers created the theological systems of the high medieval
period, the schools and cathedrals influenced the religious experience of the populace.
One can imagine the communicative effect of these structures on the worshipers as they
participated in the mass and, awed by light filtering into the gloom below, perceived the
massive intricacy of these houses of God. The massiveness, beauty, and luminosity all
express through the structure itself religious meaning—the majesty and power of the
Divine.

[26] W. Mark Gunderson, "On Light," unpublished working notes, October 9, 1991. (Used by permission.)

Figure 5.10 Cathedral of Notre Dame, Paris, north rose window. At center the Virgin Mary holds the Christ child on her knee and is surrounded by prophets, kings, ancestors of Christ, patriarchs, and high priests of Israel. (Giraudon/Art Resource, New York.)

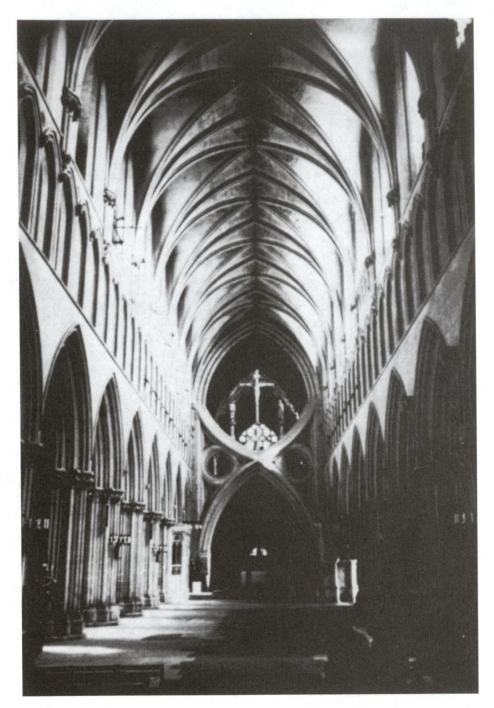

Figure 5.11   Cathedral Church of St. Andrew, Wells, England; nave with choir and sanctuary beyond double arch. (Photo by Kenneth Lawrence.)

Figure 5.12   Facade, Cathedral of Siena, Italy. (Photo by Kenneth Lawrence.)

CHAPTER 6

❧

History, Revelation, and the Knowledge of God

Introduction

In Part II of *Exploring Religious Meaning,* we examined a number of religious experiences of individuals and groups; presented an analysis of some of the characteristic features and elements of religious experience; and articulated the broad aspects of religious experience, especially through art and architecture.

Part III shifts from the more subjective dimension of personal—individual or group—experience to the more objective side of that which is experienced. That is, in Part III we characterize what people who have had such experiences have believed to be their object, source, or goal. In Western religious traditions the object, source, or goal of religious experience is often characterized in personal terms, as God. Since some religions do not conceive of the ultimate reality in strictly personal terms, we ordinarily use the term *the Divine* to indicate that which is sought in religious experience.

Many have argued that the concepts religious persons use to indicate or to characterize the Divine and the relations that humans have to the Divine arise from the experiences of mundane human life—from the interaction of human beings with their natural environment and from the realm of interpersonal relations. Thus, the Divine may be characterized with images derived from the forces or phenomena of nature, like lightning or a storm, or from human relationships or phenomena, such as a king or an all-powerful father. Because human images of the Divine are based on or derived from human experience of nature and social—personal and interpersonal—life, to speak of the Divine is in some sense to speak of the human. Yet religious persons are convinced that they encounter a transhuman reality, which is real regardless of the way it is imagined, conceived, or expressed.

Here we examine images and concepts of the Divine as these have been articulated in different cultural settings and periods of history. Underlying all the concerns of this chapter is the overarching question "Why should one think of the Divine at all?" Hardly a culture has existed where this question has not been raised. A hymnic statement from the Vedas of early Hinduism expresses what appears to be inherent human awareness of the Divine. At the same time it leaves open the options concerning the way in which that Divine is to be conceived—as personal or impersonal, historical or timeless, active or quiescent, one or many.

> Who truly knows, and who can here declare it?
> Whence It was born, and how this world was fashioned?
>
> . . .
>
> Whether he made the world or did not make it,
> He knows whence this creation came, he only
> Who in the highest heaven guards and watches,
> He knows indeed, but then, perhaps, he knows not![1]
> (*Rig Veda*, Book X, Hymn 129)

Three interrelated topics of particular importance to Western religious traditions—Judaism, Christianity, and Islam—are discussed in this chapter. Naturally, these concepts of history, revelation, and faith are present in other religious traditions also. In this chapter these topics are of special importance, for if we are seeking to examine and understand human concepts and experiences of the Divine, then the question of how the Divine is present in human history, how the Divine is revealed, how the Divine is known (by faith or in other ways) becomes crucial.

Every religious tradition contains some understanding of *revelation*. The meaning of revelation ranges from some form of religious insight—as experienced by a Taoist in contemplation of nature or by a Hindu in transcendental meditation—to the idea of a special communication from a personal God—as when, in Jewish, Christian, and Islamic belief, God communicates his will to particular individuals in unique events. Judaism, Christianity, and Islam have, in fact, frequently been called "historical" religions because of their belief that God does communicate to people in specific historical contexts through specific historical events. Some of the dimensions of this understanding of revelation, and some of the problems it involves, are discussed in Unit 34; faith, as discussed in Units 35 and 36, will be seen to be of universal human significance.

The relationship of faith to reason, as discussed by philosophers and theologians for centuries, is still an issue of very great importance. Also, faith is a comprehensive human possibility, a mode of existence that many have believed both undergirds and transcends the rational dimensions of life. *Faith* in this sense involves belief, at least some minimum of belief, but it means much more than that: It involves commitment, trust, and basic self-acceptance and self-understanding. The connection of faith, as discussed here, with the definition of the term *religion*, explored in the introduction, should be clear and should provide occasions for a reexamination of that definition.

---

[1] As cited in John Noss, *Man's Religions*, 4th ed. (New York: Macmillan, 1969), p. 97.

UNIT 34   Revelation: General and Special

Is God self-revealing? If so, how can we understand revelation?

> *Revelation* translates the Greek word *apokalypsis* and literally means "an uncovering, a laying bare, making naked." . . . So understood, R[evelation] presupposes (1) that someone or something is hidden and that this someone or something has not been discovered but, rather, disclosed.[2]

We cannot find a developed concept of revelation in the Bible. Although the Bible contains numerous "images and symbols for the disclosure of God's will and purposes,"[3] revelation has developed as a doctrinal concept during the history of Christianity since the writing of the Scriptures. Alan Richardson, author of *Christian Apologetics*, interprets two kinds of revelation: *general revelation*, the awareness that everyone has of God, and *special revelation*, a designation of the unique knowledge of God that comes from a particular historical experience:

> The only kind of theory of the knowledge of God which will adequately embrace all the facts of man's experience will be one which recognizes that there are two kinds of revelation or divine disclosure of truth. There is first general revelation, which pertains to the universal religious consciousness of mankind; and there is also special revelation, which is mediated through particular episodes of definite times and places in history. The broad distinction between general and special revelation is that the former is nonhistorical, in that its content is not communicated to mankind through particular historical situations but is quite independent of the accidents of time and place, whereas the latter is historical, that is, bound up with certain series of historical persons and happenings through which it is communicated to mankind. This is broadly the distinction between biblical (Jewish-Christian) religion and the non-Christian religions.[4]

So according to Richardson, general revelation allows all people in some way to know about God, but special revelation means that God is disclosed in a very special way to specific people so that they personally experience God. Special revelation is the divine confrontation of God and humankind through such actual historical events as the Israelite exodus from Egypt and the life, death, and resurrection of Jesus Christ.

There are at least three dimensions of general revelation that represent different ways of knowing God: The first is reason, our capacity to think about God, for example, when our logic tells us that there must have been an ultimate first cause of all that is. The second, artistic experience, may include the use of our minds but often relates to our emotional responses, for example, when we are moved by the beauty of visual art forms, scenes in nature, or music. The third is our sense of morality, for example, a gnawing conscience

---

[2] Van A. Harvey, *A Handbook of Theological Terms* (New York: Macmillan, 1964), p. 207.

[3] Ibid.

[4] Alan Richardson, *Christian Apologetics* (New York: SCM Press and Harper & Row, 1947), p. 117.

in the face of hard ethical choices or a case of gross injustice. Reflect on these three forms of general revelation as you read further.

> The theory of general and special revelation, however, does not restrict the general knowledge of God, to which all men have access, by limiting it to knowledge of one type only, namely, the knowledge which comes by rational reflection. It recognizes that there may be knowledge of God through general religious experience, far outside the biblical and Christian frontiers. Furthermore . . . it helps us to see that there may be a genuine knowledge of God that comes through all forms of art and artistic experience—music, poetry, drama, architecture, sculpture, painting.[5]

Thus, although a theory of general revelation may imply that strict logical analysis gives us the knowledge of God, it may also include an experience of God through art or the natural world. The key to a general revelation or knowledge of God, according to Richardson, relates to the moral experience.

> It is, however, in the moral sphere that the chief evidence of general revelation is found. Even though some might hold that there are certain people who are totally devoid of religious experience, it is indubitable that all people have had moral experience—the experience of knowing that one ought to do this and ought not to do that. Every human being who is not clearly an imbecile has knowledge of right and wrong.[6]

Alan Richardson claims that general revelation has redeeming power for those who experience God through philosophy, art forms, or nature. Other eminent theologians, however, such as Karl Barth and Emil Brunner (highly influential German theologians during post–World War I decades), hold that special revelation alone serves as the vehicle for saving grace. Barth believes that every person is a sinner, totally devoid of any natural capacity to receive God's revelation. For him, God is known by a person only because God makes that knowledge possible. Brunner agrees with Barth on this point but would argue that in every person there remains a capacity for general knowledge about God, even though such knowledge does not redeem a person from sin. Richardson feels that both Barth and Brunner neglect the saving power that comes from the knowledge of God revealed outside of Christianity.

Richardson affirms that non-Christian humanists who do good works or have some vision of God are to be considered vehicles of God's general revelation. He is quick to say, however, that Christians who recognize God-given humanist values in non-Christians should claim special revelation as essential for clarifying and correcting general revelation.

Concerning the necessity of special revelation, Richardson writes, "There is indeed a sense in which the noblest insights of the humanist are fulfilled in Christ, but there is also a sense in which they are judged and transcended by Him. . . . Although all that we have said about the necessity and value of general revelation is true, it is also true that apart from faith in Christ there is no undistorted knowledge of God or of truth at all."[7]

[5] Ibid., p. 122.
[6] Ibid., p. 124.
[7] Ibid., pp. 129–30.

∾

Do you think everyone has a religious consciousness?

Why do those, according to Richardson, under general revelation lack knowledge of God?

Could the concepts of general and special revelation as defined by Richardson be meaningful to those of religious traditions other than Christianity?

UNIT 35   Faith and Reason

We have discussed the ways in which God may be revealed—in the permanent structure and characteristics of the created world (general revelation) and in unique historical events of self-disclosure (special revelation). These categories have been particularly important to Western religious traditions (Judaism, Christianity, Islam). In this unit, we examine the same topics from the point of view of the potential receiver of revelation. That is, we consider the possible sources or faculties in human beings through which knowledge of God (or revelation) might be experienced. Particularly, we explore the possible relations between faith and reason as two human avenues to the Divine. Again, these concepts have been particularly important in Western religious traditions. Those who stress special revelation probably tend to emphasize faith as a way to know God, and those who affirm the reality and importance of general revelation place a heavy emphasis on reason.

Determining the relationship between faith and reason depends on answering this question: How shall one respond to God's revelation of himself? By faith? By reason? By both faith and reason? Or is there a dimension deeper than either faith or reason?

John Baillie, a Scottish theologian, points to the problem of relating faith and reason:

> All vital knowledge, all apprehended truth may be regarded as revealed. . . . The knowing mind is active in attending, selecting, and interpreting; but it must attend to, select from, and interpret what is presented to it; and therefore it must be passive as well as active.[8]

Here Baillie makes a distinction between the mind's active and passive behavior. When the mind acts, does this mean it reasons? When the mind remains passive, does this mean it lives by faith? Or can faith be considered the active element of humanity, whereas reason is passive? How do we gain knowledge of the Divine? By naked thought, the unaided exercise of human thinking? Or by receiving direct revelation from God himself? Or does it mislead us to distinguish between faith and reason?

The West has a long history of alternating harmony and disharmony between faith and reason. At times faith has ruled, while reason has suffered suppression. At other times reason has reigned over faith. There have been times when reason and revelation have existed together in relative peace.

[8] John Baillie, *The Idea of Revelation* (New York: Columbia University Press, 1956), p. 19.

In the following columns, faith and reason can be seen to have differing emphases:

Faith May Include an Emphasis on	Reason May Include an Emphasis on
revelation	discursive thinking
theology	philosophy
humanity's will	humanity's intellect
humanity's freedom	humanity's knowledge
trust	logic
decisive affirmation	philosophical speculations
God as personal	God as abstract and impersonal
Divine disclosure	human discovery

Comparisons between the categories suggest why faith and reason have differing roles both in religious understanding and in particular religious traditions. In the West, there have traditionally been four basic ways of relating faith and reason.

Reason Rejecting Faith

When reason rejects faith, it tends to result in skepticism about God. Reason alone has sought God but in many cases has reached an atheistic (no God) or an agnostic (no knowledge of God) position. Some interpreters who have a thoroughgoing use of reason without the help of faith have concluded that religious affirmations of God or life after death equal faith in goblins, Santa Claus, fairies, and monsters in the night. According to some thinkers, reason seeks evidence for God's existence, but in the absence of evidence for God's existence, atheism becomes obligatory.[9] A similar, though not identical, position has been proposed by A. J. Ayer:

> We conclude, therefore, that the argument from religious experience is altogether fallacious. The fact that people have religious experiences is interesting from a psychological point of view, but it does not in any way imply that there is such a thing as religious knowledge. . . . The theist, like the moralist, may believe that his experiences are cognitive experiences, but, unless he can formulate his "knowledge" in propositions that are empirically verifiable, we may be sure he is deceiving himself.[10]

Ayer refuses to accept any statements about reality as meaningful unless they are grounded in testable sense experiences. Others, such as Aristotle, Leibniz, and Hartshorne, have claimed to have knowledge of God through reason alone.

Reason Embracing Faith

A number of interpreters have held the view that reason includes the way of faith. Adherents of this position have seen a common denominator of Divine Truth in both philosophy and the Judeo-Christian tradition. Justin Martyr, a second-century

[9] Michael Scriven, *Primary Philosophy* (New York: McGraw-Hill, 1966), p. 103.
[10] A. J. Ayer, *Language, Truth and Logic*, 2nd ed. (New York: Dover, 1946), p. 120.

philosopher and Christian martyr, held "that a saving natural knowledge of God was possible through philosophy. . . ."[11] He saw a close identity between Christian teachings and much in the best philosophers. He felt Christianity inherited all the truth discerned by Greek philosophers.[12] For Justin, reason and faith represented a common ground.

Justin fathered a tradition that was articulated strongly by Clement and Origen. Clement tended to equate the saving power of philosophy with Jewish law and prophecy. He saw Plato as a Moses talking Attic Greek.[13] Origen, Christianity's earliest systematic theologian, developed a system of theology in which he saw a close proximity between the word of the Greek philosophers and the Word become flesh, Christ, the incarnation of God. In his classic work, *First Principles*, he relates in creative ways the message of scriptural faith to the teachings of philosophy and reason.

Peter Abelard, Christian philosopher of the twelfth century, refocused the emphasis on a reasoned faith. "He held that what had been revealed to the Jews by prophecy had been given to the Greeks by philosophy and that the doctrine of the Trinity, and other Christian truths, had been taught by Heraclitus and Plato. . . ."[14] Abelard's method emphasized doubt as a way to understand faith. He did not intend to make reason primary to faith, but his approach did open the way for more rationalism in theology, culminating in Immanuel Kant's attempt to confine "religion within the limits of reason alone."

Faith Rejecting Reason

In reaction to the tendency of reason to suppress faith, some people of faith have tended to negate reason altogether. At times, Tertullian, an early Christian theologian, rejected reason, "denouncing Greek philosophy as the bridal gift of the fallen angels to the daughters of men and the Greek philosophers as the patriarchs of the heretics."[15] Bernard of Clairvaux, a Christian mystic, felt that Abelard threatened the true faith with his rationalism. Doubting reason as a reliable guide to God, Bernard said, "By faith I think of God. . . ."[16] Martin Luther, father of the Protestant Reformation, held that no one can enter into a right relationship with God through good works or the power of thought. Although reason may help us in practical living, such as making clothes or doing a job, human reasoning falls short in spiritual matters; other power is required here—something given only by God and made known in divine word (See Unit 18).[17] That which God grants, in Luther's understanding, is faith alone, the gift of trust in God's saving strength.

[11] Richardson, *Christian Apologetics*, p. 228.

[12] Ibid., p. 229.

[13] Ibid.

[14] Ibid.

[15] Ibid., p. 228.

[16] Bernard of Clairvaux, "Selections from His Sermons," in *The Christian Reader: Inspirational and Devotional Classics*, ed. Stanley Irving Stuber (New York: Association Press, 1952), p. 106.

[17] Hugh Thomson Kerr, Jr., ed., *A Compend of Luther's Theology* (Philadelphia: Westminster Press, 1958), p. 3.

In our own century, the theologian Karl Barth expressed serious apprehensions about reason's ability to point adequately to God: "Knowledge of God is a knowledge completely effected and determined from the side of its object, from the side of God. . . . Our concepts are not adequate to grasp this treasure."[18] We should note, however, that Barth, as well as others who rejected reason in the realm of faith, had to depend on the expressions of reason to reject reason. Although some voices may justifiably cry out against the excesses of rationalism, no one can be free completely from the philosophy of the times.

Faith Embracing Reason

The classical Christian answer to the conflict between faith and reason finds apt expression in the words of Saint Augustine, bishop of Hippo in Africa in the fifth century:

> Understanding is the reward of faith. Therefore seek not to understand that thou mayest believe, but believe that thou mayest understand. . . . We believed that we might know; for if we wished first to know and then to believe, we should not be able to know or to believe. . . . They did not believe because they knew, but they believed in order that they might know.[19]

Here Augustine exhibits an orthodox Christian view of the relationship between faith and reason. Reason comes to creative fruition only as it is guided by faith. Faith orders understanding.

This does not mean that faith supplies factual data of sense experience. Reason must still assess and make judgments about facts of knowledge, but the power of reason to function adequately comes from faith. In knowing, "faith supplies the 'clues' or categories of interpretation by which alone the empirical *data* of science and religion can be rightly understood."[20] According to Augustine's approach, every philosophy must follow the lead of a faith principle to give valid meaning to existence. Faith serves as the condition of sound reasoning. In fact, according to Augustine, the man of faith is freed to exercise his reason more responsibly. Faith enables the believer to understand.

Further Considerations

We do not claim that our presentation of the four ways of relating faith and reason solves the problem. For some the whole idea of distinguishing between faith and reason may fracture the knowledge of God. We should point out, therefore, that thinkers in this century have endeavored to overcome the fragmentation of human personality. Not only have some psychologists and psychiatrists begun to view human life as a unified

---

[18] Karl Barth, *Dogmatics in Outline*, trans. G. T. Thomson (New York: Philosophical Library, 1949), p. 24.

[19] Saint Augustine, "In Joannis Evangelium Tractatus," *An Augustine Synthesis*, ed. Erich Pryzywara (New York: Harper & Brothers, 1958), pp. 58–59.

[20] Richardson, *Christian Apologetics*, p. 230.

whole instead of a sum of separable facets (for example, intellect, will, emotions) but also theologians have begun to reinterpret faith in a more inclusive way.

John Dillenberger, a contemporary theologian, exhibits an idea of faith that encompasses various dimensions of human response to revelation. He says that faith implies not only belief but also thoughtful discernment and an active imagination. Feeling and thinking require each other. "The great ideas move the heart. The stirrings of the heart transform and create thought."[21] Dillenberger sees faith as more than emotion, doctrine, or trust. Although he allows that faith may include feelings and intellectually defined doctrines, as well as the trust "that one has been found in the divine," he asserts that faith has roots deeper than any of its facets.[22] Faith finds its home in the human spirit, including "heart stirrings" and "thought stirrings."

The discussion of faith in the next unit attempts to explore the concept as inclusive in the way that Dillenberger and other recent theologians, Catholic and Protestant, have suggested.

∽

Can reason operate apart from faith?

Does faith undermine reason or enhance the intellectual process?

Does faith enable understanding?

Which of the categories listed on page 119 for faith and reason are most important to you? Least important?

UNIT 36   The Anatomy of Faith

In the preceding unit, it was emphasized that many contemporary theologians, influenced by twentieth-century concepts of personality as an integrated whole, have attempted to understand the concept of faith as involving more than the cognitive dimension of belief.

Faith—for many people one of the most familiar of religious concepts—is also one of the most easily and consistently misunderstood. Paul Tillich comments, "There are few words in the language of religion which cry for as much semantic purging as the word 'faith.' It is continually being confused with belief in something for which there is no evidence, or in something intrinsically unbelievable, or in absurdities or nonsense. It is extremely difficult to remove these distorting connotations from the genuine meaning of faith."[23]

The understanding of faith as a belief "in something for which there is no evidence," though common, is a most dangerous form of misunderstanding. It unwittingly pits faith against reason and knowledge. To say that you believe "by faith" in something that is unknown or cannot be rationally proved is to affirm its existence and relevance

---

[21] John Dillenberger, *Contours of Faith: Changing Forms of Christian Thought* (Nashville, TN: Abingdon Press, 1969), p. 84.

[22] Ibid., p. 85.

[23] Paul Tillich, *Systematic Theology*, Vol. III (Chicago: University of Chicago Press, 1963), p. 130.

even though you lack evidence to support your faith. In a day when rational evidence is the hallmark for accepting anything as true, it is obvious that knowledge that can be rationally validated will appear more trustworthy than faith that cannot. Therefore, in an era of expanding "knowledge," an individual with this understanding of faith assumes that he or she is less and less dependent on faith. As knowledge expands in the life of the individual, its importance tends to overpower and outweigh that of faith—faith is reduced to a wholly subjective and relatively unimportant part of life.

So it would seem that the most common understanding of faith leads to a struggle between knowledge and faith wherein faith is the inevitable loser. Perhaps this understanding has contributed to the modern relegation of religion to a secondary (or even nonexistent) role in life. In any case, it is evident that the misunderstanding of the nature and meaning of faith has important consequences.

To understand faith as the opposite of knowledge is not only misleading but also unnecessary. Much of the difficulty arises over the tendency to use the words *belief* and *faith* as synonyms. For many people, to say "I believe in America" is to say "I have faith in America", the two expressions are used without recognizable distinction. Yet the words do not mean the same thing. *Faith* connotes "reliance on," "trust in," "commitment to." On the one hand, having faith means being personally willing to trust or depend on something. On the other hand, believing in something means holding or thinking that it exists, but it does not necessarily mean trust. H. Richard Niebuhr helpfully points up this distinction:

> The belief that something exists is an experience of a wholly different order from the experience of reliance on it. The faith we speak of . . . is not intellectual assent to the truth of certain propositions, but a personal, practical trusting in, reliance on, counting upon something. So we have faith in democracy not insofar as we believe that democracy exists, but insofar as we rely upon the democratic idea or spirit to maintain itself and to influence the lives of people continuously. We have faith in the people not insofar as we believe in the existence of such a reality as "the people," but insofar as we count upon the character of what we call the people to manifest itself steadfastly in the maintenance of certain values. Faith, in other words, always refers primarily to character and power rather than to existence. Existence is implied and necessarily implied; but there is no direct road from assent to the intellectual proposition that something exists to the act of confidence and reliance upon it. Faith is an active thing, a committing of self to something, an anticipation. It is directed toward something that is also active, that has power or is power. . . . Belief as assent to the truth of propositions does not necessarily involve reliance in action on that which is believed, and it refers to propositions rather than, as faith does, to agencies and powers.[24]

Belief should be distinguished from *faith* in our common usage of the terms. Faith may entail belief—that is, the acceptance of something—but it goes beyond acceptance to actual dependence. Conversely, belief may be present without faith; that is, one may believe but not really trust. Such, in fact, is the case with the religious understanding of many people. They may believe many things—that God exists, that Jesus Christ is

[24] H. Richard Niebuhr, *Radical Monotheism and Western Culture* (New York: Harper & Brothers, 1960), pp. 116–17. Copyright © The United Methodist Church, Department of Campus Ministries. Used by permission.

Saviour, that certain religious propositions are true—yet they do not act in their daily existence on what these beliefs imply, and in failing to do so they reveal the inconsistency between their beliefs and their faith. Such inconsistency is easily recognized by others as hypocrisy, although it is seldom recognized by the individual, for the individual thinks that his or her beliefs and faith are the same.

If the distinction between faith and belief is kept in mind, we may return to the relation between faith and knowledge. Although it is true that knowledge is based on specific evidence, it is also true that knowledge relies on (trusts) certain presuppositions. The scientists build their store of knowledge on the assumption that the universe is ultimately orderly and that this order is discoverable. They place faith in that orderliness and work from this presupposition. Faith then lies behind their endeavors. Evidence from the universe and the knowledge built on it substantiates their initial trust. Religious faith follows a similar pattern. It also operates on an assumption—that the universe has meaning and purpose and that purpose is evident in human experience of life. Theologians then trust this assumption and think, like the scientists, that life provides evidence for the validity of the assumption. The religious experience, abundant throughout humanity's existence, may not be of the same form as that found in the physical world with which the scientist works, but it is no less valid because of this. Meaning in the universe may call for evidence of a different order or genre than that of function in the universe, but both are legitimate and necessary. In either case, faith is an active element in human experience. Science and religion depend on both faith *and* knowledge, and they do not oppose each other.

A more acute problem may be, instead of opposition between faith and knowledge, a conflict between opposing "faiths." We attach our trust (faith) to many objects in the course of our lives (or even in the course of one day): self, occupation, money, scientific method, distinctive religious formulations, particular political systems, and moral standards, to mention only a few. Each of these demands of us a trust and commitment resulting in the exclusion of other alternatives. We find ourselves creatures with many faiths; in Niebuhr's words, "our natural religion is polytheistic."[25] At one moment we pursue and trust one faith, and in the next another. On some occasions we find that we must choose between these faiths—one must be more important than another.

For those willing to accept a religious solution to this problem of opposing faiths, Niebuhr offers some useful insights. He points out that all of these faiths are ultimately finite—insufficient to carry the weight of full and total commitment.

> None of these can guarantee meaning to our life in the world save for a time. They are finite in time as in space and make finite claims upon us. . . . None of these beings on which we rely to give content and meaning to our lives is able to supply continuous meaning and value.[26]

When the finitude of these faiths is recognized and accepted, when each one is destroyed or loses effectiveness, we are faced with a failure of meaning or purpose. At that moment we are enabled to place our faith in "the one reality beyond all the many, which is the last

[25] Ibid., p. 119.
[26] Ibid., pp. 120–22.

power, the infinite source of all particular beings as well as their end. And insofar as our faith, our reliance for meaning and worth, has been attached to this source and enemy of all our gods, we have been able to call this reality God."[27] When all of our lesser faiths have been destroyed, we are able to trust in that which stands behind all others—the source of all meaning and purpose—God.

Such an answer is, of course, unacceptable if we affirm other faith commitments as definitive and sufficient or if we define faith as something other than trust. Nevertheless, any solution to the problem of conflicting faiths demands that the object of our faith be clearly identified and that faith be distinguished from belief and from knowledge. If that which can be distinguished from belief and knowledge—faith—can be seen as reliable, it may again be recognized for the role it actually plays in the human experience.

When in this study of religion we define *religion* as "reliance on a pivotal value," we are speaking of faith—a faith that supersedes and dominates all other claims for attention and action.

[27] Ibid., pp. 122–23.

CHAPTER 7

Ways of Conceiving
the Divine

Introduction

The nature of religious experience is often encased in descriptions of rites and rituals, credal formulations and teaching formulas, or theological concepts expressing beliefs and doctrines. Religious experience is, however, too rich and varied to be captured by such manifestations of its presence. Behind these is a primary encounter between the Divine and the individual.

The purpose of this chapter is to probe some of the ways people talk about this encounter and to examine some of the concepts by which they have sought to character-ize the one encountered. Such an encounter is not always easily described in rational terms, as the first unit makes clear. Units 38 and 39 present differing cultural views of the Divine. The chapter closes with an examination of spirit since this concept is frequently related to the Divine in human experience.

In Part I we discussed an understanding of religion that embraces not only "sacred" or "theistic" views of the Divine but also "secular" or "nontheistic" commitments. Although the following units lean toward theistic conceptions, the reader should keep in mind our definition of religion as involving a commitment to a supreme or pivotal value, which becomes the focus for the whole of life. Thus, even nontheistic religions and secu-lar movements may involve a concept of the Divine as the ultimate object or source of an individual's or a group's commitment.

UNIT 37   The Holy

Religious experience in any of its many forms is grounded in an encounter with transcendent reality, which gives it a sacredness, or holiness, that distinguishes it from other human experiences. Rudolf Otto, in *The Idea of the Holy*, says this encounter includes a "moment of consciousness or a state of mind" in which one is overwhelmed by an awareness of the Divine. Such an experience gives one a feeling of "awe"—a sense of "astonishment" or "blank wonder." For Otto this encounter with the "wholly-other" lies behind and permeates all other religious consciousness.[1] In essence it is an encounter with the mystery that lies at the core of life. Otto's name for this mysterious reality is the *mysterium tremendum*, which suggests its power and centrality.

> Let us consider the deepest and most fundamental element in all strong and sincerely felt religious emotion. Faith unto salvation, trust, love—all these are there. But over and above these is an element which may also on occasion, quite apart from them, profoundly affect us and occupy the mind with a well-nigh bewildering strength. Let us follow it up with every effort of sympathy and imaginative intuition whenever it is to be found, in the lives of those around us, in sudden, strong ebullitions [outbursts or manifestations] of personal piety and the frames of mind such ebullitions evince, in the fixed and ordered solemnities of rites and liturgies, and again in the atmosphere that clings to old religious monuments and buildings, to temples and to churches. If we do so we shall find we are dealing with something for which there is only one appropriate expression, *"mysterium tremendum."* The feeling of it may at times come sweeping like a gentle tide, pervading the mind with a tranquil mood of deepest worship. It may pass over into a more set and lasting attitude of the soul, continuing, as it were, thrillingly vibrant and resonant, until at last it dies away and the soul resumes its "profane," nonreligious mood of everyday experience. It may burst in sudden eruption up from the depth of the soul with spasms and convulsions, or lead to the strangest excitements, to intoxicated frenzy, to transport, and to ecstasy. It has its wild and demonic forms and can sink to almost grisly horror and shuddering. It has its crude barbaric antecedents and early manifestations, and again it may be developed into something beautiful and pure and glorious. It may become the hushed, trembling, and speechless humility of the creature in the presence of—whom or what? In the presence of that which is a *mystery* inexpressible and above all creatures.

Although one confronts that which is finally a mystery, Otto suggests that what is encountered here is a distinctively positive reality, even if *mystery* is normally understood to carry negative connotations.

> It is again evident at once that here too our attempted formulation by means of a concept is once more a merely negative one. Conceptually *mysterium* denotes merely that which is hidden and esoteric, that which is beyond conception or understanding, extraordinary and unfamiliar. The term does not define the object more positively in its qualitative charac-

---

[1] Rudolf Otto, *The Idea of the Holy* (Oxford: Oxford University Press, 1923), passim. Reprinted by permission. Otto's work is a thorough investigation of the phenomenon of "numinous" encounters with the Divine.

ter. But though what is enunciated in the word is negative, what is meant is something absolutely and intensely positive.[2]

As Otto indicates, such an encounter may have many different aspects—it may take place in a dynamic moment or tranquil mood or in any number of other forms. Yet the experience itself, whatever its occasion or form, leaves one with a conviction of the reality and presence of the *mysterium tremendum*—the transcendent, the divine, God.

Otto's suggestive analysis and description of the mystery that lies at the core of all religion helps to conceptualize this central element in religion. But conceptual descriptions, as important as they may be, are only part of such an experience. Whatever its occasion or form, such an experience demands not only recognition but also response—whether positive or negative, expressible or inexpressible. The following items illustrate how people from differing religious traditions have responded to and described this experience.

Jewish Example

The first illustration comes from Jewish literature. The Hebrew prophet Isaiah describes the encounter with the *mysterium tremendum* (God), which began and empowered his prophetic career.

> In the year that King Uzziah died I saw the Lord sitting upon a throne, high and lifted up; and his train filled the temple. Above him stood the seraphim; each had six wings: with two he covered his face, and with two he covered his feet, and with two he flew. And one called to another and said:
> Holy, holy, holy is the Lord of hosts;
> the whole earth is full of his glory.
> And the foundations of the thresholds shook at the voice of him who called, and the house was filled with smoke. And I said: Woe is me! For I am lost; for I am a man of unclean lips, and I dwell in the midst of a people of unclean lips; for my eyes have seen the King, the Lord of hosts!
> Then flew one of the seraphim to me, having in his hand a burning coal which he had taken with tongs from the altar. And he touched my mouth and said: Behold, this has touched your lips; your guilt is taken away and your sin forgiven. And I heard the voice of the Lord saying, Whom shall I send, and who will go for us? Then I said, Here I am! Send me. (Isaiah 6:1–8, RSV)

Chinese Example

The second example is taken from Chinese literature and art. Lao-Tzu filled the *Tao Te Ching* with pithy images suggesting how life should properly be lived. Behind these images is an acute consciousness of the Holy, the mystery that underlies life. In Chinese culture the mystery present in all of the universe is symbolized by the word *Tao*. Lao-Tzu often used the symbol in unusual ways to point beyond to the hidden mystery of the Divine found in ordinary life.

[2] Ibid., pp. 12–13.

When the highest type of men hear the Tao (truth),
  They practice it diligently.
When the mediocre type hear the Tao,
  They seem to be aware and yet unaware of it.
When the lowest type hear the Tao,
  They break into loud laughter,—
If it were not laughed at, it would not be Tao.

Therefore there is the established saying:
  "Who understands Tao seems dull of comprehension;
  Who is advanced in Tao seems to slip backwards;
  Who moves on the even Tao (Path) seems to go up and down."

Superior virtue appears like a hollow (valley);
Sheer white appears like tarnished;
Great character appears like insufficient;
Solid character appears like infirm;
Pure worth appears like contaminated.
  Great space has no corners;
  Great talent takes long to mature;
  Great music is faintly heard;
  Great Form has no contour;
  And Tao is hidden without a name.
It is this Tao that is adept at lending (its power) and bringing fullfillment.[3]

Expressions of the divine mystery are certainly not limited to poetry or prose. Traditional Chinese art radiates an awareness of the Divine—the *Tao*. In the following passage, Otto Fischer describes this element as it is expressed in Chinese paintings (see Figure 7.1).

The spectator who, as it were, immerses himself in them feels behind these waters and clouds and mountains the mysterious breath of the primeval Tao, the pulse of innermost being. Many a mystery lies half-concealed and half-revealed in these pictures. They contain the knowledge of the "nothingness" and the "void," of the "Tao" of heaven and earth, which is also the Tao of the human heart. And so, despite their perpetual agitation, they seem as remotely distant and as profoundly calm as though they drew secret breath at the bottom of the sea.[4]

Hindu Example

The third and final example is drawn from the Hindu classic *The Bhagavad-Gita*. In the philosophic tradition of Hindu holy men, the Divine is beyond description and grasp since any human attempt to express it is necessarily a part of the illusory world (see Unit 10). For the majority of Hindus, however, the Divine is often expressed through an array of gods and goddesses. Each divine being may have many representatives or embodiments, all expressing the majesty and wonder of the *mysterium tremendum*. In the passage that follows, Krishna, a popular embodiment of one of the three greatest gods of Hinduism, has been asked by his disciple, Arjuna, to reveal himself in all his glory. Krishna

[3] Lin Yutang, ed., *The Wisdom of China and India*, (New York: Random House, 1942), p. 606. Copyright 1942 and renewed 1970 by Random House, Inc. Reprinted by permission of the publisher.

[4] As quoted in Otto, *Idea of the Holy*, p. 67.

Figure 7.1
Li K'o-Jan, *The Poet T'ao Yüan-Ming.*
(Prague National Gallery. Used by
permission.)

grants the request, suggesting that this is indeed a very unusual gift, withheld even from
the other gods.

> Then, O king, when he had spoken these words, Sri Krishna, Master of all yogis, revealed
> to Arjuna his transcendent, divine Form, speaking from innumerable mouths, seeing with
> a myriad eyes, of many marvellous aspects, adorned with countless divine ornaments,
> brandishing all kinds of heavenly weapons, wearing celestial garlands and the raiment of
> paradise, anointed with perfumes of heavenly fragrance, full of revelations, resplendent,
> boundless, of ubiquitous everywhere present regard.
>
> Suppose a thousand suns should rise together into the sky: such is the glory of the Shape
> of Infinite God.
>
> Then the son of Pandu beheld the entire universe, in all its multitudinous diversity,
> lodged as one being within the body of the God of gods.
>
> Then was Arjuna, that lord of mighty riches, overcome with wonder. His hair stood
> erect. He bowed low before God in adoration, and clasped his hands, and spoke:
>
> "Ah, my God, I see all gods within your body;
> Each in his degree, the multitude of creatures;
> See Lord Brahma throned upon the lotus;
> See all the sages, and the holy serpents.

Universal Form, I see you without limit,
Infinite of arms, eyes, mouths and bellies—
See, and find no end, midst, or beginning.

Crowned with diadems, you wield the mace and discus,
Shining every way—the eyes shrink from your splendour
Brilliant like the sun: like fire, blazing, boundless.

You are all we know, supreme, beyond man's measure,
This world's sure-set plinth and refuge never shaken,
Guardian of eternal law, life's Soul undying.
Birthless, deathless; yours the strength titanic,
Million-armed, the sun and moon your eyeballs,
Fiery-faced, you blast the world to ashes,

Fill the sky's four corners, span the chasm
Sundering heaven from earth. Superb and awful
Is your Form that makes the three worlds tremble.

Into you, the companies of devas [gods]
Enter with clasped hands, in dread and wonder.
Crying 'Peace,' the Rishis and the Siddhas [disciples]
Sing your praise with hymns of adoration. . . ."[5]

Arjuna, attempting here to express the immensity of this confrontation with the Divine, clearly can only point to the fact that no description will be adequate. The power, majesty, and wonder of the God is simply overwhelming and beyond expression.

In each of these examples, drawn as they are from different religious traditions, the presence and experience of the *mysterium tremendum* is expressed. However, as Otto points out, the best and most poignant descriptions never really do justice to the inexpressible awe that humans, aware of their finitude, feel before God.

Is such an experience common to everyone?

Is it necessarily a religious experience? If so, what makes it so?

Are there more common experiences in ordinary life that incorporate the same reality and experience?

Is the consciousness of the numinous a necessary experience for valid religious encounter, as Otto appears to assume?

UNIT 38   The Divine Expressed in Religious Texts

In the preceding unit, Rudolf Otto's characterization of the feeling of awe and mystery characteristic of human experience of the Divine was discussed. This experience may be a recurring momentary event in human life. Once statements about the Divine are given

---

[5] Swami Prabhavananda and Christopher Isherwood, trans., *The Song of God: Bhagavad-Gita* (Hollywood, CA: Vedanta Press, 1951), pp. 91–97. Used by the permission of the Vedanta Society of Southern California.

textual expression, however, they take on a reality to some extent independent of momentary human experiences. As Paul Ricoeur and other contemporary philosophers have noted, the text takes on a life of its own, projecting a reality (which Ricoeur calls the world of the text) *ahead of* its readers or users (many texts concerning the Divine are primarily used for liturgical or cultic purposes) that they are invited to enter. Thus textual statements that originally expressed thoughts and feelings about the Divine become the basis for an unending human dialogue; they become both guides and criteria for later thoughts, feelings, and experiences that humans have about that which concerns them ultimately.

In this unit, a number of textually expressed ways of conceiving of God are drawn from different cultures, different religious traditions, and different historical periods. There is some overlap: The passages from the Jewish scriptures can also illustrate important dimensions of Christian and Islamic understanding since Christians and Muslims understand the God of the Jewish scriptures to be their God, too. Additional and similar Christian interpretations of God are represented in selections from the New Testament and from the medieval Christian writer Thomas Aquinas. Although these passages differ in language—the New Testament passages characterize God in very concrete personal ways, whereas the passage by Aquinas uses a more abstract, philosophical approach—most Christians would hold that they both express truths about the God worshiped and believed in by Christians.

From most of the traditions represented in this unit, other and differently expressed statements about the nature and reality of God could be found. There are other traditions, too, from which significant statements might have been taken. The statements included resemble one another in some ways; they also differ rather dramatically. Some are primarily conceptual philosophical expressions; others are more direct, poetic statements growing out of practical life and the experience of worship. But it would be difficult and perhaps false to say that even the most abstractly expressed textual statement about God—for instance, Aristotle's—did not grow out of personal experience and deep or intense concern. Since the unit is long and contains a number of texts that lend themselves to analysis and discussion, it is divided into two major sections. The following questions may help you analyze the examples:

∾

How do you respond to the different views of God presented here?

Which of the views, if any, are most like ways you have heard God spoken of?

How do they differ from, and agree with, each other?

∾

God in the Jewish Scriptures

In the Hebrew Bible (sometimes referred to by Christians as the Old Testament), repeated emphasis is placed on the perception or conception that the divine, that is, God, is personal in character. Further, this God is continually active and involved in the world and in all creation. Also, the Divine exhibits personal concern for the world and its creatures. Though writers of scripture suggest that this God is involved in the world and immanent, God is also transcendent, beyond the world and vast. Following are three examples of Jewish conceptions of the Divine. The first is from the Torah (religious law or teachings), which is most ancient in the Jewish tradition. The second two are from two different prophets, whose teachings have shaped the theology of Judaism up to the present day.

> You are the people whom the Lord brought out of Egypt . . . and took for his own possession, as you are to this day. . . . Be careful not to forget the covenant which the Lord your God made with you, and do not make yourself a carved figure of anything which the Lord your God has forbidden. For the Lord your God is a devouring fire, a jealous God. . . . When you have children and grandchildren and grow old in the land, if you then fall into the degrading practice of making any kind of carved figure, doing what is wrong in the eyes of the Lord your God and provoking him to anger . . . the Lord will disperse you among the peoples, and you will be left few in number among the nations to which the Lord will lead you. But if from there you seek the Lord your God, you will find him. . . . When you are in distress and all these things come upon you, you will in days to come turn back to the Lord your God and obey Him. The Lord your God is a merciful god; he will never fail you nor destroy you, nor will he forget the covenant guaranteed by oath with your forefathers. (Deuteronomy 4:20–32, NEB)

Do you not know, have you not heard, were you not told long ago, have
    you not perceived ever since the world began, that God sits throned
      on the vaulted roof of earth,
  whose inhabitants are like grasshoppers?

  He stretches out the skies like a curtain
  He spreads them out like a tent to live in;
  He reduces the great to nothing
  and makes all earth's princes less than nothing.
Scarcely are they planted, scarcely sown, scarcely have they taken root in the earth,
  before he blows upon them and they wither away,
  and a whirlwind carries them off like chaff.
  To whom then will you liken me,
  whom set up as my equal?
  asks the Holy One.
Lift up your eyes to the heavens; consider who created it all, led out their
    host one by one and called them all by their names;
  through his great might, his might and power,
  not one is missing.
Why do you complain, O Jacob,
  and you, Israel, why do you say,
  "My plight is hidden from the Lord
  and my cause has passed out of God's notice"?
Do you not know, have you not heard?
The Lord, the everlasting God, creator of the wide world,
  grows neither weary nor faint;
  no man can fathom his understanding.
  He gives vigour to the weary,
  new strength to the exhausted.

                (Isaiah 40:21–29 NEB)

> What shall I bring when I approach the Lord?
> How shall I stoop before God on high?
> Am I to approach him with whole-offerings or yearling calves?
> Will the Lord accept thousands of rams
> or ten thousand rivers of oil?
> Shall I offer my eldest son for my own wrongdoing,
> my children for my own sin?
> God has told you what is good;
> and what is it that the Lord asks of you?
> Only to act justly, to love loyalty,
> to walk wisely before your God.
>
> (Micah 6:6–8 NEB)

Aristotle: God as Pure Being, The Unmoved Mover

The view of God held by Aristotle, a Greek philosopher of the fourth century B.C.E., greatly influenced later Western thought. Joined or fused with the Jewish view of God as the active Creator, it influenced Jewish, Muslim, and Christian thought.

Aristotle's beginning point is with the world of nature that we observe. He sees natural entities—organisms—as having an innate tendency to develop. An acorn has within itself an innate tendency to grow into a fully developed oak tree, provided its environment is favorable. A newborn human baby will naturally develop into a full-grown human being, capable of self-sustaining life and rational activities. Even the stars and planets seem to move in accordance with a law of their being.

Aristotle was convinced that the motion and development characteristic of things we observe must have an ultimate source, or cause. This first cause of motion must be perfect and complete in every way. It must not itself be subject to change or development, for otherwise its own development would need an explanation that goes beyond it. He calls this perfect source of motion and development for the whole universe God, or the Unmoved Mover. For Aristotle, God does not create the world; the world is uncreated and exists eternally. God is the source of motion and development in the world, the perfect reality that exists as an object of love and desire, the standard of absolute perfection for all other things.

> The first mover, then, exists of necessity; and insofar as it exists by necessity, its mode of being is good, and it is in this sense a first principle. For the necessary has all these senses—that which is necessary perforce because it is contrary to the natural impulse, that without which the good is impossible, and that which cannot be otherwise but can exist only in a single way.
>
> On such a principle, then, depends the heavens and the world of nature. And it is a life such as the best which we enjoy, and enjoy for but a short time (for it is ever in this state, which we cannot be), since its actuality is also pleasure. (And for this reason are waking, perception, and thinking most pleasant, and hopes and memories are so on account of these.)

What is God's life, his activity, like, according to Aristotle?

> And thinking in itself deals with that which is best in itself, and that which is thinking in the fullest sense with that which is best in the fullest sense. And thought thinks on itself

because it shares the nature of the object of thought; for it becomes an object of thought in coming into contact with and thinking its objects, so that thought and object of thought are the same. For that which is *capable* of receiving the object of thought, i.e., the essence, is thought. But it is *active* when it *possesses* this object. Therefore, the possession rather than the receptivity is the divine element which thought seems to contain, and the act of contemplation is what is most pleasant and best. If then, God is always in that good state in which we sometimes are, this compels our wonder; and if in a better this compels it yet more. And God *is* in a better state. And life also belongs to God; for the actuality of thought is life, and God is that actuality; and God's self-dependent actuality is life most good and eternal.

We say therefore that God is a living being, eternal, and most good, so that life and duration continuous and eternal belongs to God; for this is God.[6]

Since, according to Aristotle, to know the world would mean to know change, and thus to change in his knowledge, God does not *know* the world: He knows only his own unchanging mind.

Saint Thomas Aquinas: God as He Who Is

Thomas Aquinas, one of the great theologians and philosophers of medieval Christianity, drew on Christian Scriptures and tradition, as well as on the philosophical reflections of Christian thinkers like Saint Augustine and on Aristotelian philosophy, in formulating his statements about the nature and reality of God.

This name HE WHO IS, is most properly applied to God, for three reasons:

First, because of its signification. For it does not signify form, but simply existence itself. Hence since the existence of God is His essence itself, which can be said of no other (Q. III, A, 4), it is clear that among other names this one specially denominates God, for everything is denominated by its form.

Secondly, on account of its universality. For all other names are either less universal, or if convertible with it, add something above it at least in idea; hence in a certain way they inform and determine it. Now our intellect cannot know the essence of God itself in this life, as it is in itself, but whatever mode it applies in determining what it understands about God, it falls short of the mode of what God is in Himself. Therefore the less determinate the names are, and the more universal and absolute they are, the more properly are they applied to God. Hence Damascene says (*de. Fid. Orth.* i.) that, HE WHO IS, *is the principal of all names applied to God; for comprehending all in itself, it contains existence itself as an infinite and indeterminate sea of substance.* Now by any other name some mode of substance is determined, whereas this name, HE WHO IS, determines no mode of being but is determinate to all; and therefore it denominates the *infinite ocean of substance.*

Thirdly, from its consignification, for it signifies present existence; and this above all properly applies to God, whose existence knows not past or future, as Augustine says (*De Trin.*v.)[7]

---

[6] Aristotle, *Metaphysics*, Book 12, ch. 7, 1072b; from *The Oxford Translations of Aristotle*, Vol. 3, 2nd ed., trans. W. D. Ross, (Oxford: Oxford University Press, 1928). Used by permission of the publisher.

[7] Thomas Aquinas, *Summa Theologica*, trans. Fathers of the English Dominican Provinces (London: Burns, Oates & Washbourne, 1920), Part 1, QQ I-XXXVI (abridged).

The Divine in Navaho Life

The Navaho are one of the larger groups of original inhabitants of the North American continent still living in part of their original region. They retain many elements of their ancient culture in the southwestern United States, including religious traditions. Those who have not been converted to Christianity, brought by the Europeans, remain polytheistic in their religious beliefs.

Navaho conceptions of the Divine may seem strange to those not familiar with polytheistic religions. If you are acquainted with the gods and goddesses of the ancient Greeks or with the stories of creation that appear in the early Babylonian or Japanese religions, you may notice certain remote similarities to Navaho beliefs. (The stories of the Navaho Holy People have primarily been preserved as an oral tradition passed on through the generations. More recently, the tradition has been written down by students of Navaho life.)

The universe of The People contains two classes of personal forces. There are the Earth Surface People, living and dead; these are ordinary human beings. Then there are the Holy People. They are not "holy" in the sense of possessing moral sanctity, for often their deeds have a very different odor. They are "holy" in the meaning of "powerful and mysterious," of belonging to the sacred as opposed to the profane world. They travel about on sunbeams, on the rainbow, on the lightnings. They have great powers to aid or to harm Earth Surface People. But it is better not to call them gods because the word "god" has so many connotations which are inappropriate. The Holy People are not portrayed as all-knowing or even as all-powerful. They certainly are not depicted as wholly good. While they are supplicated and propitiated, they may also be coerced. Probably coercion is indeed the dominant note. In general, the relationship between them and the Earth Surface People is very different from what Christians think of as the connection between God and man.

As described in the Navaho origin myth, the Holy People lived first below the surface of the earth. They moved from one lower world to another because of witchcraft practiced by one of them. In the last of the twelve lower worlds the sexes were separated because of a quarrel, and monsters were born from the female Holy People. Finally a great flood drove the Holy People to ascend to the present world through a reed. Natural objects were created. Then came the first death among the Holy People. About this time too, Changing Woman, the principal figure among them, was created. After she reached puberty, she was magically impregnated by the rays of the Sun and by water from a waterfall, and bore twin sons. These Hero Twins journeyed to the house of their father, the Sun, encountering many adventures and slaying most of the monsters. . . .

The Hero Twins—Monster Slayer and Child of the Water (sometimes called Reared-within-the-Earth and Changing Grandchild)—are invoked in almost every Navaho ceremonial. Their adventures establish many of the Navaho ideals for young manhood. They serve especially as models of conduct in war and can almost be called the Navaho war gods. The Hero Twins slew most of the monsters, but they did not kill all of these potential enemies of mankind. Hunger, Poverty, Old Age, and Dirt survived, for they proved to have a place in human life. The exploits of the Twins, as well as those of other Holy People, define many features of the Navaho landscape as holy places. The lava fields, which are so conspicuous in the Navaho country, are the dried blood of the slain monsters.

Changing Woman, the Sun, and the Hero Twins are four supernatural beings who seem to bulk largest in the religious thought and lore of The People. In the background are First Man and First Woman, who were transformed from two ears of white and yellow corn, and others prominent in the stories of life in the lower worlds. Most of The People believe that First Man created the universe, but another version of the incident, possibly due to Christian influence, pictures a being called *be' gochidi* as the creator of the world. . . .

But of these beings and powers, of whom we have mentioned only a few, Changing Woman alone is consistently well-wishing to the Earth Surface People. The other beings are undependable, even though they may have given mankind many of their prized possessions. The Sun and the Moon demand a human life each day: the Hero Twins are often pitiless; First Man is a witch; Coyote is a trickster.[8]

Śankara: Brahman, The One Eternal Self

Śankara, a Hindu philosopher who lived from approximately 788 to 820, describes God—Brahman—as the *One Reality*—"One without a second." Brahman is that source of the changing world of illusion, whose reality, in contrast to the One Reality, is only apparent or illusory, a product of nescience, a sort of false or mistaken knowledge that is really ignorance.

> Brahman as the eternal subject (pratyagâtman, the inward Self) is never an object, and . . . the distinction of objects known, knowers, acts of knowledge, etc. . . . is fictitiously created by Nescience.
>
> Of Brahman . . . the two following passages [from the *Upanishads*] declare that it is incapable of receiving any accretion and is eternally pure, "He is the one God, hidden in all beings, all-pervading, the Self within all beings, watching over all works, dwelling in all beings, the witness, the perceiver, the only one; free from qualities" and "He pervaded all, bright, incorporeal, scatheless, without muscles, pure, untouched by evil." . . .
>
> The Self is not to be known as manifold, qualified by the universe of effects; you are rather to dissolve by true knowledge the universe of effects, which is mere product of Nescience, and to know that one Self, which is the general abode, as uniform.[9]

Jesus: God as Loving Parent

Jesus of Nazareth, founder of the movement that became the Christian religion, exhibited in his teachings and life-style an intimate consciousness of the one God, not only as a personal God, but also as a parent. The following quotations from Matthew in the New Testament clearly present this perspective.

> You have learned that they were told, "Love your neighbor, hate your enemy." But what I tell you is this: Love your enemies and pray for your persecutors: only so can you be children of your heavenly Father, who makes his sun rise on good and bad alike, and sends the rain on the honest and the dishonest. If you love only those who love you, what reward can you expect? Surely the tax-gatherers do as much as that. And if you greet only your

---

[8] Reprinted by permission of the publisher, from *The Navaho* by Clyde Kluckhohn and Dorothea Leighton, Cambridge, MA: Harvard University Press, copyright © 1946 by the President and Fellows of Harvard College, © 1974 by Florence Kluckhohn Taylor and Dorothea Leighton.

[9] F. Max Müller, ed., *The Sacred Books of the East*, trans. George Shebaut (Oxford: Clarendon Press, 1890), p. 32.

brothers, what is there extraordinary about that? Even the heathen do as much. There must be no limit to your goodness, as your heavenly Father's goodness knows no bounds. . . . (Matthew 5:43–48, NEB)

For if you forgive others the wrongs they have done, your heavenly Father will also forgive you; but if you do not forgive others, then the wrongs you have done will not be forgiven by your Father. . . . (Matthew 6:14–15, NEB)

Surely life is more than food, the body more than clothes. Look at the birds of the air; they do not sow and reap and store in barns, yet your heavenly Father feeds them. You are worth more than the birds! Is there a man of you who by anxious thought can add a foot to his height? And why be anxious about clothes? Consider how the lilies grow in the fields; they do not work, they do not spin; and yet, I tell you, even Solomon in all his splendour was not attired like one of these. But if that is how God clothes the grass in the fields, which is there today and tomorrow is thrown on the stove, will he not all the more clothe you? How little faith you have! No, do not ask anxiously, "What are we to eat? What are we to drink? What shall we wear?" (Matthew 6:26–32, NEB)

Emptiness (Shunyata): The Void in Buddhism

Some forms of Buddhism are often described as being atheistic since beliefs about a God or gods are not given prominent attention or are looked on as idle speculation. But students of Buddhism have noted that even in so-called atheistic forms of Buddhism, there are concepts that have some resemblance to concepts of God in other religious traditions. One such Buddhist concept is that of "the Void."

The Buddhist Void is far from being a nihilistic doctrine. The Void is not nothingness or annihilation but the very source of all life. In speaking of this theory as taught in the Buddhism of China and Japan (where it has influenced the creation of a very subtle aesthetics . . .), Hajime Nakamura, the Japanese Buddhist scholar, says:

"Voidness . . . is . . . that which stands right in the middle between affirmation and negation, existence and nonexistence. . . . The void is all-inclusive; having no opposite, there is nothing which it excludes or opposes. It is living void, because all forms come out of it, and whoever realizes the void is filled with life and power and the . . . love of all beings."

This subtle doctrine is, by its very nature—expressed in the term "Void" itself—not a matter that readily lends itself to brief or simple exposition. Perhaps, however, modern science can again be brought to our aid if we remind ourselves that in this century the non-material nature of the universe has been widely accepted since Eddington in *The Nature of the Physical World* presented his two famous tables: one a seemingly solid "symbol," the other a mysteriously balanced group of invisible energies and forces. Still, though accepted as scientific fact, such knowledge as the nonsubstantiality of substance plays little part in the living of our everyday lives or the thinking of our everyday thoughts. The early Buddhists, being Indians, perhaps found less difficulty than Westerners in acceptance of the world as maya, or a kind of magical show in which what is seen is both true and not true. Buddhism would say this is not to argue that what is seen is nonexistent, but only that we take it for what it essentially is not.[10]

---

[10] Nancy Ross Wilson, *Three Ways of Asian Wisdom* (New York: Simon & Schuster, 1968), pp. 121–22.

UNIT 39   Conceptualization of the Divine

The following table may be useful for considering the concept of God found in the texts given both in the preceding unit and elsewhere.

A Framework for Conceptualizing Images and Concepts of the Divine

A *DEISTIC VIEWS*	*C* *TRANSCENDENT-IMMANENT VIEWS*	*B* *PANTHEISTIC VIEWS*
1. *Polytheistic deism:* There are many divine beings. They *belong* to the natural order.		3. *Dualistic pantheism:* The natural order is a manifestation or superficial appearance of the One Divine Reality.
	5. There is One Divine Being, who both transcends the natural order as its Creator, or source, and is present and active in it.	
2. *Dualistic deism:* There is One Divine Being transcending the natural order as its Creator, or source, with a relative separation between the Divine and the natural.		4. *Materialism:* The basic physical components (matter, energy, etc.) of the natural order are what is ultimately real.

Deistic Positions

In deistic positions, God or the gods are viewed as individual beings. In *polytheistic deism,* the gods are beings, usually possessing extraordinary powers, *within* the universe. They may create and maintain parts of it. They may come into being, that is, may themselves be created or born. Some of them may die; others may be immortal. Polytheistic deism is found in many religious traditions, including the following: popular Hinduism, popular Taoism, the Babylonian and Japanese creation stories (see Unit 82), and the Navaho religion (see the preceding unit). Ordinarily in polytheistic religions, some divine beings are male, others female; some are animals; some are other natural forms such as the sun and moon or the wind.

In *dualistic deism,* the Divine and the world are relatively separate from each other, though the Divine is ultimately the creator, or in some manner the source or sustainer, of the universe. Aristotle's concept of God, discussed in the previous unit, is an expression of dualistic deism. For Aristotle, God does not create the universe, but it is totally dependent on him. A Christian form of dualistic deism became very influential in seventeenth- and eighteenth-century Europe in response to the highly successful scientific work of Isaac Newton. According to this version of deism, God created the universe and allows it to run in accordance with the laws of nature he has established for it. God does not intervene in the natural order by means of miracles or a direct presence. He does guarantee reward for the good, however, and punishment for the evil in a future life. Many outstanding intellectual figures of eighteenth-century Europe and North America accepted this form of deism, among them Thomas Jefferson, author of the Declaration of Independence and third president of the United States.

Dualistic deism is always *monotheistic*. Many forms of dualistic deism have spoken of the Divine in masculine terms, but this probably was the result of cultural influences since in the strict sense the Divine would be neither male nor female.

Pantheistic Positions

According to pantheistic positions, the Divine is the *one and only* reality. For *dualistic pantheism, everything* is a manifestation of the Divine, but moral, religious, and philosophical discipline and insight are required before this can be realized (in the form of enlightenment) by individuals. For philosophical Hinduism, Brahman is the sole reality. The many gods of Hinduism are merely manifestations of the one Divine Being, which is neither male nor female. The texts in the previous unit from ´Sankara and Nakamura concerning the concept of the Void in Buddhism, illustrate this position. It is also exemplified in philosophical Taoism and in the classical Greco-Roman philosophical school known as Stoicism, according to which the Divine Reason or Fire is the source and inner reality of all things.

According to *materialistic pantheism* (sometimes called scientific or philosophical materialism or naturalism), only the physical universe—whether conceived of as matter, mass, or energy—is real. The Greco-Roman school of philosophy known as Epicureanism (founded by Epicurus, 341–270 B.C.E.), based on the conception of the nature of reality of the earlier Greek philosopher Democritus (460–360), held that all reality is composed of atoms moving in space. The atoms are eternal. They join by chance collisions to form objects, which endure only for a time; then their atoms separate to become temporary components of other objects. The human soul is composed of atoms and is not immortal. Even the gods are composed of atoms and endure only for a time. A powerful expression was given to Epicureanism in the Latin poem *On the Nature of Things*, by Lucretius (d. 54 B.C.E.). During the nineteenth and twentieth centuries, scientific materialism was widely accepted by educated Europeans. Marxism is one of its many transformations.

Transcendent-Immanent Positions

According to *transcendent-immanent positions*, God is viewed as an individual being both beyond and within the world. This form of theism is found preeminently in Judaism and Christianity and in some schools of philosophical thought. It is monotheistic. Although culturally it has spoken of God primarily in masculine terms, it will generally hold that God is neither male nor female but is the ground, or creator, of sexuality and may at times be symbolized by either, or by neither, masculine or feminine characterizations. (Judaism's long opposition to the polytheistic fertility cults of its neighbors in Palestine, which usually had both a male and a female deity who were consorts, may account for the heavily patriarchal language used to describe God in the Jewish scriptures.) According to transcendent-immanent positions,

1. God is understood to be the Creator or Source of the created world who transcends it in an ultimate way, as seen in the passage from Aquinas in Unit 38. If this had been the only characterization of God by Aquinas, the Divine would have been understood in a dualistic pantheistic sense.

2. According to transcendent-immanent positions, however, God in *one* aspect is fully present and manifest in the created world. For Judaism, God's wisdom is fully expressed in the Torah, the same wisdom, made explicit, that was or is expressed in the creation and ordering of the created realm. For Christianity, God's wisdom (the second Person of the Trinity, the Wisdom of God in accordance with which the world was or is created) is fully present in the human Jesus. (See the New Testament, Gospel of John, Chapter 1.)

3. According to transcendent-immanent views, the Divine is also continuously active in the created world. The Voice or Spirit of God in Judaism makes God's will known to the prophets and to others. For Christians, God as the Holy Spirit (not another Divine Being, but a genuine aspect of the one God) is understood to be present and active in the world, especially within the Christian community, making God's power and purposes known and effective. Various philosophical schools, including Platonism and Neoplatonism and the twentieth-century philosopher A. N. Whitehead's process philosophy, approximate this view, though Neoplatonism is perhaps closer in some ways to dualistic pantheism.

The preceding chart and discussion are, to some extent, oversimplification. The native Japanese religious tradition, Shinto, for instance, can be claimed to belong to the polytheistic deistic type. But with its emphasis on the sacredness and interrelatedness of *all* beings, and with the many centuries of Shinto traditions blending with those of Buddhism and Taoism and even Christianity, it might be called pantheistic or it may be said not to "fit" the chart at all. Nevertheless, the chart may prove useful in considering both the texts concerning the Divine given in Unit 39 and earlier and later discussions of the Divine— for instance in the chapter on religious traditions (Chapter 3).

Unit 40   Spirit

The human experience of a transcendent reality is not easily expressed. It may take many forms, and any conceptualization of it is inadequate and circumscribed by the limitations of human existence and language. Typologies, analogies, and metaphors that attempt to express both personal awareness of an encounter with a transcendent reality often do not retain the dynamic vitality of these experiences.

However, most human cultures have attempted to conceptualize these dynamic, transient elements. In Western cultures the word *spirit* has been traditionally used to refer to this reality. Drawn from the Latin *spiritus*, which originally referred to human breath, it designates the vitality empowering and activating all of life. The Hindu Sanskrit word *atman*, the Hebrew *ruah*, and the Greek πνευμα carried similar meanings. In early civilizations breath was understood to be the essential element of life; when breath was no longer present, life ceased. One's spirit, breath, was the activator of life.

The word *spirit* has through the centuries taken on other meanings. When we speak of someone's spirit we may be speaking of vigor or zest. For example, if we ask, "Will you do it?" and the reply is "I will try!" we might well respond, "That's the *spirit!*"

We are referring to the vitality, the energetic action, or strong intent that motivates and empowers someone. In a similar way, spirit has sometimes come to include such nonmaterial aspects of human experience as awareness, intellect, understanding, judgment, and will, although the emphasis has remained on its designation of the vital, empowering reality of life.

When used in connection with the Divine, *spirit* usually refers to the divine agency that enlivens or empowers life itself. As such it is seen as the power or force, the vitality that is at the center of all existence. This *divine spirit* also often serves as the dynamic interconnection between the transcendent realities of life and the finite world in which these experiences take place. Using the metaphor of breath, the Hebrew tradition vividly expresses this interconnection:

> Then the Lord God formed man from dust from the ground, and breathed into his nostrils the breath of life, and man became a living being. (Genesis 2:7, RSV)

Spirit, in this passage, clearly enters the body and imparts identity and the capacity to act.

Whether *spirit* is used to refer to a divine presence or to the life force present in humanity and in the natural world (neither of the meanings necessarily excludes the other), its intent is to point to that which gives vitality or power to life. This is its primary meaning.

As noted, in the Jewish and Christian traditions the metaphor of breath has often been used to speak of the role of spirit. Wind and fire are other prominent metaphors for the mystery of the spirit:

> When the day of Pentecost had come, they were all together in one place. And suddenly a sound came from heaven like the rush of a mighty wind, and it filled the house where they were sitting. And there appeared to them tongues of fire, distributed and resting on each one of them. And they were all filled with the Holy Spirit and began to speak in other tongues, as the Spirit gave them utterance. (Acts 2:1–4, RSV)

These images and others like them speak of the mysterious power of contact between humans and God. This experience of mystery is also understood to bestow on believers new possibilities, as seen in these passages drawn from Christian Scriptures: "You shall receive power when the Holy Spirit has come upon you" (Acts 1:8); "For the law of the Spirit of life in Christ Jesus has set me free from the law of sin and death" (Romans 8:2).

Ancient and Preliterate Thought

Each culture seeks to express the reality of spiritual encounter from its own perspective and experience. Ancient cultures, and many present-day cultures that do not depend extensively on writing for communication, live in a world alive, a world in which all objects, events, and people have an inherent power. The inner mysterious power that impels, dominates, and directs the thought and action of a person is his or her *spirit*. The spirit is understood to transcend the physical body and may come to us from outside ourselves. It may be either good or evil, as in many of these cultures gods may be either good or evil. Chinua Achebe, writing about the African Igbo people in his novel *Things Fall*

Apart, captures this sense of personal spiritual reality as he includes the *chi,* or personal god, in any description of a character.[11]

Since spirits often come from without, they are not understood to be physically limited and are seen as supernatural and often divine. Because in these cultures all aspects of nature may also be enlivened by spirits, all of reality is dependent on the power and influence of spirits. The particular form of such "spirit power" varies greatly from culture to culture, but its presence is seldom doubted. In its varied forms, spirit is the vitality empowering and activating all of life.

Japanese Patterns

The early views of spirit carry over into most contemporary religions in some form. Shinto, a native Japanese religion grounded in nature and ancestor worship, continues to focus all understanding of life on the presence and role of spirits, known as *kami.* Without a concept of a particular deity or divine being, all reality is thought to be spiritual and spirit driven. Generally understood as benevolent, these spirits are seen by the Japanese as protective, gracious, and helpful. The *kami* assure harmony and blessings in life. Sokyo Ono describes the general pattern:

> Among the objects or phenomena designated from ancient times as kami are the qualities of growth, fertility, and production; natural phenomena, such as wind and thunder; natural objects, such as the sun, mountains, rivers, trees and rocks; some animals; and ancestral spirits. In the last-named category are the spirits of the Imperial ancestors, the ancestors of noble families, and in a sense all ancestral spirits. Also regarded as kami are the guardian spirits of the land, occupations, and skills; the spirits of national heroes, men of outstanding deeds or virtues, and those who have contributed to civilization, culture, and human welfare; those who have died for the state or the community; and the pitiable dead. Not only spirits superior to man, but even some that are regarded as pitiable and weak have nonetheless been considered to be kami.
>
> It is true that in many instances there are kami which apparently cannot be distinguished from the deities or spirits of animism or animatism, but in modern Shinto all kami are conceived in a refined sense to be spirits with nobility and authority. The kami-concept today includes the idea of justice, order, and divine favor (blessing), and implies the basic principle that the kami function harmoniously in cooperation with one another and rejoice in the evidence of harmony and cooperation in this world.[12]

Jewish Concepts

Among Jews the image of breath and wind are prominent metaphors for spirit. In this tradition, the term *spirit* also signifies the "soul" or "heart" of a human, that is, something that gives people their identity and psychic strength. Even though Judaism is a monotheistic faith, its earliest beliefs allowed for supernatural beings (angels and devils), which although ultimately subservient to God, were influential in human life. Jew-

---

[11] Chinua Achebe, *Things Fall Apart* (Greenwich, CT: Fawcett, 1959).

[12] Sokyo Ono, *Shinto: The Kami Way* (Rutland, VT, and Tokyo: Charles E. Tuttle, 1962), p. 7.

ish thinkers refined and altered these elemental understandings of spirit by elaborating on the concept of the Spirit of the Lord. Molded by their vision of one God, the Spirit of God signifies the force or power that issues from God, sent into the created order among humans. In this tradition God's spirit has many modes: It is the creative and sustaining force within the universe; provides extraordinary endowments of leadership to Jewish priests and kings; grants wisdom and discernment; and serves as the agent of communication with humans, particularly through the prophets. The prophets of Israel presumed they were speaking for God, that they were agents of God's spirit. Through such manifestations the transcendent God is immanently present in human life. The imagery is clearly that of the human spirit centered in and directed by one all-powerful, divine spirit overarching and influencing all of life.

Islamic Patterns

Among Muslims the prophetic role is a central feature of the faith, and it is here that they emphasize the presence of the divine spirit. Muhammad is understood by Muslims to be the channel or vessel through whom the spirit of Allah speaks to humanity. The Qu'ran, the Islamic scripture, is a "recitation" by Allah's "spirit," represented by the angel Gabriel through his prophet Muhammad. Muslims who follow Sufi patterns of thought also emphasize the possibility that a believer has direct personal contact with the divine spirit (see Unit 16).

Christian Thought

Christian thought on the spirit is grounded in the Jewish precepts described above. Many of the nuances and dimensions of the phrase *Spirit of God* in Jewish usage were appropriated by early Christians to talk about God's action in human life. Two other elements, however, became important in Christian thinking. First, Jesus is seen as God's very presence in the world; therefore, many of the traditional attributes of spirit are used by early Christian writers to characterize the forceful, impressive ministry of Jesus. Jesus's power and authority were identified with the work of the Spirit.

> And when Jesus was baptized, he went up immediately from the water, and behold, the heavens were opened and he saw the Spirit of God descending like a dove, and alighting upon him. (Matthew 3:16, RSV)

The second element of Christian understanding of the spirit arose from Jesus's teachings concerning the Spirit. In John's gospel, Jesus promises that a "Counselor . . . even the Spirit of Truth" who will dwell in his disciples will be sent by the Father (God) when Jesus is physically gone from their midst (John 14:15–17). The experience of the early church convinced the disciples that God was uniquely with them, guiding and fulfilling their ministry. Remembering this teaching of Jesus, they began to speak of the presence of the Holy Spirit. For the church, the Holy Spirit came to be understood as the unique presence of the divine spirit of Jesus. Irenaeus, a second-century church father, stated the concept this way:

Know thou that every man is either empty or full. For if he has not the Holy Spirit, he has no knowledge of the Creator; he has not received Jesus Christ the Life; he knows not the Father who is in heaven.[13]

Here the Spirit's role is given prominence equal to that of the Father and the Son and is made the channel by which humans may come to know God.

In the main, Christians have taken the Spirit for the "whole nature of God."[14] The name Spirit defines the nature of God by gathering together in one name the leading attributes of God: power, purity, invisibility, vitality, freedom, love, and so forth. Spirit means God as all-sufficient, almighty, infinite, perfect, the mover of all things. The Spirit for Christians indicates the living action of God in history. That action or movement is understood to take place in a dynamic relationship between God and one's own vitality—spirit.

∾

In what context do you most often use the word *spirit?*

Does the *kami* understanding of the Japanese differ from that of the Jewish or Christian traditions? How?

Are there similarities between some of the ideas found in Unit 34 and those discussed in this unit?

[13] Irenaeus, *Fragments XXVI*, quoted in *Handbook of Christian Theology*, eds. Marvin Haverson and Arthur A. Cohen (New York: Meridian Books, 1958), p. 170.

[14] Richard Sibbes, *The Complete Works of Richard Sibbes, D.D.*, Vol. V, ed. Alexander B. Grosart (Edinburgh: James Nichol, 1863), p. 487.

CHAPTER 8

❧

The Problem of Evil

Introduction

The preceding two chapters have sought to explore concepts and images of the Divine as expressed in scriptures of the world's religious traditions and in theological and philosophical reflections on human religious experience. In this chapter we seek to examine the problem of evil—that is, discuss and analyze questions related to the experience of a disruptive and destructive force (or forces) encountered by human beings—and inquire about the relationship between this force and that which is experienced as Divine.

The awareness of evil—the sense that there are personal moral, religious, and philosophical problems about evil—may arise in various ways. Unit 41 discusses the problem of suffering, probing both philosophical and religious answers. Unit 42 focuses on evil as a moral problem that raises questions about the relation of humanity to the Divine.

For some, evil is encountered in interpersonal relationships that assume transcendent significance. For others, evil is perceived as an autonomous force either within or outside of the individual and is often personalized in the form of one or more demonic figures. The problem of evil is much more acute in the monotheistic religious traditions of the West than in other religious traditions, at least partly because the former affirm (1) that everything that exists, even what may be regarded as evil, is in some sense the result of the creative activity of one supremely wise, powerful, and good Creator; and (2) that evil is in some sense a reality, not merely an illusion. Thus, the question of how there can be a totally good and powerful Creator who nevertheless *allows* evil to exist has often been a difficult and pressing one for sensitive people in Western religious traditions. Before

146

investigating the interpretation of evil in non-Western religions, as well as in the Western religions, the reader may want to review the concepts of the Divine discussed in the previous chapter.

UNIT 41   Why Suffering?

As both units in this chapter will emphasize, life, for all its good, is often torn, full of pain and sorrow. Albert Outler interprets the way various ancients posed their answers to the question of why humans suffer:

1. *Ancient popular religions* before Christ pointed to "the careless antics of the sky-gods or the purposeful cruelties of the earth-gods" as the source of evil and thus human suffering.
2. *Platonists* identified evil (suffering) as the privation or corruption of the good (itself identified with being).
3. *Stoics* saw evil and suffering as the result of "unreason and lack of self control."
4. *Epicureans* viewed suffering as evidence of the "blind way of the world from which the wise man withdraws as far as possible."
5. *Buddhism* designated suffering as inherent in self-centered human desire.

(by Jacques Bakke)

What solutions did they propose to the problem of suffering? *Ancient religions* tried to outwit the careless and capricious gods. *Platonists* proposed a mystical escape through philosophical abstraction. *Stoics* believed that reason could order power. *Epicureans* sought serene indifference. *Buddhists* concluded that the cure for suffering is the extinction of self-interested, self-regarding, self-centered desire. The end of suffering is to be reached by extinction of the limited personal self. These responses to suffering tend "to disengage the divine from the hurly burly of ordinary life and to propose a program of aloofness as the right answer to the problem."[1]

Judeo-Christian answers to suffering do not point to an aloof God. Biblical faith presents God as sovereign over all creation, including good and evil. Suffering has a purpose under God, whether *penal* (punishment for sins) or *pedagogical* (disciplinary correction). The Old Testament emphasizes that God sends suffering as punishment for sin. The sinfulness of Israel was seen to be the cause of national disaster because sin evoked God's wrath. Sin would bring suffering both to individuals and to the community.[2]

The biblical character known as Job protested against the view that suffering was a divinely decreed penalty for sin. The Book of Job exhibits Job's suffering as the epitome of anguish and pain and then struggles with the question of whether this suffering of a righteous man is a true index of justice in the universe. Tradition had pointed to suffering as just punishment for the ungodly. Thus, along with many psalmists, Job focuses on the central theological question regarding suffering: Is God just to permit sinners prosperity while the faithful suffer? Job claims innocence before God, whereas his so-called comforters imply otherwise. Elihu, one of Job's counselors, connects suffering with transgressions but does intimate that suffering is the means by which, or the context in which, God redeems his own: "He delivers the afflicted by his affliction and opens their ear by adversity."[3] Eliphaz, another adviser, observes that "man is born to trouble as the sparks fly upward,"[4] suggesting that God structures suffering into existence and that no one can escape anguish. Eliphaz does believe, however, that each tyrant will receive just punishment and that good persons can overcome disaster, thus proving God's justice in the long run. Both the prologue and the epilogue of Job present suffering as probationary. Job's faithfulness is put to the test. Is his obedience merely self-serving, or does it result from commitment to God? But Job remains a man of his word and then God rewards him, thus corroborating the traditional Old Testament view of ultimate welfare for the righteous and wrath for the unrighteous.[5]

Although most Old Testament writers see suffering as a penalty for transgression, some suggest that suffering has a redeeming purpose (disciplinary, purificatory), as the psalmist indicates: "It was good for me that I was afflicted, that I might learn thy statutes."[6] Especially in the servant songs of Deutero-Isaiah we find suffering to be vicarious and redemptive. The Servant, whether corporate or individual, is shown as despised, rejected,

---

[1] Albert Outler, *Who Trusts in God, Musings on the Meaning of Providence* (New York: Oxford University Press, 1968), p. 84.

[2] Deuteronomy 31, 32.

[3] Job 36:15 (RSV).

[4] Job 5:7.

[5] Alan Richardson, *A Theological Word Book of the Bible* (New York: Macmillan, 1959), p. 250.

[6] Psalms 119:71.

"a man of sorrows and acquainted with grief,"[7] even though he is sinless and does not deserve to suffer. The Servant suffers for our sins. His "suffering is neither the result of his own sin nor the chastisement that might lead to his own perfection. . . . The suffering apparently gains for itself a merit that is transferable."[8]

The New Testament does include punitive theories of suffering, although pedagogical and redemptive interpretations are emphasized, especially in connection with Christ's passion. In the New Testament, God is presented more as Father than as judge or king, and from the paternal perspective suffering becomes chiefly pedagogical, corrective, or redemptive. Not only does the Fatherhood of God lend itself to this view of suffering, but also belief in a redeemed future for the faithful fosters courage and hope among the suffering. Paul's affirmation that "all things work together for good to them that love God,"[9] as well as his belief that "the sufferings of this present time are not worthy to be compared with the glory that shall be revealed to us,"[10] expresses a New Testament assurance that suffering will be overcome.[11] This redemptive meaning of suffering focuses on Jesus, who, though sinless, gives himself for others to bring deliverance for sufferers through his atoning death. "For the Son of Man also came not to be served but to serve and to give his life as a ransom for many."[12] Christians claim that the paradox and power of the New Testament faith is that God works through suffering to redeem those who suffer.

Thus, we have considered several answers to the question "Why suffering?" Which of the answers considered do you think is most viable? Can you think of others?

UNIT 42   Concepts of Evil

In his film *The Virgin Spring,* Ingmar Bergman focuses on the presence of evil in a world created by a good God. In Tore's words upon discovering his murdered daughter, Karin, we feel the impact of human anguish over God's silence when people find themselves confronted by evil. "You saw it, God. You saw it! The death of an innocent child, and my vengeance. You permitted it, and I don't understand you."[13] Tore asks questions that many have asked: Is God the source of evil? If so, or if God merely allowed evil even though he had the power to prevent it, how can God be good? For monotheistic religious traditions, such questions have been genuine. Polytheistic religious traditions have found it easier to

---

[7] Isaish 53:3.

[8] Richardson, *Theological Word Book,* p. 251.

[9] Romans 8:28.

[10] Romans 8:18.

[11] Albert C. Knudson, *Basic Issues in Christian Thought* (New York: Abingdon-Cokesbury Press, 1950), pp. 95, 96.

[12] Mark 10:45.

[13] Anthony Schillaci, Movies and Morals (Notre Dame, IND: Fides Publishers, 1968), p. 102.

accept evil as merely a part of things: Some divine beings may be evil or indifferent toward humans, others good and compassionate.

Bergman draws no easy lines between good and evil. Karin, Tore's daughter, is raped and murdered on her way to mass. When the murderers fall into Tore's hands, Tore, a confessing Christian, in turn murders them in a ceremony of pagan revenge "and proves himself worse than the lecherous murderers of his child."[14] In the end Tore seeks forgiveness: "Yet I now ask you for forgiveness—I do not know of any way to reconcile myself with my own hands. I don't know any other way to live."[15] Thus through prayer Tore is reconciled to God and yet recognizes the reality of a world in which both good and evil are present. As a sign of his renewed faith, he promises to build a church.

On the surface, the ending may seem unrealistic, but if viewed within the context of Bergman's understanding of life as embracing *both* good and evil, the realism obtains, and the film concludes in an open-ended way. Bergman gives no easy answer to why evil has permeated God's creation. He does not dub God the source of evil, nor does he give any real reason for permitting evil. "In fact, Bergman affirms the admixture of good and evil as part of that human condition of which he is so acute an observer. There is no simple dismissal of either element in reality, for maturity consists in realizing that we must expect to find the two mingled: light and dark, authentic and inauthentic, creative and destructive, good and evil."[16] Anthony Schillaci points to a symbol in *The Virgin Spring* that graphically expresses the intermingling of good and evil.

> The envious serving girl, Ingeri, reluctantly prepares the lunch for Karin's journey to Mass, hollows out a loaf of bread, greedily wolfing down its contents, and places in it an ugly toad. Later, it is at the precise moment that Karin offers this loaf to the lecherous goatherds that mischief is unleashed and the rape-murder committed. The loaf falls apart and there the toad sits obscenely in the center of the white bread. Like it or not, this is the world as it really is—a good marred by the mystery of evil.[17]

Such mystery is painful for many. If God is good and powerful, why does he allow evil? To some, God appears all-powerful but evil in allowing evil. To others, he may seem good but weak, powerless to prevent evil.

Asian religious thinkers have not dealt with the problem of evil in the same way as have many in the West who have struggled through the centuries with philosophical issues pertaining to the idea of a dualistic universe, where good and evil are in conflict. Major religions of the East are, for the most part, monistic, reflecting a view of the cosmos as a unity, a oneness of everything rooted in a primal goodness. Hinduism, in Western ways of thinking, is a pantheistic monism; the One, all-inclusive spiritual reality is everything and everyone and yet is greater than all that is, whether experienced by humans as good or evil. Although we may live in a world where wickedness and misery exist, Hinduism claims that even the evil itself, which is at most illusory in the monistic scheme of things, has a divine and good purpose.[18]

[14] Ibid., pp. 98–99.

[15] Ibid., p. 105.

[16] Ibid., p. 101.

[17] Ibid.

[18] See Ward J. Fellows, *Religious East and West* (New York: Holt, Rinehart & Winston, 1979), pp. 199–265.

Buddhism, as a reform movement in Hinduism, did not include speculations on the Divine, but it did focus on ways to become liberated from self-centered desire so that even an evil person, one in bondage to the worst expressions of self-centeredness, will reach purity. In becoming enlightened the Buddhist reaches the freedom of knowing that good and evil are not two realities but "are simply one."[19]

In Chinese Taoism and Confucianism, the forces of yin and yang may appear to be dualistic, but they are derived from and point toward an all-unifying Power or Principle, designated as the Tao in Taoism and Heaven in Confucianism. In Taoism the ultimate Power is experienced mystically by intuition, whereas in Confucianism the emphasis is given to reason and learning as ways to understand the moral goodness of Heaven, and thus be enabled to live ethically. Although Confucianists may talk about evil and sins, they can confirm religious tenets that stress the goodness of Heaven and essential human goodness. Taoism or Confucianism seem to deal with evil as the intuited impropriety that creates disharmony in living and is to be corrected by being in harmony with the ultimate Governing Power. Yet for them, persistent evil is impossible.[20]

Many Christians struggling with the logical problem of how evil can exist when everything has been created by a good and all-powerful God have accepted the position that evil comes from a real but inferior power created by God. By recognizing evil as real, Christianity differs from Eastern strategies that deny the basic reality of evil, reducing it to the status of "illusion, mirage, *maya*, giving it only a deceptive appearance of reality within a great all-encompassing monism. . . . "[21] By viewing evil as inferior to God, Christianity seeks to reject any idea of evil as one all-powerful facet of a dual reality vying on equal terms with God in a divided universe. "Thus the Christian maintains neither the monist nor the dualist solution of the problem of evil while holding it [evil] is both subordinate [to God] and perverse."[22]

Roland Frye, an interpreter of theology in literature, presents his understanding of the normative Christian view of evil as follows:

> Christianity summarizes the source of evil under the symbol of the demonic, and the essence of the demonic is the aspiration to godhead, the attempt to usurp the place of the Creator, followed by assault upon creation in a frenzy of hate which irrevocably dedicates itself to a continuous destruction of life. Satan is thus *the* continuous source of evil. . . . He is not an independent evil being set opposite an equally independent good being, and his fall from heaven comes precisely from his false claim to be just that. . . . In the Christian conception, then, evil is totally subordinate to God: it is good in its created intention, but perverted from its normative goals. In poetic terms, Satan is a perversion of the great, but subordinate, good, which was Lucifer. . . . It is thus basically a lie, carrying at the core of its existence a falsification of its own nature.[23]

According to Frye, in seeking to elevate himself above God, Satan became the symbol of the fall of all humans and the participation in evil of all humanity.

---

[19] See *Tannisho: A Primer: a Record of the Words of Shinran Set Down in Lamentation over Departures from His Teaching*, trans. Dennis Hirota (Kyoto: Ryukoku University Translation Center, 1982), p. 81.

[20] Fellows, *Religious East and West*, pp. 70, 91–96, 104–107.

[21] Roland Mushat Frye, *God, Man and Satan: Patterns of Christian Thought and Life in Paradise Lost, Pilgrim's Progress and the Great Theologians* (Princeton, NJ: Princeton University Press, 1960), p. 2. Copyright © 1960 by Princeton University Press. Used by permission.

[22] Ibid.

[23] Ibid., pp. 22–23.

Figure 8.1   M. Gustave Dore, illustration for Milton's *Paradise Lost*, Book IX, lns. 99, 100

   The belief that Satan is a powerful demonic being and enemy of God was held by many in the first-century Jewish context in which Christianity originated. Some Christians have interpreted Satan or the devil as *merely* a symbol for the sources of evil within humans that cause them to turn from God and to inflict harm on themselves, the world, and other humans through selfishness, greed, cruelty, and anger. Others have interpreted Satan as a symbol for the power of collective movements, such as extreme nationalism (as in German Nazism) or powerful institutions (as in a cruel system of punishment of offenders against the law or the recently repealed racist laws and practices of South Africa's apartheid). Most Christians have probably believed in the transhuman objective reality of Satan—a being originally good, created by God for goodness, but who through misuse of freedom became evil and, as stated by Frye, the major source of evil in the universe. Some Christians, including the great seventeenth-century French Catholic mathematician and religious thinker Blaise Pascal, have at times been willing to see their religious opponents, fellow Christians, as instruments in the hands and under the influence of Satan. Pascal

Figure 8.2
Albrecht Dürer, *The Angel with the Key* (Detail, from *Albrecht Dürer Complete Woodcuts*, ed. Dr. Willi Kurth. Copyright 1946 by Crown Publishers. Used by permission of Crown Publishers, Inc.)

accused his Jesuit opponents (members of the Catholic religious order founded by Ignatius Loyola, the Society of Jesus, who were active in political and religious controversy in Pascal's time) of having the mind of, and being the children of, the devil.

During sixteenth-century religious conflicts in Europe, not only some Protestant and Catholic leaders but also some in opposing Protestant groups accused their opponents of being instruments of Satan. Other Christians cautioned that no matter how intense differences of belief and opinion may be, attributing opponents' motives and conduct to the devil's influence is not compatible with the New Testament commandment for Christians to love one another.

Since the emergence of modern psychotherapy, there has been a tendency to understand "demonic possession" as a prescientific age's way of describing emotional or behavioral ("mental") disturbances. However, in a recent study called *People of the Lie*, M. Scott Peck, a psychoanalyst and lay Christian, has argued that there are genuine instances of people falling under the influence of demonic—objective and external transhuman—powers distinct from ordinary emotional disturbances such as neuroses and psychoses that can be medically treated. According to Peck, there are people who actually become evil by allowing themselves to become possessed by evil powers. Peck is cautious rather than sensational in the development of his theory and warns against the tendency to understand "demonic" forces as they are often represented in anthropomorphically popular and classical art and literature or in cartoons and comic strips.[24] Others warn against the theory itself as tending to produce irresponsible charges against one's opponents or to lead neurotic people to see themselves as being under demonic attack when their disorders may actually be better dealt with if seen as produced by emotional or physical disturbances.

Most Christians have understood evil as arising through a misuse of something good—the ability to make free decisions. In an influential work called *On the Free Choice of the Will*, the fourth-century North African bishop, Augustine, argued that free will is a part of human nature as humans were created by God. It is a necessary part of human nature, for without free choice, humans could neither be good nor respond to God and their fellow humans in the free choice of unselfish love. But free choice of will has been misused. In fact, Augustine was convinced that all humans misuse it because human nature has fallen away from its original goodness and has become evil—selfish and self-

Figure 8.3   *Calvin and Hobbes*, copyright by Waterson. Reprinted with permission of Universal Press Syndicate. All rights reserved.

[24] M. Scott Peck, *People of the Lie: The Hope for Healing Human Evil* (New York: Simon & Schuster, 1983).

centered. Thus, for Augustine, the problem of the existence of evil—how or why there is evil in a world created by a good and all-powerful God—ceases to be a logical problem and becomes instead a practical problem: How can humans regain their original freedom to use their capacity of free choice or free will in ways that will bring good rather than evil? This is perhaps the question that the character Tore in Bergman's film finally found himself asking. Various answers to this question, and various other ways of responding to the problem of evil, will be explored in later units of this book, especially in the chapters on sin and guilt and salvation and redemption (chapters 11 and 13).

The cartoon in Figure 8.3 perhaps sums up the difficulty presented by evil; it captures, by using an "everyday" situation, what Christian theologians have seen as a human protensity to innate selfishness and evil, whether it may be credited to the demonic or to human misappropriation of freedom.

CHAPTER 9

❧

Understanding the Self

Introduction

In the two preceding parts of the book, we explored the varieties of human religious experience and conceptions of the Divine or ultimate reality. In this chapter and the next, we focus on human existence and its religious dimensions. Chapter 9 deals with the nature of human existence and the meaning of individual selfhood as viewed from different religious and cultural points of view. In Chapter 10, we examine the social dimension of human existence—the interrelationship of the self with other selves, the social solidarity of human existence.

Human beings are, as Aristotle and other social philosophers have suggested, social animals. In a very direct and literal sense, we have to *learn* to be human, and each society develops its own models and images of what human beings should be like. Nevertheless, human beings, at least in most societies, tend to develop a sense of individuality. In some societies—including Western societies during the modern period—great emphasis has been placed on the uniqueness, the irreplaceable value, of each individual. Even in societies in which the individual's sense of unique identity is muted (as in most societies until the modern period and as in the kibbutzim of contemporary Israel, for example, where the individual tries to see everything through the eyes of the group), the importance of the individual, even if only as a part of the group, has been recognized.

What does it mean to be a person, to be (or have) a self? Throughout the history of human civilizations this question has frequently been raised. In myths of origin, from those of Babylon and Assyria to those of Japan or the Navaho Indians; in philosophical and scientific speculation, from Gautama Buddha and Socrates to twentieth-century existentialists like Martin Heidegger or behaviorists like B. F. Skinner; and in religious literature, questions about the nature and characteristics of human existence have been posed. In our own time, as in many others, these questions are of deep concern, sometimes painfully so, to individuals searching for meaning in life.

Attitudes and ideas about the meaning of human existence—what it means to be human, what it means to be a self in isolation from or in relation to other selves—have frequently become ingrained in a culture and its religions. These attitudes and ideas are transmitted to the young through cultural practices and institutions, often without conscious intent. They become such a pervasive feature of the culture that people are scarcely aware of them; they seem as natural a part of the lifescape as the air or the topography. In times of cultural crisis, people become aware of them in especially sharp ways, when critical attention is directed at their possible inadequacies or biases. One characteristic of our own time is that social unrest and expanding contacts of many different cultural traditions with one another have caused many people to question traditional assumptions about the nature of human existence and the meaning of individuality.

UNIT 43   The Nature of Humanity

A hauntingly recurrent theme in human history has been the inquiry into humanity's nature, essence, and uniqueness. The modern behavioral sciences of sociology and psychology often provide astounding insights into elements of human nature—yet they fail to give a complete definition. Perhaps this only suggests that the complexity and variety of human nature may not accommodate themselves to a rational definition. Even if this is true, human beings continue to seek explanations.

Definitions of humanity offered through history are myriad. Erich Fromm and Ramon Xirau provide a convenient set of categories describing human attributes: "reason, the capacity for production, the creation of social organization, and the capacity for symbol making."[1] To these attributes may be added many others, such as moral systems; propensity for religious affirmations; and as the insights of modern philosophy and psychology have taught us, the fact that humanity is constantly becoming—modifying, changing. Attributes, insights, beliefs, and a host of other elements all help distinguish the species.

Following are representative statements concerning the nature of humanity. Each in its own way, without attempting to be inclusive, expresses a particular understanding of what it means to be human.

[1] Erich Fromm and Ramon Xirau, *The Nature of Man* (New York: Macmillan, 1968), p. 6. Copyright © 1968 by Macmillan, Inc. Used by permission.

The Reasoning Self

Blaise Pascal's often-quoted characterization of a human being as a "thinking reed" exemplifies the Western philosophical tradition that defines human nature by the ability to reason.

> Man is but a reed, the most feeble thing in nature; but he is a thinking reed. The entire universe need not arm itself to crush him. A vapour, a drop of water suffices to kill him. But, if the universe were to crush him, man would still be more noble than that which killed him, because he knows that he dies and the advantage which the universe has over him; the universe knows nothing of this.
>
> All our dignity consists, then, in thought. By it we must elevate ourselves, and not by space and time which we cannot fill. Let us endeavour, then, to think well; this is the principle of morality.[2]

Self-Awareness

Fromm and Xirau, summarizing variant positions, maintain that human self-awareness incorporates, yet transcends, reason, becoming one's essential nature—a position hinted at in Pascal's statement.

> It can be stated that there is a significant consensus among those who have examined the nature of man. It is believed that man has to be looked upon in all his concreteness as a physical being placed in a specific physical and social world with all the limitations and weaknesses that follow from this aspect of his existence. At the same time he is the only creature in whom life has become aware of itself, who has an ever-increasing awareness of himself and the world around him, and who has the possibilities for the development of new capacities, material and spiritual, which make his life an open road with a determinable end. As Pascal said, if man is the weakest of all beings, if he is nothing but a "reed," he is also the center of the universe, because he is a "thinking reed."[3]

Self-Transcendence

Erich Fromm, working from modern psychological and philosophical insights, also suggests that the ability to transcend one's animal nature creates conflicts and questions that constantly lead to the search for answers. The essence of human nature, then, is to be always becoming: Life is a never-ending process of better answers to old and new questions caused by our unique situation of not being merely animals.

> He [Fromm] sees the essence, or nature, of man in certain contradictions in human—as against animal—existence. Man is an animal, but without having sufficient instincts to direct his actions. He not only has intelligence—as has the animal—but also self-awareness; yet he has not the power to escape the dictates of his nature. He is a "freak of nature," being in nature and at the same time transcending it. These contradictions cre-

---

[2] Blaise Pascal, *Pensées* (New York: E. P. Dutton, n. d.), para. 347. Pascal was a seventeenth-century mathematician, physicist, and theologian whose influence on French Catholicism was considerable.

[3] Fromm and Xirau, *The Nature of Man*, p. 6.

ate conflict and fright, a disequilibrium which man must try to solve in order to achieve a better equilibrium. But having reached this, new contradictions emerge and thus again necessitate the search for a new equilibrium, and so forth. In other words, the questions, not the answers, are man's "essence." The answers, trying to solve the dichotomies, lead to various manifestations of human nature. The dichotomies and the resulting disequilibrium are an ineradicable part of man *qua* man; the various kinds of solutions of these contradictions depend on socio-economic, cultural and psychic factors; however, they are by no means arbitrary and indefinite. There is a limited number of answers which have either been reached or anticipated in human history. These answers, while determined by historical circumstances, differ at the same time in terms of solutions, differ in terms of their adequacy to enhance human vitality, strength, joy, and courage. The fact that the solutions depend on many factors does not exclude that human insight and will can work towards attempting to reach better rather than worse solutions.[4]

The Self as the Divine

A different religious insight into the nature of life is provided by the following Hindu affirmation, which stresses that humanity is dependent on the Divine—the Lord—found within the Self. To discover Self in all its magnificence is to discover the Divine.

> Lords! Inspiration of sacrifice! May our ears hear the good. May we serve Him with the whole strength of our body. May we, all our life, carry out His will.
>
> Peace, peace, and peace be everywhere.
>
> Welcome to the Lord! . . .
>
> There is nothing that is not Spirit. The personal Self is the impersonal Spirit. It has four conditions.
>
> First comes the material condition—common to all—perception turned outward, seven agents, nineteen agencies, wherein the Self enjoys coarse matter. This is known as the waking condition.
>
> The second is the mental condition, perception turned inward, seven agents, nineteen agencies, wherein the Self enjoys subtle matter. This is known as the dreaming condition.
>
> In deep sleep man feels no desire, creates no dream. This undreaming sleep is the third condition, the intellectual condition.
>
> Because of his union with the Self and his unbroken knowledge of it, he is filled with joy, he knows his joy; his mind is illuminated.
>
> The Self is the lord of all: inhabitant of the hearts of all. He is the source of all; creator and dissolver of beings. There is nothing He does not know.
>
> He is not knowable by perception, turned inward or outward, nor by both combined.
>
> He is neither that which is known nor that which is not known, nor is He the sum of all that might be known. He cannot be seen, grasped, bargained with. He is undefinable, unthinkable, indescribable.
>
> The only proof of His existence is union with Him. The world disappears in Him.
>
> He is the peaceful, the good, the one without a second. This is the fourth condition of the Self—the most worthy of all. . . . He is whole; beyond bargain. The world disappears in Him. He is the good; the one without a second. (*Mandookya Upanishad*)[5]

[4] Ibid., pp. 8–9.

[5] Shree Purohit Swami and W. B. Yeats, trans., *The Ten Principle Upanishads* (London: Faber & Faber, 1937). Reprinted by permission of M. B. Yeats, Benares University, Faber & Faber, and Macmillan, Inc.

The Self as the Image of God

The following Hebrew psalm indicates wonder at the ability and place of humanity but sees this as the gift of God, on whom humanity is totally dependent. Humanity is "next to" God, but only because God so blesses it.

> O Lord, our Lord
>   how majestic is thy name in
>   all the earth!
>
> Thou whose glory above the
>   heaven is chanted by the
>   mouth of babes and infants,
> thou hast founded a bulwark
>   because of thy foes, to still
>   the enemy and the avenger.
>
> When I look at thy heavens, the
>   work of thy fingers, the moon
>   and the stars which thou has
>   established;
> what is man that thou art mindful
>   of him, and the son of man that
>   thou dost care for him?
> Yet thou hast made him little
>   less than God and dost crown
>   him with glory and honor.
> Thou hast given him dominion
>   over the works of thy hands;
>   thou hast put all things under
>   his feet,
> all sheep and oxen, and also
>   the beasts of the field,
> the birds of the air, and the
>   fish of the sea, whatever passes
>   along the paths of the sea.
>
> O Lord, our Lord,
>   how majestic is thy name in
>   all the earth!
>   (Psalm 8, RSV)

The Obedient Self

The idea that human uniqueness and meaning are found through creation in the *image of God* characterizes the Hebrew-Christian tradition. Even here, however, the image may be expressed through various emphases, as shown by Augustine, a fifth-century theologian, who stressed *obedience,* and Paul Ramsey, a modern ethicist, who describes its character as *love.*

> Now, as God also can be known by the worthy, only intellectually . . . there was danger lest the human mind, from being reckoned among invisible and immaterial things, should be

thought to be of *the same* nature with Him who created it, and so should fall away by pride from Him to whom it should be united by love. For the mind becomes like God, to the extent vouchsafed by its subjection of itself to Him for information and enlightenment. And if it obtains the greatest nearness by that subjection which produces likeness, it must be far removed from Him by that presumption which would make the likeness greater.[6]

The Loving Self

Every discussion of the "image of God" among Christians should then be this: This term cannot be defined by probing deep into the nature of man or by employing some sub-Christian sources of insight into what it means to be man. This term, like all other "Christian categories," can be defined only derivatively by decisive reference to the basic "primitive idea" in Christian ethics, i.e., the idea of Christian love which itself in turn can be adequately defined only by indicating Christ Jesus. Jesus' pure humility and prompt obedience to God and his actions expressing pure and instant love for neighbor: these were in fact the same thing, the same image, the very image of God.

Standing wholly within the relationship of imaging God's will, "with unveiled face, reflecting as a mirror the glory of God," and fully obedient love: these are in reality the same. There is no obedience, no response to God, there are no religious duties beyond this: Thou *shalt* love; and love fulfills every legitimate obedience. Existence within the image of God is the same thing as existence for another. Hence he [Kierkegaard] who wrote that "only when God has infinitely become the eternal and omnipresent object of worship, and man always a worshipper, do they resemble one another," also said with equal appropriateness that "we can resemble God only in loving."[7]

∾

Are there other definitions of humanity that are more meaningful to you?

Is it important or enlightening to discuss the nature of humanity?

Why is the nature of humanity an essential religious topic?

How do you define humanity?

UNIT 44   On the Meaning of *Person*

The preceding unit inquired into the nature of humanity—what it means to be human. The present unit continues the inquiry by investigating personhood—what it means to be a particular person.

Every person is in a constant state of becoming, an ever-developing flux of growth and change. There may be arrests and attempts at crystalization that inhibit or thwart growth, but the process continues. Gordon W. Allport described the development of personality in a broad sense as a process, normally ever in flux. One of his best-known writings is entitled *Becoming, Foundations for a Psychology of Personality.*

---

[6] St. Augustine, "The Morals of the Catholic Church," *Basic Writings of Saint Augustine*, Vol. I, ed. Whitney J. Oates (New York: Random House, 1948), pp. 329–30.

[7] Paul Ramsey, *Basic Christian Ethics* (New York: Scribner, 1950), p. 259. Used by permission.

Erik Erikson has had a significant influence on the thought of our time through his writings, which describe a model of the development of identity throughout the human life cycle. Each stage of development presents new crises of identity to be resolved through our experience, thus allowing our developing personality to emerge into a new and more complex level. Again, the negative resolution of identity crises can stand in the way of the full attainment of human potential. Erikson's model is similar to Allport's in his assertion that growth, development, and learning continue until the moment of death. In Erikson's model, achieving ego integrity as opposed to experiencing despair in old age is one of the most important possibilities for personality potential.

Generally, in models of human personality, there is some implicit or explicit goal or highest potential. One might say that most human beings seek the attainment of some form of mature personhood or, as Sigmund Freud put it, seek to achieve their own *ego ideal*. From a psychological perspective, religions provide content for the ego ideal—for the goals we accept, establish, hope for, and seek and for that which we hope to become. Specifically, the materials that follow exemplify aspects of what it means to be a person— to find a personal identity.

The search for identity by blacks continues to be an agonizing phenomenon of our day. These two very different poems reflect some of the important factors in the process. The first, by Langston Hughes, exhibits depth of experience and identification with the earth, which became a part of the perspective of many black persons who worked the land in the old American South. The poet expresses an abiding sense of being a part of the flow of history. Notice how in this poem the key to one's identity, one's personal sense of who one is, is found in the history of one's group; in the history of geographical and cultural change and tradition; in one's life space, work history; in ethnic and culturally shared struggle, endurance, and triumph.

> I've known rivers:
> I've known rivers ancient as the world and older than the flow of human
>   blood in human veins.
>
> My soul has grown deep like the rivers.
>
> I bathed in the Euphrates when dawns were young.
> I built my hut near the Congo and it lulled me to sleep.
> I looked upon the Nile and raised the pyramids above it.
> I heard the singing of the Mississippi when Abe Lincoln went down to New
>   Orleans, and I've seen its muddy bosom turn all golden in the sunset.
>
> I've known rivers:
> Ancient, dusky rivers.
>
> My soul has grown deep like the rivers.[8]

In her poem "Status Symbol," Mari Evans speaks of personal identification in an urban world. Notice how one's personal identity also comes from group history, from struggle and travail and triumph; but it is expressed in symbols of social and economic roles, higher-status roles from which members of one's group had been excluded.

[8] Copyright 1926 by Alfred A. Knopf, Inc., renewed 1954 by Langston Hughes. "The Negro Speaks of Rivers," from *Selected Poems* by Langston Hughes. Reprinted by permission of the publisher.

```
        i
Have Arrived
        i
     am the
   New Negro
        i
am the result of
President Lincoln
World War I
and Paris
the Red Ball Express
white drinking fountains
sitdowns and
sit-ins
Federal Troops
Marches on Washington
      and
prayer meetings . . .
today
They hired me
it
is a status
job . . .
along
with my papers
They
gave me my
Status Symbol
the
key
to the
White . . . Locked . . .
John[9]
```

During World War II in Germany, Dietrich Bonhoeffer, a leader of the underground church movement, was arrested and eventually killed because he participated in a plot to stop Hitler. While he was in prison, he wrote this questing poem. Notice how Bonhoeffer gives three possible answers to the question of where our identity comes from. First, he asks whether he is the self that others see. Then he asks whether he is the self he sees himself and feels himself to be. Rejecting both as being at most partial explanations of who we are and from where we receive our identity, Bonhoeffer—who was at this time imprisoned, soon to be sentenced to death for his part in the conspiracy—affirms that wherever we receive partial impressions of our identity, our selfness, self-worth, comes from the fact that we belong to God.

> Who am I? They often tell me
> I stepped from my cell's confinement
> calmly, cheerfully, firmly,
> like a Squire from his country house.

[9] Mari Evans, "Status Symbol," *I Am a Black Woman* (New York: William Morrow, 1970). Used by permission of the author.

Who am I? They often tell me
I used to speak to my warders
freely and friendly and clearly,
as though it were mine to command.

Who am I? They also tell me
I bore the days of misfortune
equably, smilingly, proudly,
like one accustomed to win.

Am I then really that which other men tell of?
Or am I only what I know of myself?

Restless and longing and sick, like a bird in a cage,
struggling for breath, as though hands were compressing my throat,
yearning for colours, for flowers, for the voices of birds,

thirsting for words of kindness, for neighbourliness,
tossing in expectation of great events,
powerlessly trembling for friends at an infinite distance,
weary and empty at praying, at thinking, at making,
faint, and ready to say farewell to it all.

Who am I? This or the Other?
Am I one person to-day and to-morrow another?
Am I both at once? A hypocrite before others,
and before myself a contemptible woebegone weakling?
Or is something within me still like a beaten army
fleeing in disorder from victory already achieved?

Who am I? They mock me, these lonely questions of mine.
Whoever I am, Thou knowest, O God, I am thine![10]

Our contemporary scene is full of examples of the human search for identity, for the establishment of personhood. What does it mean to be a person? What is a mature person? How does one's religion contribute to and shape the nature of individuality? Paul Tournier, in his book *The Meaning of Persons*, elaborates on this subject within the context of a Christian perspective, giving us a concept of identity, of a self that acquires identity, through constructive experience and personal growth. This may be called a concept of an "expanding self," or at least of a developing self, a self that becomes more mature, creative, and better related to others by expanding its capacities. (See also Carl R. Rogers, *On Becoming a Person*.)

A completely satisfied man would be a fossil. Dissatisfaction maintains the constant movement of life, like an unending search. . . . What is a child? You cannot describe him without thinking of the whole life of the man, with all its unknowns, for which he is preparing. . . .

We must resist the temptation to give a doctrinaire answer to the question . . . "Who am I?" We must give up the idea that knowing the person means compiling a precise and exhaustive inventory of it. There is always some mystery remaining, arising from the very fact that the person is alive. We can never know what new upsurge of life may transfigure it tomorrow. . . .

[10] Dietrich Bonhoeffer, *The Cost of Discipleship*, trans. J. B. Leishman (New York: Macmillan, 1959), p. 18. Reprinted by permission of Macmillan, Inc., and SCM Press Ltd.

It is a mysterious spiritual reality, mysteriously linked to God, mysteriously linked with our fellows. We are aware of these links at those privileged moments when there springs up a fresh current of life, bursting the fatal fetters of the personage, asserting its freedom and breaking out into love.[11]

Some might argue that a few religious traditions, such as some forms of Buddhism, have stressed the ideal of a contracting or diminishing self, the no-self or nonself, in which true identity and fulfillment come through nonidentity, from breaking the ties to external objects—other selves and the world—and elimination of the (false or superficial) personality or character traits that we have acquired as defensive reactions in our past misguided attempts to become and to be.

UNIT 45   Dimensions of the Self and Religion

When we inquire into the religious experience of an individual person, we often discover that experience may reflect particular emphases. The religious experience of some individuals may be highly intellectualized, dependent on or expressed according to highly theoretical concepts. The experiences of others may be primarily a matter of feeling, emotion, or affection. For centuries, people who have paused to consider such questions have described what they believed to be ideal. Among the elements identified as particularly significant for religion have been emotional involvement, firm trust and belief, and a life of actions based on these elements. A number of theologians and psychologists of religion in the Western world have emphasized the need for balance among these primary facets of religious experience.

Not realizing the extent to which his emotional (affective) and intellectual (cognitive) experiences in religion would lead to action (cognitive), the Englishman John Wesley became the founder of a reform movement in the English church that eventually would be known as *Methodism*. Below Wesley writes of the event that led him to a deeper religious experience and clarification of his spiritual life. The other quotations indicate Wesley's awareness of the role of one's intellect and the necessity for religious experience to manifest itself in action.

In the evening I went very unwillingly to a society in Aldersgate Street, where one was reading Luther's preface to the *Epistle to the Romans*. About a quarter of nine, while he was describing the change which God works in the heart through faith in Christ, I felt my heart strangely warmed. I felt I did trust in Christ, Christ alone for my salvation; and an assurance was given me that He had taken away *my* sins, *even* mine, and saved *me* from the law of sin and death.[12]

. . . We join with you, then, in desiring a religion founded on reason and every way agreeable thereto. But one question remains to be asked, "What do you mean by *reason?*" I suppose you mean the eternal reason, or the nature of things: the nature of God and the

[11] Paul Tournier, *The Meaning of Persons*, transl. Edwin Hudson (New York: Harper & Row, 1957), pp. 230–32, 232–34.

[12] John Wesley, *Journal*, Vol. I, ed. Nehemiah Curnock (London: Epworth Press, 1938), pp. 475–76.

nature of man, with relations necessarily subsisting between them. Why, this is the very religion *we* preach: a religion founded on, and every way agreeable to, eternal reason, to the essential nature of things. . . . [13]

Do you show your love by your works? While you have time, as you have opportunity, do you in fact "do good to all men" (Galatians 6:10), neighbors or strangers, friends or enemies, good or bad? Do you do them all the good you can, endeavoring to supply all their wants, assisting them both in body and soul to the uttermost of your power? [14]

. . . This religion we long to see established in the world: a religion of love and joy and peace, having its seat in the inmost soul, but ever showing itself by its fruits, continually springing forth not only in all innocence—for love worketh no ill to his neighbor—but likewise in every kind of beneficence, spreading virtue and happiness all around it. [15]

W. C. Bower, a twentieth-century philosopher of religious education, conceived of creative religion as dynamically reconstructive in nature and believed that this quality is achieved when emotion, belief, and action are integrated. Bower maintains that religion is essentially an emotional experience. The emotional manifestations of religion have been of a wide-ranging character, including a sense of dependence on some power beyond the human. They have also included what Bower calls "crasser forms" of emotional seizures, which may be characterized as both irrational and primitive. Yet emotional involvement is essential to any real participation in religion. [16]

Bower emphasizes the point that religion has always been concerned with ideas and beliefs, from which the great creeds have sprung. These creeds have served to clarify thought as well as provide legitimization for functioning ideas and for regulation of the beliefs of a religious community. [17] The cognitive and affective aspects of religion lead to a more central core. For Bower, this core lies in the conative or end-seeking aspect, which centers concern on the ultimate values in life. Thought in religion arises as meaning and serves as a direction-giving factor. Emotion gives to it warmth and vibrancy. Bower insists that it is an error to mistake either of these basic and important factors for religion itself, in its fullest sense. They are only aspects of the phenomenon. The fundamental and basic character of religion is active when *all* the aspects of religion are directed into end-seeking, integrated activity. These ends are concerned with ultimate values in human experience. [18]

Many religious traditions incorporate these dimensions into a whole religious life, as we have seen in the frequent intermixture of religious orientations—mystical, moral, ecstatic, and aesthetic—in forms of Hinduism, Islam, Christianity, Judaism, Buddhism, Taoism, and Confucianism. Sometimes, however, often to correct what are perceived as neglected aspects within a tradition, mass or elitist movements arise, emphasizing one of the dimensions to the neglect of the others. Thus many early

---

[13] From *John Wesley* by Albert C. Outler, p. 394. Copyright © 1964 by Oxford University Press, Inc. Reprinted by permission.

[14] Ibid., p. 99.

[15] Ibid., p. 386.

[16] W. C. Bower, *Religion and the Good Life* (Nashville, TN: Abingdon Press, 1933), p. 44.

[17] Ibid., p. 42.

[18] Ibid., p. 51.

Methodists—unlike Wesley—emphasized feeling at the expense of reason and intellect, and eighteenth-century Christian deists emphasized intellect at the expense of feeling.

UNIT 46   Views of Being Human, East and West

Just as one's religious experience will be shaped by the particular nature of one's encounter with religion and its subsequent expressions in life, so is it molded by views of humanity inherent in the culture of which one is a part. Eastern and Western cultures view humanity from distinctively different perspectives. As a result, their views of the value and place of humanity in the scheme of the universe contrast rather dramatically, as the following selections indicate.

East: Human Beings as One Species Among Many Natural Beings

Chinese and Japanese visual art (see Figure 9.1) illustrates well the Eastern tendency to see human beings as blending into the vastness of the natural universe, as small interdependent parts of a much larger whole. This view reveals Eastern tendencies toward monism and pantheism as well as the strong emphasis of Chinese and Japanese Buddhism, Taoism, Confucianism, and Shinto on the interrelatedness of all things.

Before assuming brush and silk painters would go out to nature, lose themselves in it, and become the bamboo that they would paint. They would sit for half a day or fourteen years

Figure 9.1   Landscape by K'un-ts'an. (Reproduced with the permission of the Museum fuer Ostasiatische Kunst Berlin, Staatliche Museen Preussicher Kulturbesitz.)

before making a stroke. The Chinese word for landscape painting is composed of the radicals for mountain and water, one of which suggests vastness and solitude, the other pliability, endurance, and continuous movement. *The human part in that vastness is small, so we have to look closely for him in the paintings if we find him at all.*[19]

We love natural truth; our philosophers were convinced that human desire has grown beyond bounds; man's eagerness to grasp the object of his desire gives rise to much unnatural and untruthful behaviour. *Man, we think, is no higher in the scale of things than any other kind of matter that comes into being;* rather, he has tended to falsify his original nature, and for that reason we prefer those things that live by instinct or natural compulsion; they are at least true to the purpose for which they were created. We paint figures occasionally, but not so much as you do in the West.[20]

West: Human Beings as God's Creation, an Exalted View of Humanity

In the West, there has been much more of a tendency to see human beings as standing out against, or even apart from, the natural universe as background. Although this view became pronounced during the European Renaissance of the fourteenth and fifteenth centuries, it is apparent even in earlier religious and artistic traditions, as in the following examples from the Hebrew scriptures and classical (Greek and Roman) visual art (see Figure 9.2).

> When I look at thy heavens, the work of thy fingers,
> the moon and the stars which thou hast established:
> what is man that thou art mindful of him,
>   and the son of man that thou dost care for him?
>
> *Yet thou hast made him little less than God,*
>   *and dost crown him with glory and honor.*
> *Thou hast given him dominion over the works of thy hands;*
>   *thou has put all things under his feet,*
>
> all sheep and oxen,
>   and also the beasts of the field,
> the birds of the air, and the fish of the sea,
>   whatever passes along the paths of the sea.
>   (Psalms 8:3–8, RSV)

> Examine carefully the photographs of the Oriental painting and the Western sculpture. What does comparison of these symbolic, artistic representations show about the differences between Eastern and Western views of humanity?

[19] Huston Smith, *The Religions of Man* (New York: Harper Collins, 1991, 1958), p. 213. Used by permission of the publisher.

[20] Chiang Yee, *The Chinese Eye: An Interpretation of Chinese Painting* (Bloomington: Indiana University Press, 1964), pp. 9–10.

Figure 9.2
Apoxyomenos (Scraper). Roman marble copy, probably after a bronze original of ca. 330 B.C. by Lysippus. (Reprinted by permission of the Vatican Museums, Vatican City.)

CHAPTER 10

❧

Freedom and the Self

Introduction

Some would say that humanity is unique—that human beings are distinguished from other animals because of their freedom to make choices. Some have said that humanity is altogether unfettered by the determinants and circumstances that limit individual and personal freedom. Others, inclined toward determinism, believe that humans have little personal freedom because of the many biological, environmental, social, and cultural factors that work together to determine their actions. If total freedom is seen as one pole on a continuum of thought and determinism as the other, in the center are those who maintain that freedom lies in what one is able to do with the determinants that have been bequeathed to each individual human.

In our modern technological world the issues surrounding an adequate understanding of human freedom are complicated by the ever-increasing pace of ordinary human life, in which the urgency and complexity of decision making threatens traditional concepts of freedom.

> Many individuals trapped in dull or slowly changing environments yearn to break out into new jobs or roles that require them to make faster and more complex decisions. But among the people of the future, the problem is reversed. "Decisions, decisions . . ." they mutter as they race anxiously from task to task. The reason they feel harried and upset is that transience, novelty and diversity pose contradictory demands and thus place them in an excruciating double bind. . . .

The rapid injection of novelty into the environment upsets the delicate balance of "programmed" and "non-programmed" decisions in our organizations and our private lives.[1]

Alvin Toffler here helps us understand some of the pressures of the present and the future that are upon us, pressures that demand countless decisions, often without the cushion of background information or an opportunity for reflection on the consequences. He calls this reality "future shock," for the future demands a reassessment of how we make decisions and how we can decide freely without becoming frenzied.

The chapter does not purport to be exhaustive on the subject of personal freedom; rather, the units are designed to help the reader consider this important aspect of human life and religion. Most religions have dealt with issues of freedom, and some of these are discussed here: the definition of freedom, freedom and decision making, responsibility and freedom, and various understandings of humankind's nature as they affect conceptions of freedom. Indeed, we can immediately see that how a particular religion answers these important questions determines its outlook on a wide range of religious issues.

UNIT 47   Responsible Freedom

To be human means to be responsible. The word *responsible* suggests being able to take responsibility, to live responsibly with others. In another sense, *responsibility* and *freedom* are equivalent concepts. One must be free to be responsible. At the same time one must use this freedom responsibly. To be mature means to be able to take responsibility for oneself and one's actions, affirmatively and actively.

All of the philosophers who have been called existentialists would accept such a statement, for one of the hallmarks of existentialist thought is the emphasis it puts on human responsibility. Responsibility, for the existentialists, is the very essence of being human. To be human means to be able to respond to the challenges of one's surroundings; it means being able to give meaning to one's life through authentic decisions and honesty toward oneself. Most of all, it means being able to respond not just superficially but on a deep personal level of commitment to other people—sometimes in cooperation, sometimes in opposition, but always with a recognition of the genuinely human personality of the other. Even when trying to escape responsibility, one cannot evade it, for there is no one who can take our responsibility from or for us. This emphasis is characteristic of the religious existentialists—of the Protestants Kierkegaard, Barth, and Tillich; the Catholic Gabriel Marcel; and the Jewish philosopher Martin Buber, who defined humans by the capacity to enter into the deeply personal I-Thou relationship. A similar emphasis on personal responsibility is found in Theravada Buddhism's insistence that one is totally responsible for one's own progress to enlightenment. This emphasis on personal responsibility is also characteristic of existentialists who ordinarily have been thought of as nonreligious or antireligious. In *Being and Nothingness*, Jean-Paul Sartre, a French philosopher, wrote,

[1] Alvin Toffler, *Future Shock* (New York: Random House, 1970), p. 355.

The essential consequence of our earlier remarks is that man being condemned to be free carries the weight of the whole world on his shoulders; he is responsible for the world and for himself as a way of being . . . since he is also the one who makes himself be, then whatever may be the situation in which he finds himself, the for-itself [Sartre's term for human beings because they are conscious not only of their surroundings, as some animals are, but also of their subjective existence or identity] must wholly assume this situation with its peculiar coefficient of adversity, even though it be insupportable. He must assume the situation with the proud consciousness of being the author of it, for the very worst disadvantages or the worst threats which can endanger my person have meaning only in and through my project; and it is on the ground of the engagement which I am that they appear. It is therefore senseless to think of complaining since nothing foreign has decided what we feel, what we live, or what we are. . . . Thus there are no *accidents* in a life; a community event which suddenly bursts forth and involves me in it does not come from the outside. If I am mobilized in a war, this war is *my* war; it is in my image and I deserve it. I deserve it first because I could always get out of it by suicide or by desertion; these ultimate possibles are those which must always be present for us when there is a question of envisaging a situation. For lack of getting out of it, I have chosen it. This can be due to inertia, to cowardice in the face of public opinion, or because I prefer certain other values to the value of the refusal to join in the war (the good opinion of my relatives, the honor of my family, etc.). Anyway you look at it, it is a matter of choice.[2]

Sartre states the case for personal responsibility in an extreme form, which may be difficult to appropriate in modern society, in which economic, political, and cultural interdependence constantly becomes more evident and influential in determining the roles of individual responsibility.

～

For how much of our world are we responsible? For all of it, as Sartre maintains?

What can personal responsibility actually and concretely mean in the highly mechanized, rationalized world that most of us live in—a world in which people very often never encounter the concrete consequences of their acts since these acts are only links in the infinite chain of events that we call modern industrial society?

～

The contemporary American poet James Dickey has attempted to explore several aspects of this problem in his comment about one of his poems:

The protagonist of "The Firebombing" is a suburban householder bowed down with making payments, keeping track of his children's toys, getting his sons to scout meetings, mowing the lawn, and all those inconsequential things we do: these things are our lives. He can hardly believe his is the same person who got into the night aircraft and took off with napalm bombs on bomb shackles under the wings. This memory produces an extremely complex state of mind. He's now a householder, and he realizes with a shock that he's burned up women and children with napalm in his God-like phase. He's wondering how it felt for those people, but he can't really imagine it. They were Japanese, about as foreign to him and his origins as anything could possibly be. But most importantly he can't imagine the result of the mission because he never saw it.

[2] Jean-Paul Sartre, *Being and Nothingness*, trans. Hazel E. Barnes (New York: Philosophical Library, 1956), pp. 553–54. Copyright © 1956 by Philosophical Library, Inc.

In aerial warfare you can't contemplate the results of your destruction, especially at night, because they are hidden from you by distance and darkness. All you see is a flash of fire and, depending on your altitude, you don't even see that sometimes. You have a terrifying detachment from the result of what you are doing. If you had gone down there and seen your destruction of these people, then you would be able to feel guilt, easily. But it's in the nature of the operational function you're performing that you can't do this, even if you want to. This detachment produces a peculiar state of mind. The protagonist feels that his inability to imagine one of his victims knocking at his door with his ears burned off, his inability to imagine anybody knocking at his door except his neighbor coming over to borrow the lawn mower, is a kind of judgment on him—and it is. He is realistic about it, though, and says that there is nothing he can do; and there isn't. Maybe that's the worst sentence of all, to be deprived of feeling what a human being ought to be entitled to feel.[3]

Contrast what Sartre says about responsibility in the modern world with what Dickey says. Is the existentialist emphasis that a person should take full responsibility for all one's actions and their consequences a reaction (a response) to the loss of the feeling of concrete responsibility that Dickey describes?

Consider the much more recent experience of many Americans, both participants in Operation Desert Storm in the Middle East in 1990 and television viewers at home, where the use of highly sophisticated technology, radar, and "smart bombs", resulted in the deaths of tens of thousands of Iraqi soldiers and civilians with minimal loss of American lives. Many of the American casualties were in fact the result of the deadly efficient "friendly fire," in which technologically identified targets were misidentified by human executors. The media as well as the military commentators focused on the wonders of the technology, with little apparent concern for the (relatively) defenseless tens of thousands of human casualties. In the light of this recent experience, you may want to read "The Firebombing," in Dickey's book of poems *Buckdancer's Choice*.[4] The following units of this chapter explore some ways in which religious traditions have dealt with the questions raised here. See Unit 63 for a discussion of the moral and religious dimensions of warfare in the contemporary world.

UNIT 48   Human Freedom

Responsibility assumes that each person enjoys intellectual and moral freedom, the nature of which has been variously described and emphasized by the world's religions.

In Eastern religions the divine is generally understood as an all-pervasive, immanent reality that permeates the physical as well as the spiritual universe. Seldom under-

[3] From *Self-Interviews* by James Dickey, pp. 138–39. Copyright © 1970 by James Dickey. Reprinted by permission of Doubleday and Co., Inc.

[4] James Dickey, "The Firebombing," *Buckdancer's Choice* (Middletown, CT: Wesleyan University Press, 1964, 1965), pp. 11–20.

stood as distinct from everyday life, whatever particular deities may be present essentially represent this impersonal divine reality. Often humans are seen to contain within themselves this divine reality, so human responsibility includes the discovery and uncovering of the divine within. In fact, true humanity must identify and cooperate with the divine to be *freed* from the impermanence and irrelevancies of everyday physical existence. In Hinduism, *moksha* frees or releases an individual to truly identify with the divine so that all other realities become meaningless. To be truly free is to lose all personal desires and to be delivered from the endless round of physical reincarnations. Obviously, to move toward this state, a person must have the ability to make the choice for the divine, to have freedom to chose; yet the goal of freedom *from* the world in some sense gives a very different emphasis to the concept of human freedom. The emphasis is not on the human ability to decide but on the ultimate goal, where one will be *free*.

Similarly, in all forms of Buddhism there is an emphasis on the responsibility of the individual both to recognize the situation of humanity (the Four Noble Truths) and to choose the method taught by the Buddha to overcome selfish human desires (the Eightfold Path). Although the Buddha's teachings may be variously interpreted in the several branches of Buddhism, the ultimate goal is the same, enlightenment (Nirvana), wherein one's everyday existence is, as in Hinduism, freed from the traps of self-centered desires. In Buddhism, however, the emphasis is not really on escape from the daily round as much as on freedom to live that daily round without allowing its demands to overcome the true reality—the spiritual life unbound by daily physical existence. Again, one must be able to choose, but the ultimate freedom is freedom from life's entrapments.

In contrast, the understanding of the divine in Western religions raises different issues for the definition of human freedom. Since humans are understood to be creatures of a particular divine being, freedom of the will must always be defined within a context that includes divine will. For example, the Muslim definition of the relationship between the divine and the human assumes that human beings must be able to choose between the will of Allah for their individual and their own self-directed, most often sinful, will. The proper Muslim response in this context is to submit to the will of Allah. Symbolizing this reality, the word *Islam* means "one who submits." The most complete and true life is one lived within the perimeters laid down by Allah in the prophecies of Muhammad as expressed in the Qu'ran. Once one submits to Allah's will, human choice, although still present, is molded by the divine will.

Judaism, like Islam, also emphasizes the greatness of God, the holiness, wisdom, goodness, and power of God, the Creator of all things, beside whom there are no other gods. Judaism joins to this perception of God the dignity and potential greatness of humanity. Human beings are dependent on God, receiving their being and life and all things necessary to life as gifts from God. However, humans are potentially cocreators with God. They should show reverence to God but not sacrifice their own talents or lose their creative initiative in blind submission: It is God's will that people develop their creative potential to the fullest in accordance with the commandments of God.

This double aspect of the human relationship to God in Judaism is well illustrated in the Jewish scriptures. In the book of Genesis, for instance, Abraham (the patriarch of Judaism) is praised because of his faithful obedience to God. Certainly there is no lack of reverence for God on Abraham's part. Nevertheless, it is shown as entirely proper that

Abraham should attempt to persuade God to change his mind about destroying the wicked cities of Sodom and Gomorrah. Abraham succeeds in getting God to agree to spare the wicked cities, provided some good people can be found in them (see Unit 87). In the same way, Moses persuades God to change his mind about destroying the Hebrews who have worshiped a golden calf, thereby showing their lack of faith in God after he has just delivered them from slavery in Egypt (Exodus 32). In both cases, God takes counsel and accepts the suggestions of his faithful servants, his obedient and loyal friends. The same point is made in story form in the Talmud:[5]

> Rabbi Eliezer disagreed with some other rabbis about a point of law and, unable to convince them, said, "If the law is as I think it is, then this tree shall let me know." Immediately the tree jumped a hundred yards, but the other rabbis said: "One does not prove anything from a tree." Rabbi Eliezer then appealed to a brook, which immediately began to flow upstream, but his colleagues replied: "One does not prove anything from a brook." Rabbi Eliezer said: "If the law is as I think, then the walls of this house will tell." And the walls began to fall. Rabbi Joshua reprimanded the walls: "If scholars argue a point of law, what business have you to fall?" Then the walls stopped midway: to show their respect for Rabbi Joshua, they did not fall further; and in deference to Rabbi Eliezer they did not straighten up. Then Rabbi Eliezer appealed to heaven, and a voice said: "What have you against Rabbi Eliezer? The law is as he says." Rabbi Joshua, however, replied: "It is written in the Bible (Deuteronomy 30:12): It is not in heaven. What does this mean?" Rabbi Jirmijahu said: "The Torah has been given on Mount Sinai, so we no longer pay attention to voices, for on Mount Sinai already thou hast written into the Torah to decide according to the majority." Some time after this dispute, Rabbi Nathan met Elijah, the prophet, and asked him what the Holy One, blessed be His Name, had done in that hour. And Elijah replied: "God smiled and said: My children have won against me, my children have won."[6]

According to Judaism, a full illumination of true humanity can be attained when humans gain this perspective of their relationship to the one God. In the light of this distinctive Jewish understanding of freedom—an interaction with the sovereign God, even to the point of questioning and influencing God's actions—Jewish imagery of the value and place of humanity is greatly enhanced and has significantly affected Western understandings of humanity.

∽

Stated in your own words, what are the central differences between Eastern and Western religious concepts of freedom?

How does the Jewish concept of freedom differ from that of Muslims?

Are there significant contrasts in the Jewish and Christian explanations of human freedom?

Why is freedom of the will considered an essential human attribute?

[5] The Talmud is a collection, or collection of collections, of commentaries on the body of law revealed in the Jewish scriptures. It developed over a period of centuries and was handed down as oral tradition before being put in written form.

[6] An adaptation of a story from the Talmud, Baba Mezia 596, cited by Erich Fromm, *Psychoanalysis and Religion* (New Haven, CT: Yale University Press, 1950), p. 45.

UNIT 49   Concepts of Christian Freedom and the Dilemmas of Decision Making

Like Judaism and Islam, Christianity also emphasizes the majesty and greatness of God and at the same time highlights human responsibility. One of its central tenets proclaims that humanity is totally dependent on God's grace for salvation. If that is true, what is the nature of human freedom among Christians? Here we consider how some Christian theologians, ancient and modern, have interpreted freedom and what it means to decide.

Concerning Free Will

Pelagius, a British monk who came to Rome late in the fourth century, maintained that people are created free to choose good or evil and that they always have that freedom.

> We have implanted in us by God a possibility for acting in both directions. It resembles, as I may say, a root which is most abundant in its produce of fruit. It yields and produces diversely according to man's will; and is capable, at the cultivator's own choice, of either shedding a beautiful bloom of virtues, or of bristling with the thorny thicket of vices. . . . But that we really do a good thing, or speak a good word, or think a good thought, proceeds from our own selves. . . . Nothing good, nothing evil, on account of which we are deemed either laudable or blameworthy, is born with us, but is done by us: for we are born not fully developed, but with a capacity for either conduct; we are formed naturally without either virtue or vice. . . .[7]

Concerning the "Unfree" Will

Augustine, Christian bishop of Hippo in North Africa during the fifth century, vehemently rejected Pelagius's position. Augustine felt that Pelagius neglected the grace of God in human actions; although humanity (Adam) originally had freedom to sin or not to sin, because of their pride people sinned by choosing themselves over God and therefore lost their freedom to choose between the alternatives of good and evil. Since this original choice, according to Augustine, individuals have no freedom of their own to choose good or evil; they choose only the evil. Humanity's only hope of freedom to choose goodness depends on God's grace—his willingness to restore human ability to do good. This restoration emphasizes humanity's dependence on God for any ability to do good. John Calvin, the sixteenth-century Protestant reformer, agreed with Augustine, as the following statement indicates:

> The will, therefore, is so bound by the slavery of sin, that it cannot excite itself, much less devote itself to any thing good. . . . We must . . . observe this point of distinction, that man, having been corrupted by his fall, sins voluntarily, not with reluctance or constraint; with the strongest propensity of disposition, not with violent coercion; with the bias of his

---

[7] Paul Lehmann, "The Anti-Pelagian Writings," *A Companion to the Study of St. Augustine*, ed. Roy Battenhouse (New York: Oxford University Press, 1955), p. 208.

own passions, and not with external compulsion: yet such is the pravity of his nature, that he cannot be excited and biased to any thing but what is evil. If this be true, there is no impropriety in affirming, that he is under a necessity of sinning. . . .

Man is so enslaved by sin, as to be of his own nature incapable of an effort, or even an inspiration, toward that which is good.[8]

Concerning Freedom in a New Context

The positions of Pelagius and Augustine have often been seen as the poles of a continuum on the question of freedom. Each position contains truth but can be criticized for being dogmatic. On the one hand, Pelagius has often been criticized for defining freedom in a manner that may negate the necessity of God's grace, that is, that humans are simply free and really not dependent on God. Augustine and Calvin, on the other hand, in their stress on the necessity of God's grace threaten the very existence of freedom. Christian thinkers have often agreed with and consequently argued for one or the other of these positions or, just as frequently, have taken a position between them.

A modern theologian, Carl Michalson, wishing to move beyond the limits of these age-old arguments, suggests that the event of Jesus—his teachings, witness, and death and resurrection—creates a new context for human decision making. According to Michalson, through faith in the God revealed in Jesus, Christians are not merely limited by their previous conditions, the set of determinates given in any human life. Christians also can in faith decide about their actions within the limitations of birth, sin, and social condition, but with a new reality of freedom for their destiny as defined by God's love revealed in Jesus. Such a freedom incorporates several features:

> Let me test the sense of the Christian meaning of freedom through a series of illustrations. The Japanese daughter of a Samurai was once sent to a mission school where she was given a plot of ground a yard square with which to do entirely as she chose. It was called a "do as you please" garden. She planted it according to her own design and afterward exclaimed it was the first time in her life she had known what it meant to be free. Christian freedom is like that, to be sure, but it is more.
>
> Radhakrishnan, the Indian philosopher and statesman, has likened freedom to being dealt a hand of cards and being allowed to play out the game, but strictly within the limits of the cards in hand. Christian freedom also includes this sense of a certain latitude within prescribed limits.
>
> Pascal's analogy of the wager comes even closer to what Christians mean by freedom. It recapitulates the others but adds still another element. The coin is tossed. One is free to do as he pleases with his decision. But he can only choose "heads" or "tails"; he must play out the game within those limits. What is added by Pascal, however, is urgency. One *must* call out before the coin has fallen. That is to say, man is not free not to choose. He is not free to filibuster with destiny beyond the deadline for authentic resolution.[9]

A Christian is given by these realities a sense of real freedom from those elements of life that so often limit loving action, even though this freedom is still within the limits of human life.

---

[8] John Calvin, *A Compend of the Institutes of Christian Religion*, ed. Hugh Thomson Kerr, Jr. (Philadelphia: Presbyterian Board of Education, 1939), pp. 49, 51.

[9] Carl Michalson, *World Theology* (New York: Scribner, 1967), pp. 168–69.

Michalson further suggests that under these conditions love allows one to be free to serve in the world without yielding to its usual binding demands or concerns. Love thereby allows creativity in each new situation of life without depending on a rigid set of rules or laws. The Christian is in addition freed from the sin of rebellion against God. One may authentically live within the world as God intended. And finally, one's identification with God's will and love frees one from the fear of death—for God will be then as he is now, all in all. With these suggestions Michalson focuses on the nature and function of a Christian life lived in freedom rather than arguing about whether, or to what extent, a human has free will.

As the examples show, freedom has been understood in a variety of ways by Christian theologians. It has been defined in still other ways by philosophers and by other cultures, where the stress on individual freedom has not been as significant as it has been in Western religions, particularly Judaism and Christianity.

∽

In the light of these interpretations of freedom, what does it mean to decide?

Do you agree or disagree with Pelagius that we are born without either virtue or vice and can choose between the alternatives of doing good or evil? Why?

Do you agree or disagree with Augustine's understanding that we have no real freedom in doing good or evil? Why?

If there are elements of truth in both positions, what resolution would you propose to rectify the seeming contradictions found between the two positions?

Does Michalson offer you new insights into the nature of Christian freedom? If so, what might these be?

CHAPTER 11

❧

Sin and Guilt

Introduction

Most religions have provided some direction to adherents regarding what is considered right or appropriate behavior in one's basic attitudes toward life as well as in social relationships. Failure to live by these standards often produces guilt or shame, and these feelings play a decisive role in personal direction and control.

Religions thus inculcate the sense of what is appropriate or right and what is wrong. In the Western world, this process has frequently been referred to as the development of conscience. *Guilt* is understood to be a primary motivational factor in one's attitudinal and behavioral functioning. Students of oriental religion and culture have sometimes referred to *shame*, as differentiated from guilt in the Western connotation, as the underlying motivation of appropriate behavior. This chapter is designed to explore briefly the concepts of shame and guilt in oriental and Western contexts. Attention is also given to the concept of sin as developed within the Judeo-Christian heritage.

UNIT 50   Roles of Shame and Guilt

A pompously, pretentiously dressed individual, through no fault of his own, slips on a banana peel and careens into a mud puddle. He looks quickly and furtively around and is relieved that no one has seen his fall.

A woman sends a large check to a bank, explaining that years ago a teller had given her twenty dollars too much. Though no one else has ever known about it, she explains that over the years she has come to feel increasingly guilty and is now returning the original sum with the correctly calculated interest.

These two incidents illustrate the contrasting attitudes of shame and guilt as discussed by Ruth Benedict in the passage that follows. The man who would have been ashamed if others had seen his disgrace, since no one did see, felt relief, not shame. The woman was burdened by guilt, even though no one else knew she had accepted the overpayment. Her guilt could be relieved only by confession (even if she remained anonymous) and restitution.

At the time of writing *The Chrysanthemum and the Sword,* Ruth Benedict believed that Western societies relied heavily on guilt, perhaps as a part of their Puritan heritage, and less on the sense of shame to regulate behavior. Some recent observers have suggested that perhaps a shift has occurred, that there is more tendency now than formerly for many in Western societies to be shame oriented rather than guilt oriented. As you read Benedict's discussion, ask yourself whether the distinction between the two attitudes and the corresponding contrast between Western and Eastern orientations are as clear today.

> In anthropological studies of different cultures the distinction between those which rely heavily on shame and those that rely heavily on guilt is an important one. A society that inculcates absolute standards of morality and relies on men's developing a conscience is a guilt culture by definition, but a man in such a society may, as in the United States, suffer in addition from shame when he accuses himself of gaucheries which are in no way sins. He may be exceedingly chagrined about not dressing appropriately for the occasion or about a slip of the tongue. In a culture where shame is a major sanction, people are chagrined about acts which we expect people to feel guilty about. This chagrin can be very intense and it cannot be relieved, as guilt can be, by confession and atonement. A man who has sinned can get relief by unburdening himself. This device of confession is used in our secular therapy and by many religious groups which have otherwise little in common. We know it brings relief. Where shame is the major sanction, a man does not experience relief when he makes his fault public even to a confessor. So long as his bad behavior does not "get out into the world" he need not be troubled and confession appears to him merely a way of courting trouble. Shame cultures therefore do not provide for confessions, even to the gods. They have ceremonies for good luck rather than for expiation.
>
> True shame cultures rely on external sanctions for good behavior, not, as true guilt cultures do, on an internalized conviction of sin. Shame is a reaction to other people's criticism. A man is shamed either by being openly ridiculed and rejected or by fantasying to himself that he has been made ridiculous. In either case it is a potent sanction. But it requires an audience or at least a man's fantasy of an audience. Guilt does not. In a nation where honor means living up to one's own picture of oneself, a man may suffer from guilt though no man knows of his misdeed and a man's feeling of guilt may actually be relieved by confessing his sin.
>
> The early Puritans who settled in the United States tried to base their whole morality on guilt and all psychiatrists know what trouble contemporary Americans have with their consciences. But shame is an increasingly heavy burden in the United States and guilt is less extremely felt than in earlier generations. In the United States this is interpreted as a relaxation of morals. There is much truth in this, but that is because we do not expect shame to do the heavy work of morality. We do not harness the acute personal chagrin which accompanies shame to our fundamental system of morality.
>
> The Japanese do. A failure to follow their explicit signposts of good behavior, a failure to balance obligations or to foresee contingencies is a shame (*hajj*). Shame, they say, is the

root of virtue. A man who is sensitive to it will carry out all the rules of good behavior. "A man who knows shame" is sometimes translated "virtuous man," sometimes "man of honor." Shame has the same place of authority in Japanese ethics that "a clear conscience," "being right with God," and the avoidance of sin have in Western ethics. Logically enough, therefore, a man will not be punished in the afterlife. The Japanese—except for priests who know the Indian sutras—are quite unacquainted with the idea of reincarnation dependent upon one's merit in his life, and—except for some well-instructed Christian converts—they do not recognize post-death reward and punishment or a heaven and a hell.[1]

UNIT 51   Guilt and Religious Experience

When we say that humans are "ethical animals," we refer to the reality that humans know right from wrong and are able to choose between good and evil. The personal responsibility that arises out of this freedom to choose is part of what it means to be human and to act ethically. In religious language, *righteousness* denotes proper ethical actions and *guilt* is associated with actions that do not conform to the ethical principles of the religion. Guilt, arising from improper or evil action, is therefore one expression of the personal ethical principles operative through an individual's conscience. Guilt may lead to contrition, confession, and restitution, to make amends for improper action.

Although guilt may be examined and at least partially explained through an intellectual process, its foundation is in the feelings: It is a part of the subconscious that activates our daily lives, a powerful psychological phenomenon. Because of its power and usefulness, it is a significant element in the religious experience of many cultures, particularly in Western religious traditions.

Among the early Jews, the nature of an offense defined the degree of guilt, making it possible for some forms of guilt to become an objective contamination. Johannes Pedersen, a biblical scholar, describes this ancient Jewish understanding:

> It follows from the psychological conception of the Israelites that a man is responsible for all his actions. Every action must exercise its effect, also in the soul of the person who acts. . . . The decisive thing is what is the relation of the action to the acting soul: does it arise in the central will of the soul, or does it merely lie in the periphery of the soul? If the latter is the case, then it can be wiped out and be removed before it gains ground. . . . But if an infringement upon the law of righteousness is more deeply seated in the soul, then it is not to be removed.[2]

In other words, one may remove the guilt of minor acts through confession and restitution; however, in more serious offenses a person is not necessarily able to remove the guilt; it becomes an objective reality. For example, in the case of murder, the guilt is so intense that it not only shapes the reality of the murderer but also becomes attached to his or her fam-

[1] Ruth Benedict, *The Chrysanthemum and the Sword: Patterns of Japanese Culture* (Boston: Houghton Mifflin, 1946), pp. 222–24. Used by permission of the publisher.

[2] John G. McKenzie, *Guilt: Its Meaning and Significance* (Nashville, TN: Abingdon Press, 1962), pp. 40–49. Copyright © 1962 by Abingdon Press.

ily. It also demands reciprocal action, which may not take place for generations. This is the basis of the teaching that "the sins of the fathers shall set the teeth of the children on edge" and "an eye for an eye" and "a tooth for a tooth." In early Judaism this concept of objective guilt was sometimes used by a violated family to destroy the offending party. More often guilt became a consuming poison to the offender, recompensing the violated family by destroying the unregenerate soul and thereby ridding the Jewish community of a danger. This understanding is in accordance with the fundamental Jewish law of the soul. In Israel's conception of the psychic life, guilt produces misfortune, just as righteousness undergirds happiness.

> But the wicked are like the tossing sea; for it cannot rest, and its waters toss up mire and dirt. There is no peace, says my God, for the wicked. (Isaiah 57:20–21, RSV)

In Judaism's prophetic period (from 750 B.C.E.), the emphasis began to shift from objective guilt to the more subjective or psychological elements of guilt, which results from and expresses itself in wrong or rebellious attitudes rather than objective acts of revenge which arise from such attitudes. The prophets taught that such attitudes had to be changed. The emphasis was no longer on the contagion of an objective guilt that could not be removed (as in early Judaism) or on a debt that could be paid or canceled only by God (as in medieval Christian teaching).

These psychological and subjective aspects of guilt have been emphasized in Christianity from the New Testament period to the present. Guilt, and the human responsibility it incorporates, became a central issue for Saint Augustine of Hippo (354–430) and the Danish Christian philosopher Søren Kierkegaard (1819–1855). Without guilt individuals cannot recognize or appropriate true responsibility for their actions and remain totally selfish—unable to accept God's grace offered in forgiveness.

Modern theological study of the role of guilt and conscience in personality development draws on the traditions within Judaism and Christianity that have emphasized the subjective and psychological character of guilt as well as on recent psychological models of personality development. John G. McKenzie, an English psychotherapist and adherent of Christianity, distinguishes between a socially created and immature conscience (Freud's concept of the superego), which often functions on the level of taboos and neurotic (false) guilt, and a mature conscience able to be self-governing in accordance with the authentic needs of (and duties to) the self and others. McKenzie suggests that a child's morality begins when he or she becomes conscious of approval and disapproval from those surrounding the child, usually parents and teachers. Since parents and teachers are not always with the child, he or she internalizes their teachings and prohibitions, and these become the basis of moral action; however, they are still adopted from others.

> Now, many people never outgrow this infantile Super-ego. Unconsciously they strive to obey the prohibitions and conform to the commands. Inwardly they rebel against its rigidity and compulsions; and they may develop . . . a perfectionist character-trend, or a dynamic trend to restrict their lives within narrow limits. The least deviation from perfection and they are full of guilty-feelings, recriminations, and yet at the same time a raging hostility has to be kept repressed, or projected.
> Thus we come, again, up against the ambivalence which lies at the root of the origin of guilt-feelings. I would not say that the child or the adult wants to comply with the Super-

ego, but he or she fears the guilt-feelings. He or she is afraid of freedom; they are afraid lest the impulses prove too strong for the Ego to control. Hence unconsciously they cling to the authoritative conscience. . . .

The problem of moral growth is simply the problem of growing up. . . . We have to pass from Super-ego control to conscience-control. . . . It is doubtful whether the Super-ego ever withers away entirely; but with the development of the adult or positive conscience it performs a different role. Instead of repressing through the guilt-sense an offending line of behaviour, it pulls us up, compels us to reflect upon what we are tempted to do; and then exercises control through reason rather than through feeling. If we cross the "barrier" and fall then there is a consciousness of objective guilt, but instead of morbid guilt-feelings with all their threats there is sincere contrition . . . that is to say, there is sorrow for the guilty behaviour and a turning away from such behaviour. . . . It is the passing from the "borrowed morality" of the Super-ego to the free morality of conscience where *oughts, commands* and *prohibitions* have become moral guides and not moral policemen. We accept these not in virtue of external authority, but because we *see* they are true . . .[3]

Similarly, in religious traditions a mature believer not only accepts responsibility for his or her actions but also develops a "mature morality" based on the ethical teachings of the tradition, not as something imposed from outside by religious teachers but because such teachings are true and lead to a fruitful and joyous life. Transgression of the religious teachings may lead to guilt, but in a mature believer these become avenues for returning to responsible action, often through contrition and restitution.

∽

Do you distinguish between types of guilt, for example, healthy and unhealthy guilt?

Do religions play a constructive role in society by providing some content for the conscience?

Do you agree with McKenzie that "appropriate" or "healthy" guilt experiences are necessary for people to live in a social context?

In your judgment, have contemporary changes in family structures and educational patterns modified the role of guilt in the development of ethical behavior?

UNIT 52   Judeo-Christian Concepts of Sin

A central emphasis in the Judeo-Christian tradition has been the broken relationship between God and humankind denoted by the word *sin:* Most Christians have connected the concept of sin with disobedience to the commandments or laws of God. The Ten Commandments given by God to the descendants of Israel (see Exodus 20) have often been taken as a prototype of God's commandments, in that they contain in broad outline an indication of the conduct God desires and forbids. Primarily, God's will has been interpreted to include the exclusive devotion to God and justice and love toward one's fellow humans. Christianity, departing from Judaism, has laid great stress on *original sin,* an attitude involving self-will

[3] McKenzie, *Guilt,* pp. 32, 34, 35, 40, 48, 49.

and self-indulgence held to be characteristic of *all* fallen humanity that precedes and causes specific acts of sinfulness. Thus, medieval Christianity stressed as deadly sins seven dispositions or character traits—pride, covetousness, lust, envy, gluttony, anger, and sloth—which as particular manifestations of the underlying original sin (an attitude or disposition rather than an act) are motivating causes of sinful acts both in the unredeemed and in Christians who have fallen away from the restored innocence given them by baptism.

The following passage from Genesis gives an account of the fall of Adam and Eve, a symbol to many Christians and Jews of the fall of all humans.

> Now the serpent was more subtle than any other wild creature that the Lord God had made. He said to the woman, "Did God say, 'You shall not eat of any tree of the garden'?" And the woman said to the serpent, "We may eat of the fruit of the trees of the garden; but God said, 'You shall not eat of the fruit of the tree which is in the midst of the garden, neither shall you touch it, lest you die.' " But the serpent said to the woman, "You will not die. For God knows that when you eat of it your eyes will be opened, and you will be like God, knowing good and evil." So when the woman saw that the tree was good for food, and that it was a delight to the eyes, and that the tree was to be desired to make one wise, she took of its fruit and ate; and she also gave some to her husband, and he ate. Then the eyes of both were opened, and they knew that they were naked; and they sewed fig leaves together and made themselves aprons. And they heard the sound of the Lord God walking in the garden in the cool of the day, and the man and his wife hid themselves from the presence of the Lord God among the trees of the garden. But the Lord God called to the man, and said to him, "Where are you?" And he said, "I heard the sound of thee in the garden, and I was afraid, because I was naked; and I hid myself." He said, "Who told you that you were naked? Have you eaten of the tree of which I commanded you not to eat?" The man said, "The woman whom thou gavest to be with me, she gave me fruit of the tree, and I ate." Then the Lord God said to the woman, "What is this that you have done?" The woman said, "The serpent beguiled me, and I ate." (Genesis 3:1-13 RSV)

This passage describes actual disobedience but also—and more important—the desire to be like God or to be God, a wish that separates humanity from God.

Reinhold Niebuhr, a contemporary theologian, expands on this interpretation.

> Since Augustine it has been the consistent view of Christian orthodoxy that the basic sin of man was his pride. In this view Christian thought agreed with the conception of the Greek tragedies, which regarded *hybris* as man's most flagrant fault and one which was invariably followed by punishment or *nemesis*. The basic sign of pride does not mean some conscious bit of exaggerated self-esteem, but the general inclination of all men to overestimate their virtues, powers, and achievements. Augustine defined sin as the "perverse desire of height," or as man's regarding himself as his own end, instead of realizing that he is but a part of a total scheme of means and ends.[4]

Although Niebuhr stresses sin as pride, he also finds another basic mode of human sinfulness in sloth or self-indulgence.

Harvey Cox, another contemporary theologian, offers yet another explanation of sin—one that contrasts with the broadly accepted concept of sin as pride but to some extent resembles Niebuhr's concept of sin as sloth.

---

[4] Reinhold Niebuhr, "Sin," *A Handbook of Christian Theology*, ed. Marvin Halverson and Arthur A. Cohen (New York: World Publishing Company, 1958), p. 348.

Man-as-sinner has usually been pictured by religious writers as man-the-insurrectionary, the proud heaven-storming rebel who has not learned to be content with his lot. Refined and escalated in literature, this image blossoms in the heroic Satans and Lucifers of Goethe and Milton. No wonder we find sin so interesting and sinners more attractive than saints. No wonder we secretly admire Lucifer while our orthodox doctrine condemns him to the lake of fire. This misleading view of sin as pride and rebelliousness has given the very word sin an intriguing lustre: a naked Eve with moist bedroom eyes guiltily tasting the forbidden apple; a slithery, clearly phallic, serpent; man defying the petty conventions imposed on him by small-minded people. In these terms why shouldn't we be in favor of sin? The only trouble is this mish-mash of sex and self-affirmation images has almost nothing to do with the biblical idea of sin. It is basically a Greek, or more precisely, promethean notion larded with remnants of medieval folk piety, Victorian antisexuality, and the bourgeois obsession with orderliness.[5]

. . . Apathy is the key form of sin in today's world. . . . For Adam and Eve, apathy meant letting a snake tell them what to do. It meant abdicating what the theologians have called *gubernatio mundi,* the exercise of dominion and control over the world. For us it means allowing others to dictate the identities with which we live out our lives.[6]

. . . I believe a careful examination of the biblical sources will indicate that man's most debilitating proclivity is *not* his pride. It is *not* his attempt to be more than man . . . it is his sloth, his unwillingness to be everything man was intended to be.[7]

Is it necessary to have a concept of sin or wrongdoing in a religion? If so, why is it necessary? If not, how can broken human relationships be explained?

What does Niebuhr mean by sin as pride?

Which of the explanations of sin presented here do you find most appropriate?

---

[5] Harvey Cox, *On Not Leaving It to the Snake* (New York: Macmillan, 1964), pp. xi, xii. Copyright © 1964, 1965, 1967 by Harvey G. Cox. Used by permission.

[6] Ibid., p. xviii.

[7] Ibid., p. xi.

CHAPTER 12

❧

Death and the Self

Introduction

In every society, in every period of human history, people have been preoccupied with the experience and meaning of death. It is a custom among some Christian groups for individuals to remind each other on Ash Wednesday each year, "Recall, O man, thou art mortal. Dust thou art, and to dust thou shalt return." There is hardly any reality of which human beings in their long history have been more aware than the fact, the inevitability, of death. Death, its meaning, its mystery, and the uncertainty or promise of what may come after, has been the subject of wide-ranging speculation and deepest interest.

A student wrote in a journal entry,

> Why are some people so sure they will find the answers to life when they die? I asked one person why she was sure. She said, "Because Jesus said so in the Bible." Faith is their answer. Faith is not my answer. I have heard people witness of God's part in their lives, and how they could feel his presence. But I haven't felt Him directly in my life. I have experienced the love of people. I guess that's how He works. God is very vague to me. I guess that is why I'm not sure I'll find the "whys" of life when I die. I don't have any idea of what is after death, as some people think they do. Perhaps that is why death scares me. I talked to a girl one time who believes there is nothing after death. I can't believe that either. I can't imagine a nothing. I can't feature a complete end to everything.

The ambiguity of feelings toward life and death expressed in this statement is not an uncommon human experience. The reality of death is recognized and there is little assurance of an afterlife; nevertheless, there is still the hope and anticipation of continuance. Religions have usually embraced a more positive stance toward death and its consequences.

Every religious tradition has interpreted the meaning of death. Most have contained teachings about the meaning of existence beyond the present one, in the continuity of future generations; in an afterlife; in a succession of rebirths; or in a restored or resurrected, totally renewed existence.

This chapter explores the phenomenon of death as a fundamental human experience, giving examples of various religious interpretations of death and an afterlife.

UNIT 53   How It Feels to Die

The reality of death has always been intriguing, and the event itself has been surrounded in all cultures by ritual preparation, elaborate burial practices, and stylized grief formulas. Accounts of death and the anticipated afterlife have been numerous throughout history; for example, the ancient Tibetan *Book of the Dead* contains elaborate descriptions of the patterns of death and methods for contacting the dead.

Attention has been focused more recently on "near-death" experiences as the advances of modern medicine have made the phenomenon of "clinical death" more common. Accounts of such experiences have become popular reading, and the frequency of the phenomenon has opened discussions of life after death among psychologists and medical professions in ways unanticipated a few years ago. These accounts inevitably raise anew images and questions that have been an integral part of religious traditions throughout human history. The following account of such an episode contains many features that have been reported by others who have had similar experiences: enhanced awareness, a sense of detachment, euphoria, dying by stages and from the extremities, and an encounter with *something* greater than life.

A little more than 24 hours ago, as I write this, I learned what it is like to die.

By nearly every clinical standard an arresting of life did occur. The cause of my "death" was a condition known to doctors as anaphylactic shock. This is a rapid failure of vital functions induced by an acute allergic reaction to an alien protein introduced into the tissues—as, for example, the extreme reaction that sometimes occurs when a person has been stung by a bee.

In my case, the alien substance was penicillin. For most people, a dosage of this drug, properly administered, does the job expected of it. For me, with long-dormant allergic factors lurking in my system, the dosage could hardly have been more hostile had it been spat from the fangs of a cobra. . . .

The allergic onslaught was massive and swift. At the last possible moment it was neutralized and reversed by specific counteragents. Had I reached the doctor a minute or two later, or had there not been a supply of the counteragents on hand, I could not have survived. A busy telephone line, a low battery in the car, a misplaced ignition key, a blocked street—any number of things could have made the difference.

Slumped upon a chair in . . . [the Doctor's] residential consulting room, I was slipping across the honed edge of death. For a period of some minutes there had been no pulse, no blood pressure, no pronounced stirring of the heart. My eyes, I have been told, were glazed. My limbs were flaccid, my face swollen and ashen. In the last extreme seconds, only *awareness* remained of the vital functions. As the crisis deepened, I was acutely, almost electrically, aware of things around me and then, when this awareness receded, of things *within* me. I was an enthralled eyewitness and mind witness to my own rapidly advancing demise.

It was a turbulent experience but not at all terrifying—and it had its moments, as I recall them now, of pure black humor. At the end I gazed into something that I believe to be life's supreme mystery. . . .

The nasal irritation had come upon me earlier in the week. I thought it was a cold. But it dragged on, with none of the other, droopy symptoms of a cold, and on Saturday morning I awoke with a raw and scratchy throat. I suspected that this could be a strep infection, and made a mental note to give the Doctor a call later in the day.

Then I looked in the medicine cabinet for some throat lozenges. My eyes fell upon a bottle containing a dozen or so penicillin tablets left over from a pediatrician's prescription for my two small children. The bottle still had its factory label, which recommended a dosage of two tablets four times a day. So why bother the Doctor on her weekend? Although I was aware that self-prescription was poor business for the layman, I took two tablets and noted the time. It was 7:03 a.m.

During the next half-hour or so, I went through the morning routine of feeding the dog and putting her into the fenced-in backyard and brewing the coffee. While listening to news broadcasts, I became aware of a prickly itching sensation on my ankles and legs. It spread rapidly to the wrists and palms, then across the shoulders, lower back and chest. With a cup of coffee for myself and a wake-up one for my wife, I started up the stairs. The itching was taking fire. Halfway up, I set the cups and saucers on the step ahead and went into a frenzy of scratching. I could see coin-size white blotches rising on the backs of my hands. I remembered that long-forgotten reaction to the first penicillin. . . .

I became increasingly aware of a thickening and stiffening of the facial features, and a wheezing of the breath. Turning to the mirror, I scarcely recognized the swollen, crimson-splashed face that stared back at me.

My wife called the Doctor and told her about the penicillin and the reaction, listened a moment, said, "All right, we'll do our best," and hung up.

"The Doctor said we must come at once," she said quietly. . . .

Then I was inside the car, lying on my back across the middle row of seats. The car was bumping along and I heard the clatter of the engine. Behind me, in the third row, my 5-year-old daughter was prattling. My 7-year-old son was commanding her to be quiet. I remember thinking what a nice ad it would make: *A Volkswagen bus is a handy family car to die in*.

We had stopped. As the door spilled open and my wife started tugging me out, I saw a flash of color at the head of the walkway, atop the steps at the patients' side entrance to the big cream stucco house. It was the Doctor in her red-and-blue-plaid dressing robe, looking decidedly unprofessional against the backlight of the morning glare. She was standing in the doorway, leaning out.

As my wife pulled me to my feet, the Doctor, from a distance of 15 or so yards, sized up my condition. She could see the un-coordinated rolling of my eyes, the death pallor of my face, the wobble of my legs. These indications told her that the shock was far advanced and that I might pass out before I could reach the consultation room. For her to try to drag my 200-pound bulk up the five steps and inside would be a futility. So she went back to retrieve the setup in case she had to perform the treatment on the sidewalk.

Momentarily rejuvenated by the rest during the car trip, I was able to make it up the walk. Supported by my wife, I climbed the steps, crossed through the waiting lounge into the consultation room and sank into a green leather-covered armchair. . . .

The hour was 8. Nine minutes had elapsed since my wife's call to the Doctor. I was approximately three minutes away from my confrontation with death.

"Poor Doctor," I said, through a swollen smile, "what an hour for friends to drop in." . . .

For me, a kind of euphoria was setting in. It was marked by exaggerated good humor, a sense of detachment and, I noted even as I experienced it, a hyper-alertness which seemed to furnish me with superior logic and reason. . . .

Then, from far away, as though on some disembodied arm, I felt the tickle of the hypodermic and a tightening little knot as the solution of adrenalin flowed into the muscle. And I observed, but thought it curious that I did not feel, that the Doctor was taking my pulse.

As I was to learn subsequently, her emergency treatment was based on a strategic concept, with allowance for tactical variations as the need might arise.

The adrenalin had to go in first, to start my heart which now was all but dormant. . . .

Now the strategy would proceed to its second phase. When an allergic reaction has set in, a chemical called histamine is excessively generated within the body, causing an increase in the permeability of cells throughout the body. This produces the effects commonly associated with allergy—a rash, an asthmatic swelling of the respiratory passages or a fit of sneezing. In acute cases the overproduction of histamine is enormous. The blood's serum and lymph spill through capillary walls in a floodtide and the blood itself tends to pile up in pools rather than return to the heart. This is the swift chain-reacting characteristic of anaphylactic shock, and it has any number of destructive side effects. The condition can still be reversed until, with cell and tissue death, the shock enters its so-called stagnant stage. Then the body must die.

To buy a little time by attacking the histamine, the Doctor sponged my upper right arm and injected the high-potency antihistamine, Chlor-Trimeton.

In a military sense the injection of adrenalin and antihistamine had been tactical and defensive. Now it was time for the all-out assault with the Neutrapen. In reserve was the cortisone, which might tip the balance in any close engagement. But the Neutrapen was the big one, a mechanism of strategic overkill aimed squarely at the penicillin. It was the ultimate weapon on which the war within my system could be won or lost.

Dimly now, for my external awareness was receding, I saw the Doctor probing for a vein in the crook of my left arm—for years the despair of blood samplers who have tried there first, give up and switched over to the big vein in my right arm.

"Try the right arm, Doctor," I said. "No one can ever find the vein in the left."

"Perhaps God has pointed the way," she said. She had hit the left's elusive vein on the very first try. The dosage went in, 800,000 units of Neutrapen—all she had on hand—to seek and destroy the 500,000 units of penicillin. Now it was up to the bloodstream to deliver.

But at that moment, the Doctor later said, there was no pulse, no discernible pressure, movement or flow of blood. The adrenalin, lost in a limbo of its own, had not taken effect.

Suddenly I knew.

"Am I dying, Doctor? Is it now?"

No reply, or rather, none that I could hear.

"Tell me truly. Am I dying now?"

"Now, we aren't going to let you," she said, though I did not hear her.

"Listen, I want to tell you just how it is, describe it to you . . . please write it down. . . ."

External awareness had slipped away—I heard, saw nothing. I sagged forward as my wife held my head to keep me from pitching from the chair. To the Doctor I had reached clinical death. But for me there was a surge of internal awareness—magnified, finely focused, brilliant.

It is a progressive thing, this death. You feel the toes going first, then the feet, cell by cell, death churning them like waves washing the sands. Now the legs, the cells winking out. Closer now, and the visibility is better. Hands, arms, abdomen and chest, each cell flaring into a supernova, then gone. There is order and system in death, as in all that is life. I must try to control the progression, to save the brain for last so that it may know. Now the neck. The lower jaw. The teeth. How strange to feel one's teeth die, one by one, cell igniting cell, galaxies of cells dying in brilliance.

Now, in retrospect, I grope for this other thing. There was *something* else, something that I felt or experienced or beheld at the very last instant. What was it? I knew it so well when it was there, opening before me, something more beautiful, more gentle, more loving than the mind or imagination of living creature could ever conceive.

But it is gone.

The thunderclap of adrenalin into the heart, reverberations through all the grottoes and canyons and cliffs and peaks of the body. Sprays of sleet, gale-driven against my nakedness, stinging, slashing. Then blurs of motion, sounds of voices.

It is only three or four minutes since I first settled into the green leather chair. The Doctor is at my right side, feeling my pulse as I stir from the coma. Her husband, the surgeon, in his blue terry-cloth dressing robe, has appeared from somewhere and is at my left, holding the other pulse. As I was to learn, in the moments of extremity, as my eyes rolled back in my head, she had run to a hall doorway and shouted for her husband, a tall and powerful man, to come down. She wanted him to do a heart massage. Then she started to prepare the long intracardiac needle. As he entered, however, the earlier dosage of adrenalin took effect.

"Well," he is saying, "we're getting a good pulse now. Good and strong."

The ambulance moves, sunlight through the windows, glimpses of trees in chartreuse bud. An oxygen cup is placed over my nose and mouth. I suck hungrily at the odorless nothingness.

Now the bump-bump-bump of potholes, the honk-honk-honk of the ambulance horn as traffic is encountered. The good sounds, sounds of life and the living.

"No siren?" my wife asks.

"We don't have one," says the woman in white.

Inside the oxygen mask I raise my voice in a wild howl. The woman in white takes alarm, but my wife gets the message. She smiles and blinks back the tears.

"He's supplying the siren," she says.[1]

∽

What is your reaction to such descriptions? Do you think the content of the experience was real or the product of hallucination?

To what extent, if any, have Snell's own background, insights, and sensitivity contributed to this account of his experience?

Compare Snell's experience of the mysterious "something else" with (1) Gautama's comments concerning Nirvana, Unit 19; (2) Zen enlightenment, Unit 28; and (3) mystical experience of God, Unit 28.

UNIT 54   Attitudes Toward Death

Life in all its aspects has been greatly modified by the scientific and technological developments of the past century, particularly in the West. This is most obvious in the health-care field, where startling innovations have greatly lengthened our life span and increased

---

[1] David Snell, "How It Feels to Die," *Life*, May 26, 1967, pp. 38–40, 42, 44, 49. © 1967 Time Inc. Used with permission. Similar experiences, in which there are discernible patterns in the near-death process, are described and analyzed in Elisabeth Kübler-Ross's *On Death and Dying* (New York: Macmillan, 1969), Raymond Moody's *Life after Life* (New York: Bantam Books, 1975), and Craig R. Lundahl's *A Collection of Near-Death Research Readings* (Chicago: Nelson-Hall Publishers, 1982). These works themselves have been analyzed and discussed in such works as Hans Küng's *Eternal Life?* (Garden City, NY: Doubleday, 1984).

our control over disease. Such advances are seldom without their price, however. One has been the need to modify and change the patterns by which we deal with death. Death now usually occurs in a hospital or nursing home, often in an impersonal intensive-care unit. Family, patients, and friends are often cut off from one another. The traditional grief processes are interrupted and sometimes eliminated. The medical community, to a large degree, takes death as a sign of failure since the goal of medicine is to sustain life. The result is the establishment of patterns of behavior that remove us from the death process.

In the last several years, people working with the dying have come to recognize that these changing patterns have turned us into a society that denies the reality of death, creating for itself enormous psychological, emotional, and religious problems. This recognition has led to an immense amount of investigation and writing on death, with workshops and seminars for health professionals, social workers, chaplains, pastors, and laity. There has arisen among some of the professionals who work with the dying a renewed consciousness that society as a whole needs to admit the reality of death and to accept it as a part of life. The awareness of death may indeed mean the growth and expansion of meaning for life as it is lived each day.

Dr. Kübler-Ross, after extensive study of the dying, suggests that there are five stages through which dying patients and their loved ones normally pass:

1. *Denial*—"No, not me." This is a typical reaction when a patient learns that he or she is terminally ill. Denial, says Doctor Ross, is important and necessary. It helps cushion the impact of the patient's awareness that death is inevitable.

2. *Rage and anger*—"Why me?" The patient resents the fact that others will remain healthy and alive while he or she must die. God is a special target for anger, since He is regarded as imposing, arbitrarily, the death sentence. To those who are shocked at her claim that such anger is not only permissible but inevitable, Doctor Ross replies succinctly, "God can take it."

3. *Bargaining*—"Yes me, but. . . ." Patients accept the fact of death but strike bargains for more time. Mostly they bargain with God—"even among people who never talked with God before."

They promise to be good or to do something in exchange for another week or month or year of life. Notes Doctor Ross: "What they promise is totally irrelevant, because they don't keep their promises anyway."

4. *Depression*—"Yes, me." First, the person mourns past losses, things not done, wrongs committed. But then he or she enters a state of "preparatory grief," getting ready for the arrival of death. The patient grows quiet, doesn't want visitors. "When a dying patient doesn't want to see you any more," says Doctor Ross, "this is a sign he has finished his unfinished business with you, and it is a blessing. He can now let go peacefully."

5. *Acceptance*—"My time is very close now and it's all right." Doctor Ross describes this final stage as "not a happy stage, but neither is it unhappy. It's devoid of feelings but it's not resignation, it's really a victory."

These stages provide a very useful guide to understanding the different phases that dying patients may go through. They are not absolute; not everyone goes through every stage, in this exact sequence, at some predictable pace. But this paradigm can, if used in a flexible, insight-producing way, be a valuable tool in understanding why a patient may be behaving as he does.[2]

[2] Summarized by Hans O. Mauksch, "The Organizational Context of Dying," in Elisabeth Kübler-Ross, *Death: The Final Stage of Growth* (Englewood Cliffs, NJ: Prentice-Hall, 1975), p. 10. Used by permission.

Dr. Kübler-Ross has also pointed out that the bereaved normally go through these same stages. How well one handles this grief work, whether before or after the death of a loved one, depends on a number of factors, including personality, training, emotional stability, and religious faith. Healthy grief work is necessary to achieve the position in which a person can accept and find meaning in death.

The title of one of Dr. Kübler-Ross's books, *Death: The Final Stage of Growth*, expresses her conviction that the acceptance of our own death and that of loved ones is ultimately a growing experience wherein we come to recognize the importance of each day of our lives. Growth here means awareness of ourselves and our situation, acceptance of ourselves and others, embracing our own value structures and not merely those of other people, and willingness to share ourselves and our insights with others. Out of this growth, life becomes meaningful just when it seems to have lost all meaning.

> Dying is something we human beings do continuously, not just at the end of our physical lives on this earth. The stages of dying that I have described apply equally to any significant change (e.g., retirement, moving to a new city, changing jobs, divorce) in a person's life, and change is a regular occurrence in human existence. If you can face and understand your ultimate death, perhaps you can learn to face and deal productively with each change that presents itself in your life. Through a willingness to risk the unknown, to venture forth into unfamiliar territory, you can undertake the search for your own self—the ultimate goal of growth. Through reaching out and committing yourself to dialogue with fellow human beings, you can begin to transcend your individual existence, becoming at one with yourself *and* others. And through a lifetime of such commitment, you can face your final end with peace and joy, knowing that you have lived your life well.[3]

> It is the denial of death that is partially responsible for people living empty, purposeless lives; for when you live as if you'll live forever, it becomes too easy to postpone the things you know that you must do. You live your life in preparation for tomorrow or in remembrance of yesterday, and meanwhile, each today is lost. In contrast, when you fully understand that each day you awaken could be the last you have, you take the time *that day* to grow, to become more of who you really are, to reach out to other human beings.[4]

Insights such as these into the meaning of everyday life and the function of death in life have historically been taught by the various religious traditions. As modern society has placed less emphasis on religion for meaning and purpose in life, these insights and the patterns of behavior they cultivate have often been abandoned—now to be rediscovered by psychologists and others who deal with the difficulties that abandonment creates.

The phenomenon of detachment from death and the inability to deal constructively with it is not limited to modern industrial societies. Yet it seems to be most acute in the societies in which medical advances and death patterns have removed family members and friends from the actual death event. In recent years, attempts to counteract this disengagement have arisen in renewed education about death and in such movements as hospice groups, which provide homelike alternatives to hospital deaths for terminally ill patients.

---

[3] Kübler-Ross, *Death*, p. 145.
[4] Ibid., p. 164.

∾

What is your attitude toward death? How have your experiences with death shaped that understanding?

Do you think that the death of the person closest to you could bring growth to your life?

Is Kübler-Ross correct when she says that acceptance of death can mean acceptance of life, making it more meaningful?

UNIT 55   Death and the Afterlife: Cultural Perspectives

Responses to and treatment of death vary among cultures, as seen in the following descriptions. Belief in an afterlife has been almost universal among religious traditions and is often an important feature of cultural attitudes toward death. Although the following examples are drawn from several cultures and their religious traditions, it should be noted that philosophical systems that incorporate monism and pantheism also display a belief in forms of immortality.

Judaism

As Judaism firmly believes in the God-given soul, bestowed pure on every man, it also maintains a firm faith in *Olam Haba*, the world to come. This is not the same as the time of the Messiah, or the Resurrection. It is the sheltering of souls in God's eternal dwelling forever. There they will share the joys of their closeness to the divine glory.

Again, Maimonides [a Jewish philosopher] warns against the formulation of any picture. As we do not know God, we know not what He has in store for us. But Judaism does not devote excessive thought to the question of the "salvation" of souls. "All of Israel will have a share in the world to come." "All the righteous of the peoples of the world have a share in it."[5]

As Leo Trepp suggests, the expectation of a Messiah who would right the evils of the world and of a resurrected state in which good would be triumphant have historically been prominent features of Jewish belief (see Unit 56). Yet many modern Jews reject concepts of an afterlife, believing that the present life is a sufficient field of encounter with God and there is no necessity for continuation. Jewish tradition does not stress doctrinal agreement over such questions.

Christianity

In the light of the Christian gospel death appears both as the penalty of sin and as the means of salvation. As the penalty of sin it brings estrangement from God. Not spatial separation from Him . . . but spiritual and moral remoteness from God which makes the sinner's inability to escape from God a torment. . . .

[5] Leo Trepp, *Judaism: Development and Life* (Belmont, CA: Dickenson Publishing Co., 1966), p. 135.

The death of Christ, the second Adam, transforms death, sin's penalty, into a means of deliverance from its guilt and power. Because Christ "has tasted death for every man," He has made death the gateway into eternal life. The crucified Son of God has drawn the sting of death—which is sin. The believer must still undergo "natural" death, but he has been delivered from "the second death" of final estrangement from God. He lives in newness of life, because by the saving grace of God in Christ *he has learned how to die.*[6]

Hinduism

The Hindu believes in *samsara*, that the present life is the result of previous existences bound by the law of *karma*. The law is based on the causal relationship in which what one does in the present form of existence determines what one will be in the next form of existence (see Figure 12.1). This endless cycle of birth, growth, decay, and death will not be broken until one experiences *moksha*—release from *samsara*. Thus, to one who believes in reincarnation, death is just another phase in the endless cycle of rebirths. "Death is the separation of the soul [Atman] from the physical body; it becomes a starting point for a new life with fresh opportunities. It opens the door for higher forms of life; it is a gateway to fuller life."[7] (See also Unit 10).

Figure 12.1
The wheel is one of the symbols used in Hindu religion and represents the cyclical nature of existence. This is one of a number on the temple of Surya, Konarak, India. (Reproduced with permission of the Hamlyn Group.)

[6] H. F. Lovell Cocks, "Death," *A Handbook of Christian Theology*, ed. Marvin Halverson and Author A. Cohen (New York: World Publishing Co., 1958), p. 73.

[7] Frederick H. Holck, ed., *Death and Eastern Thought* (Nashville, TN: Abingdon Press, 1974), p. 194.

Taoism

Since man is an aspect of Tao, death is but another incident in the eternal movements of nature. It is told of Chuang Tzu that he sang and beat time on a wooden bowl, when his wife lay dead. Reproached for this apparent callousness, he replied that her death was but a change into a new aspect, as fall merges into winter, as a leaf drops from a tree to become leaf mold. For him to grieve over her death would be to show himself ignorant of Tao. In original Taoism, therefore, there is no positive view of life after death, but only the idea of changing into a new aspect of the monistic principle of Tao.[8]

Shintoism

Since one's kami nature will survive death, a man desires to be worthy of being remembered with approbation by his descendants. Therefore it is preferable to die than to fail in duty to one's family or nation. The famous kamikaze pilots of World War II acted on this principle. . . . A kamikaze pilot, by his brave but suicidal action in the national cause, exemplified the height of loyalty to the emperor and his people. He then became an illustrious ancestor, joining the eight hundred myriads of kami beings in the spirit world.[9]

Other religious traditions have similar or unique concepts of rebirth and afterlife. In the various forms of Buddhism, for example, there is a generalized sense that (in a way similar to Hinduism) what one is in one life is transmitted to succeeding lives. With the Buddhist concept of the no-self or nonself, successive rebirths present a series of challenges and tasks since what is transmitted from life to life tends to be the pattern of false and superficial characteristics of the (false) self. The task is to work through, untangle, and eliminate them until the self becomes what it truly is, the nonself. However, there is great diversity within the different varieties of Buddhism, ranging from the teachings of the Japanese Pure Land sect,—that there is life after life in the Great Western Paradise—to the more austere no-self and Nirvana of traditional Buddhism to the esoteric (to most Westerners) teachings of the Tibetan *Book of the Dead.*

UNIT 56   Resurrection and Monotheistic Faith

In Western cultures the reality of death and the emphasis on hope have often been accompanied by the belief in the resurrection of the dead. Resurrection is an ancient concept shared by several Near Eastern religions—among them Judaism and Christianity. In Egypt, Mesopotamia, and Canaan, the seasonal cycle of nature became the basis for religious affirmations of an interconnection between the annual dying and rising of the gods and the natural productivity of the land. The idea of rising from the dead was then part of the common culture that surrounded Israel from its earliest days. It is not surprising to find Hebrew scriptures, depending on an utter confidence in the sovereignty of God, referring

---

[8] Bradley, D.G., *Guide to the World's Religions* (Englewood Cliffs: Prentice Hall, 1982) p. 138. See also Unit 12.

[9] Ibid., p. 154. *Kami* is a Shinto word denoting the spiritual force in all things (see Unit 40).

to dying and rising by God's power (I Samuel 2:6; Deuteronomy 32:39). The story of Elijah's restoration of the life of a widow's son goes further to imply a conception of resurrection, although it is not very clearly developed (I Kings 17:17–24).

The Hebrew idea of resurrection and restoration is most vividly portrayed in the writings of the prophets. Grounding their ideas on God's covenantal promises to sustain and not desert Israel—especially the promise made to uphold David's household—the prophets saw the only hope of their fulfillment in a great day of restoration and renewal. "In that day, I will raise up the booth of David that is fallen and repair its breaches, and raise up its ruins, and rebuild it as in the days of old" (Amos 9:11, RSV). Ezekiel's valley of dry bones (31:1–14) carries the symbolism to the point of restoring dead Israel. From the threat of death and complete extinction, the prophet constantly looks to the day of restoration. In the prophetic treatment, the concept generally remains that of anticipated communal resurrection of Israel as a faithful and blessed community of God.

Death by Jacques Bakke.

After the Israelite exile to Babylon, the concept of resurrection began to change in that the communal restitution was now joined to a belief in the resurrection of the individual. The books of Daniel and the Maccabees, written during a national crisis, when extinction of the community was a clear possibility, contain affirmations of individual resurrection within a communal hope. Here also the concept of a great day of renewal, when all Israel's enemies would be overcome and Israel would be restored, was joined with the idea of a last day of judgment, when each individual would be judged on the basis of his or her faithfulness or unfaithfulness to God. How much this latter concept can be credited to the influence of Persian religion is debatable. It is clear that Persian Zoroastrianism did contain the basic concept of a final great battle of good and evil wherein good would triumph and there would be a general resurrection of the dead. Israelite elaboration on similar concepts came to full fruition in the period after the exile and lengthy contact with the Persian community.

> At that moment Michael shall appear,
> Michael the great captain,
> who stands guard over your fellow-countrymen;
> and there will be a time of distress
> such as has never been . . .
> But at that moment your people will be delivered,
> every one who is written in the book:
> many of those who sleep in the dust of the earth will wake,
> some to everlasting life
> and some to the reproach of eternal abhorrence.
> The wise leaders shall shine
> like the bright vault of heaven,
> and those who have guided the people in the true path
> shall be like the stars for ever and ever.
> (Daniel 12:1–3, NEB)

By the New Testament period, resurrection of both the individual and the community was accepted broadly in the Hebrew community, although not necessarily embraced by all Jews. The attempt of the Sadducees (one of the religious parties that rejected resurrection) to trap Jesus over a question about resurrection illustrates that the concept was disputed during the time of Jesus (Mark 12:18–27).

In Hebrew thought, the body meant the whole person, for no distinction was made between the physical body and the spiritual soul. Resurrection, then, was a resurrection of the entire person. Unlike the Greek concept of an immortal soul, which continued after the death of the physical body, the Hebrew understanding envisioned a renewal—a new beginning—for the person. Immortality was, therefore, not a part of original Hebrew belief. Resurrection did not represent a continuation of life but a renewal made possible only through the grace of God and dependent on his initiation and his sovereignty.

Christianity, arising in the Hebrew milieu, appropriated this belief in both individual and communal resurrection. In Christianity it formed the background for the early church emphasis on the second coming of Christ and became a prominent part of Christian eschatology, as expressed, for example, in the Revelation to John.

However, Christianity did not simply adopt the ancient ideas. The Christian testimony and affirmation that the man Jesus had been resurrected carried the concept to a new and unique dimension. Christianity did not apply resurrection to the distant future but declared that it was now present in history itself. God's sovereignty over life *and* death was evident within historical life as a dynamically different testimony to God's love. The death and then the resurrection became the climactic act in the drama of Jesus's revelation of God's love and power. It served as the central sign of God's power over human sin and over the demons and powers of the universe. Jesus's exaltation, through resurrection, as the Lord of life came to symbolize the new life of a Christian believer. "So you must consider yourselves dead to sin and alive to God in Christ Jesus" (Romans 6:1, RSV). In this central act the Christian saw God's ultimate sovereignty, his gracious love of humankind, and humanity's dependence on his grace. Belief in this unique act carried a new realization of one's own relationship to God and dependence on the love revealed in Jesus's life, death, and resurrection. For the Christian, the concept of resurrection was no longer limited to that which had been accepted by the Jews but was significantly and decisively expanded. It now constituted a new revelation of God's love and therefore became a unique event. Resurrection of Jesus, then, was and is a central precept of ancient and modern Christian belief; it gave new understanding of God and became the basis of Christian trust (faith) in him.

Christianity has also conceptualized Jesus's resurrection as testimony to the reality of the more ancient concepts of resurrection. Jesus's resurrection—an example of God's might, power, and inexhaustible love—has become the touchstone of belief in personal and communal resurrection appropriated from the Jewish culture. (It is interesting that modern Judaism has, to a large degree, rejected the belief in individual resurrection, although the messianic expectation of communal renewal is still widely accepted.) The ancient concepts and the new understanding of resurrection as revealed in Jesus, though distinguishable in Christianity, are closely related. They have occasionally been confused with each other, causing variant understandings to arise.

∼

Why do Christians insist that belief in resurrection is necessary to Christian faith?

For further comments on resurrection, see Paul's commentary in I Corinthians 15 and I Thessalonians 4.

CHAPTER 13

❧

Salvation and Redemption

Introduction

Heaven, Nirvana, enlightenment, wholeness, self-actualization, absorption into the ultimate, concord, reconciliation between humans and God—these and many other terms refer to the ultimate goal, or destiny, of human beings as proclaimed in the various religious traditions. The term *salvation* itself is closely identified with the Christian religious tradition. It connotes a process, event, state of healing, health, fulfillment, and wholeness. But every religion has a concept of wholeness and fulfillment, and most religions stress the need to arrive at this state from one of brokenness or lack or separation.

In this chapter, we examine the concepts of salvation and redemption. They take on rich meaning and variety of use not only among different religious traditions but also within the same tradition. Some aspects of this richness and diversity are explored in the units that follow:

1. The meaning of the concept *salvation*

2. A concept of salvation that is identified with God's grace or divine action

3. Varied expressions, both religious and secular, of the transition from the present "broken" age or world to a new and transformed age or world, a vision that often expresses most fully what *salvation* means.

UNIT 57   Salvation

Salvation is a key term in Christian religious traditions. It has a variety of meanings, which partly depend on particular theological perspectives and specific historical settings. Because of its key role in dominantly Christian societies, it has sometimes been transferred to secular or nonreligious contexts. Whatever the interpretation, however, the concept signifies movement from one state or condition of being—a bad, deficient, inadequate, or "lost" state—to another—a good, fulfilled, adequate, or "saved" state. This movement may be seen as something that is suddenly grasped; or may be an unfolding and developing process, a growth into the new life through new insight or change of character. Whatever the process, salvation implies the belief that something is wrong in the present natural state of human life, that existence has gone askew. Human beings are in a "fallen" or "sinful" state and need restoration to a redeemed or God- or reality-centered state.

Redemption, or restoration, depends on some activity, process, event, or agent that can reorient one's existence. For the Christian, the agent is God's love in Jesus Christ, and the process or event of salvation involves belief and trust in God's mercy given in Christ. Salvation, in this case, means being saved from a destructive self-centeredness through repentance and faith in Jesus Christ.

> It [the gift of Jesus] is the saving power of God for everyone who has faith . . . because here is revealed God's way of righting the wrong, a way that starts from faith and ends in faith. (Romans 1:16–17, NEB)

The *religious* concept of salvation depends generally on action on behalf of an individual or society by God (or the gods). In the Christian tradition this action is denoted by the word *grace*. It is a central concept of the tradition. The basic idea is also found in other, but not in all, religions. For some in the Christian community, God's grace (God's free, unmerited love given to lost and needy humans), which bestows salvation, is understood in an objective sense, primarily signifying the beneficence of God toward the natural order—including humanity—which he has created. This view has been preserved and transmitted within the Roman Catholic tradition, in which grace has often referred to a supernatural substance bestowed on the believer to supplement and complete his or her natural being.

However, some understand grace in a subjective sense. As Hegel points out, a new awareness and concern arose in Europe, and especially Germany, in the late medieval period—the internalization both of guilt and of grace. This development set the stage for the modern Protestant exploration of the meaning of grace. Paul Tillich, in one of the most famous Christian sermons of the twentieth century, explores the idea of grace as inner experience. The sermon is called "You are Accepted" and is found in Tillich's book *The Shaking of the Foundations*. To Tillich the essential experience of God's grace is its presence, experienced—even if the recipient feels totally unworthy, unacceptable, unbelieving, and powerless—by simple acceptance of the fact that one is accepted.

> You are accepted. *You* are accepted, accepted by that which is greater than you, and the name of which you do not know. Do not ask for the name now; perhaps you will find it

later. Do not try to do anything now, perhaps later you will do much. Do not seek for anything, do not perform anything, do not intend anything. Simply accept the fact that you are accepted.[1]

Many Protestants stress an objective as well as a subjective experience of grace, as did Martin Luther, John Calvin, and Tillich himself; but for Luther and Tillich the subjective experience is crucial. Many Protestents also stress, in contrast to Tillich, a need to strive actively for the subjective sense of grace, the assurance of salvation, as John Wesley did, though Wesley also stressed the need to perform "good works" (though they did not bring either the assurance or the reality of salvation) while seeking the assurance of grace.

As we have seen, the term *salvation* as a process or event of being made whole is stressed in Christianity. However, the concept itself is not limited to Christianity but is found in one form or another in other religions, as the following example illustrates.

> The transcendental vibration established by the chanting of Hare Krishna, Hare Krishna, Krishna Krishna, Hare Hare/Hare Rāma, Hare Rāma, Rāma Rāma, Hare Hare is the sublime method for reviving our transcendental consciousness. As living spiritual souls, we are all originally Krishna conscious entities, but due to our association with matter from time immemorial, our consciousness is now adulterated by the material atmosphere. The material atmosphere, in which we are now living, is called *māyā*, or illusion. *Māyā* means that which is not. And what is this illusion? The illusion is that we are all trying to be lords of material nature, while actually we are under the grip of her stringent laws. . . . We are trying to exploit the resources of material nature, but actually we are becoming more and more entangled in her complexities. Therefore, although we are engaged in a hard struggle to conquer nature, we are ever more dependent on her. This illustory struggle against nature can be stopped at once by revival of our eternal Krishna consciousness.
>
> Hare Krishna, Hare Krishna, Krishna Krishna, Hare Hare is the transcendental process for reviving this original pure consciousness. By chanting this transcendental vibration, we can cleanse away all misgivings within our hearts. The basic principle of all such misgivings is the false consciousness that I am the lord of all I survey.[2]

For the Hindu, the movement from *maya* (illusion) to *moksha* (release from the cycle of rebirths), and for the Buddhist, the movement from bondage to destructive desire to Nirvana signify salvation, or fulfillment. Concepts of salvation appear even in secular movements and ideologies. The Marxist concept of a classless society in which there will be no oppression and in which there will be equality, material plenty, and freedom for all is an example. In Nazi Germany the concept of the thousand-year reich in which the Aryan master race would rule the world is another.

Objective and subjective understandings of what God's grace is and how it brings salvation are usually combined in Christian traditions. Grace is usually thought of as something real (objective) that God bestows either directly or through agencies he has created (the church, preaching, the sacraments). It is also usually held to be accompanied by a personal (subjective) awareness on the recipient's part. Some Christian traditions (Roman Catholic, for example, and some Protestant) have stressed the need for a cooper-

---

[1] Excerpts from *The Shaking of the Foundations*, pp. 155–56, and 160–63, by Paul Tillich are reprinted with the permission of Charles Scribner's Sons. Copyright 1948 Charles Scribner's Sons.

[2] A. C. Bhaktvedanta Swami Prabhupada, *On Chanting the Hare Krishna Mantra* (Boston: Iskcon Press, n.d.), p. 5.

ative response to God's grace (even if God has in some sense previously provided grace to enable the response). Others (especially Lutheran and Calvinist traditions) have insisted that God's grace *and* a human response to it are entirely a gift from God and that it is misleading to speak of the cooperation of those who can only passively receive. Whatever a particular Christian's definition of grace, it represents the power of God acting within life, transforming the life of the believer.

A similar concept of the graciousness of the Divine is found in those forms of Hinduism that stress reliance on the gods Vishnu and Shiva for assistance in attaining release from reincarnation. For the Mahayana Buddhist, the role of the *Bodhisattva* suggests a form of gracious love benefiting the believer in the journey toward Nirvana. Muslim and Jewish tradition incorporate similar concepts whereby salvation is dependent on God's gracious love. Even in polytheistic religions, there is frequently a concept of grace as the special unbidden, unmerited state bestowed on some individual or group by a god or goddess. A kind of grace, or healing and restoring power, may be conferred by the impersonal (divine) nature of things. This is exemplified in some of the Greek tragedies: Oedipus, after terrible suffering in expiation of a fate-ordained violation of the order of nature (by murdering his father and marrying his mother), became a source of blessing (grace) to those among whom he resided.

Unit 58   Eschatology: The Coming Fulfillment

The supreme vision of what salvation—health, wholeness, fulfillment, well-being—means in a religious or secular tradition may often be seen in its *eschatology*, literally "a study of last things." In Christian tradition it includes doctrines dealing with the end of history—both the termination and transformation of history as we know it—as well as such concepts as the second coming of Christ, resurrection of the dead, immortality of the soul, final judgment, and Heaven and Hell.

For some, Christian eschatology may be focused primarily on the destiny of individuals (the soul, what happens after death). Ordinarily, however, eschatology is centered not only on the ultimate fate of individuals in relation to good and evil and God's ultimate power but also on the ultimate destiny of the whole human race and of the cosmos. Thus, Christian eschatology reflects the earlier Jewish apocalyptic tradition, which, especially from about 170 B.C.E. until the second destruction of Jerusalem by the Romans in C.E. 135, was expressed in apocalyptic works. *Apocalypse* means "revelation," and apocalyptic writings of Judaism depict in highly symbolic form a particular moment in time in which the dominant forces of evil will be defeated by the power of God. The struggle is foreseen as bitter and intense, frequently involving terrible suffering of humans, both evil and good (those who remained faithful to God in spite of terrible persecution). The results of the struggle would be a complete, decisive, and final triumph of God and the forces of good, a cosmological victory that would end in the transition from the old, evil order of things in our world to a new and perfect realm under God's justice. Salvation would be finally real: The faithful would be vindicated and the evil judged and rendered powerless and ineffectual.

Although such an understanding of eschatology is familiar in Christian, Jewish, and Islamic traditions, it is only one pattern of eschatological thought. The following sections present religious as well as secular eschatological concepts and beliefs about human and cosmic salvation.

A New Society

Throughout history there have arisen both religious and secular groups whose dissatisfaction with what they believe to be an unjust society has led them to anticipate its dissolution and its replacement by a new, more just arrangement of social opportunities. In the nineteenth century, many American and English "communitarians" formed separated communities, often anticipating the millennium when Jesus would return to earth to establish a just and perfect society: the Shakers (so called for their incorporation of sacred dance in their worship services), German pietist groups such as the Ephrata Community in Pennsylvania, and the Church of the Latter Day Saints (Mormons). Similar groups espousing various patterns of socialism, sometimes undergirded by religious principles, organized communalistic utopian groups, the most famous of which were New Harmony in Indiana, the Oneida Community in central New York, and Brook Farm in Massachusetts. Much of the philosophical base for these groups and their advertisement of themselves included evangelistic eschatological statements; each group offered salvation from an evil world.

Such associations generally sought transformation only for those who joined their group. The general societies that surrounded them were considered beyond transformation, so they formed idealized and separated communities. In this same period, however, others were also envisioning fundamental societal change.

Although maintaining that their work was scientific rather than utopian and rejecting religion, Karl Marx and Friedrich Engels, writing in mid-nineteenth-century England, used many eschatological images and patterns to define communism. According to Marx, a vigorous struggle was underway between the forces of the workers and those of the capitalists, a struggle he expected to be soon completed. The success of the struggle against "the capitalist yoke" and the "world ruled by violence" was for communists already apparent, with final victory on the horizon. The vision of the "new world, a world of freedom" in which "those who have nothing will inherit the earth," was a bright hope that the adherents of this view looked toward with eager longing. True to the eschatological perspective, the affirmation was also a challenge to renewed action and dedication. This communistic eschatology is clearly articulated in the words of the "Communist Internationale":

> Arise, you wretched and downtrodden
> Hungry, enslaved masses of the earth.
> Our outraged spirits cry out:
> We are ready to fight to the end
> To destroy the world ruled by violence.
> We will build a new world,
> Our world of freedom.
> Those who are nothing
>   will inherit the earth.

Similar eschatological perspectives are found in the writings of Mao Tse-Tung, the leader of Chinese communism:

> People of the world, unite and defeat the . . . aggressors and all their running dogs! People of the world, be courageous, dare to fight, defy difficulties and advance wave upon wave. Then the world will belong to the people. Monsters of all kinds shall be destroyed.[3]

> The wealth of society is created by the workers, peasants and working individuals. If they take their destiny into their own hands, follow a Marxist-Leninist line and take an active attitude in solving problems instead of evading them, there will be no difficulty in the world which they cannot overcome.[4]

The failure of Russian communism to achieve a classless society and the dissolving of communism as a political alternative in the Soviet Union have not meant the complete rejection of many of the eschatological teachings of Marx. Although Chinese communism is rapidly changing as it responds to international market forces, the eschato-

(by Jacques Bakke)

---

[3] Mao Tse-Tung, *Quotations from Chairman Mao Tse-Tung* (New York: Bantam Books, 1967), p. 44.
[4] Ibid., p. 112.

logical visions of Mao still play an important role in the organization and future goals of the society. The Marxist critique of an elitist capitalism and the vision, often stated in eschatological terms, of an equitable economic distribution of scarce natural resources among all peoples has become part of much Christian liberation theology, especially in Latin America.

Protest

The civil rights movement in the United States drew on three powerful sources for its strength and impetus: the affirmations of the Constitution and of the Jewish and Christian faiths concerning the rights and dignity of individuals. Martin Luther King, committed to nonviolent love, was aware that he was involved in a life-and-death struggle. The sense of imminent victory and the vision of a day of fulfillment implicit in the eschatological perspective are apparent in the statement that follows. This sense of approaching triumph was even more intense when the speech was delivered at the civil rights march on Washington in August 1963. Approximately 200,000 persons gathered on the Mall between the Washington Monument and the Lincoln Memorial to demonstrate peacefully in support of pending civil rights legislation. To the outside observer, it seemed that there were many people involved, but the event was nothing extraordinary. To the person inside the civil rights movement, however, it was a tremendous sign of the strength of the movement and its fast-approaching victory.

> I say to you today, my friends, even though we face the difficulties of today and tomorrow, I still have a dream. It is a dream deeply rooted in the American dream.
> I have a dream that one day this nation will rise up and live out the true meaning of its creed: "We hold these truths to be self-evident; that all men are created equal."
> I have a dream that one day on the red hills of Georgia the sons of former slaves and the sons of former slaveowners will be able to sit down together at the table of brotherhood.
> I have a dream that one day even the state of Mississippi, a state sweltering with the heat of injustice, sweltering with the heat of oppression, will be transformed into an oasis of freedom and justice.
> I have a dream that my four little children will one day live in a nation where they will not be judged by the color of their skin but by the content of their character.
> I have a dream today.
> I have a dream that one day, down in Alabama, with its vicious racists, with its Governor having his lips dripping with the words of interposition and nullification, one day right there in Alabama little black boys and little black girls will be able to join hands with little white boys and white girls as sisters and brothers.
> I have a dream today.
> I have a dream that one day every valley shall be exalted, every hill and mountain shall be made low, the rough places will be made plain, and the crooked places will be made straight, and the glory of the Lord shall be revealed, and all flesh shall see it together.
> This is our hope. This is the faith with which I return to the South. With this faith we will be able to hew out of this mountain of despair a stone of hope. With this faith we will be able to transform the jangling discords of our nation into a beautiful symphony of brotherhood. With this faith we will be able to work together, to pray together, to struggle together, to go to jail together, to stand up for freedom together, knowing that we will be free one day. . . .

Let freedom ring from every hill and molehill of Mississippi. From every mountainside, let freedom ring. And when this happens—when we let freedom ring, when we let it ring from every village and every hamlet, from every state and every city, we will be able to speed up that day when all of God's children, black men and white men, Jews and Gentiles, Protestants and Catholics, will be able to join hands and sing in the words of the old Negro spiritual, "Free at last! free at last! thank God almighty, we are free at last!"[5]

Transformation of Consciousness

During the mid- and late 1960s, many Americans, especially the young, became convinced that their society was dominated by oppressive political and economic power. They protested America's prosecution of a war in Vietnam; the continued denial of equal rights to all Americans, especially blacks; and attitudes of thoughtless greed on the part of large corporations, resulting in pollution of the environment. Some became convinced that America could be saved by a transformation of consciousness, changing attitudes of selfishness, aggression, and greed to those of peacefulness and love. This notion was expressed in a book that quickly became a best-seller, *The Greening of America*, written by a Yale law school professor.[6] It probably found its most popular and effective expression in the words and music of a successful folk-rock musical called *Hair*, which was later made into a powerful film, dramatizing protest against the Vietnam war; racial discrimination; and subordination of the individual, especially the young, to harsh and puritanical moral and economic restrictions by an uncaring, older establishment. The song "Aquarius" captures what many of the young involved in "the movement" of the 1960s believed and shows how, often indiscriminately, sources of salvation were sought—in reinterpretations of traditional religious figures (Jesus, Gautama) and their teachings, in commonly rejected sources of spiritual insight (astrology), in drugs and rock music and free sexual expression as sources of consciousness transformation. In the eyes of many of the younger and some of the older generation of that time, institutionalized religion, especially Christianity and Judaism, had failed to protest the wrongs of society, indeed frequently had given moral support to war and racial injustice. "Aquarius" thus brought to bear a semireligious world view—astrology—in support of longed-for social and individual experiences.

When the moon is in the seventh house,
and Jupiter aligns with Mars,
Then peace will guide the planets
and love will steer the stars.

This is the dawning of the Age of Aquarius,
The Age of Aquarius, Aquarius, Aquarius.

Harmony and Understanding,
sympathy and trust abounding,
No more falsehoods or derisions,
golden living dreams of visions,

---

[5] Martin Luther King, Jr., "I Have a Dream." Reprinted by arrangement with The Heirs to The Estate of Martin Luther King, Jr., c/o Joan Daves Agency as agent for the proprietor. Copyright 1963 by Martin Luther King, Jr., Copyright renewed 1991 by Coretta Scott King. Copyright 1968 by The Estate of Martin Luther King, Jr.

[6] Charles A. Reich, *The Greening of America* (New York: Random House, 1970).

Mystic crystal revelation
   and the mind's true liberation,
Aquarius, Aquarius.

When the moon is in the seventh house
   and Jupiter aligns with Mars,
Then peace will guide the planets
   and love will steer the stars.

This is the dawning of the Age of Aquarius,
The Age of Aquarius, Aquarius, Aquarius
   Aquarius, Aquarius, Aquarius.[7]

Jewish Prophecy

For Jeremiah, like the prophets before him and the apocalyptic thinkers who came afterward, history was the arena in which God was at work. The purpose of his activity was the creation of a redeemed, responsive people. Yet Jeremiah believed that the history of the Hebrew nation had become the history of a continuing conflict between God and many of the people. This could not continue. Jeremiah had spent his life delivering, though reluctantly and sometimes almost bitterly, the word from God concerning his judgment. He told the people of Judah that God's judgment was against them. He prophesied an invasion of Judah from the north. Few believed him because the King of Judah had surrounded himself with false prophets of optimism who said that all was well with God's people.

Suddenly, after the destruction of Jerusalem in 598 B.C.E. and before its devastation in 587 B.C.E. by the Babylonians, everybody believed him. And just as suddenly the word of God changed from doom to hope. Jeremiah announced God's decision to fulfill his ancient purpose in the times to come. The "old" covenant would be perfected by a "new" covenant written within the heart, and God's purpose behind the old would become a reality in the new—"I will be their God, and they shall be my people." The struggle between faithful God and unfaithful people, which had infected the life of humankind and nature, would be resolved, and the Jewish nation would fully become that which God had intended: the faithful wife of a compassionate "husband."

> Behold, the days are coming, says the Lord, when I will sow the house of Israel and the house of Judah with the seed of man and the seed of beast. And it shall come to pass that as I have watched over them to pluck up and break down, to overthrow, destroy, and bring evil, so I will watch over them to build and to plant, says the Lord.
>
> In those days they shall no longer say: "The fathers have eaten sour grapes, and the children's teeth are set on edge." But everyone shall die for his own sin; each man who eats sour grapes, his teeth shall be set on edge.
>
> Behold, the days are coming, says the Lord, when I will make a new covenant with the house of Israel and the house of Judah, not like the covenant which I made with their fathers when I took them by the hand to bring them out of the land of Egypt, my covenant which they broke, though I was their husband, says the Lord. But this is the covenant

---

[7] "Aquarius" © 1966, 1967, 1968 James Rado, Gerome Ragni, Galt MacDermot, Nat Shapiro, and United Artists Music Co., Inc. All rights administered by United Artists Music Co. Inc. Used by permission.

which I will make with the house of Israel after those days, says the Lord: I will put my law within them, and I will write it upon their hearts; and I will be their God, and they shall be my people. And no longer shall each man teach his neighbor and each his brother, saying "Know the Lord," for they shall all know me, from the least of them to the greatest, says the Lord; for I will forgive their iniquity, and I will remember their sin no more. (Jeremiah 31:27–34, RSV)

Islamic Vision

The following passage from the Qu'ran is an example of one of the most common types of eschatology, one that looks for an end to the present existence and something totally new in the times to come.

Muhammad clearly announced the coming of a day of judgment by Allah, when the earth and all creation would be shaken and Allah would sit on his Throne. The judgment would follow, each person being rewarded or punished in accord with his or her actions in this world.

Muhammad had declared in pronouncements found elsewhere in Muslim scriptures that this life is a time of testing, when people must choose between submission to Allah and the doing of his will and following the way of Satan, the rebel against the All-Merciful. This struggle between the forces of good and evil, of righteousness and sin, inevitably and unalterably will end with the assertion of Allah's sovereignty and power. The wise person chooses and lives by the will of Allah and lives this life in awareness of the new life to come.

> So, when the Trumpet is blown with a single blast
> and the earth and the mountains are lifted up and crushed with a single
>   blow,
> then, on that day, the Terror shall come to pass,
> and heaven shall split, for upon that day it shall be very frail,
> and the angels shall stand upon its borders,
> and upon that day eight shall carry above them
> the Throne of the Lord.
> On that day you shall be exposed, not one secret of yours concealed.
> Then as for him who is given his book in his right hand,
> he shall say, "Here, take and read my book!
> Certainly I thought that I should encounter my reckoning." So he
>   shall be in a pleasing life
>   in a lofty Garden,
>   its clusters nigh to gather.
> "Eat and drink with wholesome appetite for that
> you did long ago, in the days gone by."
>
> But as for him who is given his book in his left hand,
> he shall say, "Would that I had not been given my book and not known
>   my reckoning! Would it had been the end!
>   My wealth has not availed me,
>   my authority is gone from me."
> Take him, and fetter him, and then roast him
> in Hell, then in a chain of seventy cubits' length
> insert him! Behold, he never believed in God

the All-mighty, and he never urged the feeding
of the needy; therefore he today has not here
one loyal friend, neither any food saving foul pus,
that none excepting the sinners eat.[8]

Early Christian Eschatology

Written some five hundred years before the ministry of Muhammad, the following passage also looks forward to the complete and final end of this world and the coming
of a new, splendid creation. Although Muhammad may have envisioned a complete
reordering of this creation, the author of the Revelation to John thought it beyond reno-
vation. This work articulates apocalyptic eschatology at its fullest. The author saw in the
historical events just before and during his time the implementation in human experience
of the cosmic, age-old plan and purpose of God. People and nations were caught up in the
pervasive struggle between God and Satan, Christ and Anti-Christ, the saints and the
wicked. Convinced that God had revealed to him the secrets of his purpose and activity,
he interpreted for his fellow Christians the hidden, "real" meaning of what appeared to be
ordinary, worldly events. And then would come the end—very shortly.

The portrayal of the end of the present heaven and earth is bluntly stated, followed by the resurrection and the judgment. But the author quickly passes to his real interest—the glorious new existence that is to come. In the new heaven and the new earth, the
"sea"—which in Jewish literature had come to stand for all that threatens human life—
would be no more. The covenant promise to ancient Israel would be fulfilled, not within
but beyond history. God—the beginning and the end of all things—would make it so.

Then I saw a great white throne
and him who sat upon it;
from his presence earth and sky fled away,
    and no place was found for them.
And I saw the dead, great and small,
    standing before the throne,
and books were opened.
Also another book was opened,
    which is the book of life.
And the dead were judged by what was written
in the books, by what they had done.
And the sea gave up the dead in it, Death and
Hades gave up the dead in them, and all were
judged by what they had done.
Then Death and Hades were thrown into the
lake of fire. This is the second death,
the lake of fire; and if any one's name was
not found written in the book of life, he
was thrown into the lake of fire.
Then I saw a new heaven and a new earth;
for the first heaven and the first earth

---

[8] Reprinted with permission of Macmillan, Inc., from *The Koran Interpreted* by Arthur J. Arberry, Sura
LXIX, verses 13–37. © George Allen & Unwin, Ltd. 1955.

had passed away,
and the sea was no more.
And I saw the holy city, new Jerusalem,
coming down out of heaven from God,
    prepared as a bride adorned for her husband;
and I heard a great voice from the throne saying,
    "Behold, the dwelling of God is with men.
    He will dwell with them,
    and they shall be his people,
    and God himself will be with them;
    he will wipe away every tear from their eyes,
    and death shall be no more.
    neither shall there be mourning nor crying
        nor pain any more,
    for the former things have passed away." . . .
And he said to me,
    "It is done!
    I am the Alpha and the Omega,
        the beginning and the end."
(The Revelation to John 20:11–21:4, 6, RSV)

～

Some Christian religious groups have almost completely ignored eschatological elements in the earlier Christian traditions; other groups—for instance, the Jehovah's Witnesses—have made them their dominant concern. Why do some religious traditions emphasize eschatological salvation as a universal, cosmic event and others do not?

In traditions emphasizing mystical religion, eschatology often takes the form of inner subjective fulfillment, union, or communion with the Divine rather than looking to a fulfilling future historical state. What forms of eschatology—visions of a fulfilled or perfected state of being involving all or most humans and the future world—other than those presented here, can you think of?

CHAPTER 14

❧

The Religious Matrix
of Interpersonal Relations

Introduction

In the preceding section, we have examined the self and the dimensions of religion that affect its sense of identity, its selfhood. Now we move to a discussion of the sociocultural setting that profoundly affects the way people define what selfhood means. The social setting of the self is important both for the sense of personal identity and for the religious dimensions of the self's experiences. Competing codes of morality and definitions of truth, competing scientific systems, and competing systems of religious beliefs and practices will be offered to the individual by the culture that the individual participates in, inherits, belongs to, or inhabits.

Religion—every religion, even the religion of a tiny minority—is a social phenomenon, and culture is a social product. Religion is a part of culture. Some anthropologists have defined culture as "the social heritage . . . the sum of the historical achievements of human social life transmitted in the form of a tradition."[1] According to this definition, the term *culture* refers to the things a society teaches the individuals who are members of that society. Culture then is something already existing that individuals absorb or passively acquire.

Other students of human behavior have questioned this definition of culture. The anthropologist David Bidney holds that humans are active creators and transformers

---

[1] David Bidney, *Theoretical Anthropology* (New York: Columbia University Press, 1953), p. 25.

of culture.[2] And the sociologists Peter Berger and Thomas Luckmann write, "Society is a human product. Society is an objective reality. Man is a social product."[3] Berger and Luckmann emphasize here that humans are created by their societies and the cultures of those societies but that ultimately the societies and cultures are created by actual, specific, individual human beings interacting with other human beings. According to this view, culture is not just something handed down from generation to generation: Each person, in interaction with other people—in interaction with the whole of society during that person's life's span—creates culture by acquiring and transforming it.

To see the connectedness of selves in society is not sufficient. We need to analyze various ways in which religious commitment enters the process of individual and group interaction. In this chapter, we consider general dimensions of individual and group, and of group and group, interaction, as well as ethical dimensions. Also, we examine the role of religion in promoting social stability, as an agent of social change, and as affected by social change.

Our concern in this chapter is to explore the context in which the self relates to other selves. Every self finds itself defined in interpersonal relationships with other selves. One is neither born nor lives in a vacuum. Most of daily living consists of interpersonal relationships with others, so the interaction among individuals is a significant element in our understanding of ourselves and our society. The units in this chapter focus on ethical issues that arise as a person relates to others—primarily on the way the individual relates to other individuals. The discussion of ethical issues involving relationships between groups will be considered in the next chapter.

The first unit deals with the tension or dynamic interplay that exists between an individual and his or her community. We then turn to an exploration of love and duty as two approaches to personal involvement in a community. Finally, we examine the connection between particular actions and the motivations for those actions.

The phrase *religious matrix* in the title of this chapter refers to the creative power of religion to give meaning to relationships between the self and others.

UNIT 59   The Individual and the Community

In the modern world the desire to preserve individual identity is seldom exactly and delicately balanced with the concurrent necessity to participate in corporate life. Each changing moment tilts the balance one way or the other, and many feel that life results in a frightening and often disorienting seesaw as we try to be ourselves in an increasingly complex world. Historically, humans seeking to escape such disorientation have emphasized one aspect of identity over the other. An emphasis on either pole reflects a particular understanding of the human role in the natural order. These interpretations of humanity in turn reflect religious beliefs or perceptions that are often illustrated in secular and religious literature.

---

[2] Ibid.

[3] Peter L. Berger and Thomas Luckmann, *The Social Construction of Reality* (Garden City, NY: Doubleday, 1966), p. 58.

William Ernest Henley, writing in the late nineteenth century, reflects the extreme individualism of the period, the roots of which reach back at least into the eighteenth century.

> Out of the night that covers me,
>   Black as the Pit from pole to pole,
> I thank whatever gods may be
>   For my unconquerable soul.
>
> In the fell clutch of circumstance
>   I have not winced nor cried aloud.
> Under the bludgeonings of chance
>   My head is bloody, but unbowed.
>
> Beyond this place of wrath and tears
>   Looms but the Horror of the shade,
> And yet the menace of the years
>   Finds, and shall find, me unafraid.
>
> It matters not how strait the gate,
>   How charged with punishments the scroll,
> I am the master of my fate;
>   I am the captain of my soul.[4]

Henley's poem emphasizes the individual's capability to determine his or her life. Little room is left for the influence of other persons and society, or for any Divine influence. For Henley, the "gods," if there be any, clearly have no final or pervasive control over life or the future: It is the individual who determines his or her own fate.

> Some thirty inches from my nose
> The frontier of my Person goes,
> And all the untilled air between
> Is private *pagus* or demesne.
> Stranger, unless with bedroom eyes,
> I beckon you to fraternize,
> Beware of rudely crossing it:
> I have no gun, but I can spit.[5]

In this brief poem, W. H. Auden also stresses the need to be an individual—everyone must have one's own space, one's own being. Yet he recognizes the concurrent reality: No individual is alone, is an island unto himself or herself; an individual is always part of some community. Although one may be responsible for maintaining personal identity in a community, one can never escape the reality of the social character of human existence.

Because of this social nature of humanity, many people put the interests, goals, and purposes of the community over those of the individual. Personal fulfillment in life does not necessarily depend on what one accrues but rather on one's contribution to the

---

[4] William Ernest Henley, "Invictus," *Poems* (New York: Scribner, 1919), p. 119.

[5] W. H. Auden, "Thanksgiving for a Habitat," *About the House* (New York: Random House, 1963), p. 4. Copyright © 1965. Reprinted by permission of Random House, Inc.

community. This interpretation led Mo-ti, an early Chinese moral philosopher, to insist that the needs of a community overarch and encompass those of an individual:

> Mo-ti said: The purpose of the magnanimous is to be found in procuring benefits for the world and eliminating its calamities.
> But what are the benefits of the world and what its calamities?
> Mo-ti said: Mutual attacks among states, mutual usurpation among houses, mutual injuries among individuals; the lack of grace and loyalty between ruler and ruled, the lack of affection and filial piety between father and son, the lack of harmony between elder and younger brothers—these are the major calamities in the world.
> But whence did these calamities arise, out of mutual love?
> Mo-ti said: They arise out of want of mutual love. At present feudal lords have learned only to love their own states and not those of others. Therefore they do not scruple about attacking other states. The heads of houses have learned only to love their own houses and not those of others. Therefore they do not scruple about usurping other houses. And individuals have learned only to love themselves and not others. . . . Therefore all the calamities, strifes, complaints, and hatred in the world have arisen out of the want of mutual love. . . .
> But what is the way of universal love and mutual aid?
> Mo-ti said: It is to regard the state of others as one's own, the houses of others as one's own, the persons of others as one's self. When feudal lords love one another there will be no more war; when heads of houses love one another there will be no more mutual usurpation; when individuals love one another there will be no more mutual injury.[6]

The ideal of social responsibility noted in Mo-ti's comments incorporates a consciousness of the self that in reality becomes the basis for relationships in the community. One does not lose one's identity in the community, but the needs of others are as important as or more important than one's own. Reinhold Niebuhr, a twentieth-century American Christian theologian, goes a step further when he maintains that love of one's fellow humans is a basic law of humanity demanded by the social character of human existence:

> [Another] source of religious vitality is derived from the social character of human existence; from the fact that men cannot be themselves or fulfill themselves within themselves, but only in an affectionate and responsible relation to their fellows. It is this fact, rather than the fiat of any scripture, which makes the law of love the basic law for man. The law is not of purely religious origin, and indeed it is not necessary to be religious to ascertain its validity.[7]

Niebuhr's suggestion assumes that an individual *only* lives purposefully and completely in interaction with others.

The contrast between positions as diverse as those of Henley and Niebuhr is obvious. Most major religious traditions agree with the insights of Mo-ti and Niebuhr that the needs of others (the community) take precedence over the wants and needs of the individual and that an individual cannot find fulfillment solely in the self.

---

[6] Mo-ti, "Universal Love II," *The Wisdom of China and India*, trans. Y. P. Mie, ed. Lin Yutang (New York: Random House, 1942), pp. 794–95.

[7] Reinhold Niebuhr, "The Religious Situation in America," *Religion and Contemporary Society*, ed. Harold Stahmer (New York: Macmillan, 1963), p. 146.

∽

Is it possible to achieve a meaningful balance between the individual and the society? Is it necessary to achieve such a balance? Why?

Which of the positions is closer to your own understanding? Why?

What value is there in each of the positions?

UNIT 60   Love and Duty

Although there are people whose self-image is uniquely individualistic and perhaps anti-social, most people find genuine fulfillment in their social relationships. The forms of involvement with others are multitudinous, but there are discernible patterns of response that tell us much about basic life attitudes and assumptions (both conscious and unconscious).

Among the many ways people relate to others and to society, two patterns are central: love and duty. In every culture, affection (love) and a sense of responsibility (duty) motivate responses to others. Love and duty often complement and support each other in daily life, but they may also be a cause of anxiety and conflict. Many times one must balance their demands, occasionally selecting one over the other. This process is often unconscious, yet it reflects basic personal assumptions about the nature of life.

Love by its very nature expresses the content of a relationship between two individuals; consequently, it is often understood to express a social attitude that begins with the individual. Although it may not be limited to one individual and may incorporate many people or a group, it usually begins with the concern of one person for another. In love one begins with the self and moves toward the other—love bridges the gap between. In this movement, the individual will and its encounter, assessment, and acceptance or rejection of another is primary to all other considerations.

Duty, in contrast, begins with the sense of responsibility for or to the other. It is the other, often the corporate group itself, that defines one's duties or responsibilities. By performing one's duties, one finds fulfillment as a part of the larger whole; therefore society—expressed in the family, village, caste, or modern industrial society—is the central focus of life. People achieve significance as they perform their duties within the larger community.

The contrast between the approach of love based on individual affection and that of duty based on social responsibility is obvious. They are both present in daily personal life and in all cultures. Sometimes they are delicately balanced and sometimes one dominates the other. Preliterate and Eastern cultures, with their emphasis on society and the family as the primary unit of human life, often stress duty to the society before personal affection. In contrast, modern Western culture, based on a belief in a personal God and his relationship to individuals, puts personal relationships and accomplishments first and tends to idealize love as the central pattern of human relationships. Illustrations of both positions and their interconnection abound in the literature of both East and West.

Love

Charlie Brown's incredulous response to a love that continues to offer itself even to the unloving suggests an insight into the unlimited nature of love (see Figure 14.1).

Christian teachings about the nature of love are found in the following comments of Jesus:

> And behold, a lawyer stood up to put him to the test, saying "Teacher, what shall I do to inherit eternal life?" He said to him, "What is written in the law? How do you read?" And he answered, "You shall love the Lord your God with all your heart, and strength, and with all your mind; and your neighbor as yourself." And he said to him, "You have answered right, do this, and you shall live." (Luke 10:25–28, RSV)

> But I say to you that hear, Love your enemies, do good to those who hate you, bless those who curse you, pray for those who abuse you. To him who strikes you on the cheek, offer the other also; and from him who takes away your cloak do not withhold your coat as well. Give to everyone who begs from you; and of him who takes away your goods do not ask them again. And as you wish that men do to you, do so to them. (Luke 6:27–31 RSV)

In Mahayana Buddhism (see Unit 11), the ideal human is a *Bodhisattva*—one who has come close to Nirvana yet delays entrance into that state to lead others compassionately (lovingly) toward it. This compassion is overwhelming and all-consuming.

Figure 14.1   *Peanuts* by Charles Schulz (© 1970 United Features Syndicate, Inc.)

A Bodhisattva resolves: *I take upon myself the burden of suffering,* I am resolved to do so, I will endure it. . . . *I have made the vow to save all beings.* All beings I must set free. The whole world of living beings I must rescue, from the terrors of birth, of old age, of sickness, of death and rebirth, of all kinds of moral offence, of all states of woe, of the whole cycle of birth-and-death, of the jungle of false views, of the loss of wholesome dharmas, of the concomitants of ignorance,—from all these terrors I must rescue all beings. . . . And I must not cheat all beings out of my store of merit. I am resolved to abide in each single state of woe for numberless aeons; and so I will help all beings to freedom, in all the states of woe that may be found in any world system whatsoever. (Sikshasamuccaya, 280–81, *Vajradhvaja Sutra*)

Duty

India's ancient caste system was founded on the principle that each person finds a productive place in society by performing the proper duties of one's caste. To break caste is to destroy self and society. (Modern developments have modified the rigidity of the caste system somewhat, but ancient concepts are slow to change and it is still highly influential.) The following passage is taken from the *Puranas* (c.350):

He best worships Vishnu who observes the duties laid down by scripture for every caste and condition of life; there is no other mode. . . .

The Brahmana [member of priestly caste] must advance the well-being of all and do injury to none—for the greatest wealth of a Brahmana consists in cherishing kind feelings towards all. He must consider with an equal eye the jewel and stone belonging to another. . . .

The duties of the Kshatriya [member of warrior caste] consist in making gifts to the Brahmanas at pleasure, in worshiping Vishnu with various sacrifices and receiving instruction from the preceptor. His principal sources of maintenance are arms and protection of the earth. But his greatest duty consists in guarding the earth. By protecting the earth a king attains his objects, for he gets a share of the merit of all sacrifices. If a king, by maintaining the order of caste, represses the wicked, supports the pious, he proceeds to whatever region he desires.

The Father of Creation has assigned to the Vaisyas [members of the merchant caste], for their maintenance, the feeding of the cattle, commerce, and agriculture. Study, sacrifice, and gift are also within the duties of the Vaisyas: besides these, they may also observe the other fixed and occasional rites.

The Sudra [member of the servant caste] must maintain himself by attending upon the three higher castes, or by the profits of trade, or the earnings of mechanical labour. He may also make gifts, offer the sacrifices in which food is presented, and he may also make obsequial offerings.

Besides these, the four castes have their other duties, namely—the acquisition of wealth for the support of servants, cohabitation with their wives for the sake of children, kindness towards all creatures, patience, humility, truth, purity, contentment, decorum of manners, gentleness of speech, friendliness, freedom from envy or avarice and the habit of vilifying. These also constitute the duties of every condition of life.[8]

Traditional Chinese culture has been built on the principle of "filial piety" (respect, honor, and obedience to one's family and ancestors). One lives fully and com-

---

[8] Excerpts from *The Vishnu Purana,* trans. H. H. Wilson, ed. M. N. Dutt (Calcutta, 1894), as cited in Lewis Browne, *The World's Great Scriptures* (New York: Macmillan, 1946), pp. 121–22.

pletely by performing all of one's proper duties to family and society. The principle of *shu*, or reciprocity, spelled out by Confucius, forms the basis of these proper relationships.

> Tzu-kung asked, saying, "Is there one word which may serve as a rule of practice for all one's life?" The Master said, "Is not Reciprocity [shu] such a word? What you do not want done to yourself, do not do to others.[9]

Confucius made this principle the basis of the widely known Five Relationships. In each set of relationships, one's duty or responsibility to the other is central to a proper and fulfilling life.

> Kindness in the father, filial piety in the
> 　son
> Gentility in the eldest brother, humility
> 　and respect in the younger
> Righteous behavior in the husband,
> 　obedience in the wife
> Humane consideration in elders,
> 　deference in juniors
> Benevolence in ruler, loyalty in
> 　ministers and subjects.[10]

The same sense of duty to family and society carried over from China to Japan, where it became incorporated in the ethical code of the Japanese warrior-knight. Known as the *Bushido Code*, it incorporates many virtues, all derivative of the proper performance of duty. The following is an analysis of the code by a Christian missionary:

1. Loyalty.
   This was due first of all to the Emperor and under him to the lord whom one more immediately serves. One of the most familiar proverbs says, "A loyal retainer does not serve two lords."

2. Gratitude.
   It may surprise some to hear that this is a Japanese characteristic, but the Christian doctrine that the spring of a right life is not duty, but gratitude, is one that is readily appreciated by the Japanese.

3. Courage.
   Life itself is to be surrendered gladly in the service of the lord. An American cannot fail to be touched by the noble words of a young warrior of ancient times to the effect that he wanted to die in battle for his lord and feared nothing so much as dying in bed before he had a chance to sacrifice his life for the object of his devotion.

4. Justice.
   This means not allowing any selfishness to stand in the way of one's duty.

5. Truthfulness.
   A knight scorns to tell a lie in order to avoid harm or hurt to himself.

6. Politeness.
   It is the mark of a strong man to be polite in all circumstances, even to an enemy.

---

[9] Robert Ballou, *The Bible of the World* (New York: Viking Press, 1939), p. 413.

[10] John Noss, *Man's Religions*, 4th ed. (New York: Macmillan, 1969), p. 285. Copyright © 1969 by John Noss.

7. Reserve.
   No matter how deeply one is moved, feeling should not be shown.
8. Honor.
   Death is preferable to disgrace. The knight always carried two swords, a long one to fight his foes, a short one to turn upon his own body in case of blunder or defeat.[11]

～

Is it correct to say that love essentially emphasizes an individual approach to one's understanding of life and its meaning? Conversely, is it correct to assume that duty stresses a community or social approach?

Which of the examples above best expresses your own ideal interpretation of life?

Is it necessary to balance love and duty? Are they exclusive of one another? If one must dominate, which do you think it should be?

If the concerns of the individual or the society cannot be perfectly balanced, which should dominate? What does your answer say of love and duty?

Unit 61   Act and Motive

The social context in which individuals live requires the development of interpersonal relationships, which are expressed through particular acts and attitudes, positive or negative. The interaction between particular acts (such as doing some service for a neighbor) and the motivations (love, duty, and so on) for them is the topic of the following discussion.

As they develop, societies normally create codes of moral conduct, a set of prescribed actions that people, depending on their social status (the various roles occupied in society—husband, wife, father, mother, uncle, warrior, and so forth), must perform as well as a set of taboos (acts forbidden to all or some). In less complex societies, the role of the taboo is very significant as it regulates a person's actions. The following passage, for example, describes some of the taboos in Navaho society.

> A very high portion of all the acts which arise out of convictions about beings and powers are negative in character. Thus lightning-struck trees must be avoided. Coyotes, bears, snakes, and some kinds of birds must never be killed. The eating of fish and of most water birds and animals is forbidden, and raw meat is taboo. Navahos will never cut a melon with the point of a knife. They never comb their hair at night. No matter how crowded a hogan may be with sleeping figures, no Navaho may step over the recumbent body of another. Mother-in-law and son-in-law must never look into each other's eyes. Any kind of sexual contact (even walking down the street or dancing together) with members of the opposite sex of one's own or one's father's clan is prohibited. Most technical processes are hedged about with restrictions: the tanner dare not leave the pole on which he scrapes hide standing upright; the potter and the basket-maker work in isolation, observing a

---

[11] Christopher Noss, *Tohoku, The Scotland of Japan* (Philadelphia: Board of Foreign Missions of the Reformed Church in the United States, 1918), pp. 87–88; quoted ibid., p. 33.

bewildering variety of taboos; the weaver shares one of these, the dread of final completion, so that a "spirit outlet" must always be left in the design.[12]

Although taboos, often unconsciously appropriated, continue to be operative in more complex societies, they tend to be replaced in importance by elaborated sets of rationally formulated, often written, moral rules. In Judaism, the earliest simple set of rules, the Ten Commandments, were extended into 613 specific laws governing all aspects of life. Similarly, for Muslims, the Qu'ran contains a specific set of rules for life; and the Eightfold Path of the Buddha is elaborately defined in the Buddhist scriptural commentaries.

Sets of rules inherently raise the problem of motivation and intention, however. If one simply follows the rules without understanding the motivation or the reason for a particular act required by the rules, they tend to degenerate into a legalism readily compromised or avoided. Therefore, with the elaboration of rules defining most actions in life, many societies also experienced a developing interest in the motivation and intention for following the rules.

In Judaism, for instance, it is not enough to fulfill the duties, moral or cultic, that the law prescribes: One must fulfill them with a right heart or a right spirit—for the right reasons and with the right intention. One should fulfill the law because of gratitude and love toward God. The following passage, an abridgment of and commentary on a halakhic discourse from the Talmud, shows how Jewish ethical reflection attempted to clarify the relation of motive (or intention) and action.[13]

> The Mishna states: "If someone blows the *shofar*[a] in a cistern, in a cellar, or in a barrel, if one heard the sound of the *shofar*, he has fulfilled his obligation; but if he heard the echo, he has not fulfilled his obligation." Then it adds: "And also, if one was passing behind a synagogue, and he heard the sound of the *shofar* or the reading of the *megillah*,[b] if one set his mind to it, he fulfilled his obligation; if one has not, he has not fulfilled his obligation—even though the one heard and the other heard, the one set his mind to it, but the other did not set his mind to it."
>
> The subject to be explored, then, is "intention" or to be exact, whether in the carrying out of a religious duty it is necessary to intend to carry out the duty or not.[14]

[a]The ram's horn sounded in the services on Rosh Hashana, the New Year. On the requirement to hear the sound of the *shofar*, see Leviticus 23:24 and Numbers 29:1.
[b]The Book of Esther, read on the festival of Purim.

Clearly, the Jews understood that one's motivation for particular acts was as important as the act itself.

The same concern was raised by Christian theologians and philosophers like Augustine (353–430) and Abelard (1079–1142). Although both insisted that right actions are important, the intention or motivation behind the act is even more important. According to Augustine, the traits of character—habits or dispositions—that Greek phi

---

[12] Clyde Kluckhohn and Dorothea Leighton, *The Navaho* (Cambridge, MA: Harvard University Press, 1946), pp. 139–40.

[13] The Talmud contains both Halakha—reflections on the requirements of the Jewish law carried on in a characteristically legal style of reasoning—and Hagada (or Agada)—nonlegal material including folklore, philosophical and theological speculation, parables, prayers, historical and legendary tales, and so forth.

[14] Judah Golden, trans., *The Living Talmud* (New York: New American Library, 1957), p. 30.

losophy held to be the highest virtues—temperance, fortitude, justice, and prudence—are empty of value, are "splendid vices," unless they flow out of and are motivated by proper love of God and neighbor. The emphasis on motive—inner attitude or disposition—as at least partly determining the value of acts and patterns of life had been present in Christianity from the beginning, as the following words of Jesus show:

> "Listen to me, all of you, and understand this: nothing that goes into a man from outside can defile him; no, it is the things that come out of him that defile a man." When he had left the people and gone indoors, his disciples questioned him about the parable. He said to them, "Are you as dull as the rest? Do you not see that nothing that goes from outside into a man can defile him, because it does not enter into his heart but into his stomach, and so passes out into the drain?" Thus he declared all food clean. He went on, "It is what comes out of a man that defiles him. For from inside, out of a man's heart, come evil thoughts, acts of fornication, of theft, murder, adultery, ruthless greed, and malice; fraud, indecency, envy, slander, arrogance, and folly; these evil things all come from inside, and they defile the man." (Mark 7:15–23, NEB)

Compare the following Zen Buddhist story, "Muddy Road," with the preceding examples:

> Tanzan and Ekido were once travelling together down a muddy road. A heavy rain was still falling. Coming around a bend, they met a lovely girl in a silk kimono and sash, unable to cross the intersection. "Come on girl," said Tanzan at once. Lifting her up in his arms, he carried her over the mud. Ekido did not speak again until that night when they reached a lodging temple. Then he could no longer restrain himself. "We monks don't go near females," he told Tanzan, "especially not young and lovely ones. It is dangerous. Why did you do that?" "I left the girl there," said Tanzan. "Are you still carrying her?"[15]

Also consider the words of Archbishop Thomas Becket in T. S. Eliot's *Murder in the Cathedral:*

> The last temptation is the greatest treason:
> To do the right deed for the wrong reason.[16]

In everyday decision making, are people normally more aware of acts or of the motives for them?

Why are religious moral thinkers more concerned with motivation than with particular moral acts?

Why is it that moral instruction is often reduced to a series of prescriptions relative to particular acts?

---

[15] Paul Reps, ed., *Zen Flesh, Zen Bones* (Tokyo: Charles E. Tuttle Co., 1960), p. 18.
[16] T. S. Eliot, *Murder in the Cathedral*, in *The Complete Poems and Plays of T. S. Eliot*, Part I. (New York: Harcourt, Brace and Company, 1952), p. 196. Used by permission of Harcourt Brace Jovanovich, Inc., publishers and Faber and Faber Ltd.

CHAPTER 15

◦ஐ

The Corporate Expressions of Ethical Concerns

Introduction

This chapter discusses relationships characteristic of groups of people and those between the ethical norms of a society (and its religion) and the social issues that arise there.

When considering a society and its ethical relationships, attention must be given not only to broad principles of right and wrong but also to the ethical norms of particular subgroups. These groups have many organizing principles including political, economic, and religious factors. Each group develops a "corporate identity," which influences the individuals within it. As such, it applies norms of ethical behavior to the social issues it confronts. In determining the norms for any such group or the society as a whole, many questions arise, the answers to which determine how individuals and groups respond to particular issues:

Is the ethical character of a group the simple sum of the character of its members?

Does each member of the group exercise equal influence on the decision-making process, good or bad, of the group itself?

Does the group have needs and goals that transcend the individual members?

Is the process of corporate identification the same regardless of whether the group is religious, political, cultural, social, or economic?

How does a group maintain its integrity in the face of conflicting claims?

In this chapter, several ethical and social issues are examined in the light of social and religious norms. Most of the examples are drawn from Western sources, but many of the issues reflect universal concerns. The difficulty in giving simple religious answers to the questions raised by these issues should be obvious. The necessity of careful and considered response in applying religious principles and norms is equally obvious. The first two units are concerned with the relationship among human need, justice, love, conflict, and peace on the collective—social and international—level. The next two units are concerned with an issue present in every society, though not always recognized—the status of women. The last two units deal with racial and ethnic differences as sources of conflict or creative opportunity in contemporary societies. With all of these issues, the major focus will be on their interaction with the religious perspectives of a society's pivotal value.

Unit 62   Love and Justice

How does one love a million needy people?

> Here is precisely the serious difficulty of love. How are its favors to be distributed among so many beneficiaries? We never have one neighbor at a time. How are we to love justice, how are we to be just about love, how are love and justice related? If to love is to seek the neighbor's welfare, and justice is being fair as between neighbors, then how do we put these two things together in our *acts* in the situation.[1]

> Various systems of Christian ethics have related love and justice: love *versus* justice (opposites), love *or* justice (alternatives), love *and* justice (complements).[2]

Joseph Fletcher, contemporary ethicist, claims that "love and justice are one and the same." He emphasizes "that love is justice or that justice loves. . . . To be loving is to be just, to be just is to be loving." To him, love equals justice; justice equals love. Fletcher explains what he means in the following paragraph:

> Justice is Christian love using its head, calculating its duties, obligations, opportunities, resources. Sometimes it is hard to decide, but the dilemmas, trilemmas, and multilemmas of conscience are as baffling for legalists as for situationists. Justice is love coping with situations where distribution is called for. On this basis it becomes plain that as the love ethic searches seriously for a social policy it must form a coalition with utilitarianism. It takes over from Bentham and Mill the strategic principle of "the greatest good of the greatest number."[3]

Fletcher points to Paul Tillich as one who comes close to expressing his understanding of the relation of love and justice. He does not feel, however, that Tillich goes far enough. Tillich states that the "relation of love to justice in personal encounters can adequately be described through three functions of creative justice, namely, listening, giving, forgiving."[4] All persons, in one way or another, yearn to be heard, to make known

[1] Joseph Fletcher, *Situation Ethics: The New Morality* (Philadelphia: Westminster Press, 1966), p. 88.
[2] Ibid., p. 93.
[3] Ibid., p. 95.
[4] Paul Tillich, *Love, Power and Justice* (New York: Oxford University Press, 1954), p. 84.

their claim for justice. One who loves others will listen and learn in order to act justly toward them. The second step in exercising creative justice is giving. Every one we meet lives with the right to call for us to meet his or her needs. The minimum of giving in certain situations may drive toward the maximum self-sacrifice. Sacrificial giving serves the love that makes whole and creates new life in another. "The third and most paradoxical form in which justice is united with love is forgiving." Here Tillich is speaking in Pauline terms of justification by grace. This means "to accept as just one who is unjust."[5] How contradictory this seems to us! The good news of Christian teaching, however, goes beyond our usual way of viewing unjust persons as subjects deserving retribution and instead demands reconciliation, acceptance of another into the wholeness and unity provided only by forgiveness.

In the light of what Fletcher and Tillich say about the relationship between love and justice, reflect further upon Reinhold Niebuhr's interpretation as explained by Gordon Harland, a contemporary church historian.

What then is the relation between *agape* and justice? The first thing to be said is that they cannot be simply identified. *Agape* is transcendent, heedless, and sacrificial. Justice is historical, discriminating, and concerned with balancing interests and claims. Love and justice are never simply the same thing. But if they must be distinguished, they cannot be torn asunder. Justice is the relative social embodiment of love and as such it is an approximation of love. Justice is love finding a relatively complete expression in the world. The terms are not interchangeable. But justice is never something apart from, or independent of, love and pertaining to another realm.

Love Demands Justice. For justice is not alien to love, it is love making its way in the world. Love thus prompts us to seek ever wider and more inclusive structures of justice. One simply cannot say that he is concerned that love may be expressed but not concerned with politics, economics, laws, and customs. To be unconcerned for the achievement of more equal justice is to deny the claims of love. Justice is the embodiment of love in complex human relations.

Love Negates Justice. For love always transcends justice. This is true for our ideas of justice as well as for historical structures of justice. Justice is discriminating, it must always calculate and weigh conflicting interests. Love transcends the calculation of more and less and does not reward according to deserts. Thus every structure and every idea of justice stand under the higher judgment of love. Justice, to remain justice, can thus never be complacent, because the norm is not in itself but in *agape*. . . .

Love Fulfills Justice. Only love can illumine and meet the special need. "A sense of justice may prompt men to organize legal systems of unemployment insurance through which a general sense of obligation toward the needy neighbour is expressed. But no such system can leave the self satisfied when it faces particular needs among those who are the beneficiaries of such minimal schemes of justice." Love fulfills justice also because love alone can meet the other in his uniqueness and freedom. "The other has special needs and requirements which cannot be satisfied by general rules of equity." Love fulfills justice because *agape* is redemptive. . . .

Agape, which demands that we ever seek justice, which judges and finds wanting our highest achievements, also redeems and thereby fulfills what remains incomplete and distorted by sin.

Love demands, negates, and fulfills justice. Thus, although love and justice are not the same they do not exist apart from each other; when they are sought apart from each other, each is destroyed.

[5] Ibid., p. 86.

Justice without love ceases to be justice. "Any justice which is only justice soon degenerates into something less than justice." Thus as mutual love needs *agape* to keep it from degenerating into a calculation of interests, so "Justice," as Niebuhr once so cryptically put it, "without love is merely the balance of power."

Love without justice ceases to be love. It becomes a vague sentimentalism that fails to come to grips with the realities of experience. Or it issues in a perverse lovelessness by refusing mistakenly, in the name of love, to deal realistically and courageously with the fact of power upon which the securing and the maintaining of justice depend. Or it becomes corrupted by being defined in terms of attitudes, and love is thereby restricted to personal relations and exercises of philanthropy, and thus the universal kingship of the Lord of the Cross is reduced to a pleasant deed transacted in a corner.

Love and justice must never be sharply separated, though they must always be clearly distinguished. They exist together in a dialectical relation of tension.[6]

Liberation Theology and Justice

An illustration of how to distribute love justly has been sharply focused in recent decades by "liberation theologians." Struggling with the vast inequities between wealthy and poor nations as well as class and economic differences within particular nations, liberation theologies seek new ways to apply justly the insights of love in modern societies. Liberation theologies have received impetus especially among Latin Americans and ethnic minorities of the United States who call for theology to start from a nontraditional starting point: the poor.[7] While utilizing the tools of the social sciences in analyzing the reality of conflict between the oppressed poor and the oppressors in a society in which the very structure of society is unjust and evil, liberation thinkers call for the engagement of *praxis*, a method of action and reflection by the community in the light of Scripture. Just love is action demanding reflective interpretation by Christians in group discussion that then compels even more just acts of love, which in turn call for reflection again, and so on in a continuous circle.

Injustices must be viewed through the eyes of the poor, who have often been disenfranchised and voiceless in society, for God is to be found among the poor and marginalized. Liberation theologies claim that God is calling and can empower the poor of the world to exercise responsibility for the future and modify and eliminate social and economic structures that presently enslave them in poverty.

The justice that comes with liberation will be a transformation not only of individuals in bondage to inward and personal sin but also of the evil structures and institutions of society that dehumanize and perpetuate poverty and corporate injustice. Further, it should be emphasized that the God in Christ revealed through the struggle of the poor is the force to liberate not only the oppressed but also the oppressors, who perhaps unknowingly are also enslaved to the unjust structures of power.

---

[6] Gordon Harland, *The Thought of Reinhold Niebuhr* (Oxford: Oxford University Press, 1960), pp. 23–26. Copyright © by Gordon Harland. Used with permission.

[7] Robert McAfee Brown, *Theology in a New Key: Responding to Liberation Themes* (Philadelphia: Westminster Press, 1978), p. 60.

UNIT 63   Peace or Justice?

Historically, religious traditions and religious groups have taken a variety of positions regarding justice in society and the need at times—desirably or undesirably—to use force to secure peace and a just social order. Within the Hindu and Buddhist traditions there have been major strands that support pacifism and nonviolence. The twentieth-century Hindu leader Mohandas Gandhi, who led the struggle for India's freedom from British colonial domination, appealed to ancient Hindu sources, including the *Bhagavad-Gita,* to advocate complete nonviolence in attitude and action toward his opponents. He even suggested during the persecution of Jews in Germany under Hitler that they should mount a campaign of massive nonviolent public protest against their Nazi persecutors.

The same *Bhagavad-Gita* that Gandhi appealed to for support of total nonviolence was originally written to show that from the Hindu perspective of the caste system, it is appropriate for those in the military or princely caste to function as warriors when their situation imposes this as a necessity for maintaining order and justice. The rise of Islam was partly accomplished by military conquest, but the teachings of Muhammad and of the Qu'ran insist that all wars must be a response to injustice and that peace should be sought and treasured.

Roland Bainton has pointed out that traditionally there have been three differing Christian positions about war.[8] One has been the pacifist position of such groups as the Society of Friends and the Church of the Brethren and of such individuals as Leo Tolstoy and Muriel Lester; since the advent of nuclear weapons, included are a number of Catholics and traditionally Protestant Christians including Martin Luther King, Jr. and the German World War I submarine commander, Pastor Martin Niemoeller, later imprisoned by the Hitler government for his resistance to the Nazi attempt to take over the churches.

A second position identified by Bainton, that of the crusade, was introduced by Christian leaders largely to account for *some* wars (mostly those of the ancient Israelites against their Canaanite enemies) believed to have been directly commanded by God. Later Christian leaders sometimes called for crusades against the Muslims during the Middle Ages, against the Germans during World War I, or against the "atheistic" Russian communists during the Cold War.

The dominant Christian position concerning war, however, has been adherence to the criteria of the just war, as set forth by ancient stoic or eclectic philosophers such as Cicero, Roman theories of the natural Law, and Christian thinkers from the time of Augustine (died 430) to Aquinas (thirteenth century) to the present. According to such theorists, these criteria are or should be recognized by all civilized nations since they are derived from universal human reason. The following conditions must be met before a war can be considered just or justifiable:

1. War must be authorized and waged under the authority of a legitimately established government. It cannot be initiated by private citizens.

[8] Roland Bainton, *Christian Attitudes Toward War and Peace* (New York: Abingdon Press, 1960).

2. War can be undertaken only if there is a just cause, a grave and unjustifiable injury done to the people of a country by the government or citizens of another country.

3. War must be waged with right intention—the intention of seeking a better, more just peace than would exist if the unjust situation were left uncorrected. (The war should also be fought with a proper motive, aiming at doing good to all who will be affected, including the enemy.)

4. War must be waged with proper means. Especially, the lives and safety of noncombatants must be protected from direct attack or harm.

5. War must be undertaken as a last resort only after all possibilities of peaceful settlement have been exhausted.

6. War can be undertaken only when there is a reasonable expectation that the just side will prevail; otherwise great harm would be done without a correction of the original evil.

7. War can be undertaken only when the good (to all affected parties) that will result from correcting the unjust situation will be greater than the destruction that the war will produce.

Past discussions of the moral problem of war have focused on several issues:

1. How can one be even reasonably sure that the cause for which a war is undertaken or risked is just?

2. Can any war between independent nation-states in a world where any international conflict *might* lead to nuclear war be justified?

3. Under what conditions is a revolutionary uprising (civil war) against an aggressive or tyrannical government justified?

4. Can a counterrevolutionary war, aided by outside powers, fought to preserve a stable international balance of power, be justified, even if it means keeping an oppressive government in power against the wishes of a large part of the population in the country involved?

Religious groups and leaders are closely examining these issues. A pastoral letter of American Catholic Bishops that many observers consider epochal has urged the reconsideration of just-war arguments that favor retention of a defense based on nuclear weapons. The continued reliance on a nuclear arsenal for deterrence can be justified, the bishops suggest, only if governments and individuals make it a matter of first priority to move away from the nuclear balance of terror through negotiation and disarmament.[9]

During the 1980s, the stability of the international system during the Cold War confrontation between the two opposing superpowers, the United States and the U.S.S.R., was thought by many to depend on the nuclear standoff policy of mutually assured destruction (MAD). Since the perceived end of the Cold War, the question of a justified use of force, nuclear or conventional, has not gone away. The dissolution of the Soviet Union and its block of supporting nations in eastern Europe has in many places produced turbulence, civil war, and anarchy (for example, the former Yugoslavia and former U.S.S.R. itself); tensions in the Middle East, including decades- or centuries-old conflicts, continue to erupt into violence, including Operation Desert Storm; and there are many areas of continuous conflict in other parts of the world. During the 1990 war, President George Bush, in a speech to a convention of evangelical Protestant leaders, cited all of the traditional just-war criteria in support of the United States and its allies, whose sol-

---

[9] The National Conference of Catholic Bishops, *The Challenge of Peace: God's Promise and Our Response, A Pastoral Letter on War and Peace, May 3, 1983* (Washington, DC: United States Catholic Conference, 1983).

diers were under the authority of the United Nations. The questions listed earlier are still being confronted by the world's religious leaders (as well as by secular leaders and ordinary citizens) and in the consciences of faithful adherents of the world's religions.

UNIT 64   Religion and the Social Status of Women

Traditional View

One of the first books of poetry by a North American writer—and the first published work by a North American poet whose works are still recognized as having literary merit—was published in England in 1650. The writer was Anne Bradstreet, daughter of Thomas Dudley, the second governor of the Massachusetts Bay Colony, and wife of a man who, after her death, also served as governor of the colony. Anne Bradstreet was the mother of eight children; devoutly Puritan in her religious outlook; and well read in religion, history, and science. She particularly admired the poetry of Sir Philip Sidney and of the French Calvinist poet Guillaume Du Bartas, well-known Puritan writers of the period.

Anne Bradstreet did not think of herself as a poet. She wrote poetry for recreation and for the edification of herself and her friends and family. The manuscript of her book *The Tenth Muse* apparently was taken to England by her brother-in-law, John Woodbridge, without her knowledge and given to a publisher. In his "Epistle to the Reader," published as a foreword to the book, Woodbridge wrote,

> I might trim this book with quaint expressions . . . but I fear 'twill be a shame for a man that can speak so little, to be seen in the title-page of this woman's book, lest by comparing the one with the other, the reader should pass his sentence that it is the gift of women not only to speak most but to speak best.

Woodbridge then goes on to suggest that male readers will not be envious of the "excellency of the inferior sex" unless "men turn more peevish than women." It would be interesting to know what Anne Bradstreet's reaction was to this half-derogatory—"women speak most"—half-self-effacing mock compliment from her brother-in-law.

Another Massachusetts poet, Nathaniel Ward, had written these lines, again without Anne's knowledge, in his introductory verse published at the beginning of *The Tenth Muse:*

> I muse whither at length these girls will go;
> It half-revives my chill frostbitten blood,
> To see a woman once do ought that's good.

Anne often wrote as if she did in fact accept the belief, recommended for good Christian women of her time—and other times—that women are "the inferior sex." But Anne seems to have accepted this belief with irony, and in at least one poem, her poem on Queen Elizabeth, she wrote,

> Nay say, have women worth? or have they none?
> Or had they some, but with our Queen is't gone? . . .
> Let such as say our sex is void of reason
> Know tis a slander now, but once was treason.

Apparently Anne Bradstreet was not entirely convinced that women really *were* the inferior sex, who only occasionally—or *once*—could come up to the high standards of the male sex.[10]

Anne Bradstreet's subtle questioning of a cultural assumption—female inferiority—was perhaps unusual in seventeenth-century America. Yet the assumption that females are inferior and subservient to males is an ancient tradition in many cultures of the world. All of the cultures from which Western civilization grew—Greek, Roman, Mesopotamian, Israelite, Egyptian—accepted such distinctions between the sexes.

Plato, in his *Republic*, is one of the few, perhaps the only figure in the ancient Western world, who argued for complete equality of women in society. The Greek philosopher Aristotle, however, wrote,

> A husband and a father . . . rules over wife and children, both free, but the rule differs, the rule over his children being a royal, over his wife a constitutional rule. For although there may be exceptions to the order of nature, the male is by nature fitter for command than the female, just as the elder and full-grown is superior to the younger and more immature. . . . The inequality is permanent.[11]

Writers on the history of Christianity have often claimed that the position of women—in contrast to their position in the Roman Empire of the first century—was significantly elevated in Christian teaching and practice. One text cited is Paul's saying that in Christ there is "neither male nor female" (Galatians 3:27–28, RSV). But Paul also had an elevated conception of male responsibility in the marriage relationship: He assumed that the male would be dominant. His teachings about the role that women should play in the life and worship of the church reflect a conservative spirit (see I Corinthians 14:33–35; I Corinthians 11:2–16).

With the rise of asceticism as a major factor in the life of the church, the conservative view of the role and status of women became more pronounced. From the standpoint of the ascetic, who had withdrawn to the desert to flee the wickedness of the world, women were sources of temptation; after all, Eve had been responsible for Adam's fall, for the entry of evil into the world. Women were blamed by such writers as John Chrysostom and Ambrose for being immature and ignorant, conditions that where they existed are easily explained by the educational neglect of, and social discrimination against, women characteristic of the period. Clement of Alexandria, however, argued that by nature there was (and ought to be) complete equality between the sexes. (He did believe that there should be some differences in vocation.) It would be fair to say that the social position of women in the Roman Empire remained largely unaffected by the spread of Christianity. In

---

[10] The materials in this unit dealing with Anne Bradstreet are partly based on Adrienne Rich, "Anne Bradstreet and Her Poetry," and Jeannine Hensley, "Anne Bradstreet's Wreath of Thyme," *The Works of Anne Bradstreet,* ed. Jeannine Hensley (Cambridge, MA: Harvard University Press, 1967), pp. ix–xxxv.

[11] Aristotle, *Politics.* Book i, Ch. 12 (1259a–1259b), trans. Benjamin Jowett, *The Modern Library* (New York: Random House, 1943).

pre-Christian Rome, women could own property and obtain divorces. In the Eastern part of the empire (and perhaps also in the West), there was regular ordination of deaconesses. Deaconesses were allowed, however, to minister only to women, and they were not allowed to perform ecclesiastical functions thought to be proper to the male, such as teaching or praying aloud in worship services or approaching the altar. This is in stark contrast to the practice of many of the heretical sects of the period, such as Montanism, in which women were allowed more active roles. With the onset of feudalism, women lost many of the rights they had had in the urban setting of the Roman Empire.[12]

The irony of Figure 15.1 is that although seventeenth-century man—in this case the French philosopher René Descartes—may have seen a man's dignity as residing in his essence as a conscious (thinking) being—"I think therefore I am"—woman's socially defined status did not allow *her* to realize this essence. Only a woman in a socially exceptional position, such as Descartes's philosophically inclined correspondent, the Princess Elizabeth, or his patroness, Queen Christina, could become conscious of her rational essence. As a matter of fact, Descartes was not married, which may make the irony of the cartoon even more biting.

Figure 15.1   Drawing by Stevenson. (© 1969, *The New Yorker* Magazine, Inc., (May 3, 1969.)

" 'Cogito, ergo sum' is all very well for you, but what about me?"

[12] Based on D. S. Bailey, *Sexual Relation in Christian Thought* (New York: Harper and Brothers, 1959).

In modern America and in some parts of Europe the time-honored tradition of female inferiority has been vociferously denied by a rising feminist movement. One of its facets has been "consciousness development"—the overcoming by women of negative attitudes about their identity that derive from traditional stereotypes and practices based on social discrimination. The movement has attracted substantial male support and so has become a major agent for change in society. Manifestations of major change have been most obvious in the modification of traditional vocational patterns. Women now participate in almost all occupations and are particularly prominent in law, medicine, higher education, scientific research, religion, and certain fields of business such as accounting. As vocational roles change, consciousness of sexual harassment, based on the traditional ideas of inferiority and dependence, becomes more pronounced. Charges of misconduct reach to the highest levels, as exemplified by the questions raised during the U.S. Senate hearings concerning Clarence Thomas's appointment to the Supreme Court.

Women in the Christian Tradition

Changes in the place of women in society have caused intense scrutiny of traditional Christian and Jewish organizational attitudes and practices, which, similar to those found in society generally, often exemplify a belief in male superiority and, correspondingly, in the inferiority of women. Criticism has been broad. The tendency of Judaism and Christianity to represent and describe God in only masculine terms has been questioned. The exclusion of women from the priesthood and ministry, the denial of their full participation in decision making by religious organizations, and the explicit and implicit assumption of male superiority have all been attacked.

Traditionally conservative denominations continue to assert that the ordination of women is not biblically sound, sometimes repeating the historical assertion that women follow in the lineage of Eve, who committed the first sin (Genesis 3:1–13). Thus, as a tainted gender, women cannot render a pure ministry (I Timothy 2:11–15). The Apostle Paul's description of the place of women in the church as subservient to that of males continues to be cited to justify limitation of women's participation in positions of church leadership. (I Corinthians 14:33–35). Roman Catholics and some Anglican communities also refuse to ordain women because of church principles, which assert that apostolic succession is limited to men.

Some conservative communities, nevertheless, have begun to reconsider their traditional understandings. While continuing to exclude women from ordination and the rights of leadership in worship services, they have begun to include women in their governance structures and publicly recognize their historically significant teaching and mission roles within the churches.

More moderate, liberal Christian denominations criticize these traditional understandings, pointing to the incomparability with much of Jesus's teaching of the historical inequities between the sexes and recognizing the effective ministries women have rendered in the churches through the ages. As a result, female participation in the governance of many Protestant denominations is now common. Educational instruction on the rights and equality of women in the church is broadly practiced. In recent years, several

Protestant denominations have accepted the position that women may be ordained as ministers on a basis of complete equality. American Methodism has elected a number of women to their highest ministerial office—that of bishop. The ordination of women has become widely accepted in America's Episcopal church since its introduction in the 1970s. In the mid-1980s, an opinion survey indicated that Anglican bishops, other clergy, and laity heavily supported ordination of women to the priesthood. Although unwilling to ordain women, in 1970 the Roman Catholic Church named two of its female saints, Teresa of Avila and Catherine of Sienna, to a very small, select group of theologians— fewer than forty from the whole history of Catholic theology—who have been given the awesome title *Doctors of the Church*. No other women had ever been given this title in the Roman church.

These modifications in the role of women in many Christian churches reflect major changes in attitude toward the role of women in many churches during the past several decades. The rising number of women in Protestant seminaries and among pastors serving local congregations as well as those in positions of general church leadership suggest that such modifications will continue to reshape Christian churches and their ministries within society.

∽

What roles in our society are regarded by society as really "first class"—as conferring maximum prestige and dignity on the individuals who fill them?

How many women, in comparison with men, are in these roles?

Are there some roles of maximum prestige value in our society that have never been filled by women?

How do you explain the bias toward male superiority and female inferiority that has characterized Western society?

Has a similar attitude been characteristic of other societies?

What factors—social, psychological, economic, ideological—have contributed to this bias?

∽

Materials in this unit have been drawn mainly from Christian history. Other religions (for example, Hinduism, Islam, and Buddhism) have by and large taken an even more conservative stance toward the status and role of women. See also Units 69 and 70 for comment on the status of women in preliterate and ancient cultures.

Unit 65   Sexuality and Human Liberation

Sally's phone conversation in Figure 15.2 concisely focuses on major issues relating to sex roles in modern society, reflecting, on the one hand, the long-standing subservience of women to men, and on the other hand, the feminist protest against having an identity only in relation to one's husband or parents.

A student in a philosophy course recently proposed the following thesis: "Human sexuality is likely to be the most enduring of all philosophical topics." His line of reasoning was as follows: In the past, differences of race, nationality, language community, educational attainment, and religion have been the basis for fundamental differences in status and treatment. We know now that these differences are not essential and that human beings can and should be treated on a basis of equality in spite of these differences, in line with one of the major moral and political goals of our time, equal opportunity and equal treatment. But one major and apparently irreducible difference between human beings does exist and seems to pose irreducible problems for the goal of equality, the difference between the sexes.

Many contemporary speakers and writers would challenge the last statement, insisting that the basic differences between the sexes, insofar as they bear on social roles, are man-created rather than natural or inevitable. One approach toward the role of women advocated by some religious leaders has been an appeal to "natural law" (see Unit 85). According to this line of thinking, the fact that women are naturally, biologically different from men indicates something of their proper role in society: Their biological nature as women indicates that morally they are best fitted to be mothers, supervisors of the home, protectors, comforters, and healers of husband and children. Against this view, many have argued that the traditional roles assigned to women, and the traditional characteristics considered feminine, are not the result of biological differences but are cultural creations, cultural stereotypes.

Adrienne Rich, a poet and an active feminist, has written,

> The patriarchy looks to its women to embody and impersonate the qualities lacking in its institutions—concern for the quality of life, for means rather than for pure goal, a connection with the natural and the extrasensory order. These attributes have been classified as "female" in part because the patriarchy relegates them to women and tends to deny them—with a certain fatalism—to men. The encouragement of such qualities as intuition, sympathy, and access to feeling by a mother in her sons is deplored because this is supposed to make them unfit for the struggle that awaits them in a masculine world. Thus the "masculinity" of the world is perpetuated.
>
> The "liberated" woman encounters male hostility in the form of psychic rape, often masked as psychic or physical seduction. It occurs overtly in the classroom where a male teacher denigrates female intellect; more subtly in the committee where she sits as token

Figure 15.2 *Sally Forth.* Reprinted with special permission of King Features Syndicate.

woman and where her intelligence is treated with benign neglect; in the magnanimous assumption that she is "not like other women" and for this reason is so desirable a colleague, figurehead, or adornment to the establishment (the pitting of woman against woman, woman against herself). At the same time that she is told about her "specialness" she is expected to be flattered, like all women, by flirtation. She is also expected to be flattered by man's sexual self-hatred and sexual confusion, his avowal "I can talk to women, but not to men," his romanticizing of his sexual dishonesty: "I can't talk to my wife, but I can talk to you." . . .

One of the devastating effects of technological capitalism has been its numbing of the powers of the imagination—specifically, the power to envision new human and communal relationships. I am a feminist because I feel endangered, psychically and physically, by this society, and because I believe that the women's movement is saying that we have come to an edge of history when men—in so far as they are embodiments of the patriarchal idea—have become dangerous to children and other living things, themselves included; and that we can no longer afford to keep the female principle—the mother in all women and the woman in many men—straitened within the tight little postindustrial family, or within any male-induced notion of where the female principle is valid and where it is not.[13]

∼

What do you think Adrienne Rich is saying about the relation of men and women in contemporary society?

In what ways does her discussion relate to the student's suggestion that there are "irreducible" differences between the sexes?

∼

It is difficult to be objective in discussing these issues. Behavioral scientists are often heavily influenced by the assumptions or presuppositions they bring to research. Behaviorism, an influential trend in American behavioral research during the past fifty years, has emphasized the role of social conditioning in shaping what is often thought of as "human nature." Thus, behaviorists have tended to see human nature as relatively open and changeable. In contrast, Freudian psychotherapists have often assumed that there are innate psychological differences between men and women that predispose them toward different personality structures and social roles. Recently a behavioral approach called "sociobiology" has emphasized genetic, biological factors that some have held fit men and women for different roles in society.

Conservative Christians sometimes appeal to the Genesis story of creation, according to which Eve was created to be a helper for Adam, so that Adam would not be alone, to argue for a basis in God's will for male superiority. In an interesting (and difficult to interpret) New Testament passage, I. Corinthians 11:8–12, Paul seems to argue that according to the original creation, woman *was* created for the sake of man and subject to man's authority, but in the new creation that has come through Christ, there is to be complete mutuality between woman and man. They are to be not independent of each other but mutually dependent.

Some feminists have stressed that as long as women are oppressed in our society, no one can be fully free. They thus see the feminist movement as working for complete human liberation. Others have expressed fears about the impact of feminism on the traditional family structure. Still others have argued that the present decay of the nuclear fam-

---

[13] From *The New York Review of Books*, 19, no. 9 (November 30, 1972), 35–40. Reprinted with permission of the author. Copyright © 1972 by Adrienne Rich.

ily in our society through divorce is a symptom of the lack of mutuality in the relations between men and women.

∾

How do you feel about this?

Do you agree that in most societies women have been oppressed and are denied the opportunity to fulfill their human potential? Is this true in our society?

UNIT 66   Poverty and Race

Increasingly common today are homeless and hungry people seeking shelter, food, and work—mostly people of color. The tragedy of such scenes is intensified when cities like Los Angeles burn and desperate people riot in angry protest against poverty and racial discrimination. Current statistics confirm what we see. The 1992 Census Bureau reports of increased poverty during 1991 indicate that 32.7 percent of African-Americans were below the government-defined poverty line of $13,924.00. Next were Hispanics, at 28.7 percent. Asians and Pacific Islanders fared better, at 13.8 percent, as did whites, at 10.7 percent.[14] Although Native Americans are not ranked in this account, they have suffered dire poverty since they were forced onto barren reservations decades ago. Since 1970, African-Americans have experienced poverty at a ratio to whites of three to one, Hispanics at a slightly lower rate. Their increased concentration in deteriorating urban ghettos signifies deep wounds in our social structure.

Why such inequality in U.S. economic life? Racism is certainly part of the answer. Although overt racism has been outlawed at certain levels since the Civil Rights Act, the continued ill effects of covert, institutionalized racism perpetuate the racial inequalities that are so difficult to correct. A brief reminder of the economic backgrounds of African-Americans and Hispanics, the two largest populations of nonwhites in the United States, will help us draw connections between poverty and race.

The African-American story, of course, recounts slavery and its horrors as an economic reality in U.S. history. Although slavery's shackles were broken by the Civil War, African-Americans are still held down by disadvantages of the past: capital deficits that limit their qualifications as workers and give them less access to opportunities because of "limited contacts and discrimination."[15] David H. Swinton, a specialist in racial economics, writes, "Because blacks experienced such pervasive inequality in the past, they have not inherited the wealth, business ownership and human capital that make it possible for them to obtain current equal incomes."[16] In other words, in a society where those who "have" gain the greater advantage for "having more," those who "have not" are perpetually disadvantaged and thus continue to "have less."

[14] Anne Reifenberg, "U.S. Poverty Rate Reaches Six Year High," *Dallas Morning News*, September 4, 1992, pp. 1A, 12A.

[15] David H. Swinton, "The Economic Status of Black Americans During the 1980's: A Decade of Limited Progress," *The State of Black America* (New York: National Urban League, 1990), p. 52.

[16] Ibid., p. 44.

The story of Hispanics in the Southwest concerns a conquered people and their losses. In 1848 when the United States defeated Mexico and annexed territories from California to Texas and from Colorado to Nevada, the Treaty of Guadalupe Hidalgo supposedly guaranteed freedom of life and religion for Mexican residents of the Southwest as well as protection of their properties. Since then most of those Mexican-Americans have lost their lands to Anglos through economic exploitation, armed confrontation, and swindles under the guise of legality. "Within decades those Hispanics who once controlled the Southwest became the laborers who enabled the Anglos to become even more powerful expressions of the racist doctrine of Manifest Destiny, the theory that White American Protestantism had a mission to control the continent, especially people of Color, for the good of all in the service of God."[17] As the fastest-growing ethnic population in the United States, Hispanics are suffering the continued disadvantages of their economic losses and the racist structures that demean them as a people.

Racial ideologies really did not emerge until the nineteenth century, when biological imagery began to supercede religious reasons for Anglo-Saxon ethnocentrism (exalting a particular group of people based on a common history, culture, and language without reference to racial traits based on skin color). The rise of the new "science of man" augmented misguided ethnocentric beliefs by the English in the innate superiority of the white race. In the New World these racial ideologies became convenient justifications for the dominance of white colonists over people of color. Although blacks were enslaved at first for economic reasons, in time racial prejudice took on a life of its own as the subsequent generations were socialized to claim white superiority over all nonwhites. It was generally believed that God was smiling on the Anglo-Saxon people and that it was the "white man's burden" to "Anglo-Saxonize" and Christianize other races. In short, it was the Manifest Destiny of white Americans to evangelize the world.[18] In the spirit of this perverted religious justification for white superiority, the racist rubrics of European colonialism motivated the rise of what has been characterized as "internal colonialism" in America.[19] White colonialists established dominance economically and otherwise over "Indians, Negroes and Mexicans" as well as the immigrant Chinese workers and others from Asia and the Pacific Islands.

Racism in the United States, which is predominantly the result of white prejudice against nonwhites, especially for the sake of economic control, in biblical terms "is sin because it violates God's will" that everyone obey "the law of love."[20] The law of love calls for justice and fairness in all relationships, whether person-to-person or collective, societal expressions. Institutionalized forms of racism, such as any law or practice that demeans a group of people on the basis of skin color, are the most difficult to change.

---

[17] Bert Affleck, "Cross-Cultural Evangelism: A Case Study in New Mexico," *Journal of the Academy for Evangelism in Theological Education*, Vol. 2, ed. David Lowes Watson (Nashville, TN: General Board of Discipleship, United Methodist Church, 1986–87), p. 62.

[18] E. C. Orosco, *Republican Protestantism in Aztlan* (Glendale, CA: Petereins Press, 1980), pp. 138–41.

[19] See Mario Barrera, *Race and Class in the Southwest: A Theory of Racial Inequality* (Notre Dame, IN: University of Notre Dame Press, 1979), pp. 188–219.

[20] William B. McClain, *Traveling Light: Christian Perspectives on Pilgrimage and Pluralism* (New York: Friendship Press, 1981), p. 75.

How can society be moved toward economic equality? Knowledge, power, and faith are crucial factors for change. Education at all levels about the past and present realities of racism can help change racist attitudes—to know, for example, that the biological designations for the three races (Caucasian, Negroid, and Mongoloid) merely refer to skin pigmentation, nature's way of protecting people from the sun's rays. Those living nearest the equator thus developed the darkest skins. In the past two centuries, with the intermixing of these races, however, a pure race cannot be easily designated. Religious proclamations that challenge everyone to treat others with love and respect can inspire harder work for justice. Calls for inclusivism in religion and society counter religious dogmatisms that exclude any race. Political power distributed more equally among people of all backgrounds allows more varied voices to be heard and to be served more fairly. However, educational, religious, and political efforts to attain equality may not address the economic inequalities so often tied to racism, an area churches and religious bodies in the United States have tended to overlook.

Some recent advocates for equality focus on economic needs. As an economist, David H. Swinton recommends a program of reparations,[21] monetary investments, and gifts to help the "have nots" gain momentum in a society of competitive economics in order to eliminate the inherited economic gaps that have been perpetuated through the years: "Any realistic prospect for equality by the year 2000 will require reparations sufficient to eliminate the gaps in ownership of businesses, human, and nonhuman wealth." He concludes that this is especially "true in a free market 'lassez faire' economy . . . those who advocate free markets and 'laissez faire' and who also support the elimination of racial inequality in economic life must support reparations for the elimination of the inherited differences in wealth and ownership."[22]

Cain Hope Felder, biblical scholar at Howard University, calls reparations a moral expression of "compensatory justice," a "process of correcting past and present injury, disposession, exploitation, and the violation of rights. It makes restitution . . . seeks to restore persons to wholeness, and grants them rightful status in the community." Felder indicates Jesus's strong advocacy for compensatory justice in "inaugurating the Kingdom of God, not the least for marginalized socioeconomic groups. . . ."[23] He refers to Jesus's central concern for the poor in Luke 4:16–30, Luke 7:22–23, and Matthew 11:4–6. Such New Testament teaching by Jesus exhibits the power and value of the prophetic vision (Isaiah 56:6, 61:1) and the Jubilee ideal (Leviticus 25:10) found in Jewish scriptures. The Levitical teaching of Jubilee stresses that God, not any human, owns all the land and that every fiftieth year debts will be forgiven; thus everyone can begin anew as stewards of the land God provides. In keeping with the spirit of Jubilee and the prophetic concern for the poor, Felder notes especially the case of Zacchaeus, a rich tax collector who embraces Jesus's call for compensatory justice and "not only voluntarily decides to distribute half of his possessions among the poor, but he also indicates a willingness to restore fourfold to anyone he has defrauded."[24]

---

[21] Reparation in this context means providing payment to blacks and others for the systematic economic disadvantages they have historically suffered because of race or ethnic origin.

[22] Swinton, "Economic Status of Black Americans," p. 52.

[23] Cain Hope Felder, *Troubling Biblical Waters: Race, Class, and the Family* (Maryknoll, NY: Orbis Books, 1989), p. 73.

[24] Ibid.

Many people would call Jesus's teaching unrealistic and unworkable for our society. Some would cite the welfare system in the United States as a failed program of reparations. Others would say that it needs reforms that would create wealth rather than welfare for mere survival. Many people would be unwilling to give up any of their economic possessions to help create economic equality. Some would hold to a racist idea that people of color are inherently deficient and thus are ordained to fill subsidiary roles in a white world. Some would look to a future kingdom, in which God alone will bring justice, and thus they would not take any action to change our economic system as they wait for God's future salvation. Some might excuse poverty in the United States by rationalizing that racial and economic inequalities are worse in other countries such as South Africa, where blacks have been systemically oppressed, or in Latin America, where Indians of darker hue are discriminated against by those of lighter skin, most often richer power brokers. Others are just plain apathetic and do not care to think about or do anything about racial economic inequality.

The issues pertaining to poverty and race are indeed complex, as we have indicated all too briefly. Clearly racism and its accompanying poverty is not simply an American problem but is present in many cultures today. To deal with these issues will require careful thought and unselfish action.

∾

Does the radical call for compensatory justice, based on Judeo-Christian literature, offer viable solutions pertaining to poverty and racism?

How do other religions consider the issues of race and poverty?

What do you think about these matters?

Unit 67   Ethnic Pluralism in Contemporary American Churches

The history of the so-called mainline churches in the United States indicates an exclusivism in which Anglo-American culture has dominated other cultures. Segregation in the United States has been reflected in the churches, separating people of color—especially Asians, blacks, Hispanics, and native Americans—into congregations apart from whites. In most cases the ethnic-minority churches have been composed of those struggling to move beyond poverty. The larger, more affluent, white churches have usually been paternalistic toward Christians of color, extending occasional charity without being inclusive.

New efforts to be inclusive began to emerge after the civil rights movement of the 1950s and 1960s. Since the 1954 Supreme Court decision striking down inequality in education, a number of denominations have adopted a policy of integration. This policy, however, has been applied for the most part from the vantage point of the more powerful white churches. Altruistic as they may have been, white Christians have tended to reflect the idea of the American melting pot, but with a racist proviso—that the melding of races in America would still turn out white. "Whiteness" as a value indicating supposed superiority has been maintained throughout the history of Western civilization and of course has been a tragic theme in the Christian religion. "White is used to express the pure, while black expresses the diabolical."[25]

Even though minorities received invitations to join white churches, they still felt excluded. In various subtle ways, they were made aware of how difficult it is to cross cultural barriers and become integrated. Too often they felt that if they were to become equal in integrated white churches, they would have to be absorbed and abandon their own cultural roots.

In recent years the idea of integration has been reevaluated. Mainline denominations in America have begun to propose pluralism as preferable to integration. *Pluralism* connotes "diversity-in-unity and unity-in-diversity"—that is, fostering diverse cultural contributions while seeking unity in the church. Some believe that ethnic minorities represent vibrant cultures through which God is renewing the total life of the church. They support and seek to nurture cultural uniqueness, although in a context that affirms equally the positive contributions of all cultures.

In an address delivered in El Paso, Texas, Woody White proposed another image to replace the melting pot—that of the "stewpot." The melting-pot metaphor signifies a melding of different races and cultures into one in which each loses its original identity. The stewpot, however, suggests that just as various vegetables and meats contribute to a delicious stew without losing their identities, so can ethnic minorities unite in "oneness" with one another and with the dominant culture while at the same time retaining their highly valuable cultural differences.

A factor that has strengthened pluralism as a significant way of viewing interethnic Christianity is the rapid growth of ethnic minorities in both numbers and influence in the United States. This has prompted mainline churches to reexamine church growth strategies, with an eye toward evangelizing ethnic minorities. Asian and Pacific Americans as well as Hispanics are expanding in numbers too quickly to enable them to be counted accurately. Although blacks are the largest ethnic minority group (which is still growing) in the United States, demographic projections indicate that Hispanics will become the largest minority in the United States, perhaps by the end of this century. Asian and Pacific Americans are immigrating by the thousands to the United States and have formed numerous new churches. Native Americans have asserted themselves throughout recent decades in search of ways to redress historical injustices, thereby pricking the consciences of some Christians.

Those advocating ethnic pluralism argue for not only inclusive worship but also interethnic cooperation in all areas of church life. This is no easy task and demands that Christians of every ethnic background learn how to listen and learn from one another without racist bias but with ears tuned to the authentic sounds of every culture. In a time when several mainline congregations have tended to settle into traditional modes of institutional existence and have even diminished in membership, it may well be that the influx of more people of color into various denominations will offer new life, variety, and enriched cultural perspectives through which the meaning of Christian commitment can

---

[25] Roger Bastide, "Color, Racism, and Christianity," *Color and Race*, ed. John Hope Franklin (Boston: Beacon Press, 1968), p. 34.

be empowered. In recent years increasing numbers of white congregations have experienced this cross-cultural ferment as they have intentionally made contact with ethnic minority churches for cross-cultural worship, interethnic education, and the more difficult task of discussing and debating the church's mission to a suffering world.

It has become clear that the future profile of at least some of the Christian churches in the United States will be pluralistic. This can provide both participants and observers a creative opportunity to examine the interaction between changing patterns of culture and the norms and values of Christian religious groups as they interact in society. Ethnic pluralism represents only one dimension of the phenomenon of pluralism and its increasing range in modern and postmodern societies (see Unit 76). In addition to ethnic pluralism, there is increasing pluralism in life-styles, culture, national and linguistic and religious backgrounds, gender, and sexual orientation. Here the term *white* has been used to refer to a single ethnic grouping, but many whites would question whether they have much in common with other whites of differing national, cultural, or religious backgrounds. Understanding the problems and opportunities that the many kinds of pluralism represent for contemporary societies is possibly the greatest challenge facing contemporary societies and the world as a whole.

CHAPTER 16

❧

Religious Traditions and Social Stability

Introduction

Religious traditions may function as integrative and stabilizing forces in society (as in individual life). They may also function as agents of change or even of conflict in society (and in individual life). In this chapter we will be concerned with the role of religion as a unifying, integrative force in society, and in the next chapter with religion as a factor in social change.

We have defined religion as "reliance on a pivotal value in which the individual finds wholeness as an individual and as a person in community." The term *religious tradition* as used in this chapter refers to any complex patterns of behavior, attitudes, and beliefs that express reliance on, or adherence to, a pivotal value (or values) by a group of people maintained and transmitted with some degree of continuity during a period of time.

In some cases a religious tradition will coincide with the value system of a whole society. In some cases it will be in tension with other value systems in the society. There may be conflicts within the value system of a religious tradition or society. In some cases a religious tradition, even that of a minority group within a larger society, endorses the dominant cultural values. Social change may come about by the adoption in the larger society of specifically religious values or attitudes belonging to what was originally a minority group. In other cases, a religious minority's system may be modified by the adoption into it of attitudes and values prevalent in the larger society.

Religious traditions very often encourage cultural and social stability. Sometimes religion serves as an integrating force in the society even when it encourages social changes. Often, however, it plays a conservative role, resisting change or at least moderating its effects.

The units in this chapter deal with (1) the nature of religious community and some of its roles; (2) the role of religion in a highly unified, traditionally oriented, simply organized Brazilian tribal society; (3) the unity of the various facets of life in classical Greek culture; and (4) one of the major integrating themes or elements of Japanese society, the theme of simplicity.

UNIT 68   Community of Faith

The experience of religion is often uniquely individual. But even in those religions that most emphasize an individualistic approach and that encourage individual beliefs, attitudes, and practices, there is a communal, or group, side to the nurturing of these attitudes and to the preservation and continuity of tradition. This is true even if the tradition being handed on is one that emphasizes and promotes change. Belief in shared objects of faith, participation in shared rituals or practices, adherence to the same pivotal value—all these create community. Again, this is true even in the traditions in which the religious hermit is seen as the highest ideal of human life (as in Christianity in Egypt during the early centuries of the Christian era, and as has frequently been the case in Hinduism). Whatever the religious tradition, the community of faith, dependent itself on individual commitment and participation, provides support and guidance for individual believers and gives them a sense of belonging that helps to define individual identity and supports them in times of personal crisis.

Buddhism is a religious tradition that in many of its forms has been highly individualistic. Theravada Buddhism, especially, has taught that the individual finally must achieve Nirvana (complete enlightenment, fulfillment, salvation) by individual effort alone. Nevertheless, as the Buddhist monk's vow vividly shows, membership in the monastic community is indispensable as a source of discipline, sustaining order, and guidance.

> I take refuge in the Buddha (the Ideal)
> I take refuge in the Dharma (the Law or the Truth)
> I take refuge in the Sangha (the Order of Monks)

Hebrew thought and experience is replete with this sense of community. One of the most ancient creeds, repeated individually through the centuries, is a striking example of the corporate nature of religion:

> A wandering Aramean was my father; and he went down into Egypt and sojourned there, few in number; and there he became a nation, great, mighty, and populous. And the Egyptians treated us harshly, and afflicted us, and laid upon us hard bondage. Then we cried to the Lord the God of our fathers, and the Lord heard our voice, and saw our affliction, our toil, and our oppression; and the Lord brought us out of Egypt with a mighty hand and an outstretched arm, with great terror, with signs and wonders; and he brought us into this place and gave us this land, a land flowing with milk and honey. (Deuteronomy 26:5–9, RSV)

A contemporary expression of the significance of community is given by Malcolm X. A leader of the black movement in the early 1960s, Malcolm X converted to the Muslim faith and traveled to Mecca to participate in the hadj (the sacred pilgrimage).

> The believers indeed are brothers; so set things right between your two brothers, and fear God; haply so you will find mercy.[1]

Impressed, as a black man, with the oneness of the brotherhood, Malcolm X commented extensively on how common belief breaks down all lines of distinction—especially that of color. Having been asked what most impressed him in the hadj, he replied,

> I said, "The *brotherhood!* The people of all races, colors, from all over the world coming together as *one!* It has proved to me the power of the One God. . . ."
>
> I have reflected since that the letter I finally sat down to compose had been subconsciously shaping itself in my mind.
>
> The *color-blindness* of the Muslim world's religious society and the *color-blindness* of the Muslim world's human society; these two influences had each day been making a greater impact, and an increasing persuasion against my previous way of thinking.
>
> Here is what I wrote . . . from my heart:
>
> Never have I witnessed such sincere hospitality and the overwhelming spirit of true brotherhood as is practiced by people of all colors and races here in this Ancient Holy Land, the home of Abraham, Muhammad, and all the other prophets of the Holy Scriptures. For the past week, I have been utterly speechless and spellbound by the graciousness I see displayed all around me by the people *of all colors. . . .*
>
> America needs to understand Islam, because this is the one religion that erases from its society the race problem. Throughout my travels in the Muslim world, I have met, talked to, and even eaten with people who in America would have been considered "white"—but the "white" attitude was removed from their minds by the religion of Islam. I have never before seen *sincere* and *true* brotherhood practiced by all colors together, irrespective of their color. . . .
>
> During the past eleven days here in the Muslim world, I have eaten from the same plate, drunk from the same glass, and slept in the same bed (or on the same rug)—while praying to the *same* God—with fellow Muslims, whose eyes were the bluest of blue, whose hair was the blondest of blond, and whose skin was the whitest of white. And in the *words* and in the *actions* and in the *deeds* of the "white" Muslims, I felt the same sincerity that I felt among the black African Muslims of Nigeria, Sudan, and Ghana.
>
> We were *truly* all the same (brothers)—because their belief in one God had removed the "white" from their *minds,* the "white" from their *behavior,* and the "white" from their *attitude.*
>
> I could see from this, that perhaps if white Americans could accept the Oneness of God, then perhaps, too, they could accept in *reality* the Oneness of Man—and cease to measure, and hinder, and harm others in terms of their "differences" in color. . . .
>
> All praise is due to Allah, the Lord of all Worlds.[2]

Is it possible to have religion without some community of faith?

Is there a central affirmation that holds the community together in the preceding examples?

[1] Arthur J. Arberry, *The Koran Interpreted*, Sura XLIX, verse 10. (New York: Macmillan, 1955).

[2] Malcolm X, *The Autobiography of Malcolm X*, with the assistance of Alex Haley, pp. 338–42. Reprinted by permission of Grove Press Inc. Copyright © 1964 by Alex Haley and Malcolm X. Copyright © 1965 by Alex Haley and Betty Shabazz.

UNIT 69   Wholeness of Life in a Simply Structured Society

The role of religion as a unifying element within society may be illustrated by a preliterate and simply structured society. In a book called *Tristes Tropiques*, the French anthropologist Claude Lévi-Strauss records observations made during his stay in a Bororo village in the interior of Brazil. The village, with a population of about 150, was a self-contained society, and at the time of Lévi-Strauss's observations it had been relatively little affected by the outside influences of European or Brazilian cultures.

One of the centers of Bororo life was the "men's house," a large building in the middle of the village. The young, unmarried males of the Bororo tribe lived there; married males often took their meals and spent much of their leisure time in the men's house. It was also the place where preparations for the religious activities of the village went on: Religious chants were sung, and the closely guarded religious implements of the community (women were not allowed to see them) were made and stored. Married women were not allowed to enter the men's house; an unmarried woman was supposed to enter the building only once, when she came to propose marriage to her future husband.

Lévi-Strauss contrasts the Bororo attitude toward the "religious" dimension of life as he observed it in the men's house with the attitude he believed to be more characteristic of contemporary European society.

> For the European observer, the apparently incompatible activities carried out in the men's house seem to harmonize in an almost shocking way. Few peoples are as deeply religious as the Bororo, and few have such a complex metaphysical system. But spiritual beliefs and everyday habits are closely intermingled, and the natives do not appear to be conscious of moving from one system to another. I found the same easy-going religiosity in Buddhist temples along the Burmese frontier, where the priests live and sleep in the same hall as is used for worship, arrange their jars of ointment and personal collections of medicines on the ground in front of the altar. . . .
>
> This casual attitude to the supernatural was . . . surprising to me . . . I lived during the First World War with my grandfather, who was Rabbi of Versailles. The house was attached to the synagogue by a long inner passage, along which it was difficult to venture without a feeling of anguish, and which in itself formed an impassable frontier between the profane world and that other. . . . Except when services were in progress, the synagogue remained empty. . . . Apart from my grandfather's silent prayer at the beginning of each meal, we children had no means of knowing that we were living under the egis of a superior order. . . .
>
> Not that religion was treated with greater reverence among the Bororo; on the contrary, it was taken for granted. In the men's house, ritualistic gestures were performed with the same casualness as all others, as if they were utilitarian actions intended to achieve a particular result, and did not require that respectful attitude which even the non-believer feels compelled to adopt on entering a place of worship. On a particular afternoon there would be singing in the men's house in preparation for the evening's public ritual. In one corner, boys would be snoring or chatting; two or three men would be humming and shaking rattles, but if one of them wanted to light a cigarette or if it were his turn to dip into the maize gruel, he would hand the instrument to a neighbour who carried on; or sometimes he would continue with one hand, while scratching himself with the other. When a dancer paraded up and down to allow his latest creation to be admired, everybody would

stop and comment upon it; the service might seem to be forgotten until, in some other corner, the incantation was resumed at the point where it had been interrupted.[3]

In another passage, Lévi-Strauss describes one part of an elaborate funeral ceremony in the Bororo village:

> Groups of men went into the forest to fetch armfuls of green palms, which were stripped of their leaves and then divided up into sections about 30 centimeters long. These were crudely tied together by the natives with dried grass, in bundles of two or three, like the rungs of a rope ladder several metres long. Two ladders of unequal length were made in this way, and then rolled up to form two solid discs, standing edgewise and respectively about 1.50 metres and 1.30 metres high. The sides were decorated with leaves held in place by a network of fine string made of plaited hair. These discs were the male and female *mariddo*, and the making of them devolved upon the *Ewaguddu* clan.
>
> Towards evening two groups, each consisting of five or six men, set out, one to the west, the other to the east. I followed the first group, and saw them making their preparations about fifty metres from the village, behind a screen of trees which concealed them from the other villagers. They covered themselves with leaves, like the dancers, and fixed their crowns in position. But this time, the secrecy of their preparations could be explained by the part they were playing: like the other group, they represented the souls of the dead which had come from their villages in the east and the west to welcome the deceased. When all was ready, they moved towards the dancing area, whistling as they went. The eastern group had already preceded them there (one group was, symbolically, going upstream, the other downstream, and the latter therefore moved faster).
>
> Their timid and hesitant gait admirably conveyed their ghostly nature; I was reminded of Homer—of Ulysses struggling to prevent the flight of the ghosts repelled by blood. But all at once, the ceremony burst into life: men seized one or other of the two *mariddo* (which were all the heavier through having been made with fresh vegetation), lifted it high in the air and, thus encumbered, danced until they were exhausted and had to allow a rival to take it from them. The scene no longer had any mystic character; it had turned into a fair, where the young men were showing off their physical prowess in an atmosphere characterized by sweat, thumpings and gibes. And yet this sport, which exists in secular forms among neighbouring communities,—for instance, in the log races practiced by the Ge tribes of the Brazilian plateau—retains its full religious significance with the Bororo: in this mood of gay abandon, the natives feel they are playing with the dead and wresting from them the right to remain alive.[4]

For Bororo society, "the religious" is not, then, one aspect or activity of life, distinct from other aspects. There is not a specifically religious attitude different from the attitude toward everyday or secular activities and events; the religious dimension of life thoroughly penetrates and is penetrated by the nonreligious dimensions; in fact, speaking of the religious and the nonreligious or secular as two different dimensions of life would probably be foreign to the Bororo way of thinking. Nevertheless, Lévi-Strauss points out that there is a social division of labor in religious matters. "The women were excluded from the [religious] rites and deceived as to their true nature—doubtless to sanction the

[3] Adapted from *Tristes Tropiques* by Claude Lévi-Strauss. Copyright © 1955 by Librairie Plon. English translation copyright © 1973 by Jonathan Cape Limited. Reprinted by permission of Georges Borchardt, Inc.

[4] Ibid., pp. 227–28.

division of rights by which [women] take priority, where housing and birth rites are in question, leaving the mysteries of religion to their men."[5]

❧

How does the Bororo attitude compare with the attitude of classical Greek society toward religion as a dimension of life?

It is interesting that a similar social division of responsibility existed in classical Greece: Women and slaves did not participate fully in the "wholeness" of Greek life, which was economically and politically more complex than Bororo society. Has this been true of most societies?

UNIT 70   Wholeness of Life in Classical Greece

Unit 69 describes the unifying effect of religion in a simple society. This same function of unification may also be observed in more complex societies such as that of the ancient Greeks. H. D. F. Kitto, in a book that studies the life and culture of Greece, focusing particularly on the classical period (especially the sixth and fifth centuries B.C.), has emphasized the *wholeness* of outlook that characterized Greek civilization. Typically, the Greeks of the classical period did not see different dimensions of life (like the religious and the secular, the moral and the aesthetic, the intellectual and the physical, the private and the social) as separated from one another. Many civilizations have made rather sharp distinctions among these areas. The wholeness, or integration, of the various areas of life in Greek civilization can be seen, Kitto thinks, if we examine some Greek terms. The word *kalos* is usually translated as "beautiful," but *kalos* is used to describe actions that we would consider heroic or noble, traits of character we would consider morally good, and instruments that are well made or useful. In fact the word means something like "worthy of warm admiration" and may be used to refer to goodness or beauty or appropriateness—anything that we might want to classify under one of the following categories: moral, intellectual, aesthetic, or practical. Kitto thinks that most civilizations, including our own, have made distinctions among these categories, but the Greeks did not. In the same way, the Greek word *aischros*, usually translated as "ugly," can be used to describe morally bad actions, physical ugliness, baseness (in the sense of lack of worth or merit), uselessness (in the practical sense) and badness of character. To look at two other terms, Kitto notes that

> The word "hamartia" means "error," "fault," "crime" or even "sin"; literally, it means "missing the mark," "a bad shot." We exclaim, "How intellectualist these Greeks were! Sin is just 'missing the mark'; better luck next time!" Again we seem to find confirmation when we find that some of the Greek virtues seem to be as much intellectual as moral—a fact that makes them untranslatable, since our own vocabulary must distinguish. There is "Sôphrosynê," literally "whole-mindedness" or "unimpaired-mindedness." According to the context it will mean "wisdom," "prudence," "temperateness," "chastity," "sobriety," "modesty," or "self-control," that is, something entirely intellectual, something entirely

---

[5] Ibid., pp. 229–30.

moral, or something intermediate. Our difficulty with the word, as with *hamartia*, is that we think more in departments. *Hamartia*, "a bad shot," does not mean "better luck next time"; it means rather that a mental error is as blameworthy, and may be as deadly, as a moral one.[6]

∾

Do you find that people in modern society tend to see religious and secular activities as separate or different from each other?

∾

Kitto finds the classical Greek understanding of life's wholeness clearly present in the Greek attitude toward athletic contests:

The sharp distinction which the Christian and the Oriental world has normally drawn between the body and the soul, the physical and the spiritual, was foreign to the Greek—at least until the time of Socrates and Plato. To him there was simply the whole man. That the body is the tomb of the soul is indeed an idea which we meet in certain Greek mystery-religions, and Plato, with his doctrine of immortality, necessarily distinguished sharply between body and soul; but for all that, it is not a typical Greek idea. The Greek made physical training an important part of education, not because he said to himself, "Look here, we mustn't forget the body," but because it could never occur to him to train anything but the whole man. It was as natural for the polis to have gymnasia as to have a theatre or warships, and they were constantly used by men of all ages, not only for physical but also for mental exercise.

∾

Is Kitto right in saying that Christianity has "normally drawn" a "sharp distinction" between body and soul, the physical and the spiritual?

Can you find aspects of Christian belief or practice that go against this kind of separation?

Do Oriental or Eastern religions—for instance, Hinduism or Zen Buddhism—make as sharp a distinction between the physical and the spiritual as Kitto suggests?

To what extent does modern society make a sharp distinction between the physical and the spiritual, the intellectual and the spiritual, or the intellectual and the moral?

∾

But it is the Games, local and international, which most clearly illustrate this side of the Greek mind. Among us it is sometimes made a reproach that a man "makes a religion of games." The Greek did not do this, but he did something perhaps more surprising: he made games part of his religion. To be quite explicit, the Olympian games, the greatest of the four international festivals, were held in honor of Zeus of Olympia, the Pythian Games in honour of Apollo, the Panathenaic Games in honor of Athena. Moreover, they were held in the sacred precinct. The feeling that prompted this was a perfectly natural one. The contest was a means of stimulating and displaying human *aretê*, and this was a worthy offering to the god. . . . But since *aretê* is of the mind as well as of the body, there was not

[6] H. D. F. Kitto, *The Greeks*. Copyright © H. D. F. Kitto, 1951, 1957, pp. 170–71. Used by permission of Penguin Books, Ltd.

the slightest incongruity or affectation in combining musical contests with athletic: a contest in flute-playing was an original fixture in the Pythian Games—for was not Apollo himself "Lord of the Lyre"?

[The Greek word *aretê* is usually translated to mean "virtue," but "excellence" is probably better since in modern English, "virtue" usually means *only* "moral goodness."]

It was *aretê* that the games were designed to test—the *aretê* of the whole man, not a merely specialized skill. The usual events were a sprint, of about 200 yards, the long race (1½ miles), the race in armour, throwing the discus, and the javelin, the long jump, wrestling, boxing (of a very dangerous kind), and chariot-racing. The great event was the pentathlon: a race, a jump, throwing the discus, and the javelin, and wrestling. If you won this, you were a man. Needless to say, the Marathon race was never heard of until modern times: the Greeks would have regarded it as a monstrosity. As for the skill shown by modern champions in games like golf or billiards, the Greeks would certainly have admired it intensely, and thought it an admirable thing—in a slave, supposing that one had no better use for a slave than to train him in this way. Impossible, he would say, to acquire skill like this and at the same time to live the proper life of a man and a citizen. It is this feeling that underlies Aristotle's remark that a gentleman should be able to play the flute—but not too well.[7]

This stress on the unity of language and on athletic competence in many sports illustrates the integration of all of one's abilities in Greek culture. Religion tended to unify or support these and other elements of life, both social and individual.

Does the fact of vocational specialization in complex, modern societies—the fact that there are religious professionals (ministers, priests, rabbis), professional athletes, military professionals, professional critics of art and literature, and so forth—necessarily lead to a division of life, a loss of the wholeness or integration of its different parts or dimensions?

Unit 71   Japanese Fondness for Simplicity

The Japanese cherish simplicity, which has been a characteristic unifying element in Japanese culture. It has helped the Japanese adapt foreign ideas, forms of expression, and practices to Japanese life, integrating them into Japanese culture and giving them a distinctively Japanese flavor. It has also helped integrate religious traditions so that both the native religions and those imported have a particular Japanese form and character.

Fondness for simplicity is seen in most areas of Japanese life and expression. For each of the examples cited in the following discussion by Hajime Nakamura, compare Western attitudes toward simplicity or the lack of it in the corresponding areas of life.

Traditionally, the Japanese have been inclined to dislike fanciful, complicated expressions and to take to simple and naive expressions. The Japanese language . . . is deficient in words expressing prolix and abstract conceptions. Consequently, even to this day, they use Chinese words, in most cases, to express abstract ideas.

[7] Ibid., pp. 173–74.

In art, also, this tendency can be discerned clearly. The Japanese are very fond of the impromptu short verse, like the *haiku* and *tanka*. In the history of Japanese poetry, the long verse . . . is reduced to a short one (*tanka*), and then to a still shorter one (*haiku*). The extremely short form of artistic expression is characteristically Japanese and the like of it cannot be found elsewhere. . . . In Japanese literature, lyric poems and scenery sketches have been highly developed, but poems of grand style, with dramatic plots full of twists and turns, have made only a poor start.

Tanka—a thirty-one-syllable poem
Haiku—a seventeen-syllable poem

The *haiku* is extraordinarily *simple,* but it is highly symbolic and suggestive. Here is an example by the poet Matsuo Bashō (1644–1694):

Breaking the surface
of a still pond a frog jumps—
    The silence echoes

Not only in poetry but also in architecture, we can recognize the characteristic love of simplicity. The Japanese imported various formative arts from Indian Buddhism, indirectly through the hands of Chinese and Koreans. As seen in the magnificent splendor of golden Buddhist altars and mural paintings of temples, the complicated sculptures of transoms, the fantastic statue of the Goddess of Mercy . . . with a thousand arms, the square diagram of figures (Mandala) with its intricate and delicate composition—all of them had, in general, a very elaborate structure. But, such an art could hardly penetrate into the life of the common people. The Japanese could not abandon the simple and unpainted wooden architecture of ancient style, in many shrines as well as in the Great Shrine of Ise. [See Figure 16.1.] And, even in the architecture of Buddhist temples, the various sects of the Kamakura period [1185–1333] turned to a rather simple style. Also, in the Zen-influenced taste of the tea-ceremony house, we can discern a naive simplicity. . . . In some cases, especially under the influence of the Zen cult, the Japanese endeavored to infuse unlimited complexity into this simplicity. This tendency emerged especially in such arts as architecture, drawing, and poetry. For example, the void of empty spaces or of silent pauses is often not devoid, in fact, of important meaning. Even in the etiquette and conversation of everyday life, silence can be a very positive expression at times. This ideal fusion of the complex and the simple was realized by the Chinese people, who loved complicated thinking and whose spiritual life was greatly influenced by the Zen cult. When introduced into Japan, however, this, too, was altered by greater simplification. . . .

Thus, because complicated symbols were not used by the Japanese in their thinking, the philosophical theories of Indian and Chinese Buddhism were too profound, abstruse, and complicated to penetrate into the life of the common people in Japan. Consequently, they had to be simplified.

The Japanese, in assimilating Buddhism, did not depend upon its philosophical doctrines. Of course, the clergymen of large temples were engaged in philosophical debates and wrote a great number of books. The common people, however, demanded concrete and empirical clues rather than philosophical theories. . . .

The tendency to fondness for simple symbols appeared in the process of adoption of Buddhist ideas by Japanese Shintoists in ancient and medieval times. . . . Shintō, in the process of its development as religion, advanced from the cleanness of the body to the idea of cleanness of spirit. This "internal cleanness" was expressed by moral virtues of "sincerity" and "honesty." The virtues of gods of Shintō were admired through these virtues. But we can find these terms in the Buddhist sūtras. Besides, the benevolence and wisdom, admired as virtues of gods, are, of course, Buddhist terms. Therefore, it is not too much to say that almost all of the terms of the central virtues of medieval Shintō were derived from Buddhist sūtras. It must be pointed out, however, that Shintoists never adopted the doctrines of Buddhism indiscriminately. Only the virtues, which had originally existed as germs in Shintō, were brought to definite consciousness and expression by the help of Buddhist philosophy. The Shintoists did not take in the speculative, schematized, and generalized classifications of virtues of the Indian Buddhism. . . . ["Virtues of the Indian Buddhism" refers to such teachings as those contained in the Four Noble Truths and the Eightfold Path. See Unit 19, Gautama's Quest for Nirvana.] They took in directly those virtues which happened to appear congenial to Shintō. Consequently, they hardly endeavored to interpret the relations among these virtues systematically and speculatively.

We have tried to demonstrate that through the process of assimilation of Buddhism many Japanese people are inclined to give direction to their practice through very simple symbols. This tendency reappeared, it seems, in the introduction of Christianity from the period of the Civil Wars [which lasted for a century] to the beginning of the Tokugawa period in the 17th century. The Japanese Christians [Roman Catholics] devoted themselves to such simple symbols of Christianity as the cross. [See Figure 16.2.] The trampling of the holy image (*Fumi-e*) sufficed, on this psychological ground, as a loyalty test at the time of the Christian Inquisition in Japan [that is, the period when Japanese Christians were being tortured and executed if they refused to renounce their Christian faith.]

We may say that religion is always simplified when it is popularized. . . . If we look back to the trend of Japanese thought in recent years, we can realize that the complete reliance upon simple symbols has been one of the most deep-rooted attitudes of the Japanese people.[8]

Figure 16.1   The Ise Shrine, in Japan, is the national shrine of Japanese Shintoism. (Courtesy Ministry of Foreign Affairs, Government of Japan.)

[8] Hajime Nakamura, *Ways of Thinking of Eastern Peoples: India-China-Tibet-Japan* (Honolulu, HA: East-West Center Press, 1964), pp. 564–65, 572–73. By permission of the University Press of Hawaii.

Figure 16.2
Sacred image, a copper or wooden tablet with a crucifix or the Virgin Mary, used by the Tokugawa government to suppress Christianity. All who refused to tread on such an image (the test was conducted every New Year after 1628) were executed as Christians. (Tokyo National Museum. Reproduced by permission.)

CHAPTER 17

❧

Religious Traditions and Social Change

Introduction

As society becomes more open, urbanized, and heterogeneous, social stability becomes more difficult to maintain. At the same time, religious institutions themselves cannot remain unaffected. They respond to change either positively or negatively—that is, either by coming to terms with the new problems or by resistance and withdrawal from them.

In this chapter we present aspects of the response religious institutions may make to the problems relating to social change. The first unit is centered on population growth and the resultant mass hunger. In Unit 73 we consider the rapid increase in the growth of technology, and in Unit 74 the process of secularization. The stress between forces of change and the reluctance of some people in every society to identify with change is the focus of Unit 75. The patterns and character of modernization and the alienation it creates are the topics of the final unit.

UNIT 72   The Challenge of World Hunger

The problem of hunger is acute and promises to become more so with each passing year. Concerned people throughout the world ponder the complexities of the food crisis, what has led to its more rapid development, and what solutions may be found. This unit looks at some of the issues raised by the problem of hunger as it causes rapid social change.

(by Jacques Bakke)

What Is Hunger[1]

Hunger is a weakened condition brought about by the prolonged lack of food. There are four basic types of hunger.

Chronic Undernutrition

Undernutrition results when people do not consume sufficient calories and protein over a prolonged period of time. This is the most widespread but least recognized form of hunger. It is invisible, persistent, and debilitating. The headlines capture dramatic images of acute starvation, but the vast majority of the hungry suffer in quiet obscurity through chronic undernutrition. The effects include

Decreased mental attentiveness
Permanent mental retardation

[1] Much of the material in this unit is drawn from *The Hunger Primer,* a publication of Food for the Hungry, a Christian hunger-relief organization. Used by permission.

Increased susceptibility to disease
Listlessness
Decreased productivity
Emotional stress

Malnutrition

Malnutrition results from specific deficiencies in essential vitamins and minerals vital to good health. Malnutrition is closely related to undernutrition, but the physical manifestations are more obvious. Common effects include

Blindness: Up to 100,000 children become blind each year because of insufficient vitamin A.
Anemia: In developing countries 500 million women are anemic because of a lack of iron in their diets.
Death: Starvation resulting in death is the ultimate consequence of extreme malnutrition.

Famine

Famine is the widespread, extreme scarcity of food, affecting an entire region. Often it is closely associated with disasters such as drought, flood, and war, which disrupt the availability of food to an area. Without social institutions able to handle the crisis, famine results. No more than 10 percent of hunger-related deaths are due to famine. Food may exist in an area struck by famine, but because of the deep poverty of the people, it is available only to the wealthy. Modern economic patterns that emphasize the global marketing of food and general agricultural products have meant a major shift in many developing countries to cash crops in areas where previously crops supported only the local economy. Consequently, decreased acreage is planted in foodstuffs for local consumption. Sometimes such changes have caused a widespread loss of productivity, and local famine now occurs even in countries where food is exported. In Africa, inappropriate agricultural technologies combined with drought have caused vast areas of productive land to become desert. Presently, the desert in some places is expanding at a rate of some 6 miles per year, threatening famine to those who live in the area.

Seasonal Undernutrition

Seasonal undernutrition occurs annually, as harvests stored from the previous year are depleted before the new crops can be harvested. Families may go hungry for weeks or even months at a time.

What is the Magnitude of Hunger?

One out of every eight people is hungry most of the time.
Four hundred fifty million people, one-fourth of the developing world, suffer from undernutrition.
Every year, almost thirteen million people die as a result of hunger and starvation—the equivalent of all the children under five in the United States. This means more people

have died from hunger in the past 10 years than have been killed in all wars, revolutions, and murders in the past 150 years.

One billion people have various degrees of brain damage because of inadequate consumption.

Who Are the Hungry?

Children

One-third of all the children in developing countries die of malnourishment before age five.

Of the twenty-four people that die from hunger each minute, eighteen are children.

One out of every four children in the developing world dies by the age of five from hunger and hunger-related causes.

According to Brazilian government data, 400,000 children less than one year old die each year, many from malnutrition and hunger.

Rural Poor

Three-quarters of the hungry live in rural areas.

Over 600 million people live in rural households that are either completely landless or near landless.

In Latin America, 7 percent of the farmers own 93 percent of the land, and more than 60 percent of the rural poor are landless altogether. Eight out of ten farmers in central America cannot grow crops for themselves.

Urban Poor

One-fourth of the hungry live in burgeoning urban slums.

Slums form up to 75 percent or more of the cities in some developing countries, with as many as twenty people living in one room.

Millions of rural landless have moved to cities in the hope of finding work but discover that jobs are not available.

Refugees

A refugee is a person who flees home to escape invasion, oppression, persecution, or natural disasters such as drought and famine.

Currently, according to the U.N. High Commission for Refugees, 17 million people are classified as refugees.

At least 1 million people a year are added to the list of refugees in the world.

Approximately 850,000 refugees have resettled in the United States.

Recent turmoil created by war and ethnic strife in eastern Europe and Africa has greatly added to the refugee population.

What Are the Causes of Hunger?

It is difficult to attribute hunger to a single cause. Much of it today arises from economic, social, technological, and demographic changes that have accompanied the development of modern civilization. A major result of these changes is a vastly increasing population and the stress it puts on food supply and distribution. Arthur Simon offers the following insights:

Almost two centuries ago, in 1798, an Englishman named Thomas Malthus warned that the population would race ahead of the food supply. It would do so, he argued, because we can only *add* to the food supply, while the population *multiplies*. At that time the world's population of less than one billion was growing at a rate of about one-half of 1 percent annually. Now the growth rate is about 2 percent for the world and 2.5 percent for poor countries as a whole. These percentages may seem small, but the increase makes a dramatic difference.

By 1930 the world had two billion people. If you were born in 1930, the world's population has already doubled within your lifetime; and if you live to the turn of the century, you will be able to add still another two or three billion people. *During your lifetime the earth's living population will have more than tripled its previous total achievement.*

That is an explosion.

It explains why the population graphs show a horizontal line veering suddenly upward—as though a cyclist, riding along a barely noticeable slope, began pedaling straight up a cliff.

The world is presently adding 70 million persons each year to its numbers: the equivalent of the entire U.S. population every three years. Most of this growth is taking place in the poor countries, among hungry people. Today's poor countries already contain more than two-thirds of the earth's population. Soon they will contain three-fourths, and by the turn of the century, four-fifths of the human race. All the while demand for the world's food supply will climb sharply each year, and—barring unprecedented global efforts—increasing numbers will wind up in the "hungry" category. No wonder the mother from the Bronx and a great many other U.S. citizens are saying: "The only solution to the hunger problem is birth control."

Consider the evidence, however:

Lower death rates, not higher birth rates, are responsible for today's population growth. Poor countries as a whole have actually lowered their birth rates slightly over the past several decades—but death rates have dropped more sharply, and that achievement has touched off the population boom. Advances in medicine and public health, along with increases in food production, account for most gains against early death. For example, while Malthus wrote his *Essay on Population,* a fellow Englishman named Edward Jenner was discovering a vaccination for smallpox. This discovery foreshadowed a long series of steps in disease control that cut back death rates.

The population explosion began in Europe. Not the "inconsiderate poor" of Asia, Africa and Latin America, but our own ancestors touched it off. A few simple statistics show this. In 1800 about 22 percent of the human race was Caucasian; but by 1930 (only five or six generations later) that percentage had jumped to about 35. This happened because the new technologies that pushed back the death rate occurred in the West. During that time the white, European peoples had two enormous advantages:

1. *Industrial growth kept ahead of population increases.* Because gains in public health occurred gradually, population growth rates also increased gradually. The Industrial Revolution had begun earlier, so the population increase was usually needed in the cities by industries, which depended upon a growing supply of unskilled workers. Although the Industrial Revolution imposed cruel hardships on those who moved from farms to sweatshops and urban slums, the suffering would have been greater and the social situation far more explosive had the population raced ahead of industrial jobs. But the jobs usually got there first.

2. *New lands opened up for colonization.* New lands, including North America, offered an important outlet to population stresses that did develop. For example after the potato famine

ravaged Ireland in the 1840s, almost a million Irish came to our shores within five years. When periods of unemployment occurred, new lands provided a place to seek work. They also handed European peoples an impressive psychological advantage by keeping hopes alive.

Poor nations face a sharply different situation today. Two centuries of public health gains were made available to them more rapidly, so their populations began to soar almost without warning. Their people now pour into the cities long before industries can possibly supply them with jobs; and for all but a few there simply is no frontier, no new lands to colonize, no safety valve.

Population growth was cushioned in the West (1) because the death rate receded gradually, and (2) because people became economically more self-sufficient and less dependent upon their offspring for security. Today's poor countries have moved quickly into the first stage: Public health measures and modern medicine have reduced the death rate—but much faster than in the West, causing their populations to multiply more swiftly. *But the second stage is not taking hold.* A majority of people in the poor countries are *not* moving toward the point where their sense of security is clearly related to having fewer children. Instead the opposite usually applies: more children mean more security."[2]

Today most experts agree that a main cause of hunger is *poverty,* or the lack of financial, material, and educational resources. The world's poor do not have enough of these resources to provide a subsistence livelihood for their families. However, hunger and poverty are not due to a simple lack of resources. Inequitable use of resources, poor stewardship, and systems that perpetuate this inequality do not allow the poor to have access to the resources that are available. Disparate patterns of land ownership, often supported by biased world trade policies, concentrate resources in the hands of the wealthy few. Agricultural technology has often been inappropriately applied to food production in poor countries, and adequate technological training has not been provided for indigenous rural populations. The interdependence of a world economy, in which the consumer demand of richer countries drives the economy of poorer countries toward the export of cash crops and natural resources, often extracts necessary resources and labor from poorer countries rather than alleviating poverty and hunger.

Population growth also contributes to the expansion of poverty. Improvements in Western medical technology shared with the developing countries has greatly diminished the death rate in many countries. Birth control has also been resisted in many cultures, resulting in a continual population increase.

Some Moral Dimensions in Solving the Problem

Although world food output has expanded impressively over the past generation, population growth so far has absorbed all but a fraction of the increase. Hundreds of millions of the world's people still do not have enough food to fully realize their genetic potential as human beings. In a situation of global food scarcity, if some of us consume more, others must of necessity consume less. The issue that some of us are forced to confront in a world where we are dependent on common resources of energy and fertilizer to produce food is whether we can realize *our* full humanity if we continue to overconsume in full knowledge that we are thereby contributing to the premature death of fellow human beings. Former Chancellor Willy Brandt of West Germany summed up this point effectively in his first address before the U.N. General Assembly in the fall of 1973: "Morally

---

[2] Arthur Simon, *Bread for the World* (New York: Paulist Press, 1975), pp. 28–31. Used by permission.

it makes no difference whether a man is killed in war or is condemned to starve to death by the indifference of others."

Altruism is a hallmark of civilized society. But in a world transformed from a collection of relatively independent, isolated nation-states to one of complex interdependence, reliant on the sharing of often scarce resources, our concept of altruism must be adjusted. It is no longer merely a matter of alms-giving but of abstaining from excessive consumption when that consumption jeopardizes the very survival of human beings elsewhere in the world. For a man with only one crust of bread, a second crust may ensure survival, but for one with a loaf of bread, an additional crust is of marginal value. What is at issue in the global politics of food scarcity is who will get the additional crust—affluent consumers . . . who do not need it, or those on the brink of survival in the Indian subcontinent and in the sub-Saharan countries of Africa. . . .

Both conventional wisdom and economics have long held that the more the rich countries consume, the greater the markets will be for products of the developing countries. This is still true in some situations, but only to a degree. If the supply of a given resource cannot be expanded easily, continuing growth in consumption in the affluent countries will drive the price beyond the reach of the poor countries.

Our intent here is not to suggest that all affluent Americans, Europeans, or Japanese should abandon their automobiles or abstain from eating meat; it is to urge those who are more affluent to re-examine the link between their consumption of material goods and their own well-being. We need to ask whether a 20 percent increase in income indeed brings a 20 percent increase in well-being, a 10 percent increase, or any increase at all. It has been said that there are two sources of unhappiness: not getting what we want, and getting it. Many of us may be in a situation where the only real satisfaction can come from trying to improve the lot of the world's most seriously deprived: those living in the Fourth World. Indeed, this could be the new moral and social frontier for mankind.[3]

Religion and Hunger

Because of their differing attitudes toward humanity and nature itself, religions vary greatly in their assessment of individual and corporate religious responsibility for social and economic conditions. Judaism, Christianity, and Islam have insisted that religion is a relevant force in all social organization—so the economy and its impact is of great moral concern. The preceding quotation on the moral dimensions of poverty and hunger reflects the type of concern raised by these traditions.

Similarly, Chinese religions and those of other nations influenced by Chinese civilization, particularly Japan and Korea, have understood religion to influence significantly the social context. In the modern world, economic issues and their consequences have been an important part of their religious concern.

Hinduism and Buddhism, with their traditional emphases on spirituality, have not usually concentrated on social issues, so modern difficulties raised by economic developments do not typically attract significant attention among adherents of these religions. However, in recent years religious leaders of these traditions, particularly Buddhism, have begun to apply their moral teachings to the social setting, including those where economic injustice produces poverty.

[3] Lester R. Brown, *By Bread Alone* (New York: Praeger Publishers, 1974), pp. 250–51. Reprinted by permission of Praeger Publishers, a Division of Holt, Rinehart & Winston.

The rising tide of hunger and poverty dramatically raises new moral and ethical dilemmas for today's religious leaders. As the economy of the world becomes even more interdependent, traditional answers and solutions will not suffice. Religious leaders are called on to rethink and adapt traditional teachings in the face of new and intensifying global problems of hunger and overpopulation.

UNIT 73   Religion, Humanity, and Technology

A prehominid, a manlike primate, is toying with a large bone from a long-dead animal; while manipulating it, he accidentally discovers a function for it. He makes of it a tool, a weapon. Another step is taken in the process of learning to manipulate the environment to satisfy personal or group needs. Others learn this new skill, and a new stage in the sophistication of the species begins.

Humans embark on the long journey to the planet Jupiter in a complex, computer-operated spacecraft. The newest accomplishment of human technology has reached an unprecedented level of sophistication. Without the efficient functioning of the intricate computer system, the life-support system as well as the transport to the distant planet would not be possible. En route, complications develop that result in the decision by the computer system to sacrifice human beings in the interest of completing the mission for which it was programmed. Human technology is then beyond control, and the passengers are at its mercy.

Stanley Kubrick, in his fascinating film *2001: A Space Odyssey*, voices a protest against humanity becoming a slave to its technology. As human beings develop new tools to meet their needs in the exploration and understanding of their immediate and distant environment, must they not also discern those points where technology no longer serves its creative purpose or where it even dehumanizes the species? The following materials elaborate on the problems raised by technology and some responses given to them.

How do different religious traditions look at technology? The answer to this question can be found perhaps by asking how the different religious traditions look at humanity in relation to nature and history. How do the different religious traditions view historical change? Will human beings have a role in shaping the future? If they do, is this a way of fulfilling their destiny or is it a kind of impiety, a way of disrupting the divinely or naturally ordained patterns of life?

The Protestant theologian Harvey Cox has argued that the Judeo-Christian tradition has been inconsistent or ambivalent in answering these questions. He has found three different positions about the role of humanity in shaping the future. In the Jewish or Christian tradition some people have held an "apocalyptic" view that foresees an imminent catastrophe brought about by direct divine intervention. This view carries a negative evaluation of the present world, of humans' ability to shape the future through their own efforts and therefore through their own technology. A second view is the "teleological." It sees the future as the certain unfolding of fixed purposes built into the structure of the universe. Present technological efforts, as a part of the automatic movement to the future, may be valued highly. But the human responsibility to exercise critical judgment about which technological possibilities to develop and how to use them tends to be ignored. Finally, some people have held a position described by Cox as "prophetic." The prophetic tradition, he believes, has emphasized that the future is open and that it will become what the human race makes of it. Thus, both human technology and the responsibility to use it wisely, with concern for its effects on the whole human community, are stressed.[4]

Cox's analysis gives us a typology defining how Protestant Christianity has responded to the problem. Two popes of the Roman Catholic church in recent years have issued encyclicals that present a particular Christian position regarding human technology in relation to God's will and purposes.

> Peace on earth, which men of every era have most eagerly yearned for, can be firmly established only if the order laid down by God is dutifully observed.
>
> The progress of learning and the inventions of technology clearly show that, both in living things and in the forces of nature, an astonishing order reigns, and they also bear witness to the greatness of man, who can understand that order and create suitable instruments to harness those forces of nature and use them to his benefit.
>
> But the progress of science and the inventions of technology show above all the infinite greatness of God, who created the universe and man himself. He created all things out of nothing, pouring into them the abundance of His wisdom and goodness, so that the holy psalmist praises God in these words: *O Lord, our Lord how glorious is your name in all the earth.* Elsewhere he says: *How manifold are your works. O Lord! In wisdom you have wrought them all.*
>
> God also created man in his own *image and likeness*, endowed him with intelligence and freedom, and made him lord of creation, as the same psalmist declares in the words: *You have made him little less than the angels, and crowned him with glory and honor. You have given him rule over the works of your hands, putting all things under his feet.*
>
> Nevertheless, in order to imbue civilization with sound principles and enliven it with the spirit of the gospel, it is not enough to be illumined with the gift of faith and enkindled with the desire of forwarding a good cause; it is also necessary to take an active part in the various organizations and influence them from within.
>
> And since our present age is one of outstanding scientific and technical progress, one cannot enter these organizations and work effectively from within unless he is scientifically competent, technically capable and skilled in the practice of his own profession. . . .
>
> In other words, it is necessary that human beings, in the intimacy of their own consciences, should so live and act in their temporal lives as to create a synthesis between scientific, technical and professional elements on the one hand, and spiritual values on the other.[5]

All of you who have heard the appeal of suffering peoples, all of you who are working to answer their cries, you are the apostles of a development which is good and genuine, which is not wealth that is self-centered and sought for its own sake, but rather an economy which is put at the service of man, the bread which is daily distributed to all, as a source of brotherhood and a sign of Providence.

With a full heart We bless you, and We appeal to all men of good will to join you in a spirit of brotherhood. For, if the new name for peace is development, who would not wish to labour for it with all his powers? Yes, We ask you, all of you, to heed Our cry of anguish, in the name of the Lord.[6]

---

[4] Harvey Cox, "Tradition and the Future," Parts I & II, *Christianity and Crisis,* 27, nos. 16–17 (1967).

[5] Pope John XXIII, *Pacem in Terris* (*Peace on Earth*) (New York: American Press, 1963), pp. 3–4, 46–47.

[6] Pope Paul VI, *Populorum Progressio* (*On the Development of Peoples*) (Boston: St. Paul Editions, 1967), pp. 50–51.

Each of these encyclicals calls for active involvement in the changes wrought by technology by people committed to a religious perspective.

C. P. Snow, a twentieth-century novelist who was trained as a physicist, expressed concern about what he understood to be a dangerous gulf between the scientific-technological world and the rest of human experience (in academic terminology, the humanities). Discussing the complicated question of how we can best utilize scientific-technological-industrial developments in a social and human world, he wrote,

> Industrialisation is the only hope of the poor. I use the word "hope" in a crude and prosaic sense. I have not much use for the moral sensibility of anyone who is too refined to use it so. It is all very well for us, sitting pretty, to think that material standards of living don't matter all that much. It is all very well for one, as a personal choice, to reject industrialisation—do a modern Walden, if you like, and if you go without much food, see most of your children die in infancy, despise the comforts of literacy, accept twenty years off your own life, then I respect you for the strength of your aesthetic revulsion. But I don't respect you in the slightest if, even passively, you try to impose the same choice on others who are not free to choose. In fact, we know what their choice would be. For, with singular unanimity, in any country where they have had the chance, the poor have walked off the land into the factories as fast as the factories could take them. . . .
>
> The industrial revolution looked very different according to whether one saw it from above or below. It looks very different today according to whether one sees it from Chelsea or from a village in Asia. To people like my grandfather, there was no question that the industrial revolution was less bad than what had gone before. The only question was, how to make it better.
>
> In a more sophisticated sense, that is still the question. In the advanced countries, we have realised in a rough and ready way what the old industrial revolution brought with it. A great increase of population, because applied science went hand in hand with medical science and medical care. Enough to eat, for a similar reason. Everyone able to read and write, because an industrial society can't work without. Health, food, education; nothing but the industrial revolution could have spread them right down to the very poor. Those are primarily gains—there are losses too, of course, one of which is that organising a society for industry makes it easy to organise it for all-out war. But the gains remain. They are the base of our social hope.[7]

Efforts must be made to direct the use of technology in appropriate, humane ways. One can argue that scientific and technological advances are themselves based on values. They are expressions of human goals for the individual and society. As such, they improve humanity's condition. Nevertheless, they also disrupt and modify our patterns of living. Inevitably, these changes cause conflict between traditional ethical values and the new possibilities offered by technology.

> Should our technology determine our future as a culture? How shall we use our technology? To what extent should it shape the direction of our lives? Who should make these decisions?

Does the use of *technology* need to be regulated?

---

[7] C. P. Snow, *The Two Cultures: And A Second Look* (New York: Cambridge University Press, 1959, 1963), pp. 30–32. Used by permission.

Should religious and ethical values regulate the use of findings of scientific investigation?

Should technological changes and advances be made merely because they are now possible?

Can we expect whole societies to have the knowledge and interest to resolve these questions according to democratic decision-making procedures?

How would persons holding each of the several differing views of religion about change in society respond to the preceding questions?

Unit 74 Secularization

The changes and modifications in the relationship of religion to modern society are often referred to as *secularization*. Depending on one's perspective, this word takes on varied meanings. To some, it may mean the fragmentation or breakup of the religious values that undergirded past experience. To others, it may mean progress in religious understanding, the movement beyond antiquated and irrelevant values.

Paul Ricoeur, a contemporary French philosopher and Christian layman, has commented on secularization as follows:

> We mean by secularization an institutional phenomenon: the emancipation of most human activities from the influence of ecclesiastical institutions. In this first sense, secularization is synonymous with laicization: the community no longer coincides with the parish, political authority dissociates itself from religious authority. This transfer of power from the churchman to the civil servant and politician has been marked by a series of crises in which communities, hospitals, and schools have been successively affected.
>
> In a second sense secularization is characterized by the erasing of the distinction between the spheres of the sacred and the profane. This distinction, applying to time (religious and non-religious holidays), space (holy places and public buildings), social roles (the priest and the layman), the world-view (the heavens and the earth), the emotions (piety and justice) has tended to disappear for modern man. Its disappearance characterizes modernity as such. To this loss of distinction is connected the dissolution of peculiarly religious traditions, which today have become merely cultural provincialisms resistant to the universal industrial society.[8]

Harvey Cox, another contemporary Christian thinker, in his book *The Secular City* commented on this sense of secularization in a similar way:

> Recently, *secularization* has been used to describe a process on the cultural level which is parallel to the political one. It denotes the disappearance of religious determination of the symbols of cultural integration. Cultural secularization is an inevitable concomitant of a political and social secularization. Sometimes the one precedes the other, depending on the historical circumstances, but a wide imbalance between social and cultural secularization will not persist very long. In the United States there has been a considerable degree

---

[8] David Stewart and Joseph Bien, eds., *Paul Ricoeur, Political and Social Essays* (Athens: Ohio University Press, 1974), pp. 182–83.

of political secularization for many years. The public schools are officially secular in the sense of being free from church control. At the same time, the cultural secularization of America has come about more slowly. The Supreme Court decisions in the early 1960s outlawing required prayers pointed up a disparity which had continued for some years. In Eastern Europe, on the other hand, the historical process has been just the opposite. A radically secular culture has been imposed very quickly in Czechoslovakia and Poland, but religious practices Americans would find strikingly unconstitutional still obtain. In Czechoslovakia, for example, all priests and ministers are paid by the state. In Poland, in some instances religious instruction is still permitted in public schools. These discontinuities are due in part to the disparate pace with which social and cultural secularization occur. . . .[9]

The situations described by Cox in Czechoslovakia and Poland refer to the time when Marxist governments were in power.

There have been debates among religious thinkers about whether secularization is a good thing or a bad thing from the religious point of view. Some have lamented the legally required removal of religious practices and symbols (such as prayer in schools or manger scenes in city parks) from American public life as a deterioration of the traditional moral and religious values that undergird our society.

In the nineteenth-century United States, there were many efforts to effect a legal, constitutional connection between religion and the state. One proposal would have made the United States officially a "Christian Commonwealth," with the right to vote restricted to "genuine Christians" (defined as Presbyterians, Congregationalists, Episcopalians, Methodists, and Baptists). In Massachusetts, Catholic children who had been told by their parish priests not to participate in reading aloud from the King James version of the Bible (regarded as a Protestant translation) were ordered by public school officials to be beaten until they agreed to take part. In response to a controversy concerning Bible reading in the public schools in Cincinnati, Ohio, Judge Alfonso Taft in 1870 ruled as follows:

> Legal Christianity is . . . a contradiction of terms. When Christianity asks the aid of government beyond mere impartial protection, it denies itself. Its laws are divine and not human. Its essential interests lie beyond the reach and range of human governments. United with government, religion never rises above the merest superstition; united with religion, government never rises above the merest despotism; and all history shows us that the more widely and completely they are separated, the better it is for both.[10]

Historically, some people have favored secularization because they believe that legally established religion has a harmful effect on government and violates the liberties of individuals and groups within society. Judge Taft obviously believed that both government and religion benefit from the separation that results from secularization. Many then, and probably many now, questioned this ruling. In the United States today, some Catholics and Protestants, including but not limited to those sympathetic to the new Protestant fundamentalism, the Moral Majority, and the prolife (antiabortion) movement, have argued that divine and human law cannot be separated in an absolute or final way. They have

---

[9] Reprinted with permission of Macmillan, Inc., from *The Secular City*, rev. ed. by Harvey Cox. Copyright © Harvey Cox 1965, 1966.

[10] Quoted in Perry Deane Young, *God's Bullies: Power, Politics, and Religious Tyranny* (New York: Holt, Rinehart & Winston, 1982), p. 170.

argued that some legally permitted rights of religious expression (such as limited times of prayer in public schools that do not require participation) should be recognized when they are wanted by a majority of citizens (see Unit 75).

In contrast, the religious thinkers Paul Ricoeur and Harvey Cox believe that the secularization process is inevitable. They, like Judge Taft, see value for both religion and government in the resulting separation. Still others have seen both losses and benefits for religion and for modern societies in the secularization process.

The question of church-state relations goes far back in Western history. In ancient societies—ancient Greece, Rome, Egypt, Babylon, and Israel—church and state were one, although as societies became more complex, there was some differentiation between religious and secular officials and institutions. Nevertheless, the "secular" government was generally seen as having a divine foundation, and often kings and other government officials had sacred, priestly roles and functions as well as secular ones.

In Western Europe during the Middle Ages, church government and secular governments were separate in theory but nearly always influenced and exerted various degrees of control on each other. By the high Middle Ages (thirteenth century), some theologians, including Thomas Aquinas, argued that in some cases the church, especially in its highest office, the papacy, had the authority from God to exercise control over secular governments when the spiritual welfare of the subjects was at stake. One tendency of the early modern period (fourteenth to seventeenth centuries) was for thinkers, religious (Marsilius of Padua) as well as secular (Thomas Hobbes), to argue that the secular government should have authority over the church. This was part of a trend toward the differentiation of Europe into separate, independent nation-states. In the new situation of national independence, at first nearly everyone thought that a society, a group, a nation, could not have the necessary unity to survive unless all of its members participated in common religious beliefs and traditions.

It was a very new development when in the seventeenth century a few religious (Roger Williams) and secular (John Locke) thinkers argued that there could be a meaningful separation of church and state, in which the state did not attempt to regulate or control the religious beliefs and practices of its citizens and religious organizations did not attempt to control or gain power from the secular government. At that time several of the American colonies had state-supported churches.

Henry David Thoreau is a nineteenth-century example of the new attitude toward church-state relations and freedom of individual religious practice from state control. Threatened with imprisonment for refusing to pay a tax to support the state-established Congregational church—and Thoreau did go to jail for his refusal to pay taxes that he believed supported the system of slavery and the war of the United States against Mexico—he was finally given the option of signing a declaration that he was not and did not intend to be a member of the church. He signed, remarking that he would gladly sign a statement that he was not a member of any of the other organizations that he had never joined if only he knew what they were.

This very much shows the new or "modern" attitude toward religious commitment. In most societies, even very recent ones, one was born into membership in a religious organization; there was no question of individual choice. To some extent this is still true for most people, even in modern societies; but the fact that religious participation has increasingly become "privatized" and that societies have become "secularized" has added many new dimensions to the role that religious traditions, organizations, and commitments have in the contemporary world. This change can be seen in the controversies about whether a religious symbol—a menorah or a cross or a Christmas crèche—can be displayed on public property, which have become legal disputes going all the way to the U.S. Supreme Court for adjudication.

UNIT 75   Religious Fundamentalism

As the world comes closer to being one community in economy, communication, and culture, traditional religions—particularly Christianity, Islam, Buddhism, and forms of Hinduism—have had phenomenal growth and geographical distribution. In many religious communities, new growth and distribution often require adjustment and adaptation in modern materialistic, scientific, secularly oriented cultures. Although these adaptations have taken place in many religions in recent years, powerful conservative groups interested in the retention and restoration of traditional beliefs, values, and cultural patterns threatened by modernization, have emerged. To protect their traditions these groups have become increasingly involved in the political and social arena—for example, Buddhist monks burning themselves in Vietnam, Shi'ite and other conservative Muslims taking aggressive measures to resist modernization, and conservative Catholics in Latin America joining in protests against political tyranny.

Western journalists and others have attached the name *fundamentalists* to representatives of these conservative groups in many differing religious communities. This word first arose in the United States in reference to a debate in the 1920s between conservative and liberal Christians over the fundamentals of the faith. In that struggle the fundamentalists defended Christianity against such innovations as scientific explanations of evolution, which were believed to threaten the biblical account of creation, and historical-critical biblical study, which was perceived to have similar destructive results. Liberals were generally willing to accept such developments as new understandings of the faith that usefully incorporated expanding human knowledge into the religion.

Similar struggles between conservatives and liberals have occurred in other major religions in the past few decades, and most religions have felt the rise of vocal and active fundamentalist groups. Fundamentalists have historically been apolitical and often "other worldly," even critical of religious involvement in politics and other structures of society. In recent decades, however, fundamentalists have come to feel that the liberal adaptation of their religion to modern society has undermined the crucial values of their faith.

In America, under leaders such as Jerry Falwell and Pat Robertson, such groups began to take an active political role, calling for the reversal of legalized abortion, restoration of legalized prayer in schools, elimination of pornography in print and electronic media, maintenance of a strong U.S. military, and stricter codes of morality for the general public. The Southern Baptist Convention, the largest Protestant Christian domination in the United States, has been effectively split between a fundamentalist branch and a more moderate group over the question of the "inerrancy" of the Bible—the belief that the Bible as the word of God is literally true, without historical or scientific error. Conservative Muslims have rejected adaptations in their culture arising out of Western cultural and political innovations, which they often relate to Christian and Jewish influence. Their goal is the reestablishment of Islamic states ruled by traditional principles and the teaching of Allah found in the Qu'ran.

Christian Fundamentalism

Fundamentalist beliefs about the Bible are detailed in an editorial in *The Southern Baptist Journal* (May 1985), proposing that the denomination adopt, among others, the following points of belief:

1. A strong conservative binding CREED for all the teachers, administrators, executives, writers of curriculum material, leaders of our programs, the trustees of the schools, boards, and agencies, and other SBC leading employees.
2. Some items for the CREED for these SBC employees will include: A 100% commitment to the bible as the infallible Word of God with no errors in the Bible.
   And they shall believe:
   a) Jesus was born of a virgin.
   b) Jesus came out of the grave and many people saw Him and talked to Him after he arose.
   c) Jesus will come back to this earth.
   d) Adam and Eve were the first human beings and that they gave birth to the first human babies.
   e) We reject any theories of evolution, or any theory that says human beings sprang from any kind of life.
   f) That the book of Jonah is true and that Jonah spent three days and three nights in the belly of a [whale] or some kind of sea creature as Jesus said that would be a sign that Jesus would be in the belly of the earth three days and three nights.
3. We reject the theory of the Historical Critical Method and the JEDP method of reading the Bible.
4. Affirm that Moses wrote most of the first five books of the Bible.

Most Christian fundamentalists would also affirm belief in Jesus's death as an atonement for human sin before the judgment seat of God, the God-given place of women as helpmates and support for their husbands, and the authenticity of divine miracles.

Islamic Fundamentalism

The ideological worldview of Muslim fundamentalists emphasizes the restoration of strong Islamic societies and states through active organizations whose beliefs include the following:

1. Islam is a total way of life. Therefore religion is integral to politics, state, and society.
2. The political, military, and economic weakness of Muslims is due to having strayed from Islam and followed western, secular, materialistic ideologies and values. Both western liberal nationalism and Marxist socialism have failed because they are antithetical to Islam.

3. Islam, as found in the guidance of the Koran, in the practice of the Prophet, and in the example of the early Islamic community/state provides the true alternative ideology for Muslim life.

4. Therefore Muslims must reestablish God's rule, the Kingdom of God on earth, by reinstituting Islamic law, the blueprint for society.

5. The method for the renewal and reform of Muslim society is an Islamic political and social revolution, like that of the Prophet Muhammad and later 18th century Islamic movements, which brings about an Islamic system of government and law.

6. This new Islamic order does not reject science and technology. However, modernization is subordinated to Islam in order to guard against the westernization and secularization of Muslim society.

7. The process of Islamization requires organizations or societies built around dynamic nuclei of committed and trained believers, who call on all to repent and turn to God's path and who are prepared, when necessary, to fight against corruption and social injustice.[11]

❦

What similarities do you find between Christian and Muslim fundamentalist groups? What differences?

For either Christian or Muslim fundamentalists, is it possible to separate religious belief and practice from its societal settings?

Why are differences between conservative and liberal groups within a religious tradition most often manifested in social issues and practices?

UNIT 76   Characteristics of Modernization

The inevitability of rapid and comprehensive change differentiates a modern society from traditional societies. This is the basis of the process of secularization. Though change has always been part of any culture, it has become so accelerated that it is now a central feature of modern societies. To change is to modernize. In light of this, the following list indicates some of the factors that sociologists have suggested are characteristic of modern societies.

1. *Urbanization:* Modernization implies not just that people live in cities (people have lived in cities since 3000 B.C.) but also that the great majority of the population is not engaged in agricultural (primary) production but in industrial (secondary) and service (tertiary) occupations. Overcoming the necessity for a majority of the population to be engaged in the production of food and basic raw materials for clothing and shelter has been one of the keys to the transition from a traditionally oriented to a modernized society.

2. *Atomization:* Modernization has resulted in a breakdown of traditional family structures and group relationships. This is seen in the shift from extended family (or clan) groupings in traditionally oriented societies to the nuclear family (parents and children). It is also seen in the tendency of modern society for one's economic role to be separated

---

[11] John L. Esposito, "Islamic Revivalism," *The Muslim World Today*, Occasional Paper No. 3 (Washington, DC: School of International Service, American University, 1985).

from family relationships—the family group does not work together as an independent economic unit. Individuals also find themselves more and more independent and capable of determining their own patterns and relationships; thus they become more and more isolated—individual atoms separated from any larger molecular structure.

3. *Rationalization:* Activities of individuals and organizations tend to be coordinated systematically in modern societies, either by semiautomatically functioning mechanisms (the market in the economic sphere in capitalist societies) or by deliberately created agencies (bureaucracies). All activities tend then to be structures in interconnected, interacting patterns that demand rational and systematic responses.

4. *Differentiation:* One of the characteristics of modernizing societies, according to a number of contemporary sociologists—including the Americans Talcott Parsons and H. W. Pfautz and the German Joachim Matthes—is that the basic institutions of the society—political, economic, educational, and religious—must undergo a process of differentiation. According to Parsons, all human institutions and all aspects of human life undergo processes of development in the course of social, cultural, and personal change. There are both internal differentiation (expansion and diversification) and differentiation in relation to (change of relation to) other factors in the system of interaction. Thus, as society evolves, the religious element (the sacred) becomes separated, or differentiated, from the nonreligious elements (the secular). Religion tends to lose some of its earlier functions—for instance, as in Western society, some of its educational, charitable, and political functions. This process is exemplified, Parsons held, in the Protestant Reformation's extension—or transfer—of autonomous responsibility, traditionally lodged in the church, to individual Christians for their activities in their secular roles. According to Parsons, in modernized European and American societies, the Christian church's role is no longer "parental." The ethical principles that had been institutionalized within the church now became the responsibility of the individual. And the present church system typical of America, which Parsons called "denominational pluralism," was interpreted by him as a further extension of the "institutionalization of Christian ethics"; each denomination differentiates and establishes its own ethical pattern.

> The denomination . . . shares with the church type the differentiation between religious and secular spheres of interest. . . . Both may be conceived to be subject to Christian values, but to constitute independent foci of responsibility for their implementation. . . . The denomination shares with the sect type its character as a voluntary association where the individual member is bound only by a responsible personal commitment, not by *any* factor of ascription.[12]

5. *Institutionalization of innovative attitude:* One further characteristic of modernizing societies, in contrast to traditionally oriented societies, is that change not only is expected but also is encouraged. This value underlies the role of science and technology in modernizing and modernized societies. Life is lived with the expectation that newer and better methods of doing things will be invented, that newer and truer knowledge will be discovered. John R. Platt has argued that modern societies are in the process of creating a

---

[12] Talcott Parsons, "Christianity and Modern Industrial Society," *Sociological Theory and Modern Society* (New York: Free Press, 1967), p. 413.

"steady-state" world, a world of societies in which there will be nothing static: "What will begin to be steady is our acceptance of . . . new ways of creative leisure and interaction as being the most interesting and most satisfying ways of life."[13] Allan R. Brockway has written,

> The cliche . . . [that the only certainty is change] points to the essential character of the age into which we are moving today. Change is no longer causing the social and psychological disruption it once produced. . . . Change, even very rapid change, is being assimilated by contemporary men and women with a facility that would have been extremely puzzling . . . to people only a few generations ago.[14]

The implications of this understanding of modernization and change for the world's religions are many. Traditional formulations of religious truths and traditional patterns of ritual will have to be constantly modified. New technological innovations that change life patterns and styles will require a rethinking of the ethical applications of religious insights. Traditional patterns of religious institutions will need adjustment. These suggestions are not intended to be exhaustive, but it should be clear that any religion, to remain relevant to a changing society, will need significant adjustments in the formulation and application of its central and unchanging truths.

∾

What changes in medical technology require the rethinking of religious and ethical definitions and teachings?

What effect does it have on religion to say, "change is a way of life"?

Why is change so much more important to religion now than it has traditionally been?

What effect do the changes in military technology have on religious concepts of, and teachings about, war?

[13] John R. Platt, *The Step to Man* (New York: Wiley, 1966), p. 200.
[14] Allan R. Brockway, *The Secular Saint* (Garden City, NY: Doubleday, 1968), pp. 22–23.

CHAPTER 18

❧

Interpretation and Verification of Religious Knowledge

Introduction

Plato, in his dialogue Theaetetus, may have suggested that when persons claim to know something—"I know that it rained last night"—they mean to assert at least three things: (1) that what they claim to know is true—"It really did rain last night"; (2) that they believe it is true; and (3) something else, something that the participants in Plato's dialogue were not able to define to their satisfaction—something that expresses a difference between *mere* belief and belief based on adequate evidence. There are many things that most people would say they believe but would not claim to know. When we claim to know something, we generally mean that we have good reasons for believing it, that our belief is more than mere belief: It is based on adequate evidence.

Every society has well-established methods of determining whether different kinds of statements—proposed beliefs, proposed knowledge—are true or not. Even within a single society there are widely different ways of verifying or testing the truth of different kinds of statements. Some depend on the kind of statement involved. (We use different methods for deciding whether it is true that "It rained last night" and " 'Beauty is truth, truth beauty'— that is all/Ye know on earth, and all ye need to know.") Some depend on the context of the statements. (For some of our beliefs the statement "Well, I've always been told that" might count as good evidence, but it would not count as good evidence in a court of law.)

Most religions include a code of conduct and involve participation in some form of worship, though this may range from communal observances to solitary meditation. But religions also involve beliefs, and every religious tradition accepts some methods as legitimate ways of interpreting and verifying religious knowledge. The religion must be able to guide its adherents toward religious truth; otherwise, a crisis of belief, a crisis of truth, would result.

A particular religion may appeal to wisdom or revelation handed down orally through the generations as containing ultimate truth. It may appeal to written documents—Judaism, Christianity, and Islam are often referred to as "religions of the Book." A religion may appeal to those who have had especially intense experiences of religious ecstasy or who have followed special religious disciplines as its interpreters of truth, or to persons who have been specially trained and selected by the official agencies of the group or to those with whom the spirit of the Divine seems to reside in a striking way. It may appeal to criteria of rational acceptability or to scientific methods of observation. But each of these sources requires a continual effort of interpretation, for traditions must be continually interpreted and reconciled to one another. (The Navaho Indians often explain divergences in oral tradition by saying, "Well, that's *one* story, that's *his* story.") Scriptures like the Jewish Torah and the Christian New Testament must be interpreted: Jews and Christians and Muslims must ask themselves first what the scriptures actually *say,* what they *mean;* then they must ask how their teachings are to be applied in present situations. Even the criteria of rational acceptability and scientific testability require a continuous effort at further clarification, reflection, and experimental observation.

Most religious traditions would insist that not all religious truth can be verified, adequately tested, established, or refuted by ordinary commonsense methods of observation or by scientific methods of experimentation. Some religions insist that much religious truth transcends and surpasses human reasoning and thus cannot be fully understood or tested by methods of reason or sense observation alone. Nevertheless, every religious tradition will make provision for methods of finding and testing proposed religious truth. It is worth noting that in a time when many contemporary societies are experiencing a profound crisis of belief, the suggestions religious traditions give about sources of truth and methods of testing it may be of the greatest value and relevance.

Most religions contain a variety of different kinds of beliefs—all of which are accepted by adherents of that tradition as containing genuine knowledge. For instance, some Christian beliefs are *historical* statements ("Jesus suffered under Pontius Pilate, was crucified, dead and buried"). Some are *metaphysical* statements ("God is the sole Creator of all that exists, and He created it out of nothing"). Some, though they sound like *predictions* or *forecasts,* are more likely intended to be understood as *promises, assurances* to sustain faith and commitment.

In this chapter, we explore some aspects of the problem of interpreting and verifying religious knowledge. In the first unit, we examined the distinction between what in ordinary usage is called "factual statements" and other kinds of expressions. Many religious traditions hold that important aspects of religious truth are not subject to factual or observational tests in the sense described but are nevertheless both true and capable of being tested and proved—verified—by those who have had appropriate religious instruction or experiences. Unit 78 deals in a more general way with the concept of verification; however, a number of questions are raised specifically about its application to religious knowledge.

Perhaps no topic has been more thoroughly investigated by contemporary theologians and philosophers of religion than the "logic" of religious language, that is, how language expressing aspects—feelings, attitudes, value judgments, beliefs—of the religious dimension of life (the dimension of ultimate or pivotal concern and commitment) is used.

Very roughly—since the issue is extremely complex—there have been four major positions taken about the logic of religious language.

1. The logical positivists, of whom A. J. Ayer is a notable example, insist that religious language (as well as moral, ethical, and aesthetic language) expresses *only* people's feelings and attitudes, and therefore there is no need to be concerned about how religious statements might be tested for truth value. Religious language does not even make claims or assertions about reality. This view has been called emotivism.

The other three views are willing to grant that some religious language may be claiming to assert truth. To oversimplify, the views might be characterized as follows:

2. There is no problem about the logic of testing the truth of at least some religious statements: We would use exactly the same kinds of procedures to discover whether they are true as we do to test statements in the sciences or history or ordinary sense experience.
3. At least some religious language makes statements that claim to be true, but the method of testing them for truth is totally unique (perhaps depending on a special kind of authority or on some inner revelation or illumination).
4. Others have argued that, though at least some expressions claim to give true accounts of reality, their logical status is neither wholly like nor wholly unlike that of statements in other areas of discourse. Although there may be some analogies between the claims made by a religious affirmation—once we have come to understand its intent and significance, say, an article of the Apostle's Creed—and the expression of a scientific hypothesis, there may also be dissimilarities. People who hold to this fourth view may argue that, though it is useful to compare the way religious statements function and are verified with the way statements in science, history, ethics, aesthetic appreciation, and the law function and are verified, there should be no attempt to impose the logic of one field on statements belonging to other fields.

Obviously, Unit 78 can only begin to explore some of the dimensions of this important topic, which not only has been of interest to contemporary students but also has excited the intellects of the great thinkers of the Jewish Christian Islamic Middle Ages as well as great Hindu thinkers like Sankara and Ramanuja.

Unit 77   Factual Statement

That is a factual statement.

This statement, commonly made, means that the speaker has related something observable and verifiable, something that could be checked by talking with people who were present when the incident occurred.

Yet seldom do we find in a statement only a description of the occurrence. Other components are almost inevitably present. The purpose of this discussion is to explore some of the components in a "factual" statement and to see if there is only one type of "fact." The reader will then be encouraged to analyze other material, using the methods of this exploration.

As the raw material for our exploration we will use the following statement.

The Church received a letter from a couple that visited our church several Sundays back. Every pastor is eternally looking for new reasons to encourage folks to come to Church. Try this one for size:

Dear Friends:
> There is more to the story of our stopping in Pecos and attending your church than you realize. We stopped near the church and entered our trailer to change from traveling to church clothes. We were going north on 385 to 66. We got as far as Littlefield that Sunday evening. If we had not stopped that 1½ hours for church we would undoubtedly have been in Hereford for the night . . . the night the tornado struck there. Therefore in our opinion it pays to go to church on Sunday even on vacations and trips.
> Sincerely,
> Mr. & Mrs. . . .[1]

The letter contains "fact" in that it refers to occurrences that could be verified by others who were present.

	line
Dear Friends,	a
~~There is more to the story of~~ our	b
stopping in Pecos and attending your	c
church ~~than you realize.~~ We stopped near	d
the church and entered our trailer to change	e
~~from traveling to church~~ clothes. We were	f
going north on 385 to 66. We got as far as	g
Littlefield that Sunday evening. ~~If we had~~	h
~~not stopped that 1½ hours for church we~~	i
~~would undoubtedly have been in Hereford for~~	j
~~the night~~ . . . the night the tornado struck	k
there. ~~Therefore in our opinion it pays to~~	l
~~go to church on Sunday even on vacations~~	m
~~and trips.~~	n
Sincerely,	o
Mr. & Mrs. . . .	p

Do you think the above accurately isolates the data that could have been verified by other people, assuming they were present when the occurrence took place?

Observation: In most instances, the factual nature (verifiable possibility) is clear. In places, however, the data seem to move out of the category of verifiability by external witnesses; for example,

---

[1] Bulletin (Pecos, TX: United Methodist Church, 1971).

Line f: The words "from traveling to church" have been deleted because they probably reflect the subjective judgment of the writer of the letter. Yet assuming that the couple wore ragged, patched, or sloppy clothes while traveling, it could be a verifiable fact. But we do not know that.

Line p: "Mr. & Mrs . . ." indicates a married relationship that presumably can be verified by examining municipal records, assuming the marriage is not by common law. Yet this type of verification, requiring special effort and intent, is to a degree different from that required from the other facts contained in this statement.

These occurrences are referred to as facts because they are known, or could be known, to have happened. They are real, true, have existence. But what about the rest of this letter? How can we characterize this material?

The remainder of this letter refers to aspects that might not be able to be verified, even by people who were present.

	line
Dear Friends,	a
There is more to the story of our	b
~~stopping in Pecos and attending your~~	c
~~church~~ than you realize. ~~We stopped near~~	d
the church and entered our trailer to change	e
from traveling to church clothes. ~~We were~~	f
~~going north on 385 to 66. We got as far as~~	g
~~Littlefield that Sunday evening.~~ If we had	h
not stopped that 1½ hours for church we	i
would undoubtedly have been in Hereford for	j
the night . . . ~~the night the tornado struck~~	k
~~there.~~ Therefore in our opinion it pays to	l
go to church on Sunday even on vacations	m
and trips.	n
Sincerely,	o
Mr. & Mrs. . . .	p

One striking thing about the material not crossed out is its diversity; all that is shared is the impossibility or difficulty of externally verifying its content. A more specific analysis may be useful.

Lines a, o: The words "dear" and "sincerely" indicate attitudes allegedly held by the authors of the letter. Yet can such attitudes be demonstrated with certainty? Or are these merely customary and ceremonial ways of beginning and ending letters that need not be taken to involve attitudes or factual claims at all? Yet they do point to attitudes that the authors might, if asked, espouse. Are there objective tests for determining whether others have affection for us, even if they say they do?

Line a: The consideration just discussed applies somewhat to the term "friends," but it also differs. This term indicates an interpersonal relationship that may be difficult to verify by observation of external behavior. Perhaps referring to the church members as "friends" is merely a conventional mode of address, just as someone else might have said, "Hi fellows." Does anything in the letter lead you to believe that the letter's authors really *feel* friendship for the people of the church in Pecos?

Lines e to f: The words "to change . . . clothes," by syntax as well as meaning, indicate a motive on the part of the authors. Now it may be that that is exactly what they did. But the actual observable occurrence does not necessarily prove the motive.

Line f: The actions referred to by the words "from traveling to church," commented on above, may possibly have been observable. The words may indicate, however, a value judgment on the part of the authors.

Lines h to k: The words "If we had not stopped . . . for the night" represent an assumption of an occurrence on the part of the authors. Obviously it did not happen. It is equally true that it might not have happened—the car might have broken down, caught fire, had a flat; the trailer might have come loose from the car; one of the persons involved might have become sick; and so forth. Yet the authors assume that none of these possibilities would have occurred. Rather, they assume that a fact that could have been verified by anyone would have occurred. This may represent a projection, based on their own intentions.

Lines l to n: The words "therefore . . . trips" clearly indicate the conclusion the couple drew. The word "therefore" labels the inference; and the words "in our opinion," the couple's acceptance of the inference. The main inference is "it pays to go to church on Sunday," an inference that they believe to hold true even in special circumstances, "even on vacations and trips." This then represents an interpretation of "fact," that is, a convincing understanding of observable occurrences and their relationship. Do you find it convincing? Do you think it found universal acceptance? Does the pastor who quotes the letter seem to accept it? To the couple, the answers to these questions might not matter—to them it is convincing.

Line d: The words "than you realize" reveal that the authors of the letter assumed that the readers did not see the full significance of the occurrences. That is, they assumed that the readers lacked insight, which they were providing.

The unverifiable or difficult to verify material, therefore, deals with different dimensions:

> Attitudes allegedly held by the authors of the letter
> Assumed interpersonal relationships
> Alleged motives
> Value judgments by the authors
> Assumptions about possibly observable occurrences
> Interpretive inferences convincing to the authors
> Assumption of a lack of insight on the part of others

The term *fact* is not commonly applied to this type of information. Yet is not the material real, true? Does it not have existence for the couple and for others who accept the accuracy of their assumptions? Is it accurate to say that these aspects of the event their story describes did not "happen"?

Is experience made up of the combination and interaction of verifiable and non-verifiable components? Or do we use many methods for verifying or attempting to verify different kinds of beliefs about different aspects of experience?

In the analysis of the letter, it may have seemed that we can often make a clear distinction between "facts" that everyone can observe and interpretations of those facts by various observers. The examples that follow are meant to suggest that such a distinction may be very difficult to make. Each of the following statements, except the first, involves interpretation, and all (except perhaps the last) claim to be factual. (They are all to be taken as intended descriptions of the same group of events.)

1. It seems to me that his body appeared in the room and that when it appeared, it jerked convulsively.

2. When his body appeared in the room, it jerked convulsively.
3. When he walked into the room, he jumped.
4. When he walked into the room, he jumped for joy.
5. When he walked into the room, he jumped in a startled, terrified way.
6. When he walked into the room, he jumped joyfully, fulfilling the saying of the prophet, "The Lord shall come leaping like a young deer."

It should be noted that statements 4 and 5 are incompatible with each other; 5 is also incompatible with 6, and 4 is compatible with all except 5. Obviously, much more interpretation seems to be occurring in statements 5 and 6, or even 4, than in 1, 2, or 3. What is the source of the claimed significance the interpreter finds in the more "interpreted" examples?

All of the following statements describing essentially the same event, the publication of a book, involve interpretation, and each might claim to be factual. (Statement 3 is incompatible with statements 2 and 4 but is compatible with 1. Statements 2 and 4 are compatible with each other; 4 entails 2, though 2 does not entail 4; and both 4 and 2 entail 1, though 1 does not entail either 4 or 2.)

1. At the age of thirty-six, X, then professor of philosophy at Y college, published his first book, *The New Phenomenology*.
2. At the age of thirty-six, X, then professor of philosophy at Y college, published his first book, a significant, indeed a magisterial, contribution to American philosophical thought. This epoch-making work was titled *The New Phenomenology*.
3. At the age of thirty-six, X, then professor of philosophy at Y college, published his first book, a confused hodgepodge of logical fallacies and linguistic errors, infected by the German Hegelian and post-Romantic existentialist tradition of scorn for clarity and analytic precision. The contribution of this book, titled *The New Phenomenology*, to significant philosophical discussion was precisely zero.
4. At the age of thirty-six—the age at which Hegel published his epoch-making first work, *Phenomenology of Spirit*—X, then professor of philosophy at Y college, published his first book. Like the Swabian Master, X had written a number of incomplete early works, but until the publication of the significantly titled *New Phenomenology*, his prestige as a philosopher had been eclipsed by the fame of his more sensational, younger contemporaries. Nor was the significance of either work recognized at once. Both philosophers remained relatively unknown for years—each languishing as high school principals—before receiving permanent university appointments—Hegel at the University of Berlin, X at Harvard. Each initiated a new age in the history of our comprehension of Being. Once, when asked by a graduate student if *The New Phenomenology* represented a twentieth-century fulfillment of the project that Hegel had carried up to the year 1807 in his *Phenomenology*, X said, "Have you read the book? What did you find in it? Did you find the activity of God as it has unfolded presented, analyzed, made available for human consciousness?" Those who have thoughtfully read *The New Phenomenology*, those who have thought on it long and have tested it against our perceptions of the times, know that a new Hegel, a greater Hegel, did appear in twentieth-century America.

Some of these statements attribute much more significance to the event being described than others do. Statement 3 expresses a sense or feeling of disgust for the book and the person who wrote it. Statement 4 describes the author with almost religious reverence. Are these merely subjective reactions, or are they objective or at least partly objective differences of opinion? How does one decide about the significance of events? In interpreting events, what are the *basic* sources that allow us to make judgments of significance? How would you decide whether reading Professor X's book would be worth the time it might take to understand it or whether it would be a useless waste of time?

Can there be an absolute distinction between the merely factual description of an event and the significance—goodness or badness, importance or unimportance—an interpreter judges it to have, or do all descriptions to some extent contain interpretations of the event's meaning or significance? We would probably think that one characteristic of *religious statements* is that they are evaluative, interpretative of the significance of what they describe or attempt to describe. Does this mean that they are more subjective than other kinds of statements? Or does it mean, rather, that they may be more complex or profound? This question is discussed in more detail in the next unit.

UNIT 78   Verification

The question of whether and how religious expressions can be judged to be *true*—whether they make truth claims, and if they do, how it can be determined whether the claims they make are in fact true—is one of the most frequently discussed issues in contemporary theology and philosophy of religion. This unit discusses the verifiability of statements expressing religious belief in the context of verifiability, or verification in general.

Some students of religious uses of language have warned us that it may be a fundamental mistake to *ask* whether uses of religious language are true or verifiable. Many twentieth-century philosophers and theologians have stressed *noncognitive* uses of religious language—that is, uses in which the speaker does not and may not intend to convey information.

> Rather, noncognitive use of language expresses feeling, makes a commitment, helps to cement the bonds of solidarity of a group, or does any other of innumerable possible things about which it would be ridiculous to suppose that questions of truth or falsity arise, as they would if the language use were assumed to have cognitive content (*i.e.*, to claim to convey information). As has often been pointed out, when a minister says the words in a marriage ceremony, "I now pronounce you united in holy matrimony," or in a baptismal service, "I baptize you in the Name of the Father, Son, and Holy Ghost," no one would think that the purpose of the minister's expressions is to give information. Rather, the minister is using language performatively, to accomplish something. Still, the position asserted by some that *all* religious language is noncognitive seems extreme and would not be accepted by most religious persons.[2]

If some religious language *is* cognitive—that is, makes claims to be true—by what methods or sources do we verify its truth claims? When is a belief *merely* a belief and when is it knowledge? When is a belief a "fact," and when is it merely opinion? Ordinarily we say that we *know* a belief is true, or we say that a belief is a fact, when we possess good reasons—a sufficient amount of the right kind of evidence (that is, a sufficient amount of relevant *other* beliefs that we have good reason to accept as true).

---

[2] Robert C. Monk and Joseph D. Stamey, *Exploring Christianity: An Introduction* (Englewood Cliffs, NJ: Prentice-Hall, 1984), p. 129.

Philosophers have sometimes attempted to establish that there are *some* facts that we know with absolute certainty, facts (beliefs) that we do not need to justify by appealing to other beliefs (facts) to support them. One candidate for a type of absolutely certain belief—a pure "fact"—has been the kind of factual statement based on immediate sense experience. How can I be mistaken that I am now seeing a patch of white or feeling a sharp pain? These philosophers argued that on the basis of such immediate sensations, we *construct* a theoretical world of objects: We infer that because we see patches of white, there is an object present *causing* us to have the experience of seeing white. The theoretical world we construct may be a world of commonsense objects—tables and chairs—or it may be the abstractly conceived, rigorously precise world of theoretical physics.

Other philosophers have argued that there is no clear-cut line between what we observe or experience and the theoretical interpretations we create to explain what we observe and experience. Ordinarily, we do not *see* patches of white; we see white objects. Thus Marx Wartofsky, a contemporary philosopher of science, points out that what we *observe* will be dependent on the language, the set of predicates, we choose to interpret the observed (and the observable).

Thus, determining what are observables may be reduced to the question of choosing the so-called basic predicates of [our] reconstructed language. For example, if one chooses as basic predicates such "phenomenal" terms as *red, heavy, hot, loud,* and such "phenomenal" relations as *longer than,* or *brighter than,* then this fixes such terms as denoting the observables for that system. The only question is whether the theoretical terms of a science may somehow be reduced to these, and thus tied to observation as stipulated. On the other hand, one may choose terms of physical measurement as the basic predicates, so that everything would in principle be reducible to such predicates as measured distances, time intervals, or measurements of mass, or of electrical charge.

It is on pragmatic or instrumental grounds, according to this view, that one chooses among alternative languages—on grounds relating to the methodology of science, involving what scientists do when they observe, measure, etc. Nor does one simply choose among prevailing languages, which may have developed haphazardly in the history of science; rather one constructs artificial languages, ideally reconstructed languages, choosing the terms and even the logical structures best suited to scientific frameworks.

What appears as an utter relativism concerning "observation" thus has certain constraints. Although someone may choose anything at all as his basic or observation predicates, in practice the choice is not haphazard. When scientists talk about observing something, the context and the operation have been delimited by the culture of science, just as when observing is spoken of in common usage there is a consensus on what this means and how it is done. The mystic may claim to have observed the face of God in his private revelation; and in delirium, someone may perfectly sincerely claim to observe figures and objects which we take to be hallucinatory. Yet we do not take these as the normal cases of observation, though we may grant that to the person involved, all the features of normal attentive perception or observation were present. The reason is that we take observables to be common and public; we begin with the expectation that what we see is what anyone would see if he were looking; and thus we take observation to be constrained by the check of reference to public objects. . . .

The public quality of observation (what we might facetiously call the communism of the observable, where no property is private and all is commonly owned; and where the maxim holds: "From each according to his ability, to each according to his need"), this open availability to all comers, is then a criterion which excludes certain experiences, such as revelation or hallucination, from being observational. Beyond this, it seems, no other constraints are definitive.[3]

Wartofsky emphasized the condition of being publicly verifiable that holds for what will be considered "observable." But similar, though perhaps less rigorously measurable, criteria of verification are often appealed to in the realm of religious experience. Thus though the experience of *satori* (enlightenment) in Zen Buddhism is ineffable and incommunicable, the Zen master is able to validate or verify the occurrence of this experience in his disciples, presumably by seeing whether the change in manner and attitude of the disciple is coherent with the master's sense of the meaning of the experience.

A further example is given by Carlos Castaneda in *The Teaching of Don Juan: A Yaqui Way of Knowledge*.[4] The book is an autobiographical account of an anthropology student's attempt to learn the techniques of sorcery from a Yaqui Indian sorcerer. To interpret his experiences, Castaneda makes a distinction between ordinary consensus—the methods we have learned to use to arrive at true (or probable) belief based on criteria of publicly observable features of a situation—and "special consensus." Special consensus is a method for verifying or establishing the truth of beliefs by tests and methods that would not depend on objective or public criteria of observation.

Thus, in one instance, Don Juan gives Castaneda peyote to eat, and under the influence of the drug, Castaneda frolics with a dog. Afterward, Don Juan tells Castaneda that it was not really a dog but the god Mescalito who had "played" with him. Don Juan claims to have seen or recognized the god. Castaneda asks if the other persons present saw Mescalito or only a dog, and Don Juan seems to suggest that what the others *saw* is irrelevant: It was the god because Don Juan had gone through certain esoteric experiences that allowed him to *know* this.

Don Juan gave Castaneda elaborate instructions on what he could expect to experience under the influence of the various hallucinogenic plants administered to him. At one point, he taught Castaneda how to turn himself into a crow and fly with other crows. Under the influence of the sacred mushroom (*psylocybe mexicana*), Castaneda did seem to himself to turn into a crow. Afterward, he asked Don Juan whether other observers would have seen him as a crow or as himself. Again, Don Juan dismissed the question as irrelevant. The special consensus—the set of beliefs held by Don Juan and communicated to Castaneda and the experiences induced in Castaneda by the hallucinogenic plants counted for Don Juan as sufficient verification for the belief that Castaneda had actually become a crow.

Apparently, the meaning of a belief to the one who holds it can be discovered by asking what that person would consider good evidence—enough evidence of the relevant kind—to establish the truth of the belief. The American philosopher Charles S. Peirce wrote,

[3] Marx W. Wartofsky, *Conceptual Foundations of Scientific Thought* (New York: Macmillan, 1968), pp. 112–13. Copyright © 1968 by Marx W. Wartofsky.

[4] Carlos Castaneda, *The Teachings of Don Juan: A Yaqui Way of Knowledge* (Berkeley: University of California Press, 1968).

Consider what effects, that might conceivably have practical bearings, we conceive the object of our conception to have. Then, our conception of these effects is the whole of our conception of the object.[5]

∽

What are some of the beliefs you hold?

What kinds of evidence do you consider to be good evidence in favor of those beliefs?

Are different kinds and different amounts of evidence involved in testing the truth of different kinds of beliefs?

[5] James Mark Baldwin, *Dictionary of Philosophy and Psychology* (New York: Macmillan, 1902).

CHAPTER 19

❦

Authority and Tradition

Introduction

This chapter continues the discussion of religious knowledge, focusing particularly on the ways in which religious interpretations may be mediated in particular structural frameworks.

Every religious community includes some concept of authority, some concept of sources—it may be people, institutions, documents, or experience of some kind—of authority. *Authority,* in this sense, refers to that which is accepted as orthodox, stable, fixed. As such it becomes the touchstone of belief and action. It is used to settle questions of religious truth, questions about right conduct and right belief. The first unit of this chapter discusses the role of authority in religion.

In this book we often use the words *religious tradition* to refer to the many facets of a distinct religion. Used in this manner, *tradition* includes beliefs, leaders, distinctive events, structural patterns, and the host of other aspects that make up a particular religion such as Christianity, Hinduism, or Islam (See Unit 6 for a discussion of religious tradition used in this sense.) *Tradition* has other meanings, however, one of which is the means by which a particular religion conveys to each new generation the knowledge and experience gained within a religious community. It is this understanding of tradition that will be the focus of our attention in Unit 80.

Although authority and tradition are principal elements in the authentication and conveyance of religious knowledge, there is another aspect of knowledge that plays an important role in religious development—doubt. The problem of doubt is critical for any society: "Can we trust our leaders?" "How do we know the media tell us the truth?" Some doubt may be beneficial to society, promoting scientific discovery, reform, and the healthy development of inquiry. In the same way, doubt may play an important role in clarifying and investigating religious truth—matters of ultimate importance and ultimate concern. Unit 81 discusses the role and significance of doubt for religious knowledge.

UNIT 79   Authority in Religion

Søren Kierkegaard, a nineteenth-century Danish thinker, was brought up by his father in a tradition of strict Lutheran orthodoxy. For a time he rebelled against the strictness of his religious upbringing, but later he embraced it fully, rejecting humanistic and liberal elements that had become popular in academic Protestant circles in his day. The humanistic liberals stressed the human capacity to understand God. They emphasized human reason and conscience and human creativity as sources of religious truth. Kierkegaard rejected all this. In the following passage he argues that genuine religious truth must come from God, by revelation. Thus a prophet or an apostle, like Paul—persons who are instruments of God's revelation—is in a very different category from wise or learned or brilliant or well-educated persons whose teachings, however brilliant they may be, are simply productions of finite human capacities. The prophet and the apostle have authority from God; the others do not.

Kierkegaard thought that a true understanding of Christianity depended on seeing that it is paradoxical, that it negates human expectations and accomplishments—human intellect, knowledge, insight, and virtue are *not* the key to religious understanding—at the same time that it fulfills the deepest hopes by speaking of a God who reaches out to people to bring them into the presence of his love. The paradox is that truth and fulfillment come by unexpected means and in ways that shock and surprise and humble. In the following passage, Kierkegaard's critique of the liberals (referred to as "clergymen") leads him to the forceful statement of his own interpretation of religious authority.

When the sphere of paradoxical religion is abolished or explained back into the ethical, then an apostle becomes nothing more nor less than a genius—and then good-night Christianity. *Esprit* and spirit, revelation and originality, a calling from God and ingeniousness, an apostle and a genius, all coalesce . . . one not infrequently hears clergymen . . . in all learned simplicity, prostitute Christianity. . . .

They talk in lofty tones of the cleverness and profundity of St. Paul, of his beautiful similes, etc.—sheer aesthetics. If Paul is to be regarded as a genius, it looks very bad for him. Only to clerical ignorance could it occur to praise Paul aesthetically, because clerical ignorance has no standard but thinks in this wise: If only one says something good about Paul, it's all to the good. Such good-humored and well-intentioned thoughtlessness is to be referred to the fact that the person in question has not been disciplined by qualitative dialectics, which would have taught him that an apostle is not served by saying something good about him when it is crazy, so that he is recognized and admired for being what in an apostle is a matter of indifference and what essentially he is not, while with that what he is is forgotten. It might just as well occur to such thoughtless eloquence to laud Paul as a stylist and for his artistic use of language, or still better, since it is well known that Paul practiced a manual trade, to maintain that his work as an upholsterer must have been so perfect that no upholsterer either before or since has been able to equal it—for, if only one says something good about Paul, then all is well. As a genius Paul can sustain no comparison with Plato or with Shakespeare, as an author of beautiful similes he ranks rather low, as stylist his is an obscure name, and as an upholsterer—well, I may admit that in this respect I don't know where to place him. One always does well to transform stupid seriousness into jest—and then comes the real serious thing, the serious fact that Paul was an apostle, and as an apostle has no affinity either with Plato or Shakespeare or a stylist or an upholsterer, who are all of them (Plato as well as the upholsterer Hansen) beneath any comparison with him.

A *genius* and an *apostle* are qualitatively distinct, they are categories which belong each of them to their own qualitative spheres: that of *immanence* and that of *transcendence*. . . . The genius may well have something new to contribute, but this newness vanishes again in its gradual assimilation by the race, just as the distinction "genius" vanishes when one thinks of eternity. The apostle has paradoxically something new to contribute, the newness of which, precisely because it is paradoxical and not an anticipation of what may eventually be developed in the race, remains constant, just as an apostle remains an apostle to all eternity, and no immanence of eternity puts him essentially on the same plane with other men, since essentially he is paradoxically different. . . . The genius is what he is by reason of himself, i.e., by what he is in himself: an apostle is what he is by reason of his divine authority. . . . A genius may perhaps be a century ahead of his age and hence stands there as a paradox, but in the end the race will assimilate what was once a paradox, so that it is no longer paradoxical.

Quite otherwise with the apostle. The word itself indicates the difference. An apostle is not born, an apostle is a man called and sent by God, sent by him upon a mission. . . .

An apostle can never in such wise come to himself that he becomes conscious of his apostolic calling as a stage in his life's development. The apostolic call is a paradoxical fact which in the first as well as the last moment of his life stands paradoxically outside his personal identity with himself as the definite person he is.

A genius is appraised on purely aesthetic grounds, according to the content and specific gravity his productions are found to have; an apostle is what he is by reason of the divine authority he has. The *divine authority is the qualitatively* decisive factor.[1]

Because the authority of the prophet or apostle rests for Kierkegaard in the Divine, and these persons are unique representatives of the Divine, their words become distinctive and binding. Only a few individuals are so called and serve as instruments of God's revelation.

In seventeenth-century England, the Quakers held a view of religious authority that, like Kierkegaard's, stressed the presence of the Divine but was also quite different. The Quakers declared that all people were blessed with divine authority: Each believer experiences the indwelling Spirit of Christ, the Inner Light, as a source of all religious truth. Embracing the Light present in all, all believers had within themselves the full religious authority of Christ. An authority on the religious history of the time has written the following:

> Many of the [seventeenth-century] Quakers took [the] doctrine of the indwelling Spirit to what by most of the [other] Puritans was felt to be a dangerous extreme. The Spirit was to be the guide by which everything, Scriptures included, was to be judged. William Penn corrected misunderstandings when he wrote: It is not our Way of Speaking to say that the Light within is the Rule of the Christian Religion; but the Light of Christ within us is the Rule of true Christians, so that it is not our Light but Christ's Light that is our rule.[2]

---

[1] Selections from Søren Kierkegaard, *On Authority and Revelation: The Book on Adler, or A Cycle of Ethico-Religious Essays,* trans. Walter Lowrie (copyright 1955 by Princeton University Press), pp. 103–107. Reprinted by permission of Princeton University Press.

[2] Hugh Martin, *Puritanism and Richard Baxter* (London: SCM Press, 1954), p. 79.

In the understanding of Kierkegaard and the Quakers, religious authority resides in the Divine even when exemplified in a human personality. Yet the words, works, and writings of those who possess divine authority often become sources of religious authority. Paul's writings, and those of other apostles and prophets, came to be accepted as sacred Scripture because of the divine authority that they possessed. Nevertheless, as Scripture, these words assumed an authority of their own. They represent the presence and the will of the Divine. Similarly, religious authority often resides in several aspects of community experience: Particular historical events take on religious authority—Gautama's enlightenment; Jesus's life, death, and resurrection. Great teachers and leaders become authorities—Confucius, Buddha, the pope in Roman Catholicism, Martin Luther in Protestantism. Orthodox beliefs are formulated into creeds and confessions—the Three Refuges of Buddhism, the Apostles' Creed of Christianity, the confessions of the Qu'ran. Authoritative moral codes define proper life—the Ten Commandments in Judaism and Christianity, the Eightfold Path in Buddhism, the Five Great Relations in Confucianism. Each of these sources of authority points beyond itself to the Divine, but for the ordinary believer each constitutes meaningful and real authority, defining belief and action. In so doing, these sources exemplify the multifaceted nature of religious authority as experienced in daily life.

∿

How does Kierkegaard's understanding of authority relate to the discussion (in Unit 34) of general and special revelation? Would it be accurate to say that Kierkegaard rejects the validity of the idea of general revelation?

What are the most significant sources of authority in the religious groups and traditions with which you are familiar?

Who can speak with authority in matters of religious truth? Those who are specially trained or appointed (ordained)? Those who live the best lives, morally or religiously? Those with a unique or distinctive religious experience? What do the main religious groups with which you are familiar say about this?

Does ultimate religious authority reside in the written words of a document (such as the Bible or the Qu'ran)? Does it come from a special experience, such as an illumination of the heart by revelation? Does it come from some other source?

UNIT 80   Tradition: Its Meaning and Function

Because of the brief span of our national history, our mobility, and the fact that we are a land of immigrants, Americans have sometimes been "antitraditional"—making a virtue out of newness and often discarding the old. Only recently have we begun to understand and use our traditions in the manner that most cultures have throughout history. It may be difficult for Americans to appreciate the significant role tradition has played in human history, yet its importance can hardly be overstated.

The term *tradition* is derived from the Latin word *traditio,* which literally means "a handing over." In Latin culture and in later cultures, this term was used to indicate (1) content—information, teachings, doctrine, behavior patterns, or other thoughts and/or practices received from previous generations—and at times (2) the process by which such material was handed down. The term thus embraces customs, doctrines, and concepts, as well as action.

Tradition understood in this way has been an ever-present reality in the great religious movements of the world. It has been the central means by which religions ensured the transmittal of religious experience, information, beliefs, and moral codes to each new generation of believers.

Tradition is so important in Judaism that in the musical *Fiddler on the Roof,* set in a late nineteenth-century Russian Jewish community, it was idealized as perhaps *the* means of defining life and its relationship to God.

> A fiddler on the roof,
> Sounds crazy, no? But in our little village of Anatevka you might say everyone of us is a fiddler on a roof, trying to scratch out a pleasant simple tune without breaking his neck. It isn't easy.
> You may ask, "Why do we stay up there if it's so dangerous?" We stay because Anatevka's our home. And "How do we keep our balance?" That I can tell you in one word: tradition.
> Tradition! Tradition! Tradition!
> Tradition! Tradition! Tradition!
> Because of our traditions we've kept our balance for many years. Here in Anatevka we have our traditions for everything—how to eat, how to sleep, how to work, even how to wear clothes. For instance, we always keep our heads covered; we wear these little prayer shawls. This shows our constant devotion to God. You may ask "How did this tradition get started?" I'll tell you, I don't know. But it's tradition. Because of our traditions everyone here knows who he is and what God expects him to do.[3]

Tradition plays an important part in Judaism in yet another way. Its festivals and holy days are to a large degree the means by which Jewish faith, life, and history are perpetuated. This is evident in the Passover celebration, in which, among the components of the ceremonial practices, there is a section that recites the ancient "four questions," usually asked by the youngest male present.

> Why is this night of passover different from all other nights of the year?
> On all other nights, we eat either Chomaytz or Matzoh,
>   but on this night we eat only Matzoh.
> On all other nights, we eat all kinds of herbs,
>   but on this night we eat only Moror.
> On all other nights, we do not dip even once,
>   but on this night we dip twice.
> On all other nights, we eat either sitting or reclining,
>   but on this night we eat reclining.

[3] "Tradition," from *Fiddler on the Roof,* a musical play based on Joseph Itkin, *Fiddler on the Roof.* Copyright © 1964 Joseph Stein. Used by permission.

The eldest male, usually the father, answers:

> Once we were slaves to Pharaoh in Egypt, and the Lord in His goodness and mercy brought us forth from that land, with a mighty hand and an out-stretched arm. Had he not rescued us from the hand of the despot, surely we and our children would still be enslaved, deprived of liberty and human dignity.
>
> We, therefore gather year after year, to retell this ancient story. For, in reality, it is not ancient, but eternal in its message, and its spirit. It proclaims man's burning desire to preserve liberty and justice for all.
>
> The first question asked concerns the use of Matzoh. We eat these unleavened cakes to remember that our ancestors, in their haste to leave Egypt, could not wait for breads to rise, and so removed them from the ovens while still flat.
>
> We partake of the Moror on this night that we might taste of some bitterness, to remind ourselves how bitter is the lot of one caught in the grip of slavery.
>
> We dip twice in the course of this Service, greens in salt water and Moror in Charoses, once to replace tears with gratefulness, and once to sweeten bitterness and suffering.
>
> The fourth question asks why, on this night, we eat in a reclining position. To recline at mealtimes in ancient days was the sign of a free man. On this night of Passover, we demonstrate our sense of complete freedom by reclining during our repast.[4]

Note that in both of these examples, tradition does not necessarily depend on cognitive or conscious transmission of information or patterns of behavior but rather is incorporated in the dynamic interplay of daily life; therefore, it is often unconsciously appropriated. Tradition plays a similar role in all religions. In Chinese and Japanese religions, it has been as important as duty (see Unit 60) in defining life. Even to an outsider, the importance of traditions of Hinduism in Indian society are obvious.

Christianity, as other religions, depends greatly on tradition to define and interpret beliefs and life-styles. Roman Catholicism and Eastern Orthodoxy heavily depend on tradition, insisting on its continuing role in defining belief and action. The following statement by the Catholic theologian Karl Adam expresses this function:

> The Church affirms, completely and entirely, the whole of holy Scripture, both the Old Testament and the New. . . .
>
> And by the side of the holy Scripture stands extra-scriptural Tradition. The Gospel itself is based upon oral teaching, upon the preaching of Christ, of his disciples and of that apostolic succession of teachers which began with the first pupils of the apostles. Therefore the formation in the Christian communities of a living stream of tradition was natural and inevitable. The New Testament is certainly an important expression, but it is by no means an exhaustive expression, of this apostolic tradition which filled and permeated the whole consciousness of the Church. Oral tradition, the apostolic teaching alive and active in the Christian communities, that is prior to and more fundamental than the Bible. It attests the Bible, both in its inspiration and in its canon. It is more comprehensive than the Bible, for it attests a mass of ritual and religious usage, of customs and rules, which is only slightly indicated in the Bible. And it possesses a quality which the Bible as a written document has not and cannot have, and which constitutes its pre-eminent merit, namely, that living spirit of revelation, that vitality of revealed thought, that "instinct of faith" which stands behind every written and unwritten word, and which we call the "mind of the church."[5]

---

[4] *Haggadah for the American Family*, English Service with directions by Martin Berkowitz. Copyright © 1958, 1963 and 1966 by Martin Berkowitz. Used by permission of the copyright owner.

[5] Karl Adam, *The Spirit of Catholicism*, trans. Dom Justin McCann, O.S.B. (New York: Macmillan, 1954). Used by permission of Sheed & Ward Ltd. and the Ampleforth Abbey Trustees.

～

What principal traditions can you identify within the religious communities with which you are familiar?

Is it possible to sustain a religion from generation to generation without the use of tradition?

Given the definition of religion used in this book, is it possible for a person to be religious with little or no dependence on tradition?

What might be the relationships, if any, between tradition and personal religious experience?

UNIT 81   Doubt

Although some religions may look on doubt as a dangerous enemy to recognized sources of authority and even to faith itself, doubt may be seen by others as a necessary stage on the way to religious maturity.

A student once asked her college chaplain, "Is it wrong to doubt faith and god? I've been religious all my life, but now I doubt my religion. It troubles me to doubt." This student raised questions that trouble many people. What is the role of doubt in life? How do individuals and groups deal with the doubt that may arise in the course of the study and practice of their religion? Ignore it? Condemn it? Welcome it? If doubt cannot be ignored, how can it be dealt with? Can they affirm with Tennyson that more faith resides in "honest doubt than in all the creeds"?

In the past four centuries, many so-called permanent values that gave certainty to believers have been called into question. Not only has the scientific picture of the universe changed, but also some philosophers and even religious thinkers have affirmed that God has died. Thus, doubts abound. If doubt cannot be eliminated by condemnation or avoidance, some have held that it can be dealt with effectively by an honest acceptance— embracing doubt bravely.

Different levels of doubt should be recognized. The theologian Paul Tillich has described four types of doubt: scientific, skeptical, existential, and redemptive.

Scientific Doubt

Scientific doubt is necessary to scholars and scientists; it is a part of their method for the discovery of truth. If they failed to doubt established facts and conclusions in the academic world, there would be no advancement in knowledge and study. The process of learning involves continual questioning of views of the universe. When Copernicus doubted that the earth was the center of the universe, he paved the way for the scientific revolution of the seventeenth century, a new astronomy, a new physics, and the technology that transformed Europe. Because the Wright brothers doubted the commonly held belief in the impossibility of successful flying machines, it has now become possible for humans to fly to the moon. Scientific doubt is essential to scientific and technological development. It has been one of the major contributors to the discovery of the laws of nature.

Skeptical Doubt

Another level of doubt is skeptical doubt, defined by Tillich as "an attitude of actually rejecting any certainty."[6] Not to be refuted logically, this attitude may reveal indifference, a superficial refusal to take serious questions seriously, or it may be an expression of genuine despair about finding anything to believe in. Skeptical doubt of "everything" may be a game that people play to protect themselves from serious claims of involvement.

This level of doubt can be destructive if it crystalizes into negativism about every aspect of life. The cynic tends finally to be self-negating, to find no exit from a feeling of worthlessness in a meaningless universe. Suicide or mental breakdown may become alternatives if the liberating function of skeptical doubt fails.

Implicit in skeptical doubt is the demand to doubt *doubts* and thus move to dimensions of doubt as a redemptive reality. If this positive aspect of skeptical doubt emerges, the doubter engages in what Tillich calls "existential doubt."[7]

Existential Doubt

The word *existential* refers to existence—the vitality and reality of life at any one moment; therefore, existential doubt operates at a different level than skeptical doubt or scientific doubt. Existential doubt is doubt about the meaning of an individual's life. It is felt in a very personal way, involving the individual's questioning of the validity of his or her own life and of its ultimate purpose or meaning. It usually arises when the individual has begun to doubt those things that have given meaning to life. "It does not question whether a special proposition is true or false. It does not reject every concrete proof, but it is aware of the element of insecurity in every existential truth." Doubt about the *meaning* of existence pertains to one's ultimate concern. Tillich calls this the doubt "which is implied in faith."[8] It is the doubt inherent in *every* human venture, in every risk of faith or commitment. It may never rise to the surface. It may be repressed or ignored; when it does emerge, it may cause panic or despair, or it may offer redemptive possibilities.

Redemptive Doubt

According to Tillich, then, doubt can become a redemptive element in faith. When existential doubt becomes the basis of a new willingness to commit oneself in faith and trust at a deeper level, it becomes redemptive. Faith can embrace doubt. Theistic believers may see their doubts as gifts from God. Here, faith means trusting or risking one's

---

[6] Paul Tillich, *Dynamics of Faith* (New York: Harper and Brothers, 1957), p. 19.

[7] Ibid., p. 20.

[8] Ibid.

life in commitment that does not close its eyes to uncertainty. Although trust emphasizes confidence, risk is always involved, and the awareness of risk brings conscious or unconscious doubts. Even the skeptic is involved in risk in holding the skeptical position. The skeptic who begins to doubt skepticism can open the door to the existential doubt that may lead to the courageous risk of faith. In the process of doubting, redemption from self-negating cynicism or indifference may be at hand.

In this unit, potentially positive as well as negative effects of doubt in relation to religious belief and commitment have been examined. An important question, then, for any religious authority system will be this: *How does it deal with existential doubt when its adherents are faced with the crises of life?* In the preceding unit we examined the role of tradition as one of the ways in which religious continuity is established. It may not be an exaggeration to say that the strength and vitality of tradition in religion provide one of the major means of dealing with the problem of doubt, sometimes even circumventing the appearance of doubts of any kind.

CHAPTER 20

Order and Origins

Introduction

When we speak of nature, the natural world, and the universe, we refer not only to the immediate physical, psychosocial, and cultural setting of human activity; in one sense we also refer to the whole of reality that can be comprehended or imagined by finite rational-experimental processes. When we use the term *natural universe*, we may at times mean the realm that we apprehend through the senses. We may also mean the realm studied by the various sciences. We will also see that religions show an interest in the natural realm. Most religious traditions have included among their cognitive features (their beliefs) concepts about the nature, origin, goal or destiny, and significance of the natural universe.

In considering the natural world, religion and science are often viewed as two separate ways of understanding reality; however, we assume that scientific understanding and religious understanding must be considered within a common context, especially since both religious vision and scientific method have influenced the modern view of the natural order.

Several modes of understanding the universe and its relationship to religion are investigated in this chapter. In asking the question of whether the meaning of the natural order has significant implications for one's religious understanding, two important considerations emerge. The prevailing view of modern science that reality is a process may give us tools for appropriating conflicting religious views about the universe. As the Eastern and Western views of life come into closer contact, their views concerning the nature of the universe become more relevant.

❧

How will contemporary persons deal with the differences between the Hebraic affirmation of the natural order as basically good and the Hindu view of the world as illusory or unreal?

What is the origin of the universe and how have various religious traditions described its beginning?

❧

The relationship of science and religion remains an important question. Kepler and Copernicus represent giant minds in the modern scientific revolution, yet we must quickly note that although they were scientists, they depended heavily on religious interpretations in spelling out their new view of the universe. In more recent times, thinkers diverse in other ways—Alfred North Whitehead, Pierre Teilhard de Chardin, Michael Polanyi—represent a similar spirit. You may want to consider the following question as you read this unit: Can science and religion work together to lead to richer and deeper understanding of the universes of our experience—the inner universe that we know in feeling and achieved self-consciousness and the external universe that we know through sense experience and the imaginative constructions of intellect? Both religion and science involve powerful impulses to creative and imaginative expression. Perhaps the connections between the two realms are becoming clearer now than ever before in human history.

UNIT 82   Religious Views on the Origin of the Universe

Although we may sometimes contrast religious approaches to the understanding of the natural universe with scientific or secular (the terms may not be interchangeable) approaches, it is important to realize that there have been and are contrasting religious attitudes toward the nature and origin of the universe.

How the universe, at least in its present configuration, originated; what its present stage of development is; and toward what future states it may be evolving—these questions have fascinated thoughtful and imaginative people in many ages. In contemporary astrophysics, the field of cosmology—the study of the structure and development of the universe—has grown excitingly in the past two decades. Scientists have been fascinated with concepts of an expanding universe. The model known as the "big bang" theory—that the expansion of the universe began as a result of the explosion of densely packed matter some billions of years ago—currently seems to have won the day, but theorists continue to elaborate on the concept.

Concepts and images relating to the origin and development of the universe have appeared in the world's religions, too. Integral to the religions has been an interest in understanding, or at least in recognizing, the power(s) or being(s) that activate(s) the process. Such interest often finds expression in images of God(s) as creator(s) and sustainer(s) of the universe. These images are numerous and yet varied in their understanding of the Divine, the process of creation, and humanity's place in it.

Egyptian Hymn to the Creator (1300 B.C.E.)

Pharaoh Amenhotep IV, in the fourteenth century B.C.E, consolidated ancient Egyptian worship into worship of one God—the sun god, Aton. The following passages praising Aton stress his creativity, which is seen as a continuing process that is constantly renewing itself. (Compare this hymn with the Hebrew Psalm 104.)

Thy dawning is beautiful in the horizon of the sky,
O living Aton, Beginning of life!
When thou risest in the eastern horizon
Thou fillest every land with thy beauty.
Thou art beautiful, great, glittering, high above every land,
Thy rays, they encompass the lands, even all that thou has made.
Thou art Re, and thou carriest them all away captive.
Thou bindest them by thy love.
Though thou art far away, thy rays are upon earth;
Though thou art on high, thy footprints are the day. . . .

Creator of the germ in woman,
Maker of seed in man,
Giving life to the son in the body of his mother,
Soothing him that he may not weep,
Nurse even in the womb,
Giver of breath to animate every one that he maketh!
When he cometh forth from the body . . . on the day of his birth,
Thou openest his mouth in speech,
Thou suppliest his necessities. . . .

How manifold are thy works!
They are hidden from before us,
O sole God, whose powers no other possesseth.
Thou didst create the earth according to thy heart
While thou wast alone:
Men, all cattle large and small,
All that are upon the earth,
That go about upon their feet;
All that are on high,
That fly with their wings,
The foreign countries, Syria and Kush,
The land of Egypt;
Thou settest every man into his place,
Thou suppliest his necessities,
Every one has his possessions,
And his days are reckoned.
The tongues are divers in speech,
Their forms likewise and their skins are distinguished.
For thou makest different the strangers.[1]

Arising from a common geographical and cultural matrix around the same time as the preceding Egyptian passage were two well-known stories of creation. The Babylo-

---

[1] "The Hymn to Aton," trans. J. H. Breasted, *Development of Religion and Thought in Ancient Egypt* (New York: Scribner, 1912).

nian *Enuma elish'* epic may be fruitfully compared with the Hebrew story as found in Genesis 1. The similarities as well as the differences are striking and attest to the distinctive religious perspectives from which each account is written.

Babylonian Story of Creation (about 2000 B.C.E.)

The story begins with a picture of the earliest imaginable period of primordial time, when only the divine pair, Apsu, the freshwater, and Tiamat, the saltwater, existed. Out of their commingling, the younger gods arose. When they began to cause disturbances, Apsu determined to destroy them, but they were able to kill him. Tiamat, the primordial saltwater, set out to avenge him. Marduk, one of the younger gods, was chosen to fight her. After extensive preparation, he engaged the primordial mother-god in battle. Marduk, referred to as "Sun of the heavens," succeeded in destroying her. What follows is the description of what he did with her body.

> Then the lord [Marduk] paused to view her dead body,
> That he might divide the monster and do artful works.
> He split her like a shellfish into two parts:
> Half of her he set up and ceiled it as sky,
> Pulled down the bar and posted guards.
> He bade them to allow not her waters to escape.
> He crossed the heavens and surveyed the regions.
> He squared Apsu's quarter, the abode of Nudimmud,
> As the lord measured the dimensions of Apsu.
> The Great Abode, its likeness, he fixed as Esharra,
>
> The Great Abode, Esharra, which he made as the firmament.
> Anu, Enlil, and Ea [gods] he made occupy their places.
> He constructed stations for the great gods,
> Fixing their astral likeness as constellations.
> He determined the year by designating the zones:
> He set up three constellations for each of the twelve months. . . .
>
> In her belly he established the zenith.
> The Moon he caused to shine, the night (to him) entrusting.
> He appointed him a creature of the night to signify the days: . . .
> When Marduk hears the words of the gods,
> His heart prompts (him) to fashion artful works.
> Opening his mouth, he addresses Ea
> To impart the plan he had conceived in his heart:
> Blood I will mass and cause bones to be.
> I will establish a savage, "man" shall be his name.
> Verily, savage-man I will create.
> He shall be charged with the service of the gods
>   That they might be at ease! . . .

The most guilty of the gods is then selected to be killed as material for the creation of humankind.

> It was Kingu who contrived the uprising,
> And made Tiamat rebel, and joined battle.
> They bound him, holding him before Ea.

They imposed on him his guilt and severed his blood (vessels).
Out of his blood they fashioned mankind.
He imposed the service and let free the gods,
After Ea, the wise, had created mankind,
Had imposed upon it the service of the gods.

Finally, after building a lofty shrine in Babylon, the gods feast.

The great gods took their seats,
They set up festive drink, sat down to a banquet.[2]

Hebrew Story of Creation (After 1300 B.C.E.)

In the beginning God created the heavens and the earth. The earth was without form and void, and darkness was upon the face of the deep; and the Spirit of God was moving over the face of the waters.

And God said, "Let there be light" and there was light. And God saw that the light was good; and God separated the light from the darkness. God called the light Day, and the darkness he called Night. And there was evening and there was morning, one day.

And God said, "Let there be a firmament in the midst of the waters, and let it separate the waters from the waters." . . . And it was so. And God called the firmament Heaven . . . a second day. And God said, "Let the waters under the heavens be gathered together into one place, and let the dry land appear." And it was so. God called the dry land Earth, and the waters that were gathered together be called Seas. . . . And God said, "Let the earth put forth vegetation. . . ." And it was so. . . . And God saw that it was good . . . a third day.

And God said, "Let there be lights in the firmament of the heavens to separate the day from the night; and let them be for signs and for seasons and for days and years, and let them be lights . . . upon the earth." And it was so. . . . And God saw that it was good . . . a fourth day. And God said, "Let the waters bring forth swarms of living creatures, and let birds fly. . . ." And God saw that it was good . . . a fifth day. And God said, "Let the earth bring forth living creatures. . . ." And it was so. . . . And God saw that it was good.

Then God said, "Let us make man in our image, after our likeness; and let them have dominion over the fish of the sea, and over the birds of the air, and over the cattle, and over all the earth, and over every creeping thing that creeps upon the earth." . . . Male and female he created them. And God blessed them. . . . And it was so. And God saw everything that he had made, and behold, it was very good. And there was evening and there was morning, a sixth day.

Thus the heavens and the earth were finished, and all the host of them.

And on the seventh day God finished his work which he had done, and he rested on the seventh day. . . . So God blessed the seventh day and hallowed it. . . . (Genesis 1:1–2:3, RSV)

❧

What is the reason for creation in each of these stories?

The nature or character of the God(s) is reflected in these stories: How is it similar or different in each?

[2] "The Creation Epic," from "Akkadian Myths and Epics," trans. E. A. Speiser, *Ancient Near Eastern Texts Relating to the Old Testament*, ed., James B. Pritchard, 3rd ed., with Supplement. (Copyright © 1969 by Princeton University Press), pp. 66–69. Reprinted by permission of Princeton University Press.

What is the character of the human being created in each account? What is the
    purpose for which the human was created?

What materials were used in creation? What is their origin?

∾

These stories comment on the beginning of the universe; creation is an event in the
past. Many interpreters regard these stories, whether Egyptian, Babylonian, or Hebrew, as
attempts to express in symbolic language a basic religious understanding of the relation of the
Divine to the natural universe and human life and activity. There are other ways to understand creation, as the following passage shows. Martin Luther (1483–1546 C.E.) believed that
the creative process continues; it is not something that happened only in the past.

> Even as God in the beginning of creation made the world out of nothing, whence He is
> called the Creator and the Almighty, so His manner of working continues still the same.
> Even now and unto the end of the world, all His works are such that out of that which is
> nothing, worthless, despised, wretched and dead, He makes that which is something, pre-
> cious, honorable, blessed and living. Again, whatever is something, precious, honorable,
> blessed and living, He makes to be nothing, worthless, despised, wretched and dying. After
> this manner no creature can work; none can produce anything out of nothing.[3]

Luther also stressed the sustaining nature of God's activity.

> "I believe in God the Father Almighty, Maker of heaven and earth." What does this mean?
> Answer: I believe that God has made me and all creatures; that He has given me my body
> and soul, eyes, ears, and all my members, my reason and all my senses, and still preserves
> them; also clothing and shoes, meat and drink, house and home, wife and children, fields,
> cattle, and all my goods; that He richly and daily provides me with all that I need to sup-
> port this body and life; that He defends me against all danger and guards and protects me
> from all evil; and all this purely out of fatherly, divine goodness and mercy, without any
> merit or worthiness in me; for all of which it is my duty to thank and praise, to serve and
> obey Him. This is most certainly true.[4]

When we turn our attention from Western concepts of creation to those of the
East, other distinctive aspects arise. Because Hindus stress the union of an individual's soul
(Atman) with the world-soul (Brahman), they are less concerned with concepts of time
and history (see Unit 10). Nevertheless, the importance of the creative process does not
escape attention, as the following passage from the *Mundaka-Upanishad* shows. Notice the
reincarnation and reunion motifs that underlie the statement.

> This is the truth. As from a blazing fire sparks, being like unto fire, fly forth a thousand-
> fold, thus are various beings brought forth from the Imperishable, my friend, and return
> thither also.
>   That heavenly Person is without body, he is both without and within, not produced,
> without breath and without mind, pure, higher than the high Imperishable.
>   From him (when entering on creation) is born breath, mind, and all organs of sense,
> ether, air, light, water, and the earth, the support of all.

[3] Martin Luther, "The Magnificat," *The Works of Martin Luther*, Vol. III (Philadelphia: Muhlenberg
Press, 1930), p. 127.

[4] Martin Luther, *Smaller Catechism* (St. Louis: Concordia Publishing House, 1943), p. 6.

Fire (the sky) is his head, his eyes the sun and the moon, the quarters his ears, his speech the Vedas disclosed, the wind his breath, his heart the universe; from his feet came the earth; he is indeed the inner Self of all things.

From him comes Agni (fire), the sun being the fuel; from the moon (Soma) comes rain (Parganya); from the earth herbs; and man gives seed unto the woman. Thus many things are begotten from the Person (purusha).

From him come the *Rig*, the Sâman, the Yagush, the Dîkshâ (initiatory rites), all sacrifices and offerings of animals, and the fees bestowed on priests, the year too, the sacrificer, and the worlds, in which the moon shines brightly and the sun.

From him the many Devas too are begotten, the Sâdhyas (genii), men, cattle, birds, the up and down breathings, rice and corn (for sacrifice), penance, faith, truth, abstinence, and law.

The seven senses (prâna) also spring from him, the seven lights (acts of sensation), the seven kinds of fuel (objects by which the senses are lighted), the seven sacrifices (results of sensation), these seven worlds (the places of the senses, the worlds determined by the senses) in which the senses move, which rest in the cave (of the heart), and are placed there seven and seven.

Hence come the seas and all the mountains, from him flow the rivers of every kind; hence come all herbs and juice through which the inner Self subsists with the elements.

The Person is all this, sacrifice, penance, Brahman, the highest immortal; he who knows this hidden in the cave (of the heart), he, O friend, scatters the knot of ignorance here on earth.[5]

Although Hinduism's picture of creation magnifies the mystery of the Brahman-Atman nature, Japan's ancient Shinto religion embodies a creation myth comparable to those in many Western traditions. Concerned only with the islands of Japan and not the universe, it accounts for creation from a distinctively nationalistic viewpoint. The following summarization of this complicated Japanese tradition is by John Noss.

The Japanese islands are a special creation of the gods. After the primal chaos had in the course of events separated into heaven and ocean, various gods appeared in the heavenly drift-mist, only to disappear without event, until finally there came upon the scene the two deities who produced the Japanese islands and their inhabitants. These were the primal male and female, Izanagi, the Male-Who-Invites, and Izanami, the Female-Who-Invites. Their heavenly associates commanded them to "make, consolidate, and give birth to" the Japanese islands. These two beings descended the Floating Bridge of Heaven (a rainbow?), and when they reached its lower end, Izanagi pushed down his jeweled spear into the muddy brine and stirred it until the fluid below them became "thick and glutinous." Then he drew the spear up, whereupon "the brine that dripped down from the end of the spear was piled up and became an island." Stepping down on the island, they came together, and Izanami bore from her womb the eight great islands of Japan. . . . [After the creation of a number of lesser deities Izanami dies and goes to the underworld. Izanagi unsuccessfully attempts to rescue her and a period of conflict and disorder ensues. During this period Izanagi produces the goddess of the sun, the moon-god, and the storm-god.]

Years later, we find the sun-goddess, Amaterasu, looking down from her seat in heaven and becoming concerned about the disorder in the islands below. The storm-god's son was ruling there, but she was not satisfied. She finally commissioned her grandson Ni-ni-gi to descend to the islands and rule them for her. . . . [In later times Ni-ni-gi's great grandson Jimmu Tenno became the first human emperor of the islands and established his capital on the central island, Honshu, in 660 B.C.]

---

[5] *The Unpanishads*, E. Max Müller, trans., Vol. II (New York: Dover, n.d.), pp. 34–35.

Meanwhile, the leading families of Japan and the whole Japanese people descended from the minor deities, or lesser kami, residing on the islands.

Thus, we are to understand that the emperor of Japan is a descendant in an unbroken line from the sun-goddess, Amaterasu, and that the islands of Japan have a divine origin, and so also the Japanese people.[6]

❧

Why have the world's religions been occupied with the attempt to explain the origin of the universe?

How many different accounts of the "nature and destiny of humanity and natural order" do you find in the accounts in this unit?

What is the relation of humans to God and to the natural universe in each account?

❧

Recent scientific developments have added great interest to questions about the origin and nature of the universe. There is now perhaps a greater awareness of cosmology than has existed since the time of Copernicus, Kepler, Galileo, and Newton. In the next unit we will examine the role of religious components in the creation of a new cosmology in the scientific work of one of the great scientific investigators of an earlier period and in the relation of scientific thought to religious vision in our time.

UNIT 83   Religious Vision and Scientific Method

Religious concepts and images have been used as a basis for scientific work and may well be continuing to function in the creative imagination that leads to scientific discovery.

For example, Johann Kepler was one of the founders of exact modern science, an astronomer who not only championed but also corrected and refined the Copernican model that placed the sun, rather than the earth, at the center of our planetary system. E. A. Burtt has described how a number of essentially religious conceptions about the nature of the universe (or cosmos) influenced Kepler to adopt the revolutionary new theory.

> In his subsequently expressed reasons for accepting Copernicanism this central position of the sun is always included, usually first. This ascription of deity to the sun was covered over by Kepler with such mystical allegorization as was necessary to give it a hearing in the prevailing theological environment, with especial reference to the doctrine of the Trinity. The sun, according to Kepler, is God the Father, the sphere of the fixed stars is God the Son, the intervening ethereal medium, through which the power of the sun is communicated to impel the planets around their orbits, is the Holy Ghost. To pronounce this allegorical trapping is not to suggest, of course, that Kepler's Christian theology is at all insincere; it is rather that he had discovered an illuminating natural proof and interpretation of it, and the whole attitude, with its animism and allegoriconaturalistic approach, is

---

[6] John B. Noss, *Man's Religions,* 4th ed. (New York: Macmillan, 1969), pp. 320–21. © John B. Noss, 1969. Used by permission.

quite typical of much thinking of the day. . . . But the connexion between Kepler, the sun-worshipper, and Kepler, the seeker of exact mathematical knowledge of astronomical nature, is very close. It was primarily by such considerations as the deification of the sun and its proper placing at the centre of the universe that Kepler in the years of his adolescent fervour and warm imagination was induced to accept the new system: But, his mind immediately proceeded, and here his mathematics and his Neo-Pythagoreanism come into play, if the system is true, there must be many other mathematical harmonies in the celestial order that can be discovered and proclaimed as confirmation of Copernicanism, by an intensive study of the available data. This was a task in exact mathematics, and it was very fortunate for Kepler that he was just plunging into such profound labours at the time when Tycho Brahe, the greatest giant of observational astronomy since Hipparchus, was completing his life-long work of compiling a vastly more extensive and incomparably precise set of data than had been in the possession of any of his predecessors. Kepler had joined Tycho Brahe the year before the latter's death and had full access to his magnificent accumulations. . . . Both Copernicus and Kepler were firmly convinced for religious reasons of the uniformity of motion, *i.e.*, each planet in its revolution is impelled by a constant and never failing cause, hence Kepler's joy at being able to "save" this principle as regards the areas even though it had to be surrendered as regards the planet's path. But the discovery which yielded Kepler the most inordinate delight and to which he referred for many years as his most important achievement, was the discovery published in his first work, the *Mysterium Cosmographicum* (1597), that the distances between the orbits of the six planets then known bore a certain rough resemblance to the distances which would be obtained if the hypothetical spheres of the planets were inscribed in and circumscribed about the five regular solids properly distributed between them. . . . Of course, this performance has remained entirely unfruitful—the correspondence is rough, and the discovery of new planets has quite upset its underlying assumptions—but Kepler never forgot the pristine enthusiasm which this achievement awoke in him.[7]

Kepler wrote:

> The intense pleasure I have received from this discovery can never be told in words. I regretted no more the time wasted; I tired of no labour; I shunned no toil of reckoning, days and nights spent in calculation, until I could see whether my hypothesis would agree with the orbits of Copernicus or whether my joy was to vanish into air.[8]

Kepler's close identification of religion and science has often been lost in the modern world. Many people see a conflict between the knowledge gained through scientific investigation and that found in religious insights.

Particularly in the eighteenth and nineteenth centuries, many educated people felt that there was conflict and antagonism between the Newtonian concept of the natural order—often interpreted as leading to a view of the universe as a completely mechanical, "clockwork," deterministic machine—and religious views of the universe as alive and the scene of encounter between the human spirit and the Divine. The revival of attacks on Darwinian concepts of evolution by "scientific creationists" reflects the belief of some Christians that there are conflicts between biblical accounts of creation and God's role in it and widely accepted results of modern scientific inquiry.

[7] E. A. Burtt, *Metaphysical Foundations of Modern Physical Science*, 2nd rev. ed. (London: Routledge & Kegan Paul, 1932), p. 48. Used by permission of Humanities Press, Inc., New York.

[8] Ibid., pp. 47–52.

Yet this understanding of a conflict—alleged or real—is not shared by everyone. Interpreters of Hinduism and Buddhism have pointed to what they consider to be profound analogies between modern scientific cosmology and microphysics and concepts of Hinduism and Buddhism involving space, time, the evolving universe, and the self. After an initial impulse in late nineteenth- and early twentieth-century theology to separate science from religion (by saying that science deals with facts whereas religion deals with values, or value-laden interpretations of the significance of facts), an increasing number of Jewish and Christian thinkers have been interested in exploring the relationship between religious belief and the new science.

The Catholic priest and paleontologist Pierre Teilhard de Chardin (d. 1955) interpreted the evolutionary process, as disclosed in geological, biological, and cosmological sciences, as under the guidance of the divine Spirit; he believed that contemporary scientific insight can sensitize us to the Divine's presence and purposes.[9]

The writings of another contemporary thinker, Michael Polanyi, also contain interesting speculations concerning the relation in contemporary scientific work of an intuitive vision of reality to exact scientific procedures. In *The Tacit Dimension*, Polanyi explores a dimension, or process, of mind that he calls "tacit knowing." According to Polanyi, tacit—intuitive, nonreflective—knowing plays an essential role in scientific discovery, especially in guiding scientists to the problems that lead to new discoveries. Flashes of insight, hunches, lucky guesses, and intuitions are examples of tacit knowledge emerging into consciousness—in much the same way that new forms of life emerge from simpler forms.[10]

Alfred North Whitehead was another twentieth-century thinker who shared Polanyi's belief that exact scientific theorizing begins at an intuitive, feeling-level relationship to nature that may be called *religious* since it involves a sense of a relationship that can never be given complete and exact conceptual expression to the whole and potential wholeness of things. Mathematician, logician, philosopher of science, and metaphysician, Whitehead wrote,

> Nature is a process. As in the case of everything directly exhibited in sense-awareness, there can be no explanation of this characteristic of nature. All that can be done is to use language which may speculatively demonstrate it, and also express the relation of this factor in nature to other factors.
>
> It is an exhibition of the process of nature that each duration happens and passes. The process of nature can also be termed the passage of nature. I definitely refrain at this stage from using the word "time," since the measurable time of science and of civilised life generally merely exhibits some aspects of the more fundamental fact of the passage of nature. I believe that in this doctrine I am in full accord with Bergson, though he uses "time" for the fundamental fact which I call the "passage of nature." Also the passage of nature is exhibited equally in spatial transition as well as in temporal transition. It is in virtue of its passage that nature is always moving on. It is involved in the meaning of this property of "moving on" that not only is any act of sense-awareness just that act and no other, but the

[9] See especially Pierre Teilhard de Chardin, *The Future of Man* (New York: Harper & Row, 1964).

[10] See Michael Polanyi, *The Tacit Dimension* (New York: Doubleday, 1966), and *Personal Knowledge* (Chicago: University of Chicago Press, 1958).

terminus of each act is also unique and is the terminus of no other act. Sense-awareness seizes its only chance and presents for knowledge something which is for it alone.[11]

Many have found that not only the new cosmology, with its vision of a dynamic universe that embraces evolutionary processes on a physical-universal as well as biological-terrestrial scale, but also the newer theories of the microcosm, begun with Max Planck's and Albert Einstein's quantum physics (1900–1905) and continuing to the latest experimental and speculative theories concerning the physics of elementary particles, partly derive from and possibly support a dynamic religious vision of reality.[12]

Some time ago, one of the authors of this book asked a friend, an outstanding physicist, what an atom looks like. With great patience he replied, "I don't know; I've never seen one. I can't tell you where one is. I can only tell from a cloud chamber where something has been." From subatomic particles to clusters of galaxies, all are examined not in terms of what they are as static entities but as interacting participants in a cosmic drama. For many people, contemporary physics discloses a sense of grandeur and mystery in its emerging vision of reality. Such elements constantly challenge traditional interpretations of the relationship of science and religion and perhaps leave room for a much closer identification of religion with science than has often been assumed.

Is Polanyi's theory about "tacit knowing" at least in part a theory about the role of religious vision in scientific knowledge?

Do Polanyi's and Whitehead's theories about tacit, or intuitive, knowing rest on a religious vision—or at least an intuitive vision about reality, the nature of human life, and its relationship to the rest of nature?

Examine how the discussion of Kepler's scientific theorizing illustrates the interaction of religious and aesthetic values with the observational and mathematical exactness so often considered the special characteristics of scientific method.

---

[11] From Alfred North Whitehead, *The Concept of Nature* (Cambridge: Cambridge University Press, 1920), pp. 53–54. Used by permission of publisher.

[12] See especially, from the scientific side, such works as Nigel Calder, *The Key to the Universe* (New York: Viking Press, 1977); Robert Jastrow, *God and the Astronomers* (New York: Warner Books, 1978); Gary Zukav, *The Dancing Wu Li Masters: An Overview of the New Physics* (New York: Bantam Books, 1980); John Gribbin, *In Search of Schrödinger's Cat* (New York: Bantam Books, 1984); Ilya Prigogine, *Order Out of Chaos: Man's New Dialogue with Nature* (New York: Bantam Books, 1984); John Boslough, *Stephen Hawking's Universe* (New York: William Morrow, 1985); Kitty Ferguson, *Stephen Hawking: Quest for a Theory of Everything* (New York: Bantam Books, 1992); and Stephen W. Hawking, *A Brief History of Time* (New York: Bantam Books, 1988). See also, from the side of religion, Roland Muskat Frye, ed., *Is God a Creationist?* (New York: Scribner, 1983).

CHAPTER 21

❧

Human Response
to the Natural Process

Introduction

The two units in this chapter focus on the religious dimensions of attitudes toward the place of human beings in the natural order. The chapter stresses contrasting attitudes—feelings, images, concepts—that different societies have taken toward nature and its impingement on and relationship to human life. In some cultures the natural process has been viewed with warmth and acceptance, in others as something impersonal to be used, and still in others as something to be downgraded and dispensed with in the human search for truth.

We can easily recognize how attitudes toward nature in the West have fostered pollution and other forms of environmental violence. We have not included descriptive material on these problems because of lack of space and the abundance of materials elsewhere. Instead we have sought to penetrate the attitudes prevalent in the West that have produced the disruptive actions in nature. We have also sought to relate these attitudes to the religious traditions that have transmitted them. A wealth of resources, contemporary and traditional, will enable the reader to go beyond the limited discussion of this chapter.

Unit 84   Humanity and the World

What is the relationship between humanity and the natural process? Different cultures and different individuals have responded to this question in diverse ways. Some responses have been analytical, some descriptive, and still others imitative. Some have emphasized the cognitive dimension, others the affective. Some responses have been given consciously, others unconsciously. We will isolate and tentatively explore three types of responses, each a basic perspective concerning the natural process: (1) symbiosis, (2) apobiosis, and (3) diabiosis.

Symbiosis

The term *symbiosis,* derived from the field of biology—the study of living things—is widely used to stress the interrelatedness of all living things. The prefix *sym-* is a Greek preposition used as part of a compound word and signifies "together, interdependent, mutual, reciprocal." The morpheme *-bios-* in Greek signifies "life in all of its appearances and expressions." Hence the term *symbios-* literally means "life together, interdependent life, life lived mutually or reciprocally." When used to characterize a type of attitude toward the natural process, *symbiosis* denotes the accommodation of humanity to the natural process in a relationship of harmony, unity, and organic wholeness. Symbiotic persons regard themselves as one with the natural world, from which they draw their sustenance and meaning with a minimum of disruption and interference.

This type of relationship is exemplified by how most animals behave in their natural environment. Few animals kill for the sake of killing. Animals will kill out of hunger, sometimes out of fear, in self-defense, or perhaps as a part of a life ritual such as mating. But few ravage for the sake of ravaging.

Some cultures strongly reflect this type of primary understanding. The cultures of the American Indians are and were symbiotic in relation to the natural process. Likewise, the Chinese and Japanese cultural ethos, the bygone culture of ancient Egypt, and many isolated Western cultures today reflect this mentality. More developed expressions of symbiotic awareness may be found in aspects of popular Hindu religion—veneration of animals, especially the cow; reverence toward rivers and lakes, especially the Ganges; the recognition of the process of life/death, creation/destruction, within the natural process, as mediated through the worship of Shiva; *ahimsa,* nonviolation of living things; and the extremely profound recognition of the continuity and interdependence of human existence, *samsara,* or rebirth/redeath. This symbiotic attitude is not absent in Western culture: Rod McKuen's *The Earth* and other poems, much of Robert Frost and Thoreau, and the strain of nature-mysticism within Christianity. Even the preoccupation of many Westerners with sex—including its mutation in advertising—may be only a disguised expression of the ancient, symbiotic nature/human fertility cult. But on the whole, Western culture, unlike the cultures of the East, has not been dominated by the symbiotic consciousness.

This mentality, therefore, is seldom found in pure form. Even in the cultures and for those individuals most shaped by symbiotic awareness, a distinction is noted—in varying degrees—between humanity and the rest of nature. The totem of an Eskimo tribe may be one of the community, even as in prehistoric Nile culture a village appears to have identified with a particular animal; but the existence of the totem itself reflects at least an unconscious awareness that the totem animal or plant is distinguishable from the group. Black Eagle (note the name) in Figure 21.1 expresses this idea. Even where the affirmation of the natural process is depicted in religious or divine imagery, the distinction between

Figure 21.1 Rick O'Shay by Stan Lynde. (Copyright © 1970 by *The Chicago Tribune*. Used by permission.)

humanity and the world is preserved. Yet the symbiotic perspective persists as the dominant tone of humanity's sense of relationship to the natural process. And this perspective values stability and order and tends to encourage the status quo. Change—when it means interference or manipulation or reordering of the natural process—is resisted. One is encouraged to observe and to adjust to the natural process rather than to manipulate it.

From a religious perspective, this mentality is based on the perception of a divine power or force that is immanent in the natural process, including humanity. This divine power may be depicted in many ways: the Japanese veneration of *kami*, the precommunist Chinese reverence for Heaven and the ancestors, *shaktism* in India, the love of natural order and beauty in the West, the experience of the psychic powers of sexuality. These are only a few examples. In any case, nature itself—including humanity—is considered an expression or materialization of the divine presence.

> Nature is an indispensable part of me, especially mountains. I am really looking forward to this summer when I can again be in the mountains. It is in the mountains where I find real peace. I can feel life and really be aware of it, and not just take it for granted. I feel closer to God when I am alone in the mountains than any other time. Then I know there is a God who is still active whereas at other times I'm not really sure.[1]

Apobiosis

The term *apobiosis*, coined for our purposes, signifies the antithesis of symbiosis. The prefix *apo-* is the Greek preposition meaning "apart, separate from, alienated." Hence the compound *apobiosis* reflects humanity's apartness, its separation, its lack of oneness with the natural order. Or more positively, people see themselves as detached from the natural process, and not only free from it, but also impelled to oversee, manipulate, and exploit it for their own ends.

This mentality is one of the wellsprings of the technological thrust of European and North American culture and has at least two sources in its history: on the one hand, the affirmation in Greek culture of humanity's capacity to understand and to order phenomena through reason; on the other hand, the conviction drawn from the Jewish tradition and mediated through Christianity that God and humanity stand somewhat apart from the natural process. Examples of this attitude are seen in the "naming" of the animals in the creation story of Genesis 2 and the injunction to humans to "fill . . . subdue . . . have dominion" in Genesis 1. Both of these components issued eventually in the rebirth called the Renaissance; in exploration, settlement, and development of new political and social patterns; in the industrial revolution; and in the awesome development of modern science and technology. The apobiotic mentality is a requisite for the conquest of space, disease, and all other frontiers.

Yet it is striking that only in western Europe and North America do we find the birth of science and technology; only recently, along with the spread of Western culture, has it appeared in India, China, and Japan. Nor has it been present in the Near Eastern countries. The reason for this may be found in the observation that although Islam has a

---

[1] Unpublished student journal of Beth Utton. Used by permission.

deity who is transcendent, a human being is not understood as an independent agent, manipulating and ordering the natural process. At this point we need to distinguish between the apobiotic mentality and modern scientific mentality. The Muslim cultures have not given birth to modern science in the full sense of the term. Yet in these cultures people often see themselves as opposed to the natural process; they are reconciled to it only through submission to the sovereignty of Allah, who has created, controls, and provides for those who abide by his covenant. As Harvey Cox has noted (see below), both the Jewish and the Christian heritages contain a strong emphasis on a transcendent deity. Cox sees in this conviction the basis for the disenchantment of the natural process. This is correct, at least in part. A transcendent deity to whom humanity is related does issue in a semitranscendent understanding of humanity in these religious traditions. And it is with respect to the understanding of humanity that Judaism and Christianity differ from Islam. But not until the Renaissance—and the rediscovery of the Greek emphasis on rationality—did the Jewish and Christian understanding of humanity generate the apobiotic mentality that is reaching its fruition in Western science and technology. Technology means "building knowledge," and apobiotic individuals are the builders.

Again, one may not find a pure expression of apobiosis. The contrast with symbiosis lies not in the means but in the objective. Both rely on observation (note how Black Eagle calls Rick O'Shay only by the name "Yellow Hair"), but symbiotic people observe so that they may participate. Apobiotic people observe so that they may manipulate, although in their apobiotic efforts they are often caught up in the order and beauty they are seeking to understand and then harness. Affective involvement fostering harmony and identification with the natural process has no place in a scientific experiment or technological application. The astronauts of the Apollo series, looking out at the lunar terrain, may have been awestruck by the sight, but this was extracurricular as far as their mission was concerned: They were after rocks, not scenery. Their response to the moonscape was symbiotic, but their mission was apobiotic. As men they combined the two. The apobiotic mentality aims at conquest and change, harnessing the powers (no longer divine) of nature. Exploitation, frustration, disorder, or failure may occur, but only as the price of humanity's creativity, a creativity that transcends the natural order.

Thus the natural process itself does not contain a divine presence. Humanity, by becoming master of nature, shares in the transcendent power of God.

> Presecular man lives in an enchanted forest. Its glens and groves swarm with spirits. Its rocks and streams are alive with friendly or fiendish demons. Reality is charged with a magical power that erupts here and there to threaten or benefit man. Properly managed and utilized, this invisible energy can be supplicated, warded off, or channeled. If real skill and esoteric knowledge are called into play, the energies of the unseen world can be used against a family foe or an enemy of the tribe. . . .
>
> Many historians of religion believe that this magical world-view, although developed and organized in a very sophisticated way, was never really broken through until the advent of biblical faith. The Sumerian, Egyptian, and Babylonian religious systems, despite their fantastically complicated theologies and their enormously refined symbol systems, remained a form of high magic, relying for their cohesion on the integral relation between man and the cosmos. . . . Both god and man were part of nature.
>
> This is why the Hebrew view of Creation signals such a marked departure. It separates nature from God and distinguishes man from nature. This is the beginning of the disen-

chantment process. . . . Whereas in the Babylonian accounts, the sun, moon, and stars are semidivine beings, partaking the divinity of the gods themselves, their religious status is totally rejected by the Hebrews. . . . None of the heavenly bodies can claim any right to religious awe or worship.

Nor is man tied to nature by kinship ties. The lines of kinship in the Bible are temporal, not spatial. Instead of reaching out to encompass kangaroos and totem shrubs, they reach back to the sagas of the fathers and forward to the fortunes of the children's children. . . . Just after his creation man is given the crucial responsibility of naming the animals. He is their master and commander. It is his task to subdue the earth. Nature is neither his brother nor his god. As such it offers him no salvation. . . . For the Bible, neither man nor God is defined by his relationship to nature. This not only frees both of them for history, it also makes nature itself available for man's use.[2]

The contrast between symbiosis and apobiosis may be illustrated by the response to the following situation: A certain city was located on a large river that received water from a large watershed. At intervals the watershed far above the city would receive large amounts of rainfall, causing the river, without perceptible reason, to overflow, resulting in severe damage to the urban area. The symbiotic inhabitants tried to combat the problem by clearing the channel of underbrush and building their houses on stilts. Yet to a large measure, they remained vulnerable to the threat of the river. The apobiotic inhabitants were not opposed to these measures but in addition sought to build dams upstream to control the flow of water. In so doing, they created an even greater hazard if one of the dams should break. Both had at least one thing in common: Both symbiosis and apobiosis regard the natural process as having reality. The third mentality differs on this point.

Diabiosis

The term *diabiosis* also coined for our purposes, is compounded from the noun *bios* and the prepositional prefix *dia-*. This preposition is used in Greek to signify movement through a place, duration through a time, or the agent or instrument by which something is accomplished. *Diabiosis*, therefore, regards nature as that through which one must move if one is to reach reality. In this view, the natural process is regarded as changing, impermanent, imperfect, and of secondary importance at best. The diabiotic person believes that one must penetrate or survive the natural order to arrive at that which is real and eternal.

The culture of India most consistently exhibits diabiosis as the dominant mentality. As Heinrich Zimmer states, the natural process, including human existence itself, is considered "as fugitive and evanescent as cloud and mist." Humanity may be deluded by the seductiveness of *maya*, but in the end, that which is ultimate and real can be known only when the illusion dissolves. This Indian perspective continues in the movement of Mahavira, Jainism. In this tradition, the natural process is identified with "matter," which attaches itself to the soul through sin and can be purged only through asceticism and the practice of nonviolence toward all living things. Only then can the soul become free. Another child of Indian culture, Buddhism, also exhibits this mentality toward the natural process, including humanity's ego and culture: Gautama, the initiator, regarded not

---

[2] Harvey Cox, *The Secular City* (New York: Macmillan, 1965, pp. 21–23. Copyright © Harvey Cox, 1965, 1966.

matter but destructive craving as that which perpetuated one's egoistic existence and bound him or her to the world of illusion. Later Buddhists held to this position. Yet, unlike Gautama, they returned to the conviction that beyond this illusory existence is cosmic reality, be it compassion or energy, and only by penetrating through *maya* can this reality be reached. In the philosophical form of Taoism in China we also encounter the conviction of a reality beyond. Yet unlike Indian culture, this reality—or Tao—is also within the natural process. Thus the knowledge of Tao informs and transforms one's relationship to the natural process. Nature, then, is not unreal; rather, it is dependent for its existence and meaning on the Tao inherent in it.

This diabiotic mentality is not absent from Western culture, especially in the Christian tradition. From the very earliest times some Christians have seen the natural process as irretrievably corrupted by human sin. The natural process, therefore, is regarded as temporary, as that which must soon pass away. People, in this view, are at best pilgrims in a strange land, and at worst victims of the natural order. The Revelation to John of Patmos is the strongest New Testament example; contemporary examples may be found on the radio, TV and in the newspapers. Other non-Christian Western expressions of this diabiotic view may be noted in Greco-Roman times in Platonism and neo-Platonism, Stoicism, Gnosticism, and Manicheanism. Modern non-Christian Western expressions may be found in the alcohol and drug cultures, in which one attempts to escape the world as one experiences it.

Diabiotic people seek release from a natural process that is regarded as corrupt, illusory, or secondary. Because they seek reality beyond, they tend to neglect and abandon societal problems and values. The quest is an individual one: One is primarily concerned with saving oneself, and the rest, if necessary, must look out for themselves.

> The *māyā* of the gods is their power to assume diverse shapes by displaying at will various aspects of their subtle essence. But the gods are themselves the productions of a greater *māyā*: the spontaneous self-transformation of an originally undifferentiated, all-generating divine Substance. And this greater *māyā* produces, not the gods alone, but the universe in which they operate. All the universes co-existing in space and succeeding each other in time, the planes of being and the creatures of those planes where natural or supernatural, are manifestations from an inexhaustible, original and eternal well being, and are made manifest by a play of *māyā*.
>
> . . . Māyā is Existence: both the world of which we are aware, and ourselves who are contained in the growing and dissolving environment, growing and dissolving in our turn. At the same time, Māyā is the supreme power that generates and animates the display: the dynamic aspect of the universal Substance. Thus it is at once, effect (the cosmic flux), and cause (the creative power). In the latter regard it is known as Shakti, "Cosmic Energy." . . .
>
> . . . Enthralled by ourselves and the effects of our environment, regarding the bafflements of Māyā as utterly real, we endure an endless ordeal of blandishments, desire and death; whereas, from a standpoint just beyond our ken (represented in the perennial esoteric tradition and known to the illimited, supraindividual consciousness of ascetic, yogic experience) Māyā—the world, the life, the ego, to which we cling—is as fugitive and evanescent as cloud and mist.[3]

[3] Heinrich Zimmer, *Myths and Symbols in Indian Art and Civilization*, ed. Joseph Campbell, Bollingen Series VI (copyright © 1946 by Bollingen Foundation), reprinted with permission of Princeton University Press, pp. 24–26.

It should be noted again that most societies manifest contrasting attitudes toward nature. Perhaps nowhere would one of the three types discussed in this unit be found in an entirely pure form. However, cultures may, over a long period of time, be characterized in a fairly definite way by one of the forms. India, for instance, and the Europe of the Patristic and early Middle Ages were essentially diabiotic in attitude and ideology, if not always in life-style. A society like that of contemporary Japan is interesting. With its mixture of Eastern religious traditions—Shinto (symbiotic) and Buddhism (with Zen, especially, characterized by both diabiotic and symbiotic streams)—and the emulation of Western technical-manipulative attitudes (apobiotic), one finds a stimulating, sometimes confusing, and possibly fruitful intermingling of attitudes.

Do you find one dominant attitude, a conflict of attitudes, or a mixture of attitudes about the relation of human beings to the natural order in contemporary American society?

Unit 85   Nature and the Natural

There is a profound religious dimension to our concepts of and attitudes toward the natural realm. Even our feelings about nature express this. When we respond to nature—whether we mean the world that the astronomer and physicist present in their highly abstract theories or the concrete experience of a sunset—the way that we *feel* embodies our commitment to and understanding of what seems to us to be of supreme value. In this unit, we attempt to explore some of the ambiguities—the many not always harmonious meanings—of the term *nature* as it is reflected in contrasting religious attitudes.

What do the terms *nature* and *natural* mean? Is nature the world of living things that the biologist studies, or is it the abstract, mathematically stated laws that the physicist gives us as a description of "reality"? Is nature what Romantic poets like Wordsworth wrote about? Is nature the realm of the sounds, scents, and colors that we experience? Or is it only the motion and interaction of events, waves, and particles—sound waves rather than sounds? Is it the sunsets and mountain peaks that the tourist sees? Is it what the hippie or the hermit who has abandoned the world of suburbia or the industrial centers returns to, a realm of cosmic and personal harmony? Is it the world of the jungle that the explorer seeks to conquer, where animal species struggle for survival?

Does nature include humanity's social institutions: Are civilizations, humane societies, "natural"? Or is nature whatever exists independently of, or apart from, human activity? We speak of natural rather than artificial (manufactured) products. But are people a part of nature? Or do they stand over against it, different from it, opposed to it? Are people at war with nature? Or is nature, in people, at war with itself? Some religious traditions speak of humanity as evil by nature. Others speak of humanity as naturally good. One thing is certain: Not only must we ask whether different cultures and different traditions (or the same cultures in different moods or at different periods of time) have a positive or a negative attitude toward nature; we must also ask what they think of as *natural* and what they think *nature* includes.

Modern Western Views of Nature

Alfred North Whitehead described a view of nature that arose as Western scientific thought took a new approach to physics and chemistry in the seventeenth century.

> Nature is that which we observe in perception through the senses. In . . . sense-perception we are aware of something which is not thought and which is self-contained for thought. This property of being self-contained for thought lies at the base of natural science. It means that nature can be thought of as a closed system whose . . . relations do not require the expression of the fact that they are thought about.[4]

This rather abstract definition is perhaps typical of what nature, as described by the laws of physics, has meant to many Western thinkers since the seventeenth century.

Describing the view of nature held by such seventeenth-century philosophers and scientists as Galileo, Descartes, Locke, and Newton, Whitehead wrote,

> We then ask in what sense are blueness and noisiness qualities of the body. By analogous reasoning, we also ask in what sense is its scent a quality of the rose.
>   Galileo considered this question, and at once pointed out that, apart from eyes, ears, or noses, there would be no colours, sounds, or smells. . . . The occurrences of nature are in some way apprehended by minds, which are associated with living bodies. Primarily, the mental apprehension is aroused by the occurrences in certain parts of the correlated body, the occurrences in the brain, for instance. But the mind in apprehending also experiences sensations which, properly speaking, are qualities of the mind alone. These sensations are projected by the mind so as to clothe appropriate bodies in external nature. Thus the bodies are perceived as with qualities which in reality do not belong to them, qualities which in fact are purely the offspring of the mind. Thus nature gets credit which should in truth be reserved for ourselves: the rose for its scent: the nightingale for his song: and the sun for his radiance. The poets are entirely mistaken. They should address their lyrics to themselves, and should turn them into odes of self-congratulation on the excellence of the human mind. Nature is a dull affair, soundless, scentless, colourless; merely the hurrying of material endlessly, meaninglessly.
>   However you disguise it, this is the practical outcome of the characteristic philosophy which closed the seventeenth century.[5]

The Romantic poets Wordsworth and Coleridge, at the end of the eighteenth century, reacted against this way of conceiving nature, as did Whitehead himself in his philosophical writings. The Romantics and Whitehead conceived of nature as dynamic and alive, as a realm of feeling and meaning and value in which we are involved not first as abstract observers but as sentient participants.

---

[4] Alfred North Whitehead, *The Concept of Nature* (Cambridge: Cambridge University Press, 1920), p. 3.
[5] Alfred North Whitehead, *Science and the Modern World* (New York: Macmillan, 1948), pp. 78–80.

Eastern Understandings of Nature

In contrast to both these Western approaches, in the Hindu civilization of India nature has been viewed negatively, as illusory or unreal—including the whole of existing reality, the natural *and* the social spheres. In China, nature has been viewed positively. According to the Confucians, nature is inclusive of the social order and its institutions and relationships: One is living "naturally" (harmoniously, as one ought to live) when one lives according to the rational and traditional precepts that make one a properly and actively functioning member of the social order. However, the Taoists regard the world of social institutions and moral precepts as artificial: Humanity lives naturally when it returns to the passive and harmonious simplicity of communion with mountain, flower, animal, and stream.

Jewish, Christian, Romantic, and Anti-Romantic Views of Nature

Even before the post-seventeenth-century tendency to look at nature abstractly (see the quotations from Whitehead), there had been an ambivalence toward nature in Western thought. Both Judaism and Christianity emphasize that the created order—including the social order—is (or should be) good.

> And God saw all that He had made, and it was very good. (Genesis 1:31, NEB)

This is certainly true of the "natural" world of cosmos and minerals, plants and animals (see Genesis 1). But Christianity especially has been inclined to suggest that nature was involved in the calamity of humanity's historical (individual and social) fall. Thus not only has humanity, through its sin, become alienated from nature (its own and that of the rest of the universe) but also the rest of nature has suffered.

> And to the man God said:
>   "Because you have . . . eaten from the tree which I forbade you, accursed shall be the ground on your account. . . . It will grow thorns and thistles for you, none but wild plants. . . ." (Genesis 3:17–18 NEB)

Paul in Romans 8:19–23 writes that the whole of creation, which has been subject to bondage and decay, is longing to be set free. Other Christian thinkers—for instance, John Milton in Adam's speech in the Tenth Book of *Paradise Lost*—develop the idea that nature and its order have been upset as a result of Adam's sin. Both Paul and Milton also suggest that nature is in fact being restored through God's redemptive activity in Christ.

Not only Romantic poets and writers like the American transcendentalist Thoreau but also contemporary poets have suggested that participation in a complex urban and industrialized society represents a fall from a harmonious relationship with nature and have called for a return to "natural simplicity." The American poet James Dickey has said,

> I'm much more interested in a man's relationship to the God-made world, or the universe-made world, than to the man-made world. The natural world seems infinitely more impor-

tant to me than the man-made world. I remember a statement of D. H. Lawrence's; he said that as a result of our science and industrialization, we have lost the cosmos. The parts of the universe we can investigate by means of machinery and scientific empirical techniques we may understand better than our predecessors did, but we no longer know the universe emotionally. It's a great deal easier to relate to it as a collocation of chemical properties. There's no moon goddess now. But when men believed there was, then the moon was more important, maybe not scientifically, but more important emotionally. It was something a man had a personal relationship to, instead of its being simply a dead stone, a great ruined stone in the sky. The moon has always been very important to me. The astronauts have introduced me to a new kind of mythology about the moon. This may in the end be greater than the old Greek one.[6]

In contrast, according to Enid Starkie, the nineteenth-century French poet Charles Baudelaire believed

> that art existed only by reason of what man added of his own substance, of his own soul, to the raw material of nature. He could not endure the Romantic idealisation of nature, nor the Rousseau myth of the nobility of natural man, uncorrupted by civilisation. He believed, on the contrary, that the only value in man consisted in his spiritual essence, which only self-discipline and self-culture could develop, and that this was of greater price than anything which could be discovered in nature. . . . Baudelaire . . . tried to put nature in her proper place, for he thought that man lost his pride and dignity by being too humble with her. The violence of his opinions is due to his reaction against sentimentality.[7]

How one understands nature profoundly affects how one lives and thinks. Religion and every other aspect of life are influenced by one's understanding of nature.

[6] From *Self-Interviews* by James Dickey, pp. 67–68. Copyright © 1970 by James Dickey. Published by Doubleday & Company, Inc.

[7] Enid Starkie, *Baudelaire* (New York: New Directions, 1958), p. 293.

CHAPTER 22

❦

Time and Eternity

Introduction

Crucial to human views of nature and natural processes is the concept of time, which is related to human purposes: We measure time because we are interested in temporal sequences related to our hopes, fears, needs, goals, and desires. Time in nature also seems measurable in terms of purposive sequences. As the Jewish scriptures say, "There is a season and a time for everything under heaven . . . a time to plant, and a time to harvest what has been planted" (Ecclesiastes 3:1–2).

Thus nature itself, in the seasonal cycles and the seemingly endless generational cycles of birth, maturity, and procreation, seems to show that the passage of time measures an orderly sequence. But in the natural order that transcends our own earth, the cosmos itself, time must certainly be understood differently; it is not limited by the rotation of our earth, the basis of our earthly time. Similarly, many human societies have questioned whether in the larger, universal order of nature the passage of time is meaningful or goal-oriented. This question reveals a religious dimension to the human experience of time.

In considering the religious significance of time, one must explore several possibilities. Is it leading toward an ultimate fulfillment, as has been commonly understood in Western religions? If so, what aspects of human reality that involve time can be eternal? What realities of human life are not involved in or affected by time? What realities are beyond time? Is time only a convenient human construct that has no relevance to ultimate realities or meanings?

The purpose of this chapter is to probe the religious dimensions of the human experience of time and of the concepts of time and the eternal as they have been expressed in a variety of religious-cultural traditions. Here again we are using the term *religious* in the broad sense that denotes belief in a pivotal or supreme value—the fundamental purpose to which individuals or groups may be committed.

The first unit examines concepts of time, giving attention to the distinction between typical Eastern and Western views and attitudes. The second unit considers a possible contrast between traditions that emphasize time, history, and a personalized concept of the Divine and those that stress a timeless eternal, the natural order, and an impersonal deity.

Unit 86   The Mystery of Time

What is time? Do we exist in time? Is time a reality? Numerous questions may be asked regarding the mystery of time. Such questions are both asked and answered differently in the Eastern and Western worlds.

Hermann Hesse, in his novel *Siddhartha*, gives the flavor of an Eastern response to the question of time.

> "When the Illustrious Buddha taught about the world, he had to divide it into Samsara and Nirvana, into illusion and truth, into suffering and salvation. One cannot do otherwise, there is no other method for those who teach. But the world itself, being in and around us, is never one-sided. Never is a man or deed wholly Nirvana; never is a man wholly a saint or a sinner. This only seems so because we suffer the illusion that time is something real. Time is not real, Govinda. I have realized this repeatedly. And if time is not real, the dividing line that seems to lie between this world and eternity, between suffering and bliss, between good and evil, is also an illusion."
>
> "How is that?" asked Govinda, puzzled.
>
> "Listen, my friend! I am a sinner and you are a sinner, but someday the sinner will be Brahma again, will someday attain Nirvana, will someday become a Buddha. Now this 'someday' is illusion; it is only a comparison. The sinner is not on the way to a Buddha-like state; he is not evolving, although our thinking cannot conceive things otherwise. No, the potential Buddha already exists in the sinner; his future is already there. The potential hidden Buddha must be recognized in him, in you, in everybody. The world, Govinda, is not imperfect or slowly evolving along a path to perfection. No, it is perfect at every moment; every sin already carries grace within it, all small children are potential old men, all sucklings have death within them, all dying people—eternal life. It is not possible for one person to see how far another is on the way; the Buddha exists in the robber and dice player; the robber exists in the Brahmin. During deep meditation it is possible to dispel time, to see simultaneously all the past, present and future, and then everything is good, everything is perfect, everything is Brahman."[1]

Conversely, Westerners emphasize time as real and of great importance. Let us consider some of the issues significant to the Western frame of reference.

[1] Herman Hesse, *Siddhartha*, trans. Hilda Rosner. Copyright 1951 by New Directions Publishing Corporation. Reprinted by permission of New Directions Publishing Corporation. Pages 143–44.

We are constantly reminded by clocks, calendars, and schedules that we exist in time and that time is in us. Whereas non-Western religions tend to deemphasize time, Western religions experience the Divine as revealed in time, in and through events of history.

> Time, a problem pervading our existence
> Demands our allegiance,
> But remains a mystery eluding our understanding.

The ancient Greeks pictured time in two figures: *Chronos*, an old gray-headed man, bent with a burden of time grown old (Figure 22.1), and *Kairos*, a young man running swiftly, the back of his head shaven smooth (Figure 22.2). Chronos, old Father Time, represents our preoccupation with clock-time, the time that passes and sucks us into the past. Through the eyes of Chronos we see the world growing old, and we become weary with the burden of time. If we run with Kairos we know time as opportunity, to be seized in the moment that it comes to meet us. Through the eyes of Kairos we see the significance of the present and the future. Kairos will run by us if we do not grasp his forelock quickly at the right moment.

Paul Tillich comments on the *mystery* of time:

> Augustine points to the depth of this mystery, when he says, "If nobody asks me about it, I *know*. If I want to explain it to somebody who asks me about it, I do not know." There is

Figure 22.1   *Chronos*, by Jacques Bakke.

Figure 22.2 *Kairos,* by Jacques Bakke.

something unspeakable about time, but this has not prevented the most profound religious minds from thinking and speaking about it. . . .

Mankind has always realized that there is something fearful about the flux of time, a riddle which we cannot solve, and the solution of which we could not stand. We come from a past which is no more; we go into a future which is not yet; *ours* is the present. The past is ours only in so far as we have it still present; and the future is ours only in so far as we have it already present. We possess the past by memory, and the future by anticipation. But what is the nature of the present itself? If we look at it closely, we must say: it is a point without extension, the point in which the future becomes the past; when we say to ourselves, "This is the present," the moment has already been swallowed by the past. The present disappears the very instant we try to grasp it. The present cannot be caught; it is always gone. So it seems that we have nothing real—neither the past nor the future, nor even the present. Therefore, there is a dreaming character about our existence, which the psalmist indicates, and which religious visionaries have described in so many ways.

Time, however, could not even give us a place on which to stand, if it were not characterized by that second mystery, its power to receive eternity. There is no present in the mere stream of time; but the present is real, as our experience witnesses. And it is real because eternity breaks into time and gives it a real present. We could not even say "now," if eternity did not elevate *that* moment above the ever-passing time. Eternity is always present; and its presence is the cause of our having the present at all. . . . In every moment that we say "now," something temporal and something eternal are united. Whenever a human being says, "Now I am living; now I am really present," resisting the stream which drives the future into the past, eternity *is*. In each such "now," eternity is made manifest; in every real "now," eternity is present. Let us think for a moment of the way in which we are living our lives in our period of history. Have we not lost a real present by always being driven forward, by our constant running, in our indefatigable activism, toward the future? We suppose the future to be better than any present; but there is always another future beyond the next future, again and again without a present, that is to say, without eternity. According to the Fourth Gospel eternal life is a *present* gift: he, who listens to Christ, has eternity already. He is no longer subject to the driving of time. In him the "now" becomes a "now eternal." We have lost the real "now," the "now eternal"; we have, I am afraid, lost eternal life in so far as it creates the real present.

There is another element in time, its third mystery, which makes us look at the future; for time does not return, nor repeat itself: it runs forward; it is always unique; it ever creates the new. There is within it a drive toward an end, unknown, never to be reached in time itself, always intended and ever fleeing. Time runs toward the "future eternal." This is the greatest of all the mysteries of time. . . . The eternal is the solution of the riddle of time. Time does not drive toward an endless self-repetition, nor to an empty return to its beginning. Time is not meaningless. . . . It brings about a hidden reality—the new creation. The infinite significance of every moment of time is this: in it we decide, and are decided about, with respect to our eternal future.[2]

Although Tillich supports the goal-oriented view of time emphasized in the West, he seeks to correct false hopes for future fulfillments by stressing the "now" in which eternity is present. Meaningless waiting or frantic striving for unfulfilled futures can be transformed into "meaning-filled" moments uniting the temporal and eternal when one affirms "now" as real. In his understanding of "now," eternity is present; the temporal and the eternal unite when a person affirms "now" as real. Here Tillich criticizes the way Westerners push toward the future and thus fail to realize the gifts of the present. Tillich does not neglect the future, however. He sees time as dynamic, moving toward the "future eternal" wherein the mystery of time is solved. Since that future has not arrived, time remains a mystery.

∾

In what ways do we constantly run into a future?

Can the present moment be all-significant, as Tillich suggests?

How do you understand a meaningful present?

In what ways do we run from time?

In what ways do we confront time?

[2] Reprinted by permission of Charles Scribner's Sons, an imprint of MacMillan Publishing Company, from *The Shaking of the Foundations*, pp. 34–37 by Paul Tillich. Copyright 1948 Charles Scribner's Sons; copyright renewed 1976 Hannah Tillich.

UNIT 87   The Temporal and the Eternal

Religions may be divided into at least two distinct types: those that understand the Divine as wholly or primarily eternal and those that believe the Divine has significant temporal as well as eternal aspects.

The Divine as Personal

Judaism, Zoroastrianism, Christianity, and Islam illustrate the first type. These religions speak of the Divine in terms derived from personal experience, interpersonal relations, and the interaction of nations. Generally understood as a *personal deity*, the Divine may be characterized with words descriptive of human personality and can enter into personal relationships with individuals and groups. Being thus related to human concerns, he acts within the setting of earthly existence; therefore, he acts within time. This fact infuses time itself with divine significance.

There are numerous examples of this interplay and personal contact between the Hebrew leaders and Yahweh, the God of the Israelites. In Genesis 18, Yahweh has decided to destroy the cities of Sodom and Gomorrah because their inhabitants have participated in gross moral sin. He shares his intent with Abraham, and the following conversation ensues:

> Then Abraham drew near, and said "Wilt thou indeed destroy the righteous with the wicked? Suppose there are fifty righteous within the city; wilt thou then destroy the place and not spare it for the fifty righteous who are in it? Far be it from thee to do such thing, to slay the righteous with the wicked! Far be that from thee! Shall not the Judge of all the earth do right?" And the Lord said, "If I find at Sodom fifty righteous in the city, I will spare the whole place for their sake." . . . Then he [Abraham] said, "Oh let not the Lord be angry, and I will speak again but this once. Suppose ten are found there?" He [Yahweh] answered, "For the sake of ten I will not destroy it." And the Lord went his way, when he had finished speaking to Abraham; and Abraham returned to his place. (Genesis 18:23–33, RSV)

This example of an interpersonal relationship, wherein Abraham is not only in God's presence and talking to him but even challenges him to be fully righteous, suggests how clearly the Israelites understood their relationship to God to be one of direct, personal contact, much like that with other humans. Note that Yahweh—the transcendent, all-powerful God of all creation—acts directly in history, creating, destroying, ruling, chastening. Yet it is clear that Yahweh is not understood by Abraham as an equal: Abraham is anxious not to anger God. God is transcendent, not bound by human affairs or human history. Abraham may speak his mind and be heard by God, but it is God who acts in and controls history.

In contrast, the Hebrew realization of the transcendent nature of Yahweh, wherein the Divine is beyond comprehension or description, is expressed in the following passage from the prophet Isaiah:

> Have you not know? Have you not heard?
>   Has it not been told you from the beginning?
>   Have you not understood from the foundations of the earth?

> It is he who sits above the circle of the earth,
>   and its inhabitants are like grasshoppers;
>   who stretches out the heavens like a curtain,
>   and spreads them like a tent to dwell in;
>   who brings princes to nought,
>   and makes the rulers of the earth as nothing.
> Scarcely are they planted, scarcely sown,
>   scarcely has their stem taken root in the earth,
>   when he blows upon them, and they wither,
>   and the tempest carries them off like stubble.
> To whom then will you compare me,
>   that I should be like him?
>   says the Holy One,
> Lift up your eyes on high and see: who created these?
>   . . .
> The Lord is the everlasting God,
>   the Creator of the ends of the earth.
>   (Isaiah 40:21–26, RSV)

As Isaiah indicates, the transcendent aspect of God is as important to the Hebrew understanding of God as is the concept of his relating to individuals and the nation on a personal basis.

Thus God is understood by the Israelites as transcending creation—including time—and at the same time as being involved in time and history. Such a concept is not without its tensions, for it requires a timeless transcendent Deity, unbound by creation and its time sequence, to be involved in the very history of that creation. In this tension, timeless transcendence threatens to overwhelm the concept of a personal historical involvement by God and the significance of human beings, creatures confined with the limits of time. Yet the Hebrews, along with Christians, Muslims, and Zoroastrians, maintain that the Divine manifests both elements so that people experience a personal God who is nevertheless transcendent; therefore, human beings can enjoy the fruits of a personal relationship to the Divine.

The Divine as Impersonal

Hinduism, Buddhism, philosophical Taoism, and Shinto speak of the Divine in terms derived from natural process. Generally understood as an *impersonal* power, the essence of the Divine is characterized with words not associated with human personality. Being impersonal, it does not enter into personal relationships with individuals and groups. Thus the essence of the Divine transcends this existence and is therefore timeless, without beginning and without end. Time itself becomes only a passing episode in an unending, eternal process.

Heinrich Zimmer calls attention to an intriguing story in one of the *Puranas*, a story that speaks forcefully to our concern; "The Parade of Ants" opens with the figure of Indra, king of the Gods, after he has slain the Dragon who pent up the life-giving waters. Indra, to express and celebrate his kingly glory and splendor, has ordered Vishvakarman, the god of arts and crafts, to build splendid gardens, palaces, lakes, and towers. As he works, Indra's vision of what he desires gets bigger and bigger, so that finally Vishvakarman, in desperation, appeals to the "demiurgic creator, Brahmā, the pristine embodiment of the Universal Spirit, who abides far above the Olympian sphere of ambition, strife, and glory," for help. Brahmā himself appeals to Vishnu, the Supreme Being, who by a mere nod of his head indicates that the wish of Vishvakarman will be fulfilled. The next day a brahmin boy, "slender, some ten years old, radiant with the luster of wisdom," appears at Indra's gate. After inviting the boy into his palace, Indra asks, "O Venerable Boy, tell me the purpose of your coming."

> This beautiful child replied with a voice that was as deep and soft as the slow thundering of auspicious rain clouds. "O King of Gods, I have heard of the mighty palace you are building, and have come to refer to you the questions in my mind. How many years will it require to complete this rich and extensive residence? What further feats of engineering will Vishvakarman be expected to accomplish? O Highest of the Gods,"—the boy's luminous features moved with a gentle, scarcely perceptible smile—"no Indra before you has ever succeeded in completing such a palace as yours is to be."
>
> Full of the wine of triumph, the king of the gods was entertained by this mere boy's pretension to a knowledge of Indras earlier than himself. With a fatherly smile he put the question: "Tell me, Child! Are they then so very many, the Indras and Vishvakarmans whom you have seen—or at least, whom you have heard of?"
>
> The wonderful guest calmly nodded. "Yes, indeed, many have I seen." The voice was as warm and sweet as milk fresh from the cow, but the words sent a slow chill through Indra's veins. "My dear child," the boy continued, "I knew your father, Kashyapa, the Old Tortoise Man, lord and progenitor of all the creatures of the earth. And I knew your grandfather, Marīchi, Beam of Celestial Light, who was the son of Brahmā. Marīchi was begotten of the god Brahmā's pure spirit; his only wealth and glory were his sanctity and devotion. Also, I know Brahmā, brought forth by Vishnu from the lotus calix growing from Vishnu's navel. And Vishnu himself—the Supreme Being, supporting Brahmā in his creative endeavor—him too I know.
>
> "O King of Gods, I have known the dreadful dissolution of the universe. I have seen all perish, again and again, at the end of every cycle. At that terrible time, every single atom dissolves into the primal, pure waters of eternity, whence originally all arose. Everything then goes back into the fathomless, wild infinity of the ocean, which is covered with utter darkness and is empty of every sign of animate being. Ah, who will count the universes that have passed away, or the creations that have risen afresh, again and again, from the formless abyss of the vast waters? Who will number the passing ages of the world, as they follow each other endlessly? And who will search through the wide infinites of space to count the universes side by side, each containing its Brahmā, its Vishnu, and its Shiva? Who will count the Indras in them all—those Indras side by side, who reign at once in all the innumerable worlds; those others who passed away before them; or even the Indras who succeed each other in any given line, ascending to godly kinship, one by one, and one by one, passing away? King of Gods, there are among your servants certain who maintain that it may be possible to number the grains of sand on earth and the drops of rain that fall from the sky, but no one will ever number all those Indras. This is what the Knowers know.
>
> "The life and kingship of an Indra endure seventy-one eons, and when twenty-eight Indras have expired, one Day and Night of Brahmā has elapsed. But the existence of one Brahmā, measured in such Brahmā Days and Nights, is only one hundred and eight years. Brahmā follows Brahmā; one sinks, the next arises; the endless series cannot be told. There is no end to the number of those Brahmās—to say nothing of Indras.
>
> "But the universes side by side at any given moment, each harboring a Brahmā and an Indra: who will estimate the number of these? Beyond the farthest vision, crowding outer space, the universes come and go, an innumerable host. Like delicate boats they float on the fathomless, pure waters that form the body of Vishnu. Out of every hair-pore of that

body a universe bubbles and breaks. Will you presume to count them? Will you number the gods in all those worlds—the worlds present and the worlds past?"

A procession of ants made its appearance in the hall during the discourse of the boy. In military array, in a column four yards wide, the tribe paraded across the floor. The boy noted them, paused, and stared, then suddenly laughed with an astonishing peal, but immediately subsided into a profoundly indrawn and thoughtful silence.

"Why do you laugh?" stammered Indra. "Who are you, mysterious being, under this deceiving guise of a boy?" The proud king's throat and lips had gone dry, and his voice continually broke. "Who are you, Ocean of Virtues, enshrouded in deluding mist?"

The magnificent boy resumed: "I laughed because of the ants. The reason is not to be told. Do not ask me to disclose it. The seed of woe and the fruit of wisdom are enclosed within this secret. It is the secret that smites with an ax the tree of worldly vanity, hews away its roots, and scatters its crown. This secret is a lamp to those groping in ignorance. This secret lies buried in the wisdom of the ages, and is rarely revealed even to saints. This secret is the living air of those ascetics who renounce and transcend mortal existence; but worldlings, deluded by desire and pride, it destroys."

The boy smiled and sank into silence. Indra regarded him, unable to move. "O Son of a Brahmin," the king pleaded presently, with a new and visible humility, "I do not know who you are. You would seem to be Wisdom Incarnate. Reveal to me this secret of the ages, this light that dispels the dark."

Thus requested to teach, the boy opened to the god the hidden wisdom. "I saw the ants, O Indra, filing in long parade. Each was once an Indra. Like you, each by virtue of pious deeds once ascended to the rank of a king of gods. But now, through many rebirths, each has become again an ant. This army is an army of former Indras.

"Piety and high deeds elevate the inhabitants of the world to the glorious realm of the celestial mansions, or to the higher domains of Brahmā and Shiva and to the highest sphere of Vishnu; but wicked acts sink them into the worlds beneath, into pits of pain and sorrow, involving reincarnation among birds and vermin, or out of the wombs of pigs and animals of the wild, or among trees, or among insects. It is by deeds that one merits happiness or anguish, and becomes a master or a serf. It is by deeds that one attains to the rank of a king or brahmin, or of some god, or of an Indra or a Brahmā. And through deeds again, one contracts disease, acquires beauty and deformity, or is reborn in the condition of a monster.

"This is the whole substance of the secret. This wisdom is the ferry to beatitude across the ocean of hell.

"Life in the cycle of the countless rebirths is like a vision in a dream. The gods on high, the mute trees and the stones, are alike apparitions in this phantasy. But Death administers the Law of time. Ordained by time, Death is the master of all. Perishable as bubbles are the good and the evil of the beings of the dream. In unending cycles the good and evil alternate. Hence, the wise are attached to neither, neither the evil nor the good. The wise are not attached to anything at all."

The boy concluded the appalling lesson and quietly regarded his host. The king of gods, for all his celestial splendor, had been reduced in his own regard to insignificance.[3]

In this story the Divine Reality is timeless, impersonal, solitary, and removed from the passing into and out of existence of the multitudinous universes. The Divine is oblivious to and detached from the concerns of "ambition, strife, and glory," exemplified by the god Indra.

---

[3] Heinrich Zimmer, *Myths and Symbols in Indian Art and Civilization,* ed. Joseph Campbell, Bollingen Series VI (copyright © 1946 by Bollingen Foundation), reprinted with permission of Princeton University Press, pp. 4–8.

Yet it is significant that the concern of the story is the meaning of individual identity, as expressed in Indra's desire for palaces, gardens, lakes, and towers celebrating his glorious achievements. Thus within the worldview that espouses timeless, eternal reality, a pressing problem is the significance of time and human achievement.

Meanwhile, another amazing apparition had entered the hall.

The newcomer had the appearance of a kind of hermit. His head was piled with matted hair; he wore a black deerskin around his loins; on his forehead was painted a white mark; his head was shaded by a paltry parasol of grass; and a quaint, circular cluster of hair grew on his chest: it was intact at the circumference, but from the center many of the hairs, it seemed, had disappeared. This saintly figure strode directly to Indra and the boy, squatted between them on the floor, and there remained, motionless as a rock. The kingly Indra, somewhat recovering his hostly role, bowed and paid obeisance, offering sour milk with honey and other refreshments; then he inquired falteringly but reverently, after the welfare of the stern guest, and bade him welcome. Whereupon the boy addressed the holy man, asking the very questions Indra himself would have proposed.

"Whence do you come, O Holy Man? What is your name and what brings you to this place? Where is your present home and what is the meaning of this grass parasol? What is the portent of that circular hair-tuft on your chest: why is it dense at the circumference but at the center almost bare? Be kind enough, O Holy Man, to answer, in brief, these questions. I am anxious to understand."

Patiently the old saint smiled, and slowly began his reply. "I am a brahmin. Hairy is my name. And I have come here to behold Indra. Since I know that I am short-lived, I have decided to possess no home; to build no house, and neither to marry nor to seek a livelihood. I exist by begging alms. To shield myself from sun and rain I carry over my head this parasol of grass.

"As to the circle of hair on my chest, it is a source of grief to the children of the world. Nevertheless, it teaches wisdom. With the fall of an Indra, one hair drops. That is why, in the center all the hairs have gone. When the other half of the period allotted to the present Brahmā will have expired, I myself shall die. O Brahmin Boy, it follows that I am somewhat short of days; what therefore, is the use of a wife and a son, or of a house?

"Each flicker of the eyelids of the great Vishnu registers the passing of a Brahmā. Everything below that sphere of Brahmā is as insubstantial as a cloud taking shape and again dissolving. That is why I devote myself exclusively to meditating on the incomparable lotus-feet of highest Vishnu. Faith in Vishnu is more than the bliss of redemption; for every joy, even the heavenly, is as fragile as a dream, and only interferes with the one-pointedness of our faith in Him Supreme.

"Shiva, the peace-bestowing, the highest spiritual guide, taught me this wonderful wisdom. I do not crave to experience the various blissful forms of redemption: to share the highest god's supernatural mansions and enjoy his eternal presence, or to be like him in body and apparel, or to become a part of his august substance, or even to be absorbed wholly in his ineffable essence."

Abruptly, the holy man ceased and immediately vanished. It had been the god Shiva himself; he had now returned to his supramundane abode. Simultaneously, the brahmin boy, who had been Vishnu, disappeared as well. The king was alone, baffled and amazed.[4]

This portion of the story not only reinforces the previous emphasis but also declares that the humanlike Indra and the Creator-God Himself—Brahmā—are both ruled by the timeless, inexorable wheeling of eons.

[4] Ibid., pp. 8–10.

Yet the story does not end here. And the ending itself underscores the demand within timelessness for temporal significance.

The king, Indra, pondered; and the events seemed to him to have been a dream. But he no longer felt any desire to magnify his heavenly splendor or to go on with the construction of his palace. He summoned Vishvakarman. Graciously greeting the craftsman with honeyed words, he heaped on him jewels and precious gifts, then with a sumptuous celebration sent him home.

The king, Indra, now desired redemption. He had acquired wisdom, and wished only to be free. He entrusted the pomp and burden of his office to his son, and prepared to retire to the hermit life of the wilderness. Whereupon his beautiful and passionate queen, Shachi, was overcome with grief.

Weeping, in sorrow and utter despair, Shachi resorted to Indra's ingenious house-priest and spiritual advisor, the Lord of Magic Wisdom, Brihaspati. Bowing at his feet, she implored him to divert her husband's mind from its stern resolve. The resourceful counselor of the gods, who by his spells and devices had helped the heavenly powers wrest the government of the universe from the hands of their titan rivals, listened thoughtfully to the complaint of the voluptuous, disconsolate goddess, and knowingly nodded assent. With a wizard's smile, he took her hand and conducted her to the presence of her spouse. In the role, then, of spiritual teacher, he discoursed sagely on the virtues of the spiritual life, but on the virtues also, of the secular. He gave to each its due. Very skillfully he developed his theme. The royal pupil was persuaded to relent in his extreme resolve. The queen was restored to radiant joy.

This Lord of Magic Wisdom, Brihaspati, once had composed a treatise on government, in order to teach Indra how to rule the world. He now issued a second work, a treatise on the policy and stratagems of married love. Demonstrating the sweet art of wooing ever anew, and of enchanting the beloved with enduring bonds, this priceless book established on sound foundations the married life of the reunited pair.

Thus concludes the marvelous story of how the king of gods was humiliated in his boundless pride, cured of an excessive ambition, and through wisdom, both spiritual and secular, brought to a knowledge of his proper role in the wheeling play of unending life.[5]

About this story, Zimmer says,

The two great gods, Vishnu and Shiva, instruct the human hearers of the myth by teaching Indra, king of the Olympians. The Wonderful Boy, solving riddles and pouring out wisdom from his childish lips, is an archetypal figure, common to fairy tales of all ages and many traditions. He is an aspect of the Boy Hero, who solves the riddle of the Sphinx and rids the world of monsters. Likewise an archetypal figure is the Old Wise Man, beyond ambitions and the illusions of ego, treasuring and imparting the wisdom that sets free, shattering the bondage of possessions, the bondage of suffering and desire.

But the wisdom taught in this myth would have been incomplete had the last word been that of the infinity of space and time. The vision of the countless universes bubbling into existence side by side, and the lesson of the unending series of Indras and Brahmās, would have annihilated every value of individual existence. Between this boundless, breath-taking vision and the opposite problem of the limited role of the short-lived individual, this myth effected the reestablishment of a balance. Brihaspati, the high priest and spiritual guide of the gods, who is Hindu wisdom incarnate, teaches Indra (i.e., ourself, the individual confused) how to grant to each sphere its due. We are taught to recognize the divine, the impersonal sphere of eternity, revolving ever and agelessly through time. But

---

[5] Ibid., pp. 10–11.

we are also taught to esteem the transient sphere of the duties and pleasures of individual existence, which is as real and as vital to the living man, as a dream to the sleeping soul.[6]

The contrast between the worldview based on time and that based on timelessness is sharply drawn in the following passage from Zimmer.

> This vast time-consciousness, transcending the brief span of the individual, even the racial biography, is the time-consciousness of Nature herself. Nature knows, not centuries, but ages—geological, astronomical ages—and stands, furthermore, beyond them. Swarming egos are her children, but the species is her concern; and world ages are her shortest span for the various species that she puts forth and permits, finally, to die (like the dinosaurs, the mammoths, and the giant birds). India—as Life brooding on itself—thinks of the problem of time in periods comparable to those of our astronomy, geology, and paleontology. India thinks of time and of herself, that is to say, in biological terms, terms of the species, not of the ephemeral ego. The latter *becomes* old: the former *is* old, and therewith eternally young.
>
> We of the West on the other hand, regard world history as a biography of mankind, and in particular of Occidental Man, whom we estimate to be the most consequential member of the family. Biography is that form of seeing and representing which concentrates on the unique, the induplicable, in any portion of existence, and then brings out the sense-and-direction-giving traits. We think of egos, individuals, not of Life. Our will is not to culminate in our human institutions the universal play of nature, but to evaluate, to set ourselves against the play, with an egocentric tenacity.[7]

In this unit we have discussed, on the one hand, the way the Divine is conceived as personal, temporal, and in interaction with persons and nations, noting especially how Christianity, Judaism, Islam, and Zoroastrianism reflect this perspective. On the other hand, we have shown the Divine to be timeless and impersonal, as understood by Hinduism, Buddhism, and Taoism. Thus we have set the contrast between the temporal and the eternal in the world's major religions; we would emphasize, though, that all religions apparently maintain a dialectic between the temporal and the eternal to one degree or another.

[6] Ibid., p. 22.
[7] Ibid., pp. 20–21.

Index of Religious Traditions

American Indian:
Bororo, 244–46
Mexican, Our Lady of
    Guadalupe and, 63–64
Navaho:
    the Divine, 136–37
    magic, 91–92
    oral tradition, 271
    taboos, 219–20
Pueblo, 7
return to tribal ceremonies, 1
symbiosis, 302, 303

Buddhism, 25–30
afterlife, 195
architecture, 250
basic tenets, 48
bodhisattva, 29, 202, 216–17
branches, 28–29
code, 48
community, 48, 242
creed, 48
cult, 48
diabiosis, 306–7
the Divine, 27, 318
dukkha, 27, 58

Eightfold Path, 27, 58–59,
    220
enlightenment, 14, 27–28, 34,
    58, 174
evil, 151
Four Noble Truths, 27, 57, 58,
    174
freedom, 174
Gautama Buddha, 8, 14, 16,
    22, 26–28, 56–59, 157,
    284, 306–7
grace, 202
Hinayana, 28–29, 48
love, 216–17
Mahayana, 29, 48, 202, 216–17
mysticism, 81, 83–86
Nirvana, 27–29, 56–59, 174
nonviolence, 226
origins, 14, 25–26, 28
pantheistic position, 140
persons-in-community, 8
salvation, 201
Samyutta-nikaya:
    I:39, 58
    II:117, 58
    IV:251–52, 58
sangha, 26

satori, 279
schools, 28–29
science and religious vision,
    299
social conditions, 258
suffering, 147, 148
tanha, 27, 58, 249
Theravada, 28–29, 171, 242
Vajrayana, 29
the Void, 138, 140
Zen, 29, 33, 52, 84–86, 221,
    250, 279

Christianity, 39–42
Abelard, Peter, on faith, 120
act and motive, 220–21
Acts:
    1:8, 67, 142
    2:1–4, 142
    2:4, 67
Adam, Karl, on tradition, 286
afterlife, 193–94
apobiosis, 304, 305
Aquinas, Saint Thomas, on
    nature and reality of God,
    135

Augustine, Saint:
  on act and motive, 220–21
  on conversion, 76–77
  on evil, 154–55
  on faith and reason, 121
  on free will, 176–77
authority, 282–84
Baillie, John, on faith and reason, 118
Barth, Karl, on faith and reason, 121
basic tenets, 50
Bernard of Clairvaux, on faith and reason, 120
Betjeman, John, on religious nurture and conversion, 76
Bower, W. C., on religious experience, 166
Bultmann, Rudolf, on myth, 87
Bushnell, Horace, on religious nurture and conversion, 75–76
church organization, 41–42
code, 50
I Corinthians:
  12:10, 67
  12:12,13,27, 8
  12:14, 67
commitment, 16
community, 41, 50
conversion, 75–77
Cox, Harvey:
  on human technology, 259–60
  on secularization, 262–64
  on sin, 184–85
creed, 50
cult, 50
diabiosis, 307
dialogue, 19
Dillenberger, John, on faith, 122
the Divine as personal, 317, 318
Eastern Orthodox Church, 41, 42, 286
eschatology, 209–10
ethical pluralism, 238–40
Eucharist, 41, 42
evil, 151–55
Ferguson, Earl, on conversion, 77
Fletcher, Joseph, on love and justice, 223

freedom, 176–78
Frye, Roland, on evil, 151
fundamentalism, 265–66
Galatians 3:27–28, 228–32
Genesis:
  1:31, 310
  3:1–13, 184
  3:17–18, 310
Gospel, 41
Holy Spirit, 40, 144
human technology, 259–60
image of God, 160–61
Irenaeus, on spirit, 144–45
Jesus Christ, 39–41
  artistic images of, 83, 95–103
  compensatory justice of, 237–38
  disciples of, 13–14, 41
  freedom and, 177
  Gandhi on, 65, 66
  on God as loving parent, 137–38
  Hindu recognition of, 22
  love and, 161, 216
  motive and, 221
  resurrection of, 40, 42, 197–98
  suffering and, 149
  teachings of, 40, 65, 66, 137, 144–45
John 1:40–51, 13–14
Juan Diego, religious experience of, 61–63
justice, 223–27, 237–38
Justin Martyr, on faith and reason, 119–20
Kierkegaard, Søren, on authority, 282–83
Knox, John, on myth, 87
love, 216, 223–25
Lowrie, Walter, on orants, 98
Luther, Martin:
  on creation, 295
  on faith and reason, 120
  religious experience of, 55–56
McKenzie, John G., on guilt, 182–83
Mark:
  7:15–23, 221
  12:18–27, 221
Matthew:
  3:16, 144
  5:43–48, 137–38

  6:14–15, 138
  6:26–32, 138
Michalson, Carl, on freedom, 177–78
mysticism, 81
New Testament, 13–14, 41, 149
Niebuhr, Reinhold:
  on individual and community, 214
  on love and justice, 224–25
  on sin, 184
Old Testament, 40
origins, 13–14, 39–40
Pascal, Blaise, on evil, 152–53
Peck, Scott, on evil, 153–54
Pelagius, on free will, 176
Pentacostalism, 52, 66–67
persons-in-community, 8–10
pivotal value concept, 6–7
Protestantism, 42, 201–2, 232, 236, 259–60, 263
Psalm 42, 81
Ramsey, Paul, on nature of humanity, 160–61
resurrection, 197–98
revelation, 115, 116
Revelation to John
  20:11–24:4,6, 209–10
Richardson, Alan, on revelation, 116, 117
Ricoeur, Paul, on secularization, 262, 264
ritual, 41, 74
Roman Catholic Church, 41, 42, 201–2, 231, 232, 260, 263, 286
Romans:
  6:1, 198
  6:16–17, 200
  8:2, 142
sacraments, 41
salvation, 40, 200–203, 209–10
science and religious vision, 299
scriptures, 41
secularization, 262–65
sin, 183–85
social conditions, 258
spirit, 144–45
suffering, 149
symbols, 12, 79
Teilhard de Chardin, Pierre, on evolution, 299

Christianity (*cont.*)
  Teresa of Avila, Saint, religious
      experience of, 61–63,
      80–81
  Tertullian, on reason, 120
  Tillich, Paul:
    on doubt, 287–89
    on grace, 200–201
    on love and justice, 223
  Timothy 6:18–19, 16
  Tournier, Paul, on meaning of
      person, 164–65
  tradition, 286
  transcendent-immanent posi-
      tion, 140–41
  Trinity, 40
  Underhill, Evelyn, on mysti-
      cism, 81
  war, justifiable, 226–27
  Wesley, John:
    on grace, 201
    on religious experience,
      165–66
  women's status, 228–32, 234

Confucianism, 33–35
  basic tenets, 49
  chun-tzu, 34–35
  code, 49
  community, 49
  Confucius, 14, 32–35, 218, 284
  creed, 49
  cult, 49
  doctrine, 34–35
  duty, 218
  emphasis, 33
  evil, 151
  Five Relationships, 218
  influence, 35
  interaction with Taoism, 32–33
  jên, 34
  li, 34
  nature, 310
  as religious tradition, 35

Hinduism, 21–25
  afterlife, 194
  Atman, 22, 141, 194
  avatara, 22, 23
  basic tenets, 48
  Bhagavad Gita, 6, 129–31, 236
  Bhakti yoga, 24

Brahma, 22–23, 319–22
Brahman, 22, 24, 25, 137, 140
caste system, 24–25
code, 48
community, 48
creation, 295–96
creed, 48
cult, 48
diabosis, 307
the Divine, 22, 24, 129–31,
    137, 140, 159, 318–23
duty, 217
evil, 150
freedom, 174
Gandhi, Mahatma, religious
    experience of, 64–66
gods, 22–24
grace, 202
history, 21
interconnection of all things, 25
Jainism, 306
karma, 24, 26, 194
karma yoga, 24
Mandookya Upanishad, 159
maya, 26, 201, 307
moksha, 24, 201
Mundaka-Upanishad, 295–96
mysticism, 81–83
nonviolence, 226
organization, 21–22
pantheistic position, 140
pivotal value concept, 6
Puranas, 217, 318–23
raja yoga, 24
revelation, 115
rituals, 25
salvation, 201
samsara, 24, 26, 73, 194
Sankara, on Brahman, 137
science and religious vision, 299
scriptures, 24
sects, 21
Śiva, 22–23
social conditions, 258
symbols, 79
Upanishads, 24
Vedantic, 82–83
Vedas, 24, 115
Vishnu, 22–23, 217, 319–22

Islam, 43–47
  Allah, 7, 43, 45, 71–72, 144, 174
  apobiosis, 305

basic tenets, 50
branches, 46–47
code, 50
community, 50, 243
creed, 50
cult, 50
duties, 45–46
eschatology, 208–9
Fifth Pillar, 46
freedom, 174
fundamentalism, 266–67
history, 43–46
Ka'ba, 43, 44, 46
Malcolm X:
    on hadj, 243
Muhammad, 14, 43–45, 144,
    208–9, 226
pivotal value concept, 7
Qu'ran, 43, 45, 208–9
revelation, 115
ritual, 46, 71–72
salvation, 202
Shiites, 46, 47
social conditions, 258
spirit, 144
Sufis, 47, 59–61, 81
Sunnis, 46, 47
symbols, 12, 79

Judaism, 36–39
  Abraham, 36, 174–75, 217
  act and motive, 220
  afterlife, 193
  Amos:
    5:21–24, 15
    9:11, 196
  apobiosis, 304–6
  basic tenets, 36, 50
  Buber, Martin, on religious dis-
      agreement, 17–18
  code, 50
  commitment, 15
  community, 38, 50, 242
  Conservative, 39
  Cox, Harvey, on apobiosis,
      305–6
  creed, 50
  cult, 50
  Daniel 12:1–3, 197
  Deuteronomy:
    4:20–32, 133
    26:5–9, 242
    32:39, 196

the Divine, 128, 132–34,
     317–18
eschatology, 207–8
Exodus:
     2:15–22, 54
     3:4–6, 54
     3:7–10, 54
family, 37–38
freedom, 174–75
Genesis:
     1:1–2:3, 294
     1:31, 310
     2:7, 142
     3:1–13, 184
     18:23–33, 142
guilt, 181–82
Hanuka, 38
humanity, 37, 160, 169
Isaiah:
     40:21–29, 133
     57:20–21, 182
Jeremiah 31:27–34, 207–8
I Kings 17:17–24, 196
Messiah, 40, 193
Micah 6:6–8, 133
Moses, 16, 36, 53–55, 59–60
nature, 310
origins, 36
Passover, 38
Pederson, Johannes, on guilt,
     181
Pentateuch, 36
Psalm 8, 160
Psalms 8:3–8, 169
Purim, 38
Rabbinic, 37, 39
Reform, 39

resurrection, 195–97
revelation, 115
rites and festivals, 37–38
Rosh Hashana, 38
salvation, 202
I Samuel 2:6, 196
self as image of God, 160
Simchat Torah, 38
sin, 183–85
social conditions, 258
spirit, 143–44
suffering, 148–49
Sukkot, 38
symbols, 12, 79
Talmud, 37, 175, 220
Ten Commandments, 36, 183
Torah, 12, 37, 40, 41
tradition, 285–86
transcendent-immanent posi-
     tion, 140–41
Trepp, Leo, on expectation of
     Messiah, 193
women's status, 231
Yahweh, 36, 317
Yom Kippur, 38

Shinto:
     afterlife, 195
     basic tenets, 49
     code, 49
     community, 49
     creation, 296–97
     creed, 49
     cult, 49
     the Divine, 318
     kami, 143, 304

polytheistic deistic position, 141
simplicity, 251
Taoist elements, 33

Taoism, 30–33
     afterlife, 195
     basic tenets, 49
     Chuang Tzu, on ritual patterns
          in daily life, 73–74
     code, 49
     community, 49
     creed, 49
     cult, 49
     diabiosis, 307
     the Divine, 128–29, 318
     doctrine, 32–33
     esoteric, 32
     evil, 151
     Fischer, Otto, on the Divine in
          art, 129
     history, 30
     influence, 33
     interaction with Confucian-
          ism, 32–33
     Lao-Tzu, on the *Tao,* 128–29
     mysticism, 81
     nature, 31, 310
     origins, 31
     philosophical, 32
     popular, 32
     revelation, 115
     ritual, 31, 73–74
     Tao Te Ching, 31, 32
     worship, 31
     wu-wei, 31
     yin and *yang,* 30–31, 151

Index of Names and Subjects

A

Abbey Church of St. Denis, 104–6
Abelard, Peter, 120, 220
Abraham, 36, 174–75, 317
Abu Bakr, 46
Acceptance of death, 191, 192
Achebe, Chinua, 91, 142–43
Acts, interaction between moti-
    vations and, 219–21
Adam, Karl, 286
Adam and Eve, 184, 234
Aesthetic orientation to religion,
    6, 52, 69, 70, 79–80
Affleck, Bert, 236n
African Americans:
    discrimination against, 235, 236
    search for identity by, 162
Afterlife, 193–95
Allah, 7, 43, 45, 71–72, 144, 174
Allport, Gordon W., 161
Ambrose, 229
Amenhotep IV, 292
American Religion, The (Bloom), 2
Amos, 15
Anger over death, 191
Apobiosis, 304–6
Apocolypse, 202

Apostles, authority of, 282–83
Apostle's Creed, 6–7
"Aquarius," 206–7
Aquinas, Saint Thomas, 132,
    135, 141, 226, 264
Arberry, Arthur J., 61n, 72n,
    209n, 243n
Architecture, medieval, luminous
    wholeness in, 103–13
Arhats, 28
Aristotle, 134–35, 139, 156, 229
Arnold, Sir Edwin, 6n
Arrow of God (Achebe), 91
Artistic experience, revelation
    and, 116, 117
Artistic expression, 93–113
    images of Jesus as Christ in
        early Church, 97–103
    Japanese, 249–50
    luminous wholeness in West-
        ern European Medieval
        architecture, 103–13
    as symbolic vehicle, 94–97
Asceticism, 229
Atman, 22, 141, 194
Atomization, 267–68
Auden, W. H., 213

Augustine, Saint, 76–77, 121,
    154–55, 161n, 176, 177,
    182, 220–21, 226, 314
Authority, 281–84
Avatara, 22, 23
Ayer, A. J., 119, 272

B

Babylonian story of Creation,
    293–94
Bailey, D. S., 230
Baillie, John, 118
Bainbridge, William Sims, 2n
Bainton, Roland, 226
Bakke, Jacques, 30, 147, 196, 204,
    314
Baldwin, James Mark, 280n
Ballou, Robert, 218n
Baptism, 41
Bargaining over death, 191
Bar mitzvah, 37–38
Barnes, Hazel E., 172n
Barrera, Mario, 236n
Barth, Karl, 117, 121, 171
Bashō, Matsuo, 249
Bastide, Roger, 239n
Battenhouse, Roy, 176n

Baudelaire, Charles, 311
Becket, Thomas, 221
Becoming, Foundations for a
    Psychology of Personality
    (Allport), 161
Behaviorism, 234
Being and Nothingness (Sartre),
    171–72
Beliefs:
    crisis of, 271
    faith distinguished from, 122–24
    set of (creed), 20, 48–50, 166
    verification and, 270–71,
        277–80
Benedict, Ruth, 180–81
Berger, Peter, 212
Bergman, Ingmar, 149–50
Berkowitz, Martin, 286n
Bernard of Clairvaux, 14, 120
Bernini, Gianlorenzo, 62, 63
Betjeman, John, 76
Bhagavad Gita, The, 6, 129–31,
    236
Bhakti yoga, 24
Bidney, David, 86n, 211–12
Bien, Joseph, 262n
"Big bang" theory, 291
Blake, William, 80
Bloom, Harold, 2
Bodhidharma, 84
Bodhidharma (Mushakōji), 84–85
Bodhisattva, 29, 202, 216–17
Bonhoeffer, Dietrich, 9–10, 16,
    163–64
Book of the Dead, 187, 195
Bororo culture, 244–46
Boslough, John, 300n
Bower, W. C., 166
Bradley, D. G., 195n
Bradstreet, Anne, 228–29
Brahma, 22–23, 319–22
Brahman, 22, 24, 25, 137, 140
Brahmins, 25
Brandt, Willy, 257–58
Breasted, J. H., 292n
Brockway, Allan R., 269
Brook Farm, 203
Brown, Lester R., 258n
Brown, Robert McAfee, 225n
Browne, Lewis, 217n
Brunner, Frederick D., 67n, 68n
Brunner, Emile, 117
Buber, Martin, 16–18, 171

Buddha (*See* Gautama Buddha)
Buddhism (*See* Index of Religious
    Traditions)
Bultmann, Rudolf, 87
Burtt, E. A., 297–98
Bush, George, 227–28
Bushido Code, 218–19
Bushnell, Horace, 75–76

C

Calder, Nigel, 300n
Calvin, John, 176–77, 201
Campbell, Alexander, 14
Campbell, Joseph, 320n
Castaneda, Carlos, 279
Caste system, 24–25
Cathedral Church of St. Andrew,
    111, 113
Cathedral of Notre Dame,
    107–10
Cathedral of Siena, 112
Catherine of Sienna, Saint, 232
Charismatic movement, 67–68
Chiang Yee, 168n
Chinese culture, 30–33, 35,
    128–29, 167–68, 204–5
Christian Apologetics (Richardson),
    116
Christianity (*See* Index of Reli-
    gious Traditions)
Christianity Today, 67–68
Christmas, 41
Chrysanthemum and the Sword,
    The (Benedict), 180–81
Chrysostom, John, 229
Chuang-Tzu, 32, 73–74, 195
Church of the Brethren, 226
Churches:
    architecture, medieval, 103–13
    ethnic pluralism in, 238–40
    organization of, 41–42
Church of the Latter Day Saints,
    203
Cicero, 226
Circumcision, 37
Civil rights movement, 205–6
Clark, Kenneth, 93n, 94
Clark, Walter Houston, 81n
Classical Greece, wholeness of
    life in, 246–48
Clement of Alexandria, 120, 229
Cocks, H. F. Lovell, 194n

Codes of conduct, 20, 48–50,
    219–20
Cognitive aspects of religion, 3,
    165–67
Cohen, Arthur A., 145n, 184n
Coleridge, Samuel, 309
Commitment, 4, 15–17, 75–77,
    264–65
Communication, 17–19
Communistic eschatology, 203–5
"Communist Internationale," 203
Community:
    in Buddhism, 48, 242
    in Christianity, 41, 50
    in Confucianism, 48
    of faith, 242–43
    as feature of religious tradition,
        20, 48–50
    in Hinduism, 48
    in Islam, 50, 243
    in Judaism, 38, 50, 242
    pivotal value and, 7–10
    relations between individual
        and, 212–15
    in Shinto, 49
    in Taoism, 48
Compensatory justice, 237–38
Conduct, codes of, 20, 48–50,
    219–20
Confucius, 14, 32–35, 218, 284
Consciousness, transformation of,
    206–7
Conservative Judaism, 39
Constantine, 100
Conversion, 75–77
Conze, Edward, 58n
Copernicus, 287, 291, 298
Corporate expressions of ethical
    concerns (*See* Ethical con-
    cerns, corporate expres-
    sions of)
Cortez, Hernando, 63
Council of Chalcedon, 101–2
Covington, Judy, 95–97
Cox, Harvey, 184–85, 259–60,
    262–64, 305–6
Coyote Waits (Hillerman), 91–92
Creation stories:
    Babylonian, 293–94
    Egyptian, 292
    Hebrew, 294
    Hindu, 295–96
    Shinto, 296

Creed, 20, 48–50, 166
Crusades, 226
Cult, 20, 48–50
Culture, 211–12
Curnock, Nehemiah, 165n

D

Daily life, ritual patterns of,
    73–75
Dalai Lama, 29
Dali, Salvador, 95–97
Day, Dorothy, 14
Death, 186–98
    afterlife, 193–95
    attitudes toward, 190–92
    experience of, 187–90
    fear of, 178
    resurrection, 195–98
Death (Bakke), 196
Death: The Final Stage of Growth
    (Kübler-Ross), 192
De Bary, William Theodore, 71n
Decision making, Christian con-
    cepts of freedom and,
    176–78
Deistic views, 139–40
Democritus, 140
Demonic possession, 153–54
Denial of death, 191, 192
Denis, Saint, 105
Depression over dying, 191
Descartes, René, 230
Determinism, 170
Diabiosis, 306–8
Dialogue, understanding based
    on, 17–18
Dickey, James, 172–73, 310–11
Differentiation, 268
Dillenberger, John, 56n, 122
Diminishing self, 165
Discalced (Barefooted)
    Carmelites, 61–62
Divine, the, 114–45
    authority and, 282–84
    in Buddhism, 27, 318
    in Christianity, 317, 318
    deistic views, 139–40
    faith and (*See* Faith)
    in Hinduism, 22, 24, 129–31,
        137, 140, 159, 318–23
    the Holy, 127–31
    human freedom and, 173–75

in Judaism, 128, 132–34,
    317–18
pantheistic views, 139, 140
in religious texts, 131–38
revelation and (*See* Revelation)
ritual directed toward, 71–72
self as, 159
spirit, 141–45
symbols expressive of, 79
in Taoism, 128–29, 318
temporal and eternal aspects
    of, 317–23
transcendent-immanent views,
    139–41
(*See also* God)
Doctor of the Church, 61
Dole, N. H., 60n
Dome of the Rock, Jerusalem, 44
Doubt, 281–82, 287–89
Dravidians, 22
Dualistic deism, 139–40
Dualistic pantheism, 139, 140
Dukkha, 27, 58
Dürer, Albrecht, 153
Dutt, M. N., 217n
Duty, love and, 215–19

E

Earth, The (McKuen), 302
Easter, 41
Eastern Orthodox Church, 41,
    42, 286
Eastern religions:
    compared with Western reli-
        gions, 51
    human freedom and, 173–74
    views of humanity, 167–68
    (*See also* Index of Religious
        Traditions)
Eclipse of God (Buber), 17–18
Ecstatic orientation to religion, 6,
    52, 69, 70
Eddy, Mary Baker, 14
Ego ideal, 162
Egyptian hymn to the Creator,
    292
Eightfold Path, 27, 58–59, 220
Einstein, Albert, 300
Elihu, 148
Eliot, T. S., 221
Eliphaz, 148
Elizondo, Virgilio, 63–64

Emotional aspects of religion,
    165–67
Emotivism, 272
Engels, Friedrich, 203
Enlightenment, 14, 27–28, 30,
    58, 174
Ephrata Community, 203
Epicureanism, 140, 147, 148
Epicurus, 140
Erikson, Erik, 162
Eschatology, 202–10
    concept of, 202
    early Christian, 209–10
    Islamic vision, 208–9
    Jewish prophecy, 207–8
    new society, 203–5
    protest, 205–6
    transformation of conscious-
        ness, 206–7
Esoteric Taoism, 32
Esposito, John L., 267n
Eternal aspects of the Divine,
    317–23
Ethical concerns, corporate
    expressions of, 222–40
    ethnic pluralism in American
        churches, 238–40
    love and justice, 223–25
    peace and justice, 226–28
    poverty and race, 235–38
    sex roles 232–35
    social status of women, 228–32
Ethnic pluralism in American
    churches, 238–40
Ethnocentrism, 236
Eucharist, 41, 42
Evans, Mari, 162–63
Evil, 146–55
    concepts of, 149–55
    reasons for suffering, 147–49
Evolution, 299–300
Existential doubt, 288
Existentialism, 171
Expanding self, 164–65

F

Factual statement, 272–77
Faith:
    anatomy of, 122–25
    community of, 242–43
    reason and, 115, 118–22
Falwell, Jerry, 265

Family resemblance, 21
Famine, 254
Felder, Cain Hope, 237
Fellows, Ward J., 150n, 151n
Feminism, 1–2, 231, 233–34
Ferguson, Earl, 77
Ferguson, Everett, 103n
Ferguson, Kitty, 300n
Festivals of Judaism, 38
Fifth Pillar of Islam, 46
Fischer, Otto, 129–31
Five Relationships, 218
Fletcher, Joseph, 223
Four Noble Truths, 27, 57, 58, 174
Fox, George, 14
Freedom:
   Marx on, 203
   self and, 170–78
      Christian freedom and the
         dilemmas of decision mak-
         ing, 176–78
      human freedom, 173–75
      responsible freedom, 171–73
Free will, 154–55, 176
Freud, Sigmund, 162
Fromm, Erich, 157–59, 175n
Frost, Robert, 302
Frye, Roland, 151, 300n
Fundamentalism, 46, 265–67

G

Galileo, 309
Gandhi, Mahatma, 14, 16, 64–66,
   226
Gautama Buddha, 8, 14, 16, 22,
   26–28, 56–59, 157, 284,
   306–7
Geertz, Clifford, 3
General revelation, 116–17
Ghazali, Abu Hamid al-, 61
God:
   Aquinas on nature and reality
      of, 135
   Aristotle's view of, 134–35
   Buber on existence of, 16–18
   in Jewish scriptures, 132–34
   Luther's concept of, 4
   scepticism about, 119
   self as image of, 160
   (See also Divine, the; specific
      names)
Gold, Karen, 16n
Golden, Judah, 220n

Goldman, Ari, 19
Good Shepherd, 99
Good Shepherd, Jesus portrayed
   as, 98, 99, 101–3
Gospel, 41
Gothic architecture, 103–13
Grace:
   freedom and, 176–77
   salvation and, 200–202
Greece, ancient:
   concept of time in, 314
   wholeness of life in, 246–48
Greening of America, The (Reich),
   206
Gribbin, John, 300n
Grief, 191, 192
Guilt, 179–83
Gunderson, W. Mark, 109, 113n

H

Hadj, 46, 243
Haiku, 249
Haley, Alex, 243n
Halverson, Marvin, 184n, 194n
Hammarskjöld, Dag, 12, 16
Hanuka, 38
Hare Krishna, 21
Harland, Gordon, 225n
Harvey, Van A., 116n
Haverson, Marvin, 145n
Hawking, Stephen W., 300n
Hazelton, Roger, 94n
Hebrew story of Creation, 294
Hegel, G. W. F., 200
Heidegger, Martin, 157
Henley, William Ernest, 213, 214
Hensley, Jeannine, 229n
Hesse, Herman, 313
Hillerman, Tony, 91–92
Hinayana Buddhism, 28–29, 48
Hinduism (See Index of Religious
   Traditions)
Hirano, Umeyo, 85n
Hirota, Dennis, 151n
Hispanics, 235, 236, 239
Historical statements, 271
Hobbes, Thomas, 264
Holck, Frederick H., 194n
Holy, the, 127–31
Holy Spirit, 40, 144
Hudson, Edwin, 165n
Hughes, Langston, 162
Human existence (See Self)

Human freedom, 173–75
Humanity:
   Confucian concept of, 34–35
   Eastern views of, 167–68
   in Judaism, 37, 160, 169
   natural process and, 310–8
      apobiosis, 304–6
      diabiosis, 306–8
      symbiosis, 302–4
   nature of, 157–61
   technology and, 259–62
   Western views of, 169
Hunger, world, 252–59
Hzün Tzu, 71

I

I Ching, 35
Icons, 95
Idea of the Holy, The (Otto),
   127–28
Identity, 162–65, 212–14
Impersonal power, 318–23
Individual:
   conceptualizations of
      encounter between the
         Divine and, 126–45
      deistic views, 139–40
      the Holy, 127–31
      pantheistic views, 139, 140
      in religious texts, 131–38
      spirit, 141–45
      transcendent-immanent
         views, 139–41
   relations between community
      and, 212–15
   (See also Self)
Integration, 238–39
Interpersonal relations:
   act and motive, 219–21
   corporate expressions of ethical
      concerns (See Ethical con-
      cerns, corporate expres-
      sions of)
   individual and the community,
      212–15
   love and duty, 215–19
   religious traditions and (See
      Social change, religious
      traditions and; Social sta-
      bility, religious traditions
      and)
Irenaeus, 145n
Irkin, Joseph, 285n

Isaiah, 128
Isherwood, Christopher, 131n
Islam (*See* Index of Religious Traditions)
Israel, 36

J

Jack, Homer A., 65n
Jainism, 306
James, William, 81n, 82
Janson, H. W., 104, 106n
Japanese culture:
    duty in, 218–19
    fondness for simplicity in, 248–51
    shame in, 180–81
    views of humanity, 167–68
Jastrow, Robert, 300n
Jefferson, Thomas, 140
Jên, 34
Jeremiah, 207–8
Jesus Christ (*See* Christianity: Jesus Christ in Index of Religious Traditions)
Jiva, 24
Jnana yoga, 24
Job, 148
John the Baptist, 13–14
John XXIII, Pope, 260n
Juan Diego, 63–64
Judaism (*See* Index of Religious Traditions)
Justice:
    compensatory, 237–38
    love and, 223–25
    peace and, 226–28
Justin Martyr, 119–20
Just-war arguments, 226–28

K

Ka'ba, 43, 44, 46
Kadowaki, S. J., 84n
Kahler, Erich, 78n
Kami, 143, 304
Kapleau, Philip, 73n
Karma, 24, 26, 194
Karma yoga, 24
Kepler, Johann, 297–98
Kerr, Hugh Thomson, Jr., 120n, 177n
Kierkegaard, Søren, 171, 182, 282–83

Kildahl, John, 67
King, Martin Luther, Jr., 9, 16, 205–6, 226
Kitto, H. D. F., 246–48
Kluckhohn, Clyde, 137n, 220n
Knowledge, religious, 270–89
    authority, 281–84
    doubt, 281–82, 287–89
    factual statement, 272–77
    tradition, 281, 284–87
    verification, 277–80
    (*See also* Revelation)
Knox, John, 87
Knudson, Albert C., 149n
Krishna, 6, 129–31
Krishna Consciousness, 21
Kshatriyas, 25
Kübler-Ross, Elisabeth, 190n, 191–92
Kubrick, Stanley, 259
Küng, Hans, 190n
K'un-ts'an, 167

L

Language, religious:
    logic of, 272–80
    use of term "religion" in various cultures, 2–3
Lao-Tzu, 31–32, 128–29
Lawrence, Brother, 74
Lawrence, D. H., 311
Lawrence, Kenneth, 101n, 102n, 103n
Legal orientation to religion, 69–70
Leighton, Dorothea, 137n, 220n
Leishman, J. B., 164n
Lester, Muriel, 226
Lévi-Strauss, Claude, 87, 91, 244–46
Li, 34
Liberation theology, 225
Life of Teresa of Jesus: The Autobiography of St. Teresa of Avila, 62
Li K'o-Jan, 130
Lin Yutang, 214n
Locke, John, 264
Love:
    duty and, 215–19
    justice and, 223–25
    nature of humanity and, 160–61

Lowrie, Walter, 98, 283n
Loyola, Ignatius, 153
Luckmann, Thomas, 212
Lucretius, 140
Luminous wholeness in Western European Medieval architecture, 103–13
Lundahl, Craig R., 190n
Lun yü (*The Sayings of Confucius*), 35
Luther, Martin, 4, 14, 16, 55–56, 120, 201, 284, 295
Lynde, Stan, 303

M

MacDermot, Galt, 207n
MacIver, R. M., 86
"Magic, Science and Religion" (Malinowski), 89–90
Magical orientation to religion, 6, 70, 88–92
Mahayana Buddhism, 29, 48, 202, 216–17
Maimonides, 193
Malcolm X, 243
Malinowski, Bronislaw, 86, 89–90
Malnutrition, 254
Malthus, Thomas, 256
Mandalas, 29
Mandookya Upanishad, 159
Mantras, 29
Mao Tse-tung, 33, 35, 204–5
Marcel, Gabriel, 171
Marsilius of Padua, 264
Martin, Hugh, 283n
Marx, Karl, 203
Marxism, 10–11, 201
Mason, James, 16n
Materialistic pantheism, 139, 140
Mathnavi (Rumi), 59–60
Matthes, Joachim, 268
Mauksch, Hans O., 191n
Mausoleum of Galla Placidia, 100–101
May, Rollo, 78n
Maya, 26, 201, 307
McCann, Dom Justin, 286n
McClain, William B., 236n
McKenzie, John G., 181n, 182–83
McKuen, Rod, 302
Meaning of Persons, The (Tournier), 164–65
Mecca, 12, 43–44, 46

Medieval architecture, luminous
    wholeness in, 103–13
Mencius, 35
Merton, Thomas, 74n, 84n
Messiah, 40, 193
Metaphysical statements, 271
Michalson, Carl, 177–78
Miller, Max, 104
Milton, John, 310
Modernization, characteristics,
    267–69
Mohammed (*See* Muhammad)
Moksha, 24, 201
Monk, Robert C., 277n
Moody, Raymond, 190n
Morality:
    guilt and, 182–83
    revelation and, 116–17
Moral orientation to religion, 6,
    69–70
Moses, 16, 36, 53–55, 59–60
Mosques, 45
Mo-ti, 214
Motivations, interaction between
    acts and, 219–21
Mudras, 29
Muezzin, 45
Muhammad, 14, 43–45, 144,
    208–9, 226
Müller, E. Max, 137n, 296n
Mundaka-Upanishad, 295–96
Murder in the Cathedral (Eliot), 221
Mushakōji, Saneatsu, 84–85
Muslims (*See* Islam in the Index
    of Religous Traditions)
Mysterium tremendum, 127–31
Mystical orientation to religion,
    6, 52, 69, 70, 80–86
Myth, 86–88

N

Nakamura, Hajime, 138, 248–51
Native Americans, 235, 239
Natural process, 301–11
    humanity and, 301–8
        apobiosis, 304–6
        diabiosis, 306–8
        symbiosis, 302–4
    views of nature, 308–11
Natural universe, 290–300
    concept of, 290
    religious views on origin of,
        291–97

religious vision and scientific
    method, 297–300
Navaho culture:
    the Divine in, 136–37
    magic in, 91–92
    oral tradition in, 271
    taboos in, 219–20
Near-death experiences, 187–90
Needham, Joseph, 89n
New Testament, 13–14, 41, 149
Newton, Isaac, 139
Nichol, John Thomas, 68n
Niebuhr, H. Richard, 4n, 5–6,
    123, 124
Niebuhr, Reinhold, 184, 214,
    224–25
Niemoeller, Martin, 226
Nirvana, 27–29, 56–59, 174
Noss, Christopher, 219n
Noss, John B., 8n, 115n, 218n,
    296–97
Novak, Michael, 88n
Nurture, religious, 75–76

O

Oates, Whitney J., 161n
Obedient self, 160–61
Objective guilt, 181–82
Old Testament, 36, 41, 132–34,
    148
Oliver, Robert T., 206n
Oneida Community, 203
On the Free Choice of the Will
    (Augustine), 154
On the Nature of Things
    (Lucretius), 140
Ono, Sokyo, 143
Orant, 100
Orants, 98, 100
Origen, 120
Original sin, 183–84
Orosco, E. C., 236n
Otto, Rudolf, 127–28, 129n
Our Lady of Guadalupe, 63–64
Outler, Albert, 147, 148n, 166n

P

Pacific Americans, 239
Pacifist groups, 226
Panofsky, Edwin, 104, 105
Pantheistic views, 82, 139, 140
Pantocrator, Jesus portrayed as,
    99, 101, 103, 104

Parsons, Talcott, 268
Pascal, Blaise, 152–53, 158
Passover, 38
Paul, Saint, 8, 9, 229, 231, 234,
    282–83, 310
Paul VI, Pope, 260n
Peace, justice and, 226–28
Peck, M. Scott, 153–54
Pederson, Johannes, 181
Peers, E. Allison, 62n
Pelagius, 176, 177
Pentacostalism, 52, 66–67
Pentateuch, 36
People of the Lie (Peck), 153–54
Personal identity, 162–65, 212–14
Personality development, 161–62,
    182
Personhood, 161–65
Persons-in-community, 7–10
Pesach (Passover), 38
Pfautz, H. W., 268
Philosophical Taoism, 32
Picasso, Pablo, 94
Pierce, Charles S., 279–80
Pivotal value:
    authenticity of, 12–13
    as central value, 10–12
    commitment to, 15–16
    of individual, 4–10
    person-in-community and, 7–10
    sharing of, 13–14
Planck, Max, 300
Plato, 81, 229, 270
Platonism, 147, 148
Platt, John R., 268–69
Pluralism, 239
Polanyi, Michael, 291, 299
Polytheistic deism, 139
Popular Taoism, 32
Population growth, hunger and,
    256, 257
Poverty:
    hunger and, 255, 257
    racism and, 235–38
Prabhavananda, Swami, 131n
Prabhupada, A. C. Bhaktvedanta
    Swami, 201n
Prayer:
    in Islam, 45
    in schools, 263, 264
Prigogine, Ilya, 300n
"Prince Wen Hui and His Cook"
    (Chuang Tzu), 73–74
Pritchard, James B., 294n

Protest, 205–6
Protestantism, 42, 201–2, 232, 236, 259–60, 263
Puranas, 217, 318–23
Purim, 38

Q

Quakers, 283
Quasi-religions, 11, 12
Qu'ran, 43, 45, 208–9, 220

R

Rabbinic Judaism, 37, 39
Racism, 235–38
Radhakrishnan, 14
Rado, James, 207n
Rage over death, 191
Ragni, Gerome, 207n
Ramadan, 45–46
Ramsey, Paul, 160–61
Rationalization, 268
Reason:
    faith and, 115, 118–22
    human nature defined by ability to, 158
    revelation and, 116
Reciprocity, 218
Redemption, 200
Redemptive doubt, 288–89
Reform Judaism, 39
Reich, Charles A., 206n
Reifenberg, Anne, 235n
Religion:
    commitment to, 4, 15–17, 75–77, 264–65
    communication about, 17–19
    defining, 1–14
    functions of, 3
    traditions (*See* Index of Religious traditions)
Religious Crossroads (Tsanoff), 2–3
Religious experience:
    in artistic expression (*See* Artistic expression)
    cases of, 52–68
        Charismatics, 67–68
        framework for, 53
        Gandhi, 64–66
        Gautama Buddha, 56–59
        Juan Diego, 63–64
        Luther, 55–56
        Moses, 53–55
        Pentacostalists, 66–67

Saint Teresa, 61–63
Sufi encounters, 59–61
conceptualizations of encounter between the Divine and the individual, 126–45
    deistic views, 139–40
    the Holy, 127–31
    pantheistic views, 139, 140
    in religious texts, 131–38
    spirit, 141–45
    transcendent-immanent views, 139–41
elements of, 69–92
    conversion, 75–77
    magic, 88–92
    myth, 86–88
    religious nurture, 75–76
    ritual, 70–75
    symbols, 78–80
guilt and, 181–83
self and:
    emotional and cognitive aspects, 165–67
    views of humanity, 167–69
types of, 52, 69–70
Religious language (*See* Language, religious)
Religious nurture, 75–76
Religious texts, the Divine expressed in, 131–38
Religious traditions, 20–51
    basic tenets of, 48–51
    defined, 20
    descriptions of, 21–47
    phases of, 13–14
    religious truth and, 271
    social change and, 252–69
        characteristics of modernization, 267–69
        fundamentalism, 265–67
        humanity and technology, 259–62
        secularization, 262–65
        world hunger, 252–59
    social stability and, 241–51
        community of faith, 242–43
        Japanese fondness for simplicity, 248–51
        wholeness of life, 244–48
    (*See also* Index of Religious Traditions)
Religious vision, scientific method and, 297–300

Reparations, economic, 237
Reps, Paul, 221n
Republic (Plato), 229
Responsibility, 213–21
Responsible freedom, 171–73
Resurrection, 40, 42, 195–98
Revelation, 115–17
    faith and, 118–25
    general and special, 116–17
    religious truth and, 282–83
Rich, Adrienne, 229n, 233–34
Richardson, Alan, 116–17, 120n, 121n, 148n, 149n
Ricoeur, Paul, 78n, 132, 262, 264
Righteousness, 181
Rites (*See* Ritual)
Ritual, 20
    Christian, 41, 74
    Hindu, 25
    Islamic, 46, 71–72
    Jewish, 37–38
    role of, 70–75
    Taoist, 31, 73–74
    Zen Buddhist, 73
Robertson, Pat, 265
Rogers, Carl R., 164
Roman Catholic Church, 41, 42, 201–2, 231, 232, 260, 263, 286
Rosh Hashana, 38
Ross, W. D., 135n
Ruah, 141
Rumi, Jalal al-Din, 59–60
Rural poor, hunger among, 255
Ruskin, John, 93–94

S

Sacrament of the Last Supper, The (Dali), 95–97
Sacraments, 41
Salvation, 199–210
    concept of, 200–202
    eschatological, 202–10
        concept of, 202
        early Christian, 209–10
        Islamic vision, 208–9
        Jewish prophecy, 207–8
        new society, 203–5
        protest, 205–6
        transformation of consciousness, 206–7
Samsara, 24, 26, 73, 194
Sangha, 26

Sansom, Art, 18
Sartre, Jean-Paul, 171–72
Satan, 151–52
Satori, 279
Satyagraha, 64
Schillaci, Anthony, 149n, 150
Schools:
    Buddhist, 28–30
    prayer in, 263, 264
Schulz, Charles, 216
Science:
    religious vision and, 297–300
    role in modernization, 268
    views about natural universe,
        290, 291, 309
    (*See also* Technology)
Scientific doubt, 287–88
Scriven, Michael, 119n
Search for God at Harvard, The
    (Goldman), 19
Secular City, The (Cox), 262–63
Secularization, 262–65
Self, 156–69
    death and, 186–98
        afterlife, 193–95
        attitudes toward, 190–92
        experience of, 187–90
        fear of, 178
        resurrection, 195–98
    freedom and, 170–78
        Christian freedom and the
            dilemmas of decision mak-
            ing, 176–78
        human freedom, 173–75
        responsible freedom, 171–73
    guilt and, 179–83
    nature of humanity, 157–61
    personhood, 161–65
    religious experience and, 165–67
    salvation (*See* Salvation)
    shame and, 179–81
    sin and, 183–85
    social setting of (*See* Interper-
        sonal relations)
    transformation of, 72–73
    views of humanity, 167–69
Self-awareness, 158
Self-transcendence, 158–59
Sex roles, 232–35
Shakers, 203
Shaking of the Foundation, The
    (Tillich), 200–201
Shaktism, 304
Shamans, 90–91

Shame, 179–81
Shapiro, Nat, 207n
Shavuot (Pentecost), 38
Shibayama, Zenkei, 86n
Shi'ites, 46, 47
Shu, 218
Sibbes, Richard, 145n
Siddhartha (Hesse), 313
Simchat Torah, 38
Simon, Arthur, 256–57
Simplicity, Japanese fondness for,
    248–51
Sin, 183–85
Śiva, 22–23
Skeptical doubt, 288
Skinner, B. F., 157
Smith, Huston, 168n
Smith, Joseph, 14
Snell, David, 190n
Snow, C. P., 261
Social change, religious traditions
    and, 252–69
    characteristics of moderniza-
        tion, 267–69
    fundamentalism, 265–67
    humanity and technology,
        259–62
    secularization, 262–65
    world hunger, 252–59
Social relations (*See* Interper-
    sonal relations)
Social responsibility, 213–21
Social stability, religious tradi-
    tions and, 241–51
    community of faith, 242–43
    Japanese fondness for simplic-
        ity, 248–51
    wholeness of life, 244–48
Social status of women, 228–32
Society of Friends, 226
Southern Baptist Convention,
    265–66
Southern Baptist Journal, The, 266
Special revelation, 116–17
Speiser, E. A., 294n
Spirit, 141–45
Stamey, Joseph D., 277n
Stanford, Derek, 76
Stark, Rodney, 2n
Starkie, Enid, 311
"Status Symbol" (Evans), 162–63
Stewart, David, 262n
Stoicism, 147, 148
Stookey, Paul, 16n

Structural Anthropology (Lévi-
    Strauss), 91
Stuber, Stanley Irving, 120n
Śudras, 25
Suffering:
    Buddhism and, 27
    reasons for, 147–49
Sufis, 47, 59–61, 81
Suger, Abbot, 105–6
Sukkot (tabernacle), 38
Sun Myung Moon, 14
Sunnis, 46, 47
Swami, Shree Purohit, 159n
Swinton, David H., 235, 237
Symbiosis, 302–4
Symbols, 12
    in art, 94–97
    role in religion, 78–80

T

Taboos, 219–20
Tacit Dimension, The (Polanyi),
    299
Tacit knowing, 299
Taft, Alfonso, 263
Talmud, 37, 175, 220
Tanha, 27, 58, 249
Tantric religious patterns, 29
Taoism (*See* Index of Religious
    Traditions)
Tao Te Ching (Lao-Tzu), 31, 32
Teaching of Don Juan, The: A
    Yaqui Way of Knowledge
    (Castaneda), 279
Technology:
    humanity and, 259–62
    role in modernization, 268
    scientific doubt and develop-
        ment of, 287–88
Teilhard de Chardin, Pierre, 291,
    299
Ten Commandments, 36, 183
Tenth Muse, The (Bradstreet), 228
Teresa of Avila, Saint, 14, 16,
    61–63, 80–81, 232
Tertullian, 120
Theory of Religion, A, 2
Theravada Buddhism, 28–29,
    171, 242
Things Fall Apart (Achebe),
    142–43
Thomas, Clarence, 231
Thomas, Edward J., 57n

Thomson, G. T., 121n
Thoreau, Henry David, 264, 302
Tillich, Paul, 78n, 87, 122, 171,
    200–201, 223–24, 287–88,
    314–16
Time, 312–23
    mystery of, 313–16
    temporal and eternal aspects of
        the Divine, 317–23
Tokusho, Bassui, 73
Tolstoy, Leon, 14, 226
Torah, 12, 37, 40, 41
Tournier, Paul, 164–65
Tradition, 281, 284–87
Transcendent-immanent views,
    139–41
Tran Van Dinh, 88
Trepp, Leo, 193
Trinity, Christian, 40
Tristes Tropiques (Lévi-Strauss),
    244–46
Trotsky, Leon, 10–11
Tsanoff, Radoslav, 2–3
Tussell, Charles Taze, 14
2001: A Space Odyssey, 259
Tycho Brahe, 298

U

Under God, 2
Underhill, Evelyn, 81
Undernutrition, 253–54
Universe (*See* Natural universe)
Upanishads, 24
Urbanization, 267
Urban poor, hunger among, 255
Utton, Beth, 304n

V

Vaisyas, 25
Vajrayana, 29

Vedantic Hinduism, 82–83
Vedas, 24, 115
Verification, 270–71, 277–80
Vietnamese origins, myth of,
    87–88
Virgin Spring, The, 149–50
Vishnu, 22–23, 217, 319–22
Void, in Buddhism, 138, 140

W

Walker, Belle M., 60n
Walker, Williston, 101n
War, 226–28
Ward, Nathaniel, 228
Wartofsky, Marx, 278–79
Watson, David Lowes, 236n
Weightman, Doreen, 245n
Weightman, John, 245n
Wesley, John, 14, 165–66, 201
Western European Medieval
    architecture, 103–13
Western religions:
    compared with Eastern reli-
        gions, 51
    human freedom and, 174–75
    views of humanity, 169
    (*See also* Index of Religious
        Traditions)
White, Eugene E., 206n
White, Woody, 239
Whitehead, Alfred North, 141,
    291, 299–300, 309
Wholeness:
    individual, 4–10
    of life:
        in Classical Greece, 246–48
        in a simply structured soci-
            ety, 244–46
    luminous, in Western European
        Medieval architecture,
        103–13

as person-in-community, 7–10
    (*See also* Salvation)
Williams, Roger, 264
Wills, Gary, 2n
Wilson, H. H., 217n
Wilson, Nancy Ross, 138n
Wittgenstein, Ludwig, 21
Women:
    sex roles of, 232–35
    social status of, 228–32
Woodbridge, John, 228
Wordsworth, William, 309
World hunger, 252–59
Wu wei, 31

X

Xirau, Ramon, 157–59

Y

Yahweh, 36, 317
Yahya Ibn Mo'adh, 60–61
Yathrib, 44
Yeats, Y. B., 159n
Yinger, J. Milton, 11
Yin and *Yang,* 30–31, 151
Yoga, 24
Yohannan, John D., 60n
Yom Kippur, 38
Young, Brigham, 14
Young, Perry Dean, 263n
Yutang, Lin, 129n

Z

Zaehner, R. C., 82–83
Zen Buddhism, 29, 33, 52, 84–86,
    221, 250, 279
Zimmer, Heinrich, 306, 307n,
    318–23
Zoroastrianism, 197
Zukav, Gary, 300n